Grand Challenges for
Social Work and Society

GRAND CHALLENGES FOR SOCIAL WORK AND SOCIETY

Edited by Rowena Fong

James E. Lubben

and

Richard P. Barth

Oxford University Press is a department of the University of Oxford. It furthers
the University's objective of excellence in research, scholarship, and education
by publishing worldwide. Oxford is a registered trade mark of Oxford University
Press in the UK and certain other countries.

Published in the United States of America by Oxford University Press
198 Madison Avenue, New York, NY 10016, United States of America.

CIP data is on file at the Library of Congress
ISBN 978-0-19-085898-8

CONTENTS

ABOUT THE EDITORS

Rowena Fong, EdD, MSW, is the Ruby Lee Piester Centennial Professor at the University of Texas at Austin, School of Social Work. A Fellow of the Society for Social Work and Research (SSWR) and the American Academy of Social Work and Social Welfare (AASWSW), she is the Treasurer of AASWSW, co-principal investigator of a $23 million grant for the National Quality Improvement Center for Adoption and Guardianship Support and Preservation, and has authored more than 100 publications, including 10 books.

James E. Lubben, PhD/DSW, MPH, MSW, is the Louise McMahon Ahearn Professor of Social Work at Boston College and Professor Emeritus at UCLA. He has edited five books and authored more than 100 articles and chapters. He has been principal investigator of over $35 million of extramural grants. He is a Fellow of AASWSW and the Gerontological Society of America.

Richard P. Barth, PhD, MSW, is Dean of the University of Maryland School of Social Work and Past President of AASWSW. He has written more than 10 books and 200 articles and chapters about children's services. He has twice served as a Fulbright Scholar, received a Lifetime Achievement Award from SSWR, and is a Fellow of the American Psychological Association and SSWR.

ABOUT THE CONTRIBUTORS

Heidi L. Allen, PhD, MSW, is an associate professor at Columbia University School of Social Work. Her research is situated at the intersection of poverty and health and focuses on innovative policy approaches to eliminating disparities.

Christina M. Andrews, PhD, MSW, is Assistant Professor of Social Work at the University of South Carolina. Her scholarship focuses on improving access to high-quality addiction treatment in the Medicaid program.

Audrey Begun, PhD, MSW, is Professor of Social Work at The Ohio State University and a SSWR Fellow. Her recent scholarship focuses on intervening around substance misuse and preparing the professional workforce to develop and deliver evidence-supported interventions to underserved population.

Stephanie Cosner Berzin, PhD, is Assistant Dean, Doctoral Program, at Boston College School of Social Work. As Director of the Center for Social Innovation, her research focuses on organizational capacity building around innovation, intrapreneurship, and technology. Complementary research explores services to combat poverty and support vulnerable youth.

Julie Birkenmaier, PhD, LCSW, is Professor of Social Work at Saint Louis University School of Social Work. Her research focuses on financial capability, financial access, and financial credit. Her publications include *Financial Capability and Asset-Building in Vulnerable Households* with Margaret S. Sherraden and J. Michael Collins (Oxford University Press, 2017).

Suzanne Brown, PhD, LMSW, is Assistant Professor of Social Work at Wayne State University in Detroit. Her research focuses on women and parenting among mothers with addictions and trauma histories. She is especially interested in the ways in which social support enhances parenting success among mothers with vulnerabilities associated with trauma and addiction and also the ways in which these same vulnerabilities may erode vital social supports.

Teri Browne, PhD, MSW, is an associate professor at the University of South Carolina College of Social Work and Co-Director for Interprofessional Education for the Health Sciences at the University of South Carolina. She is co-editor of the *Handbook of Health Social Work* (2nd ed., Wiley, 2012) and a SSWR Fellow.

Sarah Christa Butts, MSW, is the Executive Director of the Grand Challenges for Social Work and Senior Administrator to the Dean's office at University of Maryland, School of Social Work (UM SSW). She is the Founding Administrator to the AASWSW, and played a significant role in the organization's development and launching of Grand Challenges from 2013–2017. She is a co-author on the AASWSW working paper to End Homelessness and serves on the UM SSW Homelessness Council where she chairs a subcommittee on Government and Inter Professional Partnerships. Prior experience include roles at the Family League of Baltimore, Maryland Department of Human Services, and Baltimore County Department of Social Services.

Christine Callahan, PhD, is a research assistant professor with the Financial Social Work Initiative (FSWI) at the University of Maryland School of Social Work. She joined the FSWI in July 2012 and conducts research and teaches in order to grow the FSWI as a national leader in financial capability.

Rocío Calvo, PhD, is an associate professor at the Boston College School of Social Work and the founding director of the Latino Leadership Initiative. Her research focuses on how access to social services contributes to the incorporation of immigrants and on the determinants of immigrants' happiness. Her work has been featured in the *Journal of Happiness Studies, Health & Social Work, PLoS One, Social Science & Medicine*, and the *British Journal of Social Work*.

John D. Clapp, PhD, MSW, is Professor and Executive Vice Dean at the Suzanne Dworak-Peck School of Social Work at the University of Southern California. His research is in the area of alcohol and drug epidemiology and prevention, and he is a Fellow of the American Academy of Health Behavior.

Claudia J. Coulton, PhD, is the Distinguished University Professor and Co-Director, Center on Urban Poverty and Community Development, Jack, Joseph and Morton Mandel School of Applied Social Sciences, Case Western Reserve University. Her research focuses on neighborhood effects on families and applications of big data and spatial analysis to understand these issues.

Sandra Edmonds Crewe, PhD, ACSW, is Professor and Dean of Social Work at Howard University. Consistent with the long-standing mission of the university, she is strongly committed to social justice and addressing equity and disparities for African Americans and other historically oppressed or marginalized populations. Her current scholarship primarily relates to ethnogerontology and caregiving. As the director of the Multidisciplinary Gerontology Center, she has served as principal investigator for professional development of aging network providers in the District of Columbia for more than 10 years.

Mathieu R. Despard, MSW, PhD, is an assistant professor at the University of Michigan School of Social Work with a research focus on the financial security of lower income families and on the capacity and effectiveness of nonprofit organizations serving these families. He teaches courses on management, community, and policy practice.

Diana DiNitto, PhD, is the Cullen Trust Centennial Professor in Alcohol Studies and Education and Distinguished Teaching Professor at the University of Texas at Austin School of Social Work and a Fellow of the American Academy of Social Work and Social Welfare. Her books include *Social Welfare: Politics and Public Policy* (8th ed., Pearson, 2016) and *Chemical Dependency: A Systems Approach* (4th ed., Pearson, 2012).

Joanna Doran, PhD, is an assistant professor at the California State University in Los Angeles, where she teaches policy, community organizing, and MSW thesis. She is also Founding Director of the Asset Building Clinic and Co-Chair of the Grand Challenge Work Committee to Advance FCAB Through Education.

Matthew W. Epperson, PhD, is an associate professor at the University of Chicago School of Social Service Administration and Co-Founding Director of the Smart Decarceration Initiative. His research centers on developing, implementing, and evaluating interventions to reduce disparities in the criminal justice system, with a focus on individuals with serious mental illnesses.

Marilyn L. Flynn, PhD, is Dean and 2U Chair of Educational Innovation and Social Work in the Suzanne Dworak-Peck School of Social Work at the University of Southern California. She is most noted for her transformational leadership in graduate education and institution building in the profession of social work.

Terri Friedline, PhD, is an assistant professor at the University of Kansas School of Social Welfare. She is Faculty Director at the Center on Assets, Education, and Inclusion, Faculty Affiliate at the Institute for Policy & Social Research, and Research Fellow at New America in Washington, DC.

Melanie Gironda, PhD, MSW, is an associate research professor in the School of Gerontology at the University of Southern California and Clinical Director of the University of Southern California Family Caregiver Resource Center. She has authored a number of articles and chapters on the centrality of social networks to the health and well-being of underserved adults.

Jeremy Goldbach, PhD, is an assistant professor at the University of Southern California Suzanne Dworak-Peck School of Social Work. His research is broadly focused on the relationship between social stigma, stress, and health among minority populations. His work seeks to identify and measure stigma and to develop interventions that address these unique determinants of health. His work has been funded by the Eunice Kennedy Shriver National Institute of Child Health and Human Development, the National Institute on Minority Health and Health Disparities, the Department of Defense, and The Trevor Project.

Ernest Gonzales, PhD, MSSW, is an assistant professor and Peter Paul Professor at Boston University, School of Social Work. He is Chair to the AGE*SW*-Productive Aging Group and Faculty Director of Health Equity and Productive Engagement at Boston University's Center for Innovation in Social Work and Health.

Annie Grier, MSW, is a project manager at the Center for Social Development, George Warren Brown School of Social Work Washington University in Saint Louis, where her work focuses on reversing mass incarceration in the United States. She oversees applied research projects and leads efforts to build social capacity in order to implement and sustain early stage criminal justice interventions.

J. David Hawkins, PhD, is the Endowed Professor of Prevention and Founding Director of the Social Development Research Group, University of Washington School of Social Work. His research, which appears in more than 300 publications, including four books, focuses on understanding and preventing child and adolescent health and behavior problems. He is a member of the National Academies of Science, Engineering, and Medicine's Forum on Promoting Children's Cognitive, Affective, and Behavioral Health; leader of the Collaborative for Healthy Parenting in Primary Care; and a Fellow of AASWSW, SSWR, and the American Society of Criminology. He is a co-developer of the following preventive interventions: Guiding Good Choices, Supporting School Success, Staying Connected with Your Teen, Raising Healthy Children, and Communities That Care.

Julia Henly, PhD, is an associate professor at the University of Chicago School of Social Service Administration, where she directs the Employment Instability, Family Well-Being, and Social Policy Network. She studies the economic and caregiving strategies of low-income families, examining how employment conditions, public benefits (especially child care assistance), and social networks interact to support and complicate family well-being.

Benjamin F. Henwood, PhD, MSW, is an assistant professor at the University of Southern California, a National Institutes of Health-funded researcher, and a Fellow of the SSWR. He is also a recognized expert in mental health and housing services research whose work connects clinical interventions with social policy.

Jin Huang, PhD, MSW, is an associate professor at Saint Louis University School of Social Work. He co-leads the Financial Capability and Asset Building for All initiative, one of social work's 12 Grand Challenges, and is a faculty director of Inclusion in Asset Building at the Center for Social Development, Washington University in St. Louis.

Jacquelyn B. James, PhD, is Co-Director of the Boston College Center on Aging & Work, Research Professor in the Lynch School of Education, and Director of the international, multidisciplinary Sloan Research Network on Aging & Work. She is also past president of the Society for the Study of Human Development.

Jeffrey M. Jenson, PhD, is the Philip D. and Eleanor G. Winn Endowed Professor for Children and Youth in the Graduate School of Social Work, University of Denver. He has published seven books and numerous articles and chapters on topics of prevention and child and adolescent development. He is Editor-in-Chief of the *Journal of the Society for Social Work and Research* and a Fellow of the SSWR and the AASWSW.

Carrie Johnson, MSW, LCSW, is the past assistant director of the Hartford Center of Excellence in Geriatric Social Work at Boston College. She is currently a special consultant for the University Institute on Aging and a field advisor in the School of Social Work at Boston College. She has more than 17 years of geriatric social work experience.

Raven Jones, MSW Candidate December 2017, is a graduate student at the University of Michigan School of Social Work, where she is National Community Scholar and a 16-month Community Organization major with a minor in management. She is passionate about researching the various aspects of economic inequality with the hope of creating legislation briefs to better inform policymakers.

Susan P. Kemp, PhD, is the Charles O. Cressey Endowed Professor at the University of Washington School of Social Work and Professor at the University of Auckland Faculty of Education and Social Work. Her scholarship focuses on place and environment as foci of social intervention, community-based social services, public child welfare, and social work history.

Jooyoung Kong, PhD, MSW, is a recent graduate of Boston College and currently a postdoctoral fellow in the Center for Healthy Aging at the Pennsylvania State University. Her primary research area is later-life family relationships. She has published several papers regarding the long-term impact of parental childhood maltreatment on later-life relationships with an abusive parent.

Laura Lein, PhD, is the Katherine Reebel Collegiate Professor of Social Work and Professor of Anthropology at the University of Michigan. Her work examines the relationships between families in poverty and the programs, policies, and institutions that are intended to address poverty. Her books include *Community Lost: The State, Civil Society, and Displaced Survivors of Hurricane Katrina* (with Ronald Angel, Julie Beausoleil, and Holly Bell; Cambridge University Press, 2012) and *Life After Welfare* (with Deanna Schexnayder, Karen Douglas, and Daniel Schroeder; University of Texas Press, 2007).

Rebecca J. Macy, PhD, is the Preyer Distinguished Chair for Strengthening Families at the University of North Carolina at Chapel Hill School of Social Work. She is currently Editor-in-Chief of the *Journal of Family Violence*. She has 15 years' experience conducting community-based studies that focus on intimate partner violence, sexual violence, and human trafficking.

Peter Maramaldi, PhD, MPH, LCSW, is a professor at the Simmons College School of Social Work, adjunct professor at the Harvard University T. H. Chan School of Public Health, and instructor at the Harvard School of Dental Medicine in Oral Health Policy and Epidemiology. As a behavioral scientist, he collaborates extensively with interprofessional teams conducting National Institutes of Health- and foundation-funded research.

Christina Matz-Costa, MSW, PhD, is an assistant professor in the Boston College School of Social Work and a senior research associate at the Center on Aging & Work. Her research focuses on meaningful engagement in later life and its effects on individuals, families, organizations, communities, and society at large.

Robin McKinney, MSW, is Director and Co-Founder of the Maryland CASH Campaign, which promotes programs, products, and policies that increase the financial security of low-income individuals and families. CASH's network annually serves 26,000 residents through free tax preparation, financial education, and coaching. She has a MSW from the University of Maryland School of Social Work, where she currently teaches.

Ruth McRoy, PhD, MSW, is the Donahue and DiFelice Endowed Professor of Social Work at Boston College and Ruby Lee Piester Centennial Professor Emerita at the University of Texas at Austin. She has authored 12 books and more than 100 articles and book chapters. She has received a US Children's Bureau's Adoption Excellence Award, a Distinguished Achievement Award from SSWR, and is a Fellow in the AASWSW and the SSWR.

Nancy Morrow-Howell, MSW, PhD, holds the Bettie Bofinger Brown Distinguished Professorship at the George Warren Brown School of Social Work at Washington University. She also directs the university's Harvey

A. Friedman Center for Aging. She is a Fellow and past president of the Gerontological Society of America.

Michelle R. Munson, PhD, MSW, is an associate professor at the New York University Silver School of Social Work and the Saul Cohen Chair of Child and Family Mental Health at The Jewish Board in New York City. She has written more than 45 articles and book chapters about child and adolescent services and interventions, many of which include social support components such as youth mentors and peer support specialists.

Deborah K. Padgett, PhD, has a doctorate in anthropology and is a professor at the Silver School of Social Work at New York University. She has written extensively on mental health services for underserved populations and is known for her expertise in qualitative/mixed methods and the "housing first" approach to ending homelessness.

Yolanda C. Padilla, PhD, is the Clara Pope Willoughby Centennial Professor in Child Welfare at the University of Texas at Austin School of Social Work and Director of the Council on Social Work Education's Center for Diversity and Social & Economic Justice. She studied social work and sociology at the University of Michigan and is an expert in social inequality and poverty.

Lawrence A. Palinkas, PhD, is the Albert G. and Frances Lomas Feldman Professor of Social Policy and Health and Chair of the Department of Children, Youth and Families in the Suzanne Dworak-Peck School of Social Work and professor in the Departments of Anthropology and Preventive Medicine at the University of Southern California.

Carrie Pettus-Davis, PhD, is the founding director of the Institute for Advancing Justice Research and Innovation and the Smart Decarceration Initiative. Her portfolio of research and practice experience is centered on decarceration through policy and practice innovation. She seeks to redress race, behavioral health, and economic disparities within the criminal justice system.

Michelle Putnam, PhD, is a professor at Simmons College, School of Social Work. She is Editor-in-Chief of the *Journal of Gerontological Social Work* and a Fellow of the Gerontological Society of America.

Lisa Reyes Mason, PhD, is Assistant Professor at the University of Tennessee College of Social Work and Faculty Director of the Environment and Social Development initiative at the Center for Social Development, Washington University in St. Louis. Her research is funded by the National Oceanic and Atmospheric Administration and the US Environmental Protection Agency.

Jennifer Romich, PhD, is Associate Professor of Social Work and Director of the West Coast Poverty Center at the University of Washington. Her research examines resources and economic in families, with a particular emphasis on low-income workers, household budgets, and families' interactions with public policy.

David Rothwell, PhD, studies and teaches courses on families, poverty, and social policy at Oregon State University. He has a PhD in social welfare from the University of Hawaii and an MSW from Tulane University.

Erika L. Sabbath, ScD, is an assistant professor at Boston College School of Social Work. She is currently the principal investigator of a K01 grant from the National Institute for Occupational Safety and Health (NIOSH) and the principal investigator of a major project within the NIOSH-funded Harvard Center for Work, Health, and Wellbeing.

Leon Sawh, MPH, is Project Manager at the Smart Decarceration Initiative, based at the University of Chicago's School of Social Service Administration. His work focuses on the development, adaptation, and evaluation of integrated mental health and substance use disorder treatment interventions for use with justice-involved and homeless populations.

Trina Shanks, PhD, is an associate professor at the University of Michigan School of Social Work. Her research interests include the impact of poverty and wealth on child well-being, asset-building policy and practice across the life cycle, and community and economic development. She has two books and numerous articles in print.

Margaret S. Sherraden, PhD, is a Founders Professor at the University of Missouri–St. Louis and a research professor at Washington University in St. Louis. She co-leads the Financial Capability and Asset Building for All initiative, one of social work's 12 Grand Challenges, and currently sits on the St. Louis Federal Reserve's Community Development Advisory Council.

Michael Sherraden, PhD, is the George Warren Brown Distinguished University Professor and is Founding Director of the Center for Social Development at Washington University in St Louis. Sherraden's early research on civic service—*National Service* (Pergamon, 1982) and *The Moral Equivalent of War?* (with Donald J. Eberly; Praeger, 1990)—contributed to the creation of AmeriCorps in 1993. Current research on asset building—*Inclusion in the American Dream* (Oxford University Press, 2005) and *Asset Building Innovations and Strategies in Asia* (with L. Zou, H. Ku, S. Deng, and S. Wang; Routledge, 2015)—has informed asset-building policies in many countries.

Michael S. Spencer, PhD, MSSW, is the Fedele F. Fauri Collegiate Professor of Social Work at the University of Michigan. He is a native Hawaiian scholar who focuses on community-based, participatory interventions for promoting health equity among populations of color. He is an AASWSW and SSWR Fellow.

Martell Teasley, PhD, is Dean of the College of Social Work at the University of Utah and serves at Editor-in-Chief for the National Association of Social Workers' journal *Children & Schools*. His primary research interests include African American adolescent development, cultural diversity, social welfare policy, and Black studies. He is nationally known for his research on school-aged children and youth.

Amanda Tillotson, PhD, is a researcher at the University of Michigan School of Social Work. Her work focuses on the role of social and economic policies in creating poverty and inequality. She is currently studying the role of housing and housing policy in the lives of low-income families.

Elizabeth M. Tracy, MSW, LISW, PhD, is the Grace Longwell Coyle Professor in Social Work at Case Western Reserve University. Her extensive publications have focused on personal network assessment and intervention in diverse social work practice and research settings, relating to child welfare and women's substance use disorders. She is a Fellow of SSWR.

Edwina Uehara, PhD, is Professor and Ballmer Endowed Dean, University of Washington School of Social Work, and Co-Chair of the AASWSW's Grand Challenges for Social Work Executive Committee. Her research centers on understanding the interplay of social structures and the sociocultural construction of health, illness, and healing.

Karina L. Walters, PhD, MSW, is the William P. and Ruth Gerberding Endowed Professor at the University of Washington School of Social Work, Director of the Indigenous Wellness Research Institute, and an enrolled member of the Choctaw Nation in Oklahoma. She is an AASWSW and SSWR Fellow and focuses on American Indian and Alaska Native wellness.

Darrell P. Wheeler, PhD, MPH, ACSW, is Vice Provost for Public Engagement at the University at Albany–SUNY. He is an educator and researcher on HIV prevention and intervention in African American gay, bisexual, and transgender communities using evidence in developing innovative programs and policy initiatives.

Bradley J. Zebrack, PhD, MSW, MPH, is Professor of Social Work at the University of Michigan. His research interests are in the area of health, medicine, and particularly the quality of health care service delivery to cancer patients and their families.

Karen A. Zurlo, PhD, MSW, is an associate professor in the School of Social Work at Rutgers, the State University of New Jersey, and is affiliated with the Institute for Health, Health Care Policy and Aging Research. Her research primarily focuses on economic security in late life.

GRAND CHALLENGES FOR SOCIAL WORK INITIATIVE

The Grand Challenges for Social Work are designed to focus a world of thought and action on the most compelling and critical social issues of our day. Each grand challenge is a broad but discrete concept where social work expertise and leadership can be brought to bear on bold new ideas, scientific exploration, and surprising innovations.

We invite you to review the following challenges with the goal of providing greater clarity, utility, and meaning to this roadmap for lifting up the lives of individuals, families, and communities struggling with the most fundamental requirements for social justice and human existence.

The Grand Challenges for Social Work include the following:

- Ensure healthy development for all youth
- Close the health gap
- Stop family violence
- Advance long and productive lives
- Eradicate social isolation
- End homelessness
- Create social responses to a changing environment
- Harness technology for social good
- Promote smart decarceration
- Reduce extreme economic inequality
- Build financial capability for all
- Achieve equal opportunity and justice

Grand Challenges for
Social Work and Society

CHAPTER 1

Grand Challenges for Social Work and Society

JAMES E. LUBBEN, RICHARD P. BARTH, ROWENA FONG,
MARILYN L. FLYNN, MICHAEL SHERRADEN,
AND EDWINA UEHARA

Ambitious yet achievable goals for society that mobilize the profession, capture the public's imagination, and require innovation and breakthroughs in science and practice to achieve.

Kalil (2012)

The Grand Challenges for Social Work (GCSW) provides an agenda of grand challenges for all of society. GCSW is a campaign inaugurated by the social work profession, prompting social workers and allies in other fields to ponder society's most challenging problems and how best to accelerate progress toward resolving them. GCSW is designed to promote scientific innovation in social work; engage the social work profession in strengthening the ties among social work organizations; foster transdisciplinary research; expand the student pipeline into the social work profession; and create greater acknowledgment of social work science within the discipline and by other, related, disciplines. A related goal is to position social work to become a more valued science by creating a social agenda for America.

The GCSW is sponsored by the American Academy of Social Work and Social Welfare (AASWSW or "the Academy"). Established in 2009, the Academy is to provide social work—and social issues—with the significance that the National Academies of Science, Engineering, and Medicine provide to those fields. Founders of the Academy envisioned a future in which social work and social welfare science are recognized as fundamental to society. Accordingly, the charter of the Academy elaborates the mission of encouraging and recognizing outstanding research, scholarship, and practice that contribute to a sustainable, equitable, and just future. AASWSW is an honorific society, inducting new members annually through a rigorous nominations and elections process modeled after the traditions of the National Academy of Medicine. There are currently more than 110 member fellows, recognizing the highest honor of researcher and practitioner accomplishment in the profession.

The Academy also informs social policy by serving as a frontline source of information for the social work profession, for Congress, and for other public and private entities charged with advancing the public good. Its focus is to promote the examination of social policy and the application of research to test alternative policies, programs, and practices for their impact on society. The Grand Challenges for Social Work is the first major initiative of the Academy.

BACKGROUND AND HISTORY OF GRAND CHALLENGES FOR SOCIAL WORK

Success has many parents, and so it is with GCSW. Edwina Uehara, Dean at the University of Washington School of Social Work, is one of the proud parents, having become an active student of grand challenges campaigns being adopted by a number of other organizations and professions. Dean Uehara first advanced the idea of grand challenges for social work. This work built upon a strong foundation laid by John Brekke, who championed the notion that there was a *science of social work* (Brekke, 2012). Brekke showcased his thinking regarding a science of social work at the Society for Social Work and Research's (SSWR) 2011 Aaron Rosen Lecture on the Science of Social Work (Brekke, 2011, 2012; Brekke & Anastas, forthcoming). These two notions—the possibility of a grand challenge campaign for social work and the codification of a science of social work—were synergistic movements. In particular, the strong emphasis on scientific rigor for the grand challenges is due in part to the growing consensus that social work had a science. Similarly, the science of social work movement benefited from the increased attention to social work becoming a critical partner with other branches of science in solving challenging societal problems.

Capitalizing on the energy of these two related developments, a meeting was arranged with Marilyn Flynn, Edwina Uehara, and Richard Barth. Flynn and Uehara were deans of their respective schools of social work, and Barth was then President of the AASWSW and Dean of the University of Maryland School of Social Work. Among the topics discussed was the idea of launching a Grand Challenges campaign for social work under the auspices of the

Academy. To further develop this idea, a larger meeting was planned for the summer of 2012. A select group of 40 participants was invited to the 2-day conference designed to grapple with social work's role in shaping 21st-century society. The 2-day conference took place at Islandwood, a conference center located on Bainbridge Island in Puget Sound, Washington. One day of the conference was devoted to refine the development of a science of social work, and the other day focused on nurturing the idea of a grand challenges campaign for social work.

On the day devoted to grand challenges, Uehara introduced the history and concept of grand challenges and proposed that social work create a grand challenges initiative (Uehara et al., 2014). In addition to her articulation of the fit between grand challenges and the point of intersection with the progress of social work, she also illustrated the potential benefits of grand challenges by introducing University of Washington's Dean of Engineering, Matt O'Donnell, who described the National Academy of Engineering (NAE) Grand Challenges initiative. The NAE had selected 14 grand challenges to galvanize the engineering profession to recruit more female and domestically born engineers by encouraging collaborations and innovations to solve major problems. The NAE's intention was to shift the understanding of engineering from a profession that built tunnels, sewers, skyscrapers, and computer programs to one that solved such major problems as providing access to clean water, providing secure cyberspace, and advancing personalized learning.

The Islandwood meeting then reviewed strategies of other grand challenges then in progress, such as the grand challenges from the William and Melinda Gates Foundation, the National Institute for Mental Health (NIMH), and Grand Challenges Canada. Barth's presentation considered the dominant approaches previously taken—especially comparing the generation of grand challenges from one or a few experts—by a larger group of people (NIMH used a very large panel of respondents from throughout the world in their Delphi process) and suggested that we needed to find our own, third way. More background on the grand challenges and their emergence--since David Hilbert first announced his grand challenges—is provided by Uehara and colleagues (2013).

Like engineering, social work is concerned about the student pipeline and a desire to galvanize its profession to become more focused on visibility and benefit for all of society. The GCSW also provided an opportunity to work collaboratively with a problem-solving (rather than organizational) focus across social work organizations and other related scientific disciplines. The GCSW would be ambitious, bold, and uncharted. Although benefits for the social work profession were expected from a successful GCSW initiative, discussions originated and remained focused on ways to explore how social work could address social problems innovatively and transformatively, making a significant impact within a decade. The goals were to improve society while building new science, skills, and relationships that would also strengthen the profession of social work.

The Academy board enthusiastically approved the role of shepherding the grand challenges and undertook the GCSW initiative in 2013 with the appointment of a Grand Challenge Executive Committee convened by Barth and staffed by Sarah Butts, the AASWSW's first administrator. Beginning in December 2012, Barth invited John Brekke, Claudia Coulton, Diana DiNitto, Marilyn Flynn, Rowena Fong, J. David Hawkins, King Davis, James Lubben, Ron Manderscheid, Yolanda Padilla, Michael Sherraden, Edwina Uehara, Karina Walters, and James Herbert Williams to be the Grand Challenge Executive Committee.

The Executive Committee convened for the first time in early 2013 at a retreat in Chicago and elected John Brekke and Rowena Fong as co-chairs. The meeting was organized by four sessions: (1) Grand Context—Impact Model, (2) Potential Frameworks and Criteria for Developing Grand Challenges for Social Work, (3) Strategies to Foster Collaborations Among Stakeholders, and (4) Approaches to Gather and Process Input from Stakeholders.

Executive Committee members more intently studied exemplars and models of grand challenges originating outside of social work. The Bill and Melinda Gates Foundation, one of the examples, began its initiative in 2003, focused on health-related challenges throughout the world. The 2010 NIMH's grand challenges targeted global mental health. The National Science Foundation identified six research ideas and three process ideas for its grand challenges. Having reviewed the exemplars, retreat participants decided to model GCSW most closely with the discipline of engineering because of similar interest in affecting the population entering the profession and being academically and profession driven yet collaborating with the community and with other disciplines.

Executive Committee members left the inaugural committee meeting with a sense of inspiration and charge. There was agreement that the process of identifying social work's grand challenges would not be hardwired and would be representative of the values of the profession—strengths-based and inclusive. Also, the meeting engendered the recognition that the committee would continue to wrestle with framework, structure, criteria, and process in the months and possibly years ahead but would eventually develop a refined construct and process.

DETERMINING AND SELECTING
THE GRAND CHALLENGES

The GCSW initiative went through three phases. The first phase focused on the identification and selection of the 12 Grand Challenges. This phase encompassed 3 years of work. The second phase focused on a rollout of the 12 Grand Challenges, and it encompassed 2 years of work. The third phase of the GCSW began in 2016 and is ongoing. It involves a wide array of activities spawned by each of the 12 Grand Challenges.

Among the tasks accomplished in the first phase of the GCSW was the clarification of context for proposed new initiative. Seeking a historical perspective of what social work had already accomplished and had brought to national scale, the Executive Committee developed two foundational working papers.

The first foundational working paper, titled "Social Is Fundamental: Introduction and Context for Grand Challenges for Social Work" (drafted in 2012–2013 and revised in Sherraden, Barth, et al., 2015), emphasizes the importance of social factors in a broad array of ways that have advanced the evolution of society. The underlying argument is that social factors and social relationships explain more than a few of the current darlings of public attention, including genetics and technology. Insofar as social factors and social relationships are the explicit focus of social work, this positions the field to craft and implement a major social agenda like that which would emerge from the Grand Challenges.

The second anchoring working paper, titled "Grand Accomplishments of Social Work and Grand Context of Social Work" (Sherraden, Stuart, et al., 2015), lends credence to the idea that social workers have the capacity to develop innovative interventions for very challenging groups and successfully implement tests and bring them to scale. This has been going on since social workers led a national effort to reduce infant mortality by half in the early 1900s, and it continues with such international models as Assertive Community Treatment, closing of group homes for young children, and Housing First! These, and many more, historic innovations developed by social workers are part of what led us to embrace Bill Gates' maxim to never overestimate what you can do in 2 years and never underestimate what you can do in a decade.

These two foundational papers helped drive the excitement and focus of the Grand Challenges Executive Committee. The conversation never strayed far from ways that social factors were undervalued and would ultimately be a greater determinant of the future of society (and even the Earth) than any other factors. The discussion of grand accomplishments also helped to keep the importance of, and possibility for, scaling up at the tip of the conversation.

With initial conceptualization by Yolanda Padilla, the Executive Committee also developed an impact model that identified the scope, products, impacts, and timeframe for the initiative. The impact model, shown in Figure 1.1, delineates the internal and external impact grand challenges were to make in a decade and was a visual depiction much like a "logic model" to guide the grand challenge approach to solving societal problems.

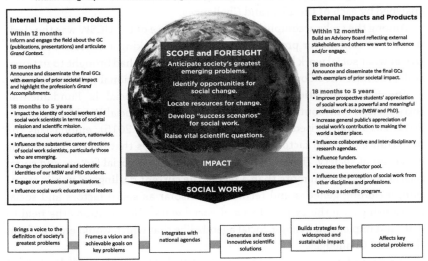

GRAND CHALLENGES OF SOCIAL WORK INITIATIVE
Impact Model: Scope, Products, Impacts, and Timeframes

Grand challenge: "a deeply significant problem widely recognized by the public whose solution is within our grasp in the next decade, given concentrated scientific and practical attention."

Internal Impacts and Products

Within 12 months
Inform and engage the field about the GC (publications, presentations) and articulate *Grand Context.*

18 months
Announce and disseminate the final GCs with exemplars of prior societal impact and highlight the profession's *Grand Accomplishments.*

18 months to 5 years
• Impact the identity of social workers and social work scientists in terms of societal mission and scientific mission.
• Influence social work education, nationwide.
• Influence the substantive career directions of social work scientists, particularly those who are emerging.
• Change the professional and scientific identities of our MSW and PhD students.
• Engage our professional organizations.
• Influence social work educators and leaders

SCOPE and FORESIGHT
Anticipate society's greatest emerging problems.
Identify opportunities for social change.
Locate resources for change.
Develop "success scenarios" for social work.
Raise vital scientific questions.

IMPACT

SOCIAL WORK

External Impacts and Products

Within 12 months
Build an Advisory Board reflecting external stakeholders and others we want to influence and/or engage.

18 months
Announce and disseminate the final GCs with exemplars of prior societal impact.

18 months to 5 years
• Improve prospective students' appreciation of social work as a powerful and meaningful profession of choice (MSW and PhD).
• Increase general public's appreciation of social work's contribution to making the world a better place.
• Influence collaborative and inter-disciplinary research agendas.
• Influence funders.
• Increase the benefactor pool.
• Influence the perception of social work from other disciplines and professions.
• Develop a scientific program.

| Brings a voice to the definition of society's greatest problems | Frames a vision and achievable goals on key problems | Integrates with national agendas | Generates and tests innovative scientific solutions | Builds strategies for widespread and sustainable impact | Affects key societal problems |

Figure 1.1 Impact model.

Although GCSW was modeled after a similar undertaking spearheaded by the NAE, the approach to identify the specific grand challenges was quite different. The NAE's 14 grand challenges were established by a small group of senior members comprising a national advisory board, and it had three major champions who were all university administrators. This approach generated criticism because it was viewed as a top-down mandate to the profession of priorities that had not been shared for input with engineers on the front lines and outside of academia.

The GCSW group learned from the engineers, and so as not to make the same errors, the GCSW opted for a more inclusive "bottom-up" approach—one that sought to cultivate ideas from the social work profession broadly. The decision proved to be worthwhile as well as arduous. The Executive Committee hosted several rounds of idea and concept generative activities, and continually sought input and feedback from the profession. A website was constructed to foster a crowdsourcing model of generating ideas for possible grand challenges. Subsequently, there was a call for formal concept papers that more explicitly articulated specific proposed grand challenges. The process was thoughtful and, at times, peppered with hot debate and deliberation.

The first announcement of the Grand Challenges in any peer-review publication was an invited paper for publication in the *Journal of the Society for Social Work and Research.* This keystone paper (Uehara et al., 2013) introduced the concept of grand challenges and began the description of how we would integrate the fundamentals of social work and social work science with the grand challenges. The paper also indicated why the AASWSW was chosen for this work. Six benefits of grand challenges were proposed: (1) providing a compelling focus, (2) bringing great minds and collaborators to focus on problem-solving, (3) providing a platform for innovative and interdisciplinary work, (4) capturing the public's imagination, (5) attracting new resources and interest, and (6) creating a platform for science diplomacy that bridges divides (adapted from Singer & Brook, 2011). The paper by Uehara et al. described the bold and historic intentions of the GCSW.

Defining Criteria and Call for Ideas and Concept Papers

The Executive Committee took great care to define criteria and a review process that would yield proposals that met appropriate standards of a grand challenge for society. A major intent of these criteria was to generate the expectation that these areas were ones for which discrete interventions and measureable progress could be generated. The committee was clear that we did not want a set of grand challenges that were characterized by massive problems with no clear scientific basis for creating measurable progress. The decision on criteria was also formulated on the basis of the purpose of the grand challenges to ensure that the science of the social work profession was strengthened along with society. For this reason, an emphasis was placed on building upon relationships with other disciplines with strong scientific traditions. The five criteria for the grand challenges were announced as follows:

1. The challenge must be big, important, and compelling.
2. Scientific evidence indicates that the challenge can be completely or largely solved.
3. Meaningful and measurable progress to address the challenge can be made in a decade.
4. The challenge is likely to generate interdisciplinary or cross-sector collaboration.
5. Solutions to the challenge require significant innovation.

Endeavoring to be as inclusive as possible, ideas for grand challenges were invited from research scholars, practitioners, students, and even the public. During the course of 3 years (2013–2016), Executive Committee members made multiple presentations to the Council on Social Work Education (CSWE), the SSWR, the National Association of Social Workers (NASW), the Association of Baccalaureate Program Directors of Social Work, the National Association of Deans and Directors (NADD), the St. Louis Group, and the NASW Social Work Pioneers to solicit input on the grand challenge ideas, concepts, and discussions. Paper cards were distributed during meetings so that participants could submit their ideas in person, e-mails were sent through NASW to state chapter directors, and a new AASWSW website was developed to provide a backbone for communications and allow members of the public to submit their challenges directly to the Academy online. The practice of soliciting input throughout the developmental stages of Grand Challenge articulation was instituted, whereby committee members used conferences as forums to provide updates, invite input, and use feedback to refine and improve the process of determining the grand challenges.

More than 80 initial ideas were proposed (see Appendix 1). Based on these ideas, a call for concept papers was issued. Guidelines outlined requirements for papers to describe how a grand challenge met the five established criteria. The committee reviewed the 80 suggested ideas for a grand challenge and invited authors to submit 6- to 10-page concept papers that further addressed each of the five essential criteria. In addition, known leaders in social work were encouraged to write concept papers on topics deemed important but not included among the 80 suggested ideas. The process was also open to new ideas as long as the authors would submit a formal concept paper to back up their concept. In the end, 38 formal concept papers were submitted and reviewed. Some of these papers were elaborations of one of the original 80 suggested ideas, and others were on totally new topics.

Review Process

A peer-review process was implemented to assess which of the concept papers met all five of the criteria. It was also important to determine if the concept papers fit with the grand accomplishments of social work, supported the grand context of social work, complemented initiatives in other fields, and offered innovations. Initially, paper review was organized much like a National Institutes of Health technical grant appraisal, but the process became much more flexible. Those selecting the concept paper as a grand challenge considered the diversity of the social work domains affected. In reviewing the concept papers, efforts were made to combine similar concept papers into more parsimonious and powerful challenges. All 38 concept papers were reviewed and scored, with the top-scoring papers identified and prioritized as promising grand challenge concepts.

The 38 well-developed concept papers were then matched against the many domains of social work to determine coverage. The Executive Committee engaged in laborious discussion about how to select and identify social work's grand challenges. There was debate about the Executive Committee's role as an evaluating committee versus creating a new group(s) for the evaluation. Scope and scale were discussed at length—whether to focus broadly or narrowly on a topic and the advantages and disadvantages of each approach. Each committee member, with his or her own subject matter expertise, developed his or her own conception of an ideal grand challenge. Some members thought we should include all the traditional areas of practice. A majority ended up pushing for new terrain and innovation. The process required careful evaluation of the merits of each individual challenge as well as the strength of the entire set of challenges collectively. A process of identifying gaps and matching the papers to the needs of the field and the grand challenges was critical in identifying an initial set of challenges and working papers.

The scoring was, some argued, perhaps too heavily weighted toward ideas that had deep scientific moorings and not sufficiently toward other equally important ideas that might be larger, policy-oriented, and perhaps transformative. Much discussion was given to how to respond to concept papers on gender equality and equity toward lesbian, gay, bisexual, transgendered, questioning, and allied (LGBTQA) identified individuals, ending poverty, responding to the needs of immigrants, and ending racism—none of which included very specific ideas about what interventions were likely to achieve these grand goals or produce objective data to determine whether progress was being made. New papers were invited on organizations and bureaucracy, as well as on severe mental illness, but these never came to completion. Ultimately, the Executive Committee decided to create grand challenges to "achieve equal opportunity and justice" and to "reduce extreme economic inequality." Furthermore, the committee reached out to support work on three position papers under "achieving equal opportunity and justice": (1) increasing success for African American students by closing the preschool to prison pipeline, one of the most influential manifestations of historic racism; (2) promoting equality by addressing social stigma; and (3) the integration of Latina/o immigrants into American society.

Thus, each grand challenge was built upon a platform of at least one working paper that laid out a scientific approach to its achievement. An exception was the challenge "harness technology for social good," which was developed based on an intense discussion among Executive Committee members about the progress and opportunities in this field. Following this discussion, Claudia Coulton agreed to develop a working paper. Although the Executive Committee is no longer searching for additional working papers—preferring instead that scholarship arising from GCSW is captured in conventional peer-review publications—the working papers provide important starting points. Working papers were developed and edited in support of each grand challenge. From 2015 to 2017, 18 papers were completed to buttress the ambitious concepts outlined in the 12 Grand Challenges. The Executive Committee always intended for the grand challenges to be much larger than any paper or authorship group. GCSW is very much a framework and scaffolding to house all the important contributions of social worker research and practitioners.

Social work had, indeed, found a way of its own to select twelve exciting and vital Grand Challenges.

Each grand challenge is a vessel that can contain many ideas, papers, and initiatives—all contributing to measurable progress on the same challenge. In some cases, primary authors of grand challenge working papers became leaders who have continued to move the campaign to address that challenge forward. In other cases, new individuals were identified who came forth to provide leadership for a grand challenge. They in turn have recruited others to join with them as grand challenge network co-leads who together are continuing to invest in the emergence of the grand challenges.

After the final 12 Grand Challenges were identified, the next step involved working with communications experts from a select group of schools of social work and a communications company (SCP Communications) to sharpen the language. The Executive Committee then prepared a brief summary of each grand challenge. The 12 Grand Challenges are listed and defined as follows (see the AASWSW website for further detailed information about each grand challenge: http://aaswsw.org/grand-challenges-initiative/12-challenges):

> *Ensure healthy development for all youth*: Each year, more than 6 million young people receive treatment for severe mental, emotional, or behavioral problems. Strong evidence shows us how to prevent many behavioral health problems before they emerge. By unleashing the power of prevention through widespread use of proven approaches, we can help all youth grow up to become healthy and productive adults.
>
> *Close the health gap*: More than 60 million Americans experience devastating one–two punches to their health—they have inadequate access to basic health care while also enduring the effects of discrimination, poverty, and dangerous environments that accelerate higher rates of illness. Innovative and evidence-based social strategies can improve health care and lead to broad gains in the health of our entire society.
>
> *Stop family violence*: Family violence is a common American tragedy. Assaults by parents, intimate partners, and adult children frequently result in serious injury and even death. Such violence costs billions of dollars annually in social and criminal justice spending. Proven interventions can prevent abuse, identify abuse sooner, and help families survive and thrive by breaking the cycle of violence or finding safe alternatives.
>
> *Advance long and productive lives*: Increased automation and longevity demand new thinking by employers and employees regarding productivity. Young people are increasingly disconnected from education or work, and the labor force faces significant retirements in the next decades. Throughout the lifespan, fuller engagement in education

and paid and unpaid productive activities can generate a wealth of benefits, including better health and well-being, greater financial security, and a more vital society.

Eradicate social isolation: Social isolation is a silent killer—as dangerous to health as smoking. National and global health organizations have underscored the hidden, deadly, and pervasive hazards stemming from feeling alone and abandoned. Our challenge is to educate the public on this health hazard, encourage health and human service professionals to address social isolation, and promote effective ways to deepen social connections and community for people of all ages.

End homelessness: During the course of a year, nearly 1.5 million Americans will experience homelessness for at least one night. Periods of homelessness often have serious and lasting effects on personal development, health, and well-being. Our challenge is to expand proven approaches that have worked in communities across the country, develop new service innovations and technologies, and adopt policies that promote affordable housing and basic income security.

Create social responses to a changing environment: The environmental challenges reshaping contemporary societies pose profound risks to human well-being, particularly for marginalized communities. Climate change and urban development threaten health, undermine coping, and deepen existing social and environmental inequities. A changing global environment requires transformative social responses: new partnerships, deep engagement with local communities, and innovations to strengthen individual and collective assets.

Harness technology for social good: Innovative applications of new digital technology present opportunities for social and human services to reach more people with greater impact on our most vexing social problems. These new technologies can be deployed to more strategically target social spending, speed up the development of effective programs, and bring a wider array of help to more individuals and communities.

Promote smart decarceration: The United States has the world's largest proportion of people behind bars. Mass incarceration and failed rehabilitation have resulted in staggering economic and human costs. Our challenge is to develop a proactive, comprehensive, evidence-based "smart decarceration" strategy that will dramatically reduce the number of people who are imprisoned and enable the nation to embrace a more effective and just approach to public safety.

Reduce extreme economic inequality: The top 1% owns nearly half of the total wealth in the United States, while one in five children lives in poverty. The consequences for health and well-being are immeasurable. We can correct the broad inequality of wealth and income through a variety of innovative means related to wages and tax benefits associated with capital gains, retirement accounts, and home ownership. Greater lifelong access to education will also provide broader economic opportunities.

Build financial capability for all: Nearly half of all American households are financially insecure, without adequate savings to meet basic living expenses for 3 months. We can significantly reduce economic hardship and the debilitating effects of poverty by adopting social policies that bolster lifelong income generation and safe retirement accounts, expand workforce training and retraining, and provide financial literacy and access to quality affordable financial services.

Achieve equal opportunity and justice: In the United States, some groups of people have long been consigned to society's margins. Historic and current prejudice and injustice bar access to success in education and employment. Addressing racial and social injustices, deconstructing stereotypes, dismantling inequality, exposing unfair practices, and accepting the super diversity of the population will advance this challenge. All of this work is critical to fostering a successful society.

The working papers were sharpened in support of each of the grand challenges. Some took many months to develop in order to finally meet the high standard of the Executive Committee and adequately address the criteria. Appendix 2 shows how the working papers were organized under each grand challenge and how each grand challenge was, ultimately, arrayed under three rubrics: individual and family well-being, stronger social fabric, and just society.

Phase 2: Rollout of the Grand Challenges for Social Work

With the decision on the final 12 Grand Challenges, the foundational papers complete, and many strong working papers in the can, the soft rollout began. A significant task was to accurately and modestly explain the selection of the grand challenges and, in so doing, to engage the other professional social work organizations, such as CSWE and NASW, whose executives served as National Advisory Board members. Stakeholder support was critical to the success of grand challenges, and affirmative buy-in was very important for this initiative to succeed and endure. We understood that we had made that effort more difficult by selecting a somewhat unconventional set of new challenges and not selecting some of social work's iconic challenges.

Wiser members of the GCSW leadership understood that we needed a strong communications plan to be able to engage our profession and others in the excitement of the GCSW. A communications contractor, SCP communications (http://www.aboutscp.com), was selected and funds were raised with a matching program anchored by a gift from the University of Southern California (USC). The match was met from willing schools of social work along with a pledge from NADD. The communications team helped generate graphics, a website (implemented by Wood Street; https://www.woodst.com), and build a social media following.

The second phase of GCSW, which began with a soft rollout at the 2015 SSWR meeting in New Orleans, concluded 1 year later with the official launch of the Grand Challenges at the 2016 SSWR in Washington, DC. AASWSW President Barth gave the keynote, which included a video on the grand challenges, with enthusiastic commentary by panelists Angelo McClain (CEO of NASW) and Darla Coffey (President of CSWE). Two major receptions afterward featured ways for attendees to get involved with the grand challenges via social media and other approaches.

The 2016 SSWR meeting marked the organization's 20th anniversary, which brought additional energy to the confab. The SSWR meeting that year was organized around the GCSW with special symposia as well as special e-poster presentations for each of the 12 Grand Challenges. All abstracts submissions were encouraged to specify how they were responsive to the grand challenges.

Phase 3: Capturing and Spreading the Synergy of the Grand Challenges for Social Work

The initiative entered the third phase that continued the social media work and focused on network generation and strengthening for each of the 12 Grand Challenges. Those involved with the 12 Grand Challenges were encouraged to mobilize activities around their specific grand challenge and elicit increased involvement of a wider cadre of constituents within social work and other professions. Similarly, it was deemed highly desirable to gain more involvement from the practice community and to build greater capacity by reaching beyond the academy to the larger social work profession. Accordingly, a new organizational structure evolved. Executive Committee co-chairs Brekke and Fong, having earned great appreciation of their colleagues, stepped down, and a new Grand Challenges Steering Committee led by Marilyn Flynn, Michael Sherraden, and Eddie Uehara was established. In January 2017, the Steering Committee added Richard Barth (past president of AASWSW) and Sarah Gehlert (current president of AASWSW). The Steering Committee was also expanded to include a select group of national leaders, including the heads of CSWE, the NASW Fund for Social Policy, and the Congressional Research Institute for Social Work and Policy (see Appendix 3). In April 2017, the

Steering Committee named Sarah Butts as Executive Director of the Grand Challenges for Social Work, Lissa Johnson as Director of Policy Initiatives, and Michele Clark as Program Associate and Strategic Liaison.

The momentum of the SSWR launch was maintained. Several special issues in professional journals showcasing the grand challenges were generated. The *Journal of the Society for Social Work and Research* (*JSSWR*) invited authors of papers at the 2016 SSWR meeting to submit articles for a special section on grand challenge implementation. The introductory paper by Uehara, Barth, Coffey, Padilla, and McClain (2017) helped connect the GCSW back to its groundwork of understanding implementation strategies under way in other grand challenges. Flynn (2017) identifies strategies for engaging the participation of academic departments in a comprehensive university and makes a compelling argument for the importance of including schools of all sizes in the grand challenges. She suggests that we attend to the critical implementation components of promoting faculty innovation and scientific development, building on student talents and capabilities, and developing university and local program initiatives. Nurius, Coffey, Fong, Korr, and McRoy (2017) focus their implementation discussion on aligning social work curricula with the grand challenges and building on the emerging reality that the future's social worker will function within interdisciplinary or interprofessional teams and have to operate with team members who are unfamiliar and may have conflicting goals. They propose that readiness for "T-shaped pedagogy" will be enhanced by building grand challenges approaches into social work education. Gehlert, Hall, and Palinkas (2017) build on this notion with a discussion of how to enhance the success of transdisciplinary and translational science and how this will, in turn, advance the grand challenges. Finally, Haggerty et al. (2017) describe their work rolling out Communities in Action, which could serve as an exemplar for other grand challenge implementation efforts.

Articles about grand challenges also appeared in the *Journal of Policy Practice* (Padilla & Fong, 2016), the *Journal of Gerontological Social Work*, the *Journal of Social Work Practice in the Addictions*, the *Journal of Social Work Education*, and *Children & Schools*. *JSSWR* will also published a special issue on ensuring healthy development for all youth, which is one of the 12 Grand Challenges and also the theme of the 2017 SSWR annual meeting.

Conferences began to arise from the grand challenge networks. The University of Chicago's School of Social Services Administration and the Brown School at Washington University in St. Louis hosted a conference on Smart Decarceration. Washington University and the University of Maryland hosted a conference in Washington, DC, titled Financial Capability for All. These conferences offered the opportunity to strengthen the working relationships between network members, to notify panelists and invited guests about the grand challenges, and to generate innovations that could help advance grand challenge goals. These GCSW-related conferences are resulting in the following forthcoming book publications: Matt Epperson and Carrie Pettus-Davis (Eds.), *Smart Decarceration*; Margaret Sherraden, Julie Birkenmeier, and Michael Collins, *Financial Capability and Asset Building*; Molly Metzger and Hank Webber (Eds.), *Inclusive Housing*; and Lisa Reyes Mason and Jonathan Rigg (Eds.), *People and Climate Change*.

In October 2016, under the leadership of Michael Sherraden and the Center for Social Development, the Grand Challenges group organized and delivered a policy conference focused on GCSW that was held at the Brown School of Social Work at Washington University in St. Louis. Titled "Social Innovation for America's Renewal," the policy conference had approximately 300 attendees, who listened and learned about as well as debated the policy recommendations for each of the respective 12 Grand Challenges. The conference brought together national experts and scholars to discuss solutions to and policy recommendations for some of society's major problems, searching for the possibility of positive social development. The purpose of the conference was to stimulate policy innovations at all levels in order to produce positive changes in people's lives.

A legacy of the conference is significant policy work from each of the grand challenge networks. Succinct, actionable policy recommendations were generated (and shown in Appendix 4). Early drafts were further refined in discussions during the conference and resulted in improvements. In addition, several networks have gone on to write more detailed policy arguments. The core of these policy ideas was eventually published in the *St. Louis Post-Dispatch* as an editorial calling for these to be the basis of a social agenda (Sherraden & Barth, 2016).

Several other conferences focused on the 12 Grand Challenges. For example, Larry Palinkas organized the Children, Youth and Families and Social Work Grand Challenges Conference held at USC, where all grand challenge co-leads were invited to present what their grand challenges were doing in relation to children, youth, and families. In addition to the grand challenge co-leads, the conference was heavily populated by USC faculty and doctoral students eager to think through educational and research implications for the grand challenges. It featured an interesting format that enabled conference participants to be quickly introduced to all 12 Grand Challenges and then meet in small café-style conversational meetings with the co-leads of up to three of the Grand Challenges. This format facilitated further thinking regarding curriculum, research, and practice implications spawned by the GCSW.

Another conference also held in 2017 at USC was organized by Marilyn Flynn, Rowena Fong, Stephanie Berzin, and Claudia Coulton. It focused on harnessing technology for social good, which had grand challenge co-leads, national and local speakers, practitioners, and community members in attendance. The conference had invited panelists and break-out discussion focusing on technologies related to geospatial technology, data linkage, predictive analytics, social media, mobile apps, and wearable technology. The conference spurred on conversations about ethics and the role it plays in the use of technology and big data challenges.

Additional meetings have been launched in response to the GCSW. One conference focused on curriculum at the Western Consortium of Schools of Social Work meeting, at which faculty and directors of schools of social work gathered to discuss integrating grand challenge curriculum into their schools of social work (Flynn, 2017). The CSWE has organized 12 pre-conference workshops featuring each of the 12 Grand Challenges to be presented at its 2017 annual program meeting.

CONCLUSION

The GCSW initiative addresses grand challenges for all of society. GCSW is about *what we can contribute to society* in new knowledge, practices, policies, and capacities developed by social work and its allies. The grand challenges will succeed if they spur specific great ideas, innovate, and create transformative solutions for some of society's large and compelling problems during the next decade. The GCSW involves everyone: families, communities, researchers, educators, practitioners, and policymakers—all working together to achieve social progress powered by evidence and effective implementation of social innovations.

REFERENCES

Brekke, J. (2011). *It's not about fish and bicycles—We need a science of social work!* Aaron Rosen Lecture, Society for Social Work and Research, Tampa, FL, January 14, 2011.

Brekke, J. S. (2012). Shaping a science of social work. *Research on Social Work Practice, 22*(5), 455–464. doi:10.1177/1049731512441263

Brekke, J. S., & Anastas, J. (forthcoming). *Social work science: Towards a new identity.* New York, NY: Oxford University Press.

Epperson, M., & Pettus-Davis, C. (forthcoming). *Smart decarceration.* New York, NY: Oxford University Press.

Flynn, M. (2017). The grand challenge concept: Campus strategies for implementation. *Journal of the Society for Social Work Research, 8*(1), 87–98.

Gehlert, S., Hall, K., & Palinkas, L. (2017). Preparing our next-generation scientific workforce to address the grand challenges for social work. *Journal of the Society for Social Work and Research, 8*(1), 119–136.

Haggerty, K., Barton, V., Catalano, R., Spearmon, M., Elion, E., Reese, R., & Uehara, E. (2017). Translating grand challenges from concept to community: The "Communities in Action" experience. *Journal of the Society for Social Work Research, 8*(1), 137–159.

Kalil, T. (2012, April). *The grand challenges of the 21st century*. Speech presented at the Information Technology and Innovation Foundation, Washington, DC.

Mason, M., & Rigg, J. (Eds.). (forthcoming). *People and climate change*. New York, NY: Oxford University Press.

Metzger, M., & Webber, H. (Eds.). (forthcoming). *Inclusive housing*. New York, NY: Oxford University Press.

Nurius, P., Coffey, D., Fong, R., Korr, W., & McRoy, R. (2017). Preparing professional degree students to tackle grand challenges: A framework for aligning social work curriculum. *Journal of the Society for Social Work Research, 8*(1), 99–118.

Padilla, Y., & Fong, R. (2016). Identifying grand challenges facing social work in the next decade: Maximizing social policy engagement. *Journal of Policy Practice, 15*, 133–144.

Sherraden, Margaret, Birkenmaier, J., & Collins, M. (forthcoming). *Financial capability and asset building*. New York, NY: Oxford University Press.

Sherraden, Michael, & Barth, R. P. (2016, October 6). 12 questions for the presidential debate [Editorial]. *St. Louis Post Dispatch*. Retrieved from http://www.stltoday.com/news/opinion/questions-for-the-presidential-debate/article_7780d1b7-44f0-5e56-9e43-a2619fd27d81.html

Sherraden, M., Barth, R. P., Brekke, J., Fraser, M. W., Mandersheid, R., & Padgett, D. K. (2015). *Social is fundamental: Introduction and context for Grand Challenges for Social Work* (Grand Challenges for Social Work Initiative Working Paper No. 1). Baltimore, MD: American Academy of Social Work and Social Welfare.

Sherraden, M., Stuart, P., Barth, R. P., Kemp, S., Lubben, J., Hawkins, J. D., . . . Catalano, R. (2015). *Grand accomplishments in social work* (Grand Challenges for Social Work Initiative Working Paper No. 2). Baltimore, MD: American Academy of Social Work and Social Welfare.

Singer, P. A., & Brook, D. (2011). *Grand Challenges Canada*. Retrieved from http://www.grandchallenges.ca/wordpress/wp-content/uploads/2011/02/thegrandchallengesapproach.pdf

Uehara, E., Barth, R., Coffey, D., Padilla, Y., & McClain, A. (2017). An introduction to a special section on grand challenges for social work. *Journal of the Society for Social Work and Research, 8*(1), 75–86.

Uehara, E., Flynn, M., Fong, R., Brekke, J., Barth, R. P., Coulton, C., . . . Walters, K. (2013). Grand challenges for social work. *Journal of the Society for Social Work and Research, 4*, 165–170. doi:10.5243/jsswr.2013.11

Uehara, E. S., Barth, R. P., Olson, S., Catalano, R. F., Hawkins, J. D., Kemp, S., . . . Sherraden, M. (2014). *Identifying and tackling grand challenges for social work* (Grand Challenges for Social Work Initiative Working Paper No. 3). Baltimore, MD: American Academy of Social Work and Social Welfare.

Grand Challenges
for Social Work
Ensure healthy development for all youth

CHAPTER 2

Ensure Healthy Development for All Youth[1]

JEFFREY M. JENSON AND J. DAVID HAWKINS

BEHAVIORAL HEALTH PROBLEMS IN CHILDHOOD AND ADOLESCENCE

Behavioral health problems in childhood and adolescence exact significant individual, social, and economic costs on millions of young people. These problems include anxiety and depression; alcohol, tobacco, and drug abuse; aggression and violence; school dropout; and risky sexual activity. Preventing behavioral health problems among young people is an urgent grand challenge for social work and the nation.

Evidence from the past three decades indicates that behavioral health problems can be prevented before they emerge in young people's lives (Elliott & Fagan, 2017; Hawkins et al., 2015; Jenson & Bender, 2014). More than 65 programs have been found effective in controlled studies of interventions aimed at preventing behavioral health problems in children, adolescents, and young adults. However, this evidence is not widely integrated or applied in most of the school, family, and community programs and policies that seek to prevent or reduce behavioral health problems. The challenge is to "scale up" or expand tested and effective preventive interventions in the many local and state systems that serve children and families.

1. This chapter draws on a paper previously published by the National Academy of Medicine: Hawkins, J. D., Jenson, J. M., Catalano, R. F., Fraser, M. W., Botvin, G. J., Shapiro, V., . . . Stone, S. (2015). *Unleashing the power of prevention* [Discussion paper]. Washington, DC: Institute of Medicine and National Research Council. Retrieved from https://nam.edu/perspectives-2015-unleashing-the-power-of-prevention

The Grand Challenge of *Ensure Healthy Development for All Youth*, selected as one of 12 Grand Challenges by the American Academy of Social Work and Social Welfare (AASWSW, 2017), includes an initiative called Unleashing the Power of Prevention (Hawkins et al., 2015). This initiative uses compelling evidence from three decades of research focused on examining the effects of preventive interventions to identify strategies that are necessary to prevent behavioral health problems in young people. The goals of Unleashing the Power of Prevention are to

- reduce the incidence and prevalence of behavioral health problems in the population of young people from birth through age 24 years by 20% from current levels over the next decade; and
- reduce racial and economic disparities in behavioral health problems by 20% over the next decade.

In this chapter, we discuss the importance and the challenge of using scientific evidence to increase the scale-up of tested and effective preventive interventions. Action steps necessary to meet the goals of Unleashing the Power of Prevention are described. The need for innovation and interdisciplinary cross-sector involvement in meeting these goals is outlined. Finally, progress in meeting the goals of the Grand Challenge of Ensure Healthy Development for All Youth by Unleashing the Power or Prevention is discussed.

ENSURE HEALTHY DEVELOPMENT FOR ALL YOUTH BY UNLEASHING THE POWER OF PREVENTION

We define *behavioral health problems* as behaviors that compromise a young person's mental or physical health and well-being. These include anxiety and depression; autistic behaviors; self-inflicted injury; risky sexual behaviors; unwanted pregnancies; obesity; risky driving; alcohol, tobacco, and other drug use; delinquent behavior, violence and aggressive behavior; and school dropout. We cast a wide net because many of these problems are predicted by shared risk factors (Hawkins et al., 2015).

The costs associated with adverse behavioral health outcomes are high. In the United States, underage drinking costs society $27 billion per year, and delinquent behavior costs society $60 billion per year (Kuklinski, Briney, Hawkins, & Catalano, 2012). Each year, more than 6 million young people receive treatment for mental, emotional, or behavioral problems. The financial costs for treatment services and lost productivity attributed to behavioral health problems such as depression, conduct disorder, and substance abuse are estimated at $247 billion per year (O'Connell, Boat, & Warner, 2009). Other costs are literally incalculable, as parents, teachers, physicians, child psychiatrists, social workers, child welfare workers, juvenile justice probation officers, and entire communities experience the adverse effects of human suffering, lost potential, and fraying social fabric.

Behavioral health problems also reflect and perpetuate social inequities. Different social groups—characterized by gender, race, ethnicity, citizenship, sexual orientation, and class—experience dramatically different levels of behavioral health. For example, almost 83% of the deaths of American Indian and Alaskan Natives are attributed to behavioral health problems (Hoyert & Xu, 2012). In 2014, homicide rates were more than 6 times higher for young males compared to females, and they were 20 times higher for African American youth compared to non-Hispanic White youth (Child Trends, 2017).

For decades, public policies have focused on protecting, treating, rehabilitating, and, often, controlling young people with identified behavioral health problems (Catalano, 2007). Billions of dollars are committed annually to rehabilitating and confining youth who exhibit mental health difficulties or engage in delinquent, aggressive, or substance-abusing behaviors (Catalano et al., 2012; Elliott & Fagan, 2017; Jenson & Bender, 2014; Woolf, 2008). Evidence suggests that these policies have increased social inequity by contributing to well-known ethnic and racial disparities in rates of incarceration between White and non-White youth (Gilman, 2014; Western & Pettit, 2010). Treatment and control strategies are clearly an important part of the continuum necessary to protect children and ensure public safety. However, there is now more than 30 years of research on effective programs and policies showing that we can prevent behavioral health problems from developing in the first place.

The Power of Prevention

Prior to 1980, few preventive interventions for behavioral health problems had been tested, and virtually no effective preventive interventions had been identified (Berleman, 1980). Beginning in the 1980s, those interested in advancing prevention turned to public health for a solution to creating a more comprehensive prevention framework (Coie et al., 1993). Public health experts had long recognized the value of identifying the individual and environmental characteristics, conditions, and behaviors predictive of illness and disease. National campaigns to inform the public of risks for and protective factors against cardiovascular disease as well as new state and local policies and regulations led to considerable reductions in cardiovascular risk factors such as smoking (Vuolo, Kadowaki, & Kelly, 2016). Identifying risks for and protective factors against health problems such as diabetes has helped countless individuals prevent, detect, or manage their diseases (Selvin, Parrinello, Sacks, & Coresh, 2014). A risk and protection focus worked to prevent illness and disease in public health. Thus, the central question for prevention scientists became: Could a risk- and protection-focused approach be effective in preventing common child and adolescent behavioral health problems such as substance abuse, delinquency, violence, and school dropout?

This question was met with a resounding "Yes" by many prevention educators, practitioners, and researchers. In fact, a framework that accounted for the presence or absence of risk and protective factors for childhood and adolescent problem behavior seemed an ideal theoretical and implementation fit for many (Botvin, 2004; Greenberg, 2010; Hawkins, Catalano, & Miller, 1992). Following 1990, the public health model of prevention received significant attention from investigators in disciplines such as education, psychology, sociology, and social work. Practitioners and policymakers identified and applied the model to practice and policy settings (Jenson & Fraser, 2016). By the end of the decade, the public health framework had become a major prevention approach in the United States (Catalano et al., 2012; Hawkins, 2006).

Interventions based on a public health approach are implemented at three levels (O'Connell et al., 2009). *Universal* prevention programs seek to reduce risk and enhance protection in the youth population without regard to the level of risk exposure of individuals in that population. Promoting Alternative Thinking Strategies (PATHS), which teaches social, cognitive, and behavioral skills to all elementary students in a local school district, is an example of a universal program (Greenberg, 2010; Greenberg, Kusché, Cook, & Quamma, 1995). *Selective* preventive interventions target youth at elevated levels of risk who do not show specific symptoms of behavioral health problems. The Big Brothers Big Sisters mentoring strategy that matches at-risk children and youth with positive adult role models is an example of a selective prevention program (DeWitt et al., 2006). Finally, *indicated* preventive interventions target children and adolescents who manifest prodromal indicators or symptoms of behavioral health problems but not diagnosable disorders or illegal or health-compromising behaviors. The Treatment Foster Care Oregon program for children in foster care is an example of an indicated prevention approach. This program seeks to avoid costly residential treatment placements for young people in foster care settings by providing skills training to youth and behavioral parent training to foster parents (Chamberlain, Leve, & DeGarmo, 2007).

More than 65 different effective individual, family, school, and community focused prevention programs have been developed and implemented at the universal, selective, and indicated levels since the 1980s. Information about effective prevention programs at each of these levels of implementation is provided in Elliot and Fagan (2017) and Jenson and Bender (2014) and is also available online at the University of Colorado's Blueprints for Healthy Youth Development website at http://www.blueprintsprograms.com.

Bringing Prevention to Scale

Evidence supporting the effectiveness of preventive interventions for reducing behavioral health problems in young people is clear and compelling. The challenge now is to scale up effective programs as part of a comprehensive strategy to achieve *population*-level reductions in behavioral health problems. This challenge is twofold:

1. Implement, at scale, effective universal promotion and preventive interventions designed to benefit all young people
2. Provide, at scale, effective selective and indicated interventions that target children, adolescents, and young adults at elevated levels of risk or early stages of problem development

Reducing risk and enhancing protection among all young people will reduce rates of behavioral health problems. Universal prevention has the potential to reach those who are not directly involved in the formal health and social service delivery sectors. Simultaneously ensuring that preventive interventions reach the highest risk children and youth, who are likely to benefit disproportionately from these efforts, will also promote health equity. Preventing problems before they occur reduces human suffering and eliminates potentially punitive responses to these problems from education, law enforcement, child welfare, or juvenile justice systems. It is imperative that strategies to bring preventive interventions to scale pursue the dual objectives of overall population health and health equity for the most vulnerable and underserved youth populations (Catalano et al., 2012; Jenson, 2010).

The Grand Challenge of Ensure Healthy Development for All Youth by Unleashing the Power of Prevention includes the following seven action steps, and related goals, that are necessary to make meaningful and measurable progress in the next 10 years (Hawkins et al., 2015):

1. Develop and increase public awareness of the advances and cost savings of effective preventive interventions that promote healthy behaviors for all.
   Goal: In a decade, more than 50% of the US adult population will report in surveys that it is possible and cost-effective to prevent behavioral health problems among children and adolescents.
2. Ensure that 10% of all public funds spent on young people support effective prevention programs.
   Goal: In a decade, at least 10% of all state and federal expenditures on the education, health, protection, and welfare of children will be allocated to effective universal, selective, and indicated interventions for preventing behavioral health problems.

3. Implement community-assessment and capacity-building tools that guide communities to systematically assess and prioritize risk and protective factors, and select and implement evidence-based prevention programs that target prioritized factors.

   Goal 1: In a decade, at least 1,000 communities in the United States will actively monitor population levels of risk and protective factors and behavioral health problems among young people.

   Goal 2: In a decade, at least 1,000 US communities will implement effective health promotion approaches and evidence-based preventive interventions.

   Goal 3: In a decade, at least 1,000 US communities will have a multisector coalition of stakeholders who actively monitor the reach and fidelity of a comprehensive system of effective interventions to promote behavioral health for young people from birth to age 24 years.

4. Establish and implement criteria for preventive interventions that are effective, sustainable, equity-enhancing, and cost-beneficial.

   Goal: In a decade, all 50 US states will use outcome data from controlled studies and information from cost–benefit analyses to inform policy decisions regarding investments in prevention, treatment, and control of behavioral health problems.

5. Increase infrastructure to support the high-quality implementation of preventive interventions.

   Goal: In a decade, 25 states will have cross-agency "backbone" organizations that provide coaching, technical assistance, and monitoring services to local community organizations that provide behavioral health promotion and prevention services for youth and their families.

6. Monitor and increase access of children, youth, and young adults to effective preventive interventions.

   Goal 1: In a decade, child welfare, disability, education, employment, health, justice, and other agencies in 20 states will use integrated data structures that enable cross-agency collaboration in monitoring the provision of effective behavioral health and preventive interventions and that promote cross-agency quality assurance in providing a full range of effective programs.

   Goal 2: In a decade, integrated data structures will have the capacity to be disaggregated by local community area and social group and will be used to monitor the provision of effective behavioral health and preventive interventions to promote health equity.

   Goal 3: In a decade, tested technology-assisted approaches will be widely used to ensure the accessibility and reach of effective preventive interventions.

7. Create workforce development strategies to prepare social work graduates and allied practitioners for new roles in promotion and preventive interventions.

   Goal 1: In a decade, 25 schools of social work will include an evidence-based behavioral health promotion and prevention curriculum track in their Master of Social Work (MSW) programs.

   Goal 2: In a decade, 20 universities will include cross-disciplinary, prevention-focused training programs in behavioral health that will include social work, primary care medicine, nursing, psychiatry, and psychology.

These goals are achievable and are consistent with the outcomes found in longitudinal studies of prevention-based programs to date (Elliott & Fagan, 2017; Jenson & Bender, 2014). To illustrate, multisite trials of community-wide prevention systems using tested and effective prevention programs have produced relative reductions of 25–33% in delinquency and drug-use indicators (Hawkins et al., 2012; Spoth et al., 2011). The Commonwealth of Pennsylvania has shown significant reductions in delinquency referrals and placements following the creation of the Evidence-based Prevention and Intervention Support Center, a resource funded primarily by the Pennsylvania Commission on Crime and Delinquency to support the implementation of tested and effective prevention programs throughout the state (Bumbarger & Campbell, 2012; Rhoades, Bumbarger, & Moore, 2012). The number of juvenile delinquency dispositions from new allegations decreased 44% and the number of delinquency placements decreased 45% in Pennsylvania between 2007 and 2014, resulting in a reduction of more than $85 million annually in juvenile incarceration costs (Bumbarger, 2016).

MEASURING PROGRESS

Measuring the impact of Unleashing the Power of Prevention will require local-, state-, and national-level data. Many states conduct annual or semi-annual surveys of health-risking behaviors among school-age children. Data from some of these surveys are helpful in assessing changes in risk and protective factors over time and in estimating the prevalence of behavioral health problems among young people. At the national level, existing national data systems are already in place to provide systematic tracking of trends in behavioral health problems to measure attainment of the goals identified in Unleashing the Power of Prevention over a 10-year span. These national databases include the following:

- *America's Children: Key National Indicators of Well-Being* (http://www.childstats.gov/americaschildren/index.asp): The *America's Children* database includes a range of behavioral health problem indicators, including substance use, delinquent conduct, violent behavior, and sexual activity. Data reflecting indicators of family and social environment, economic circumstances, health care, education, and health are also available. Most measures are collected annually and date back to approximately 1980. Selected substance use measures from the Monitoring the Future survey (http://www.monitoringthefuture.org) are included in the database.

- Centers for Disease Control and Prevention's Youth Risk Behavior Surveillance System (YRBSS) (http://www.cdc.gov/HealthyYouth/yrbs/index.htm?s_cid=tw_cdc16): The YRBSS provides annual data on the prevalence of unintentional injuries, sexual behaviors, substance use, dietary behaviors, physical activity, obesity, and asthma among youth and young adults.
- Centers for Disease Control and Prevention's National Health Interview Survey (NHIS) (http://www.cdc.gov/nchs/nhis/about_nhis.htm): The NHIS produces detailed annual estimates of the incidence and prevalence of health conditions by age, gender, and race/ethnicity for states, major metropolitan areas, and the country. Interview data are gathered to assess health care access and health-related problems and behaviors. The NHIS is used in assessing progress toward meeting the goals of Healthy People 2020.
- Substance Abuse and Mental Health Services Administration's National Survey on Drug Use and Health (NSDUH) (https://nsduhweb.rti.org/respweb/homepage.cfm): The NSDUH provides annual data on the prevalence of mental health and alcohol, tobacco, and other drug use from a random sample of approximately 70,000 individuals age 12 years or older.
- Kids Count (http://www.aecf.org/work/kids-count): Sponsored by the Annie E. Casey Foundation, Kids Count provides current and historical data on the educational, social, economic, and physical well-being of children and adolescents.
- Healthy People 2020 (HP 2020) (http://www.healthypeople.gov/2020/topicsobjectives2020/objectiveslist): The US Department of Health and Human Services has set health and behavior goals for the nation; HP 2020 includes a set of indicators for monitoring progress on each goal. These include adolescent health indicators that provide national tracking of progress toward reaching goals in underage drinking, graduation rates, suicide, depression, obesity, and smoking.
- National Survey of Children's Health (http://childhealthdata.org/learn/NSCH): This survey provides a searchable database that includes indicators of children's physical and mental health status, access to health care, and family and neighborhood influences.

Social work is ideally positioned to design, deliver, and test programs aimed at preventing behavioral health problems. Social work researchers, practitioners, and policy advocates can help establish interdisciplinary programs and training in evidence-based prevention that involve the full complement of professions concerned, including health care, public health, mental health, child welfare, education, and law enforcement. Social work can also serve as catalyst and leader for the work ahead by leveraging the latest evidence from prevention science and tracking progress toward clear, measurable goals.

Social work's history of using social ecological theories to guide epidemiological assessment of the social determinants of behavior provides a strong foundation for advancing policies, programs, and practices that promote behavioral health (Almgren, Kemp, & Alison, 2000; Bronfenbrenner, 1979). The profession's commitment to multilevel practice creates opportunities for practitioners to help individuals change their wellness behaviors. It also provides a strong underlying context for organizations to adopt and implement effective prevention programs and for communities to organize local services that promote health equity.

At the same time, it is important to note that social work has only recently begun to widely teach and implement evidence-based group, family, and individual practices that have been shown to be effective. Without more specific and better organized interventions, youth service systems are unlikely to make the changes that are necessary to improve behavioral health outcomes (Weisz, Han, & Valeri, 1997). Social work and other disciplines must continue to build capacity to deliver evidence-based practices with fidelity through intentional educational efforts with students and practitioners.

With other disciplines and professions, social work can play a transformative role in the growing focus on prevention in health care and education. The emphasis on prevention in the Patient Protection and Affordable Care Act (ACA, 2010) created new opportunities to scale up preventive interventions over the next decade. The ACA also created an opportunity for social workers to play an essential role in health care's move to integrated primary care. The social work profession should keep a watchful eye on current health reform efforts to ensure that prevention strategies receive adequate funding going forward. In the realm of education, a recent White House Early Education Summit underscored the importance of behavioral health for school success, noting the large numbers of disadvantaged children expelled and suspended from preschools for aggressive and disruptive behaviors (Samuels, 2014). Social and emotional learning (SEL) is also gaining visibility as a key to student attainment of state educational standards (Durlak, Weissberg, Dymnicki, Taylor, & Schellinger, 2011). SEL is a key ingredient of educational reforms as championed by the Collaborative for Academic, Social, and Emotional

Learning (2017). Social work researchers, educators, and practitioners can play an important role in advancing these reforms.

Working collaboratively with other practitioners, social workers can be the coordinating hub for shared efforts to prevent behavioral health problems, bringing together community residents and professionals to shape local education, health, and human service delivery and state and national initiatives to unleash the power of prevention (US Department of Health and Human Services, 2014). Together with allied professions, social work can help ensure that effective preventive interventions are supported by initiatives in health care, education, public health, mental health, child welfare, and juvenile justice. Social workers can also actively advocate for increased emphasis on preventing behavioral health problems in federal, state, and local policies and budgets.

THE NEED FOR INNOVATION

Solutions to the Grand Challenge of Ensure Healthy Development for All Youth will require significant innovation from many service sectors. Innovations necessary to bring preventive interventions and policies to scale include the following:

1. Local prevention decision and implementation support infrastructures must be created to plan, implement, and monitor evidence-based behavioral health promotion systems.

   Currently, few towns, cities, or states have created systems for promoting behavioral health. Some pioneering states and communities have established innovative efforts, including children's cabinets, city and neighborhood coalitions, interagency planning groups, and cross-cutting initiatives focused on achieving collective impact on desired outcomes (Bumbarger & Campbell, 2012; Hanleybrown et al., 2012; Kania & Kramer, 2011). Backbone infrastructure is needed to promote collaboration across agencies and organizations to use resources effectively to prevent behavioral health problems.

2. Sustainable efficient methods are needed to spread effective preventive interventions with sufficient fidelity to produce outcomes and sufficient adaptability to ensure widespread uptake.

   Scaling effective preventive interventions will require new and wider use of technology. This may involve mobile- and media-based interventions that reach entire populations and also innovations such as brief and effective systems for mental health screening in primary care settings (Gibbons et al., 2012). Innovations in methods of training, coaching, and technical assistance to support use of interactive intervention delivery systems will be required. Data-based modeling and simulation methods used in engineering should be applied to spreading and scaling preventive interventions.

3. Systems will need to be developed to monitor the epidemiology of risk, protection, and youth behavioral health outcomes in local communities, and data will need to be aggregated into national reports of trends in the epidemiology of the predictors and behavioral health of the nation's youth.

Few existing data systems that monitor epidemiologic data provide accurate community- or neighborhood-level estimates of the prevalence of behavioral health problems needed for local prevention planning. Furthermore, these databases measure only a small number of empirically validated risk and protective factors for youth behavioral health outcomes. A national data monitoring system is needed that provides community data on the prevalence of risk and protective factors and behavioral health outcomes for local prevention planning (Catalano et al., 2012).

4. Methods for creating demand, or "uptake," and policy support for tested and effective preventive interventions must be applied and used.

If effective preventive interventions are to affect levels of risk, protection, and behavioral health problems, they must be widely used. For this to happen, parents, teachers, social workers, doctors, nurses, and public health workers must be willing to use them. Important work by the Laura and John Arnold Foundation, which encourages governments and nonprofit organizations to base funding and program selection decisions on evidence, is one example of a concerted effort to increase policy support for tested and effective prevention programs. This work is increasing the potential supply of evidence-based interventions for preventing youth behavioral health problems. Information about the Foundation's Evidence-Based Policy and Innovation initiative is available at http://www.arnoldfoundation.org/initiative/evidence-based-policy-innovation.

5. Social workers and allied professions must be prepared to take on new roles in promoting behavioral health in the population.

Social work's commitment to multilevel practice creates opportunities for social workers to help individuals change their behaviors, for organizations to adopt and implement effective prevention programs and practices, and for communities to organize local services for the promotion of health and health equity. New experiential and community-based learning opportunities should be developed in MSW programs to ensure that social workers acquire skills in stakeholder and resource mapping; coalition building; using epidemiologic data to guide community prevention planning; matching community needs with suitable evidence-based interventions; and planning the introduction, delivery, and monitoring of preventive interventions (Williams, Chapa, & Des Marias, 2013).

Ensuring sustainable and equitable gains in behavioral health will also require a workforce skilled in providing tested and effective preventive interventions in health, education, and other service settings. Currently, efforts are being undertaken to scale up tested and effective healthy parenting interventions by the National Academies of Sciences, Engineering, and Medicine's Healthy Parenting Collaborative in Primary Care (Leslie et al., 2016; National Academies of Sciences, Engineering, & Medicine, 2016). Social workers can play an important role in this collaborative and in interdisciplinary teams delivering interventions in primary care settings. MSW programs must explore new opportunities to prepare students for emerging roles in health care settings to promote behavioral health for all.

6. Payment systems and resource allocation must be restructured to fund dissemination of tested and effective preventive interventions.

Most resources allocated to health, justice, and social services support work with those who already manifest behavioral health problems. Recent health care legislation recognizes that broad improvements in health outcomes will require shifting some resources from delivering treatment services to individuals toward prevention before problems develop (Cantor, Mikkelsen, Simons, & Waters, 2013). Emerging strategies and policies to pay for prevention include (1) social impact bonds that provide a market-based approach to pay for evidence-based interventions to improve social, environmental, and economic conditions essential to behavioral well-being (Hernandez, Syme, & Brush, 2012); (2) wellness trusts that create a funding pool to support prevention and improve health outcomes in a population (Lambrew, 2007); and (3) community benefit requirements made possible under the ACA and imposed on nonprofit hospitals and health plans as a condition of their tax-exempt status to provide funds for promoting behavioral health (Cincinnati Children's Hospital Medical Center, 2011).

PROGRESS AND FUTURE DIRECTIONS

Members of the Coalition for the Promotion of Behavioral Health (CPBH) have undertaken efforts to implement the seven action steps and goals of Unleashing the Power of Prevention. The Coalition was created in 2014 as the organizational entity for implementing strategies identified in the *Unleashing the Power of Prevention* report. An eight-person steering committee guides implementation of the report's seven action steps through subcommittees that aim to (1) expand the membership base and reach of the CPBH, (2) gather and disseminate information about ways to better prepare social workers for prevention practice and policy in behavioral health, (3) disseminate the principles and framework found in the Unleashing the Power of Prevention initiative to state and federal administrators and elected officials, and (4) secure funding to support the work necessary to advance the goals of Unleashing the Power of Prevention. To date, the CPBH has focused its work in the following three areas:

1. Increasing community and state infrastructure for delivering preventive interventions for behavioral health problems in children and youth

    CPBH members have been working in several states to improve infrastructure for delivering preventive interventions. In Utah, a CPBH team led a statewide prevention summit in 2015 that was attended by state policymakers, administrators, and cabinet-level officials. The summit was followed by a prevention webinar in 2016 that was organized by the Utah State Division of Substance Abuse and Mental Health. CPBH members are providing ongoing consultation in Utah to implement action steps of the Unleashing the Power of Prevention initiative.

    Members of the CPBH presented the *Unleashing the Power of Prevention* report to a Massachusetts Special Legislative Commission on Behavioral Health Promotion and Upstream Prevention in 2017. The session was organized by the Massachusetts Promote Prevent Commission recently created by the Massachusetts legislature. Efforts to establish principles of the *Unleashing the Power of Prevention* report have also been initiated in Colorado.

2. Scaling up tested and effective family-focused interventions in pediatric and health care settings

    Recent changes within health care make primary care a potential home for family-focused prevention and suggest possibilities for sustainable funding of family-focused prevention programs. As noted previously, members of the CPBH are participating in efforts to scale up healthy parenting interventions in primary health care being led by the National Academies of Sciences, Engineering, and Medicine's Forum on Promoting Children's Cognitive, Affective, and Behavioral Health. CPBH members and members of the Forum-sponsored Collaborative on Healthy Parenting in Primary Care have published an article in the *American Journal of Preventive Medicine* identifying 16 family-focused prevention programs that have been tested in controlled trials and found to be effective in reducing children's negative behavioral health outcomes and noting that few of these tested and effective programs are widely used (Leslie et al., 2016). The authors note that three obstacles inhibit the expansion of family-focused prevention programs: (1) social norms and perceptions of stigma associated with participation in parenting programs; (2) concerns about the expertise of sponsoring organizations to offer parenting advice; and (3) lack of stable, sustainable funding mechanisms. The paper is available online at http://www.ajpmonline.org/article/S0749-3797(16)30184-2/abstract.

In 2016, members of the Collaborative for Healthy Parenting in Primary Care and CPBH participated in a Congressional Briefing on Healthy Parenting aimed at informing Congress of the potential for integrating family-focused preventive interventions into primary health care. The briefing was co-sponsored by the CPBH, National Prevention Science Coalition to Improve Lives, American Academy of Pediatrics, the AASWSW, and other national organizations. The complete briefing is available at http://www.npscoalition.org/healthy-parenting-through-primary-care.

3. Preparing the social work workforce to deliver tested and effective preventive interventions for behavioral problems in children and youth

CPBH members have initiated and are collaborating on several initiatives aimed at better preparing practitioners to deliver preventive interventions in behavioral health settings. Actions of this CPBH subcommittee include coordinating with accreditation bodies of professional degree programs, creating standardized learning objectives for prevention practice courses, identifying existing prevention training programs in allied disciplines, collating a repository of prevention course syllabi, and undertaking a systematic study of the integration of prevention content into broader programs of study.

Members of CPBH co-authored a poster and paper that were featured at a 2016 workshop sponsored by the National Academies of Sciences, Engineering, and Medicine titled Training the Future Child Healthcare Workforce to Improve Behavioral Health Outcomes for Children, Youth, and Families. A co-authored paper including CPBH members has been published as a discussion paper by the National Academy of Medicine and is available online at https://nam.edu/workforce-development-to-enhance-the-cognitive-affective-and-behavioral-health-of-children-and-youth-opportunities-and-barriers-in-child-health-care-training. Detailed information about the 2016 workshop is available online at http://sites.nationalacademies.org/DBASSE/BCYF/DBASSE_173424.

Other Activities of the Coalition for the Promotion of Behavioral Health

CPBH members have delivered more than 75 presentations about Unleashing the Power of Prevention throughout the United States in the past 2 years. Members also launched the AASWSW's national webinar series on the Grand Challenges for Social Work initiative in October 2016. CPBH members participated in the 2016 Social Innovation for America's Renewal: Ideas, Evidence Action conference organized by Washington University and the AASWSW as part of an effort to advance policy strategies for the Grand Challenges of Social Work initiative. The CPHB created two policy briefs aimed at advancing the grand challenge Ensure Healthy Development for All Youth that are available at https://csd.wustl.edu/events/ConferencesAndSymposia/Pages/Grand-Challenges-Policy-Briefs.aspx and https://csd.wustl.edu/newsroom/news/Pages/Grand-Challenges-for-Social-Work.aspx.

CONCLUSION

Behavioral health problems now surpass communicable diseases as the country's most pressing health concerns for the well-being of young people. More than 30 years of evidence shows that advances in prevention and promotion research have transformative potential to prevent problems before they develop. Now our challenge is to broadly implement these recent advances at scale, developing and delivering on their potential through programs and policies that reach all young people. Given its proven ability to dramatically reduce a wide range of behavioral health problems at a fraction of the cost of more expensive treatment and control interventions, prevention is one of our nation's most valuable—and underused—resources. It is time to unleash the power of prevention—creating infrastructures, programs, and training to put prevention to work nationwide for all young people and seeing the results in the healthy development of all children.

REFERENCES

Almgren, G., Kemp, S. P., & Alison, E. (2000). The legacy of Hull House and the Children's Bureau in the American Mortality Transition. *Social Service Review*, 74, 1–27.

American Academy of Social Work and Social Welfare. (2017). *Ensure healthy development for all youth*. Retrieved from http://aaswsw.org/grand-challenges-initiative/12-challenges/ensure-healthy-development-for-all-youth

Berleman, W. C. (1980). *Juvenile delinquency prevention experiments: A review and analysis*. Washington, DC: US Department of Justice, Law Enforcement Assistance Administration, Office of Juvenile Justice and Delinquency Prevention.

Botvin, G. J. (2004). Advancing prevention science and practice: Challenges, critical issues, and future directions. *Prevention Science*, 5, 69–72.

Bronfenbrenner, U. (1979). *The ecology of human development: Experiments by nature and design*. Cambridge, MA: Harvard University Press.

Bumbarger, B. K. (2016). *Unleashing the power of prevention at scale: Researchers, communities, and public systems partnering for collective impact*. Presentation at the annual conference of the American Psychological Association, Denver, CO, August 5.

Bumbarger, B. K., & Campbell, E. M. (2012). A state agency–university partnership for translational research and the dissemination of evidence-based prevention and intervention. *Administration and Policy in Mental Health and Mental Health Services Research, 39,* 268–277.

Cantor, J., Mikkelsen, L., Simons, B., & Waters, R. (2013). *How can we pay for a health population? Innovative new ways to redirect funds to community prevention.* Oakland, CA: Prevention Institute.

Catalano, R. F. (2007). Prevention is a sound public and private investment. *Criminology and Public Policy, 6,* 377–398.

Catalano, R. F., Fagan, A. A., Gavin, L. E., Greenberg, M. T., Irwin, C. E., Ross, D. A., & Shek, D. T. (2012). Worldwide application of the prevention science research base in adolescent health. *Lancet, 379,* 1653–1664.

Chamberlain, P., Leve, L. D., & DeGarmo, D. S. (2007). Multidimensional treatment foster care for girls in the juvenile justice system: 2-year follow-up of a randomized clinical trial. *Journal of Consulting and Clinical Psychology, 75,* 187–193.

Child Trends. (2017). *Data bank indicator. Teen homicide, suicide, and firearm deaths.* Retrieved from https://www.childtrends.org/indicators/teen-homicide-suicide-and-firearm-deaths

Cincinnati Children's Hospital Medical Center. (2011). *Cincinnati Children's launches community health improvement initiative.* Retrieved from http://www.cincinnatichildrens.org/news/release/2011/community-health-10-11-2011

Coie, J. D., Watt, N. F., West, S. G., Hawkins, J. D., Asarnow, J. R., Markman, H. J., . . . Long, B. (1993). The science of prevention: A conceptual framework and some directions for a national research program. *American Psychologist, 48,* 1013–1022.

Collaborative for Academic, Social, and Emotional Learning. (2017). *CASEL.* Retrieved from http://www.casel.org

DeWitt, D. J., Lipman, E., Manzano-Munguia, M., Bisanz, J., Graham, K., Offord, D. R., . . . Shaver, K. (2006). Feasibility of a randomized controlled trial for evaluating the effectiveness of Big Brothers Big Sisters community match program at the national level. *Children and Youth Services Review, 29,* 383–404.

Durlak, J. A., Weissberg, R. P., Dymnicki, A. B., Taylor, R. D., & Schellinger, K. B. (2011). The impact of enhancing students' social and emotional learning: A meta-analysis of school-based universal interventions. *Child Development, 82,* 405–432.

Elliott, D., & Fagan, A. A. (2017). *The prevention of crime.* Hoboken, NJ: Wiley.

Gibbons, R. D., Weiss, D. J., Pilkonis, P. A., Frank, E., Moore, T., Kim, J. B., & Kupfer, D. J. (2012). Development of a computerized adaptive test for depression. *Archives of General Psychiatry, 11,* 1104–1112.

Gilman, A. B. (2014). *Incarceration and the life course: Predictors, correlates, and consequences of juvenile incarceration.* Doctoral dissertation, University of Washington, Seattle, WA.

Greenberg, M. T. (2010). School-based prevention: current status and future challenges. *Effective Education, 2,* 27–52.

Greenberg, M. T., Kusché, C. A., Cook, E. T., & Quamma, J. P. (1995). Promoting emotional competence in school-aged children: The effects of the PATHS curriculum. *Development and Psychopathology, 7,* 117–136.

Hawkins, J. D. (2006). Science, social work, prevention: Finding the intersection. *Social Work Research, 30,* 137–152.

Hawkins, J. D., Catalano, R. F., & Miller, J. Y. (1992). Risk and protective factors for alcohol and other drug problems in adolescence and early adulthood: Implications for substance abuse prevention. *Psychological Bulletin, 112*, 64–105.

Hawkins, J. D., Jenson, J. M., Catalano, R. F., Fraser, M. W., Botvin, G. J., Shapiro, V., . . . Stone, S. (2015). *Unleashing the power of prevention* [Discussion paper]. Washington, DC: Institute of Medicine and National Research Council. Retrieved from https://nam.edu/perspectives-2015-unleashing-the-power-of-prevention

Hawkins, J. D., Oesterle, S., Brown, E. C., Monahan, K. C., Abbott, R. D., Arthur, M. W., & Catalano, R. F. (2012). Sustained decreases in risk exposure and youth problem behaviors after installation of the Communities That Care prevention system in a randomized trial. *Archives of Pediatric Medicine, 166*, 141–148.

Hernandez, M., Syme, S. L., & Brush, R. (2012). *A market for health: Shifting the paradigm for investing in health*. Retrieved from http://collectivehealth.net/new/about_files/Health%20Capital%20Market%20FINAL%20March%202012.pdf

Hoyert, D. L., & Xu, J. (2012). Deaths: Preliminary data for 2011. *National Vital Statistics Reports, 61*, 1–52.

Jenson, J. M. (2010). Advances in preventing childhood and adolescent problem behavior. *Research on Social Work Practice, 20*, 701–713.

Jenson, J. M., & Bender, K. A. (2014). *Preventing child and adolescent problem behavior: Evidence-based strategies in schools, families, and communities*. New York, NY: Oxford University Press.

Jenson, J. M., & Fraser, M. W. (2016). *Social policy for children and families: A risk and resilience perspective* (3rd ed.). Thousand Oaks, CA: Sage.

Kania, J., & Kramer, M. (2011). Collective impact. *Stanford Social Innovation Review, 9*, 36–41.

Kuklinski, M. R., Briney, J. S., Hawkins, J. D., & Catalano, R. F. (2012). Cost–benefit analysis of Communities That Care outcomes at eighth grade. *Prevention Science, 13*, 150–161.

Lambrew, J. M. (2007). *A wellness trust to prioritize disease prevention*. Retrieved from https://www.brookings.edu/research/papers/2007/04/useconomics-lambrew

Leslie, L. K., Mehus, C. J., Hawkins, J. D., Boat, T., McCabe, M. A., Barkin, S., . . . Beardslee, W. (2016). Primary health care: Potential home for family-focused preventive interventions. *American Journal of Preventive Medicine, 51*(4 Suppl. 2), S106–S108.

National Academies of Sciences, Engineering, and Medicine. (2016). *Parenting matters: Supporting parents of children ages 0–8*. Washington, DC: National Academies Press.

O'Connell, M. E., Boat, T., & Warner, K. E. (Eds.). (2009). *Preventing mental, emotional, and behavioral disorders among young people: Progress and possibilities*. Washington, DC: National Academies Press.

Patient Protection and Affordable Care Act, 42 U.S.C., 1800 et seq. (2010).

Rhoades, B. L., Bumbarger, B. K., & Moore, J. E. (2012). The role of a state-level prevention support system in promoting high-quality implementation and sustainability of evidence-based programs. *American Journal of Community Psychology, 50*, 386–401.

Samuels, C. A. (2014). Pre-K suspension data prompt focus on intervention. *Education Week*. Retrieved from http://www.edweek.org/ew/articles/2014/04/02/27ocrprek.h33.html?tkn=WVUFI066aps1cjK35RCm3VfFCzGxB5x2DdAy&print=1

Selvin, E., Parrinello, C. M., Sacks, D. B., & Coresh, J. (2014). Trends in prevalence and control of diabetes in the United States, 1988–1994 and 1999–2010. *Annals of Internal Medicine, 160,* 517–525.

Spoth, R., Redmond, C., Clair, S., Shin, C., Greenberg, M., & Feinberg, M. (2011). Preventing substance misuse through community–university partnerships: Randomized controlled outcomes 4.5 years past baseline. *American Journal of Preventive Medicine, 40,* 440–447.

US Department of Health and Human Services. (2014). *The health consequences of smoking—50 years of progress: A report of the Surgeon General.* Atlanta, GA: Department of Health and Human Services, Centers for Disease Control and Prevention, National Center for Chronic Disease Prevention and Health Promotion, Office on Smoking and Health.

Vuolo, M., Kadowaki, J., & Kelly, B. C. (2016). A multilevel test of constrained choice theory: The case of tobacco clean air restrictions. *Journal of Health and Social Behavior, 57,* 351–372.

Weisz, J. R., Han, S. S., & Valeri, S. M. (1997). More of what? Issues raised by the Fort Bragg study. *American Psychologist, 52,* 541–545.

Western, B., & Pettit, B. (2010). Incarceration and social inequality. *Daedalus, 139,* 146–147.

Williams, J. H., Chapa, T., & Des Marias, E. A. (2013). *Advanced social work practice behaviors to address behavioral health disparities.* Paper presented at the National Association of Deans and Directors of Social Work, Washington, DC, October 16.

Woolf, S. H. (2008). The power of prevention and what it requires. *Journal of the American Medical Association, 299,* 2437–2439.

Grand Challenges
for Social Work
Close the health gap

CHAPTER 3

Close the Health Gap

MICHAEL S. SPENCER, KARINA L. WALTERS,
HEIDI L. ALLEN, CHRISTINA M. ANDREWS,
AUDREY BEGUN, TERI BROWNE, JOHN D. CLAPP,
DIANA DiNITTO, PETER MARAMALDI,
DARRELL P. WHEELER, BRADLEY J. ZEBRACK,
AND EDWINA UEHARA

Tāne, the deity of the forest, lived with his siblings in darkness within the eternal embrace of his parents, Ranginui (sky father) and Papatūānuku (earth mother). Becoming increasingly frustrated at living in the darkness, Tāne successfully pushed the pair apart by planting his head in the earth and using his feet to lift the sky—to expose Te Ao Mārama—the world of light.

Māori creation story

Among the Māori, the indigenous people of Aotearoa/New Zealand, Tāne serves as a model for action in the world: His roots are in earth, and his head is in the heavens. Tāne is able to bear the weight of action to procure necessary change. Similar to Tāne, social work must assert itself, bring new light, and bear the weight of action—in collaboration with allied health professions—to achieve health equity within the next generation. Social work has already had a significant impact on health interventions in the United States—from the health-policy reform efforts of the Progressive Era to the development of innovative community-based prevention interventions in modern times. Social work's perspective is in line with approaches that go beyond population surveillance, prompting action to address health inequities and social determinants of health.

Specifically, social work has an unyielding focus on lifting the health of a nation by lifting the health of the most disenfranchised and marginalized populations. Also, the profession's historical social reform efforts have sought to procure health by addressing the conditions in which people live, work, play, learn, and age. These perspectives match the calls by the World Health Organization (WHO, 2014a), Centers for Disease Control and Prevention (CDC; Brennan Ramirez, Baker, & Metzler, 2008), and the Healthy People 2020 national strategy (US Department of Health and Human Services [DHHS], 2000) to focus contemporary research and intervention efforts on the social conditions that produce health and health inequities. In addition, the reassertion of social work into the national strategy and debate is timely given the precarious position of the Patient Protection and Affordable Care Act (ACA, 2010) and the bourgeoning national effort to create culturally, linguistically, and communally grounded interventions that affect the upstream determinants of the nation's poor health.

Although the United States is among the wealthiest nations in the world and spends far more per person on health care than any other industrialized nation, the population's health is rapidly deteriorating. During the past three decades, the US population has been dying at younger ages than those of the populations in peer nations and has endured a pervasive pattern of poorer health throughout the life course, from birth to old age (National Research Council & Institute of Medicine, 2013). Moreover, population health diminishes along a social gradient: Populations that experience high rates of social, racial, and economic exclusion bear the greatest burden of poor health and premature mortality. Although poor health follows a social gradient, deteriorating US health cannot be fully explained by the health disparities that exist among people who are uninsured or poor; in fact, even the health of relatively elite Americans—those who are White, insured, and college educated, as well as those with high income—is worse than that of their peers in other industrialized countries (Avendano, Glymour, Banks, & Mackenbach, 2009; National Research Council & Institute of Medicine, 2013).

Health professions in the United States have become increasingly myopic, focusing on individualized health care rather than on population health. By prioritizing interventions that target individual behavioral change, research tends to neglect upstream opportunities to intervene upon the settings and environments in which health is produced and maintained. Attention to individual and behavioral interventions is important but alone is not sufficient to eradicate health inequities (Hood, Gennuso, Swain, & Catlin, 2016). To secure true, sustainable, population-based health changes, the health professions must unite and develop transdisciplinary approaches to examining the multilayered contributions of political, economic, and social determinants of population health inequities. Indeed, the nation's health depends on the development of this next wave of interprofessional and transdisciplinary collaboration (McGovern, Miller, & Hughes-Cromwick, 2014). Thus, if we are to truly turn the tide, health disciplines, particularly social work, must train professionals in how to invest in the social determinants of good health. We must also train professionals to develop the practice and research tools, community partnerships, and localized programs necessary to combat social and economic inequities (Hood et al., 2016; Uehara et al., 2013).

ACHIEVING HEALTH EQUITY: SOCIAL WORK ACTION PRIORITIES

We are at a critical juncture in US history. The ACA and Healthy People 2020 produced national momentum to address health inequities. However, changes in political leadership may sway this momentum away from this goal without active social work leadership. Although the ACA's primary focus is on expanding insurance coverage, it also invites innovations that fall within particular domains of social work expertise: the creation of equitable health care systems by expanding health care into and in collaboration with the communities in which people live and work, increasing health workforce diversity, improving cultural competency throughout health care delivery systems, fostering community-based approaches to prevention, and creating community health centers in medically underserved areas. All of these efforts are hallmarks of social work practice and history. Consistent with social work's approach and values, Healthy People 2020 advocates for an ecological, multilevel approach to examining health determinants. It focuses on building healthful social and physical environments that will promote health and well-being (DHHS, 2000) through place-based approaches. These approaches consist of "five key social determinants of health [areas]: economic stability, education, social and community context[s], health and health care, and the neighborhood and built environment (for example, buildings, bike lanes, and roads)" (Mitchell, 2015, p. e71). Although the ACA and Healthy People 2020 provide the impetus for addressing health inequities, neither offers "definitive strategies for communities and health professionals" (p. e71). Also, Mitchell notes, there remains limited evidence-based research on the fundamental determinants of health and limited evidence of settings-based interventions that affect population health.

   This chapter seeks to address these deficiencies through a "geography of science" approach that draws upon diverse disciplines, community leaders, and theoretical and community-centered perspectives (Logie, Dimaras, Fortin, & Ramón-García, 2014, p. 2). The American Academy of Social Work and Social Welfare (AASWSW) *Close the Health Gap* Grand Challenge Initiative is made up of three subgroups aimed at addressing health equity in the following areas through a geography of science approach: (1) Population Health

Through Community and Setting-Based Approaches, (2) Strengthening Health Care Systems: Better Health Across America, and (3) Reducing and Preventing Alcohol Misuse and Its Consequences. In this frame, social work and the health professions can activate 10 priority areas. Although they do not comprehensively address health equity in its entirety, these priorities are proposed as the first steps in initiating community and scientific conversations and launching broad, multisectorial, and interprofessional collaboration. The following are the 10 priority areas:

Population Health Through Community and Setting-Based Approaches

1. Focus on settings to improve the conditions of daily life.
2. Advance community empowerment for sustainable health.
3. Generate research on social determinants of health inequities.
4. Stimulate multisectorial advocacy to promote health equity policies.

Strengthening Health Care Systems: Better Health Across America

5. Cultivate innovation in primary care.
6. Promote full access to health care.
7. Foster development of an interprofessional health workforce.

Reducing and Preventing Alcohol Misuse and Its Consequences

8. Develop research and scholarship in alcohol misuse and its consequences.
9. Develop interdisciplinary, multisectorial, and sustainable collaborations.
10. Develop the workforce in social work to address alcohol misuse.

COMING TO TERMS: SOCIAL DETERMINANTS AND HEALTH EQUITY

In assessing population health, research has typically considered such indicators as mortality, life expectancy, morbidity, health status (physical and mental), functional limitations, disability, and quality of life (Hood et al., 2016; McGovern et al., 2014). Health determinants, also known as social determinants of health, refer to the economic and "social conditions into which people are born, grow, live, work, play, and age"—the conditions that "influence health" (Newman, Baum, Javanparast, O'Rourke, & Carlon, 2015, p. ii127). In the United States, these conditions are shaped by the specific social structures that differentiate access to and distribution of money, wealth, power, knowledge, prestige, resources, and social connectedness (Link & Phelan, 1995; McGovern et al., 2014). Health inequalities are the persistent, systematic differences in the health of social groups within a nation—differences resulting from unequal exposure to and distributions of the social determinants of health (Farrer, Marinetti, Cavaco, &

Costongs, 2015). Quite often, impoverished conditions attend populations that have endured significant legacies of discrimination based on their racial, ethnic, class, or gender identity or on their sexuality. Such conditions include unequal distribution of resources—such as quality education, culturally relevant medical care, and housing—that are typically tied to good health (Mitchell, 2015).

Racial and ethnic minorities bear the greatest burden from conditions that give rise to poor health and premature mortality. Those conditions have structural components as well as social ones (Agency for Healthcare Research and Quality, 2013; Mitchell, 2015; Smedley, Stith, & Nelson, 2003). Social determinants of health inequities are conditions of social stratification. These conditions "create . . . differences in health status between population groups that are socially produced, systematic in their distribution across the population and avoidable and unfair" (Dahlgren & Whitehead, 1992, as cited in Newman et al., 2015, p. ii127). Social determinants give rise to a common soil in which health disparities grow; health inequalities take root; and inequities become reproduced at distal, intermediate, and proximal levels.

Health equity refers to a state characterized by the "absence of systematic inequalities in health" (Farrer et al., 2015, p. 394). A large body of research has established the strong links between socioeconomic disadvantage and poor health outcomes across the lifespan (Braveman & Gottlieb, 2014; Commission on Social Determinants of Health, 2008; Kaplan, Shema, & Leite, 2008; Marmot & Bell, 2012). Although lack of access to health insurance and health services contributes to poor health outcomes, disparities in access to coverage and services also stem from significant social, economic, and environmental deprivation (i.e., social disadvantage) grounded in race- and culture-based discrimination. Those disparities often produce cumulative, intergenerational disadvantage that profoundly affects health (Braveman & Gottlieb, 2014). Such disadvantage is positively correlated with levels of debilitating chronic disease (Gordon-Larsen, Nelson, Page, & Popkin, 2006) and rates of premature mortality (Commission on Social Determinants of Health, 2008). Environmental disadvantage, a manifestation of this stratification and the underlying determinants, is a condition tied to residing in communities with concentrated poverty, food deserts, and high rates of trauma and violence.

Meeting the grand challenge of health equity and eliminating health inequities require dealing with "root causes"; focusing on what can be seen as upstream interventions and primary prevention; and addressing "unequal distribution of power, income, goods and services" (WHO, 2014a, p. 2; see also, Gehlert, Mininger, Sohmer, & Berg, 2008). This challenge entails an explicit commitment to eliminating health disparities at individual and population levels. Meeting the challenge also involves eliminating social determinants that function as precursors to adverse health conditions and outcomes. Social work's pursuit of health equity as a grand challenge means that the profession strives to ensure the highest possible standard of health and wellness for all people while prioritizing upstream interventions and primary prevention efforts among those who are at greatest risk for poor health—those who, because of social and economic disadvantage, experience the extremes of health inequalities. To be healthy, people require access to quality, culturally resonant care as well as to socioeconomic conditions that promote well-being in community, family, school, workplace, recreation, and environmental systems.

ACHIEVING POPULATION HEALTH: MOVING BEYOND THE INDIVIDUAL/CLINICAL TO THE COMMUNITY AND SOCIAL DETERMINANTS

Priority 1: Focus on Settings to Improve the Conditions of Daily Life

Combating the distal-level influence of racial and socioeconomic inequity on health and the intermediate-level consequences in a community's institutions (e.g., inadequate schools, unsafe streets, food deserts, and families with an incarcerated member) requires a sphere of interventions centered on changing the community environment to elevate the health prospects of a local population. Although large-scale social and economic (distal-level) policy changes may be the ultimate instrument for resolving the nation's health crisis, an accessible starting point for social work is to build the community-enhanced evidence base for change from the bottom up (National Research Council & Institute of Medicine, 2013).

Highly promising components of community-based research and practice for addressing social determinants of health inequities are found in the "places" and "social contexts where people engage in daily activities, in which environmental, organizational and personal factors interact to affect health and well-being, and where people actively use and shape the environment, thus creating or solving health problems" (Newman et al., 2015, p. ii127). Such settings include, but are not limited to, geographical places (e.g., cities), physical spaces where people congregate (e.g., religious centers), workplaces, green spaces (e.g., community gardens or playgrounds), and virtual worlds (i.e., social websites; Newman et al., 2015). It is critical for social work to be particularly present in settings that target and include young people—from birth to young adulthood—to address the cycle of intergenerational disadvantage.

The importance of addressing the social determinants of health inequities within settings has been highlighted by the Commission on Social Determinants of Health (2008) as well as by social determinant researchers (Marmot, 2005; Marmot & Bell, 2012). Newman and colleagues (2015) note that in addressing the social determinants of health within settings, there is room to "integrate individual behavior approaches with approaches at structural" or distal levels (p. ii135). Moreover, they note that settings approaches require cross-sectorial collaboration, committed leadership, genuine involvement of stakeholders, and strong research.

Priority 2: Advance Community Empowerment for Sustainable Health

A community organized for health improvement may work on either or both of two goals: representation in governance of the health care delivery system and interventions that create sustainable community changes. Representation in the governance of disadvantaged communities is critical for (1) efforts to ensure the enrollment in health care of as many community residents as possible and (2) active participation in evaluating services and resolving deficiencies to the community's benefit. Maximizing health care enrollment, especially among children and youth, ensures that they are counted in the assessment of efforts to improve the health of a vulnerable community. Representation in the governance of the health system may be accomplished through community organizing that strives to improve health equity. The particular task of securing representation over the long term calls for continued commitment to face-to-face, community-level education on the issues (Horton, Freire, Bell, Gaventa, & Peters, 1990). It also calls for engagement with all the organic social/cultural threads and groups in the community (e.g., religious and spiritual institutions; Stout, 2010). Community health coalitions and local learning communities can also play critical roles in developing local capacity for representation, monitoring progress, training volunteers, and demonstrating local options if reform implementations break down. By focusing on the community as the center of efforts to advance health—efforts that will complement those of the health service sector—activists build community-based interventions that are not only culturally grounded but also sustainable.

In parallel to practice-based research networks, community-oriented research networks can be developed to identify common measures and themes as well as lead in the design and development of culturally grounded health promotion interventions. Finally, social work can also partner with existing organizations, such as the National Community Building Network, the US Department of Housing and Urban Development's Office of University Partnerships, and the Alliance for Children and Families, to identify common interests and strategies for community-engaged research and action (Johnson, 2004).

Priority 3: Generate Research on Social Determinants of Health Inequities

Research on social determinants of health is essential for analyzing how environmental and traumatic stressors and racism (and other -isms) harm health and how these determinants become embodied over time, generations, and political–historical contexts. There are many social and cultural pathways by which discrimination harms health, including "economic and social deprivation; excess exposure to toxins, hazards, and pathogens; social trauma; health-harming responses to discrimination; targeted marketing of harmful commodities; and ecosystem degradation" (Krieger, 2012, p. 937). In particular, stress in response to these determinants may be an underdeveloped mechanism influencing how people respond to upstream and downstream determinants (McGovern et al., 2014).

Many emerging models of social determinants of health equity require testing. Moreover, there is quite often a gap between what is known through health equity research and what is actually taken up within communities. Davison, Ndumbe-Eyoh, and Clement (2015) identified six health equity models that bridge research and practice but require further testing: the Knowledge Brokering Framework (Oldham & McLean, 1997), the Framework for Research Transfer (Nieva et al., 2005), the Joint Venture Model of Knowledge Utilization (Edgar et al., 2006), the Translational Research Framework to Address Health Disparities (Fleming et al., 2008), the Model of Knowledge Translation and Exchange with Northern Aboriginal Communities (Jardine & Furgal, 2010), and the Ecohealth Model applied to knowledge translation (Arredondo & Orozco, 2012). The models have many strengths. They value the direct participation of community stakeholders; prioritize multisectoral engagement; recognize the importance of environmental and contextual determinants; have a proactive, collaborative, problem-solving approach; and support an inclusive conceptualization of knowledge (community and traditional, culture-based knowledge, as well as qualitative and quantitative forms).

Priority 4: Stimulate Multisectoral Advocacy to Promote Health Equity Policies

Social work's disciplinary competencies related to the person-in-environment perspective and applied ecological theory offer unique opportunities to forge broad alliances capable of advocating for a more comprehensive, multisectoral view of health determinants as well as for practices and policies to address the racial and economic injustices that form the bedrock for health inequities. Part of the strategy to close the gaps in health among subgroups is "'leveling up' the health of less advantaged groups" (Farrer et al., 2015, p. 394). WHO has demonstrated the utility of multisectoral approaches to leveling up conditions for vulnerable and marginalized populations. Government, health care, public health, and university entities have been the traditional participants in efforts to eliminate health disparities, but many settings within communities could be employed in advocacy and change efforts. According to Williams and Wyatt (2015),

> Multilevel policies . . . in homes, schools, neighborhoods, workplaces, and religious organizations can help remove barriers to healthy living and create

opportunities to usher in a new culture of health in which the healthy choice is the easy choice. (p. 556)

Multisectorial approaches have effectively translated research into action through networks of individuals, communities, government entities, health providers, institutions, businesses, and industries, but more innovation is needed. The urgency of the need to make rapid progress in the health of poor communities and communities of color calls for national collaboration both to advance the science for breaking the cycle of intergenerational disadvantage and to translate that science into action.

STRENGTHENING HEALTH CARE SYSTEMS: BETTER HEALTH ACROSS AMERICA

Priority 5: Cultivate Innovation in Primary Care

Improving the health of those suffering lifelong and even intergenerational disadvantage, especially those previously without regular primary health care, will require innovation in primary and other care. An exemplar of the viability of innovation in primary care is the emergence of accountable care organizations (ACOs) in which groups of providers agree to improve the overall health care experience of a defined patient population through efficiency of care delivery that reduces costs and improves quality of health care and health (DeVore & Champion, 2011). The first ACOs were in fact targeting what might be considered disadvantaged populations through the Centers for Medicare and Medicaid Services' Medicare Shared Savings Program (Fisher, Shortell, Kreindler, Van Citters, & Larson, 2012). ACOs have demonstrated the need for more integrated approaches in primary care. A more widely adopted and far-reaching innovation is the Substance Abuse and Mental Health Administration's (SAMHSA) SBIRT (screening, brief intervention, and referral) initiative to address substance abuse issues in primary care (Babor, Del Boca, & Bray, 2017). Given that one-third of all health care resources in the United States are spent on individuals with behavioral health needs associated with persistent medical illness (Kathol, Patel, Sacks, Sargent, & Melek, 2015), ACOs and SBIRT are timely innovations that promote health equity and benefit society.

In addition, as members of practice-based research networks, social workers now cooperate with other groups in identifying successful social innovations for medical, hospital, community, and mental health settings. Social workers examine health care processes and care of patients, designing and developing culturally grounded health interventions. Finally, social workers provide an organizational structure for surveillance and research.

Priority 6: Promote Full Access to Health Care

To achieve health equity, the profession must focus on financial and bureaucratic barriers that have plagued access to the health care system for decades and offer systemic solutions as well as interventions that are rooted in community and culture. The ACA offered unparalleled opportunities to reduce inequality in health care access and health. First, the ACA dramatically expanded health insurance coverage in the United States through major expansions of Medicaid and the creation of health insurance marketplaces. After these expansions went into full effect in 2014, more than 23 million US residents gained health insurance (Carman, Eibner, & Paddock, 2015). Second, the ACA established patient navigation funding to assist people in getting insurance and accessing health care (Andrews, Darnell, McBride, & Gehlert, 2013). Third, the ACA established new incentives to promote innovative models for coordinating and integrating health care. Such incentives were designed to make it easier for patients to find and receive the services they need. Fourth, the ACA mandated that any federally funded health care or public health care program must collect self-reported data on race, ethnicity, sex, primary language, and disability (DHHS, n.d.). Efforts to identify systemic inequality in the health care system have long been undermined by inconsistent collection and reporting of race and ethnicity data.

However, challenges remained. The ACA was not successful in obtaining universal access to insurance coverage. A 2012 Supreme Court decision allowed states to opt out of Medicaid expansion; subsequently, only 32 states expanded. This decision left millions in a "coverage gap" without access to Medicaid and too poor to be eligible for the subsidized private marketplaces (Garfield, Damico, Cox, Claxton, & Levitt, 2016). African Americans and American Indians and Alaska Natives are more likely to reside in states that have not expanded Medicaid, exacerbating within-state disparities (Andrews, 2014; Andrews, Guerrero, Wooten, & Legnick-Hall, 2015). The ACA also did not provide an avenue for undocumented immigrants to gain coverage, even without receiving government support (Joseph, 2016). Thus, it is not surprising that ACA has been effective in narrowing, but not closing, national racial and ethnic gaps in insurance coverage (Buchmueller, Levinson, Levy, & Wolfe, 2016).

Ordinarily, we would argue that social work should be targeting our advocacy efforts toward moving the ACA forward: closing the coverage gap by promoting universal adoption of Medicaid expansion; supporting states such as California and Massachusetts, which are attempting to insure undocumented immigrants (Joseph, 2016); advancing culturally specific approaches to insurance enrollment and patient navigation; and urging the use of race/ethnicity data to identify and redress disparities in quality. However, currently, the future of the ACA and its component protections is entirely uncertain. Social workers will need to unite as a profession and join forces with allies of health care justice to educate the electorate, engage communities in grassroots organizing, and petition members of Congress against ACA repeal and an inadequate replacement. We must be vigilant against policy proposals that would move access to health care and health equity back decades from the recent advancements offered by the ACA.

Priority 7: Foster Development of an Interprofessional Health Workforce

According to the US Bureau of Labor Statistics (2014), between 2012 and 2022, employment of health care social workers is projected to grow by 27%, and employment of mental health and substance abuse social workers is projected to grow by 23%. Because of these occupational trends, social work can create integrated pathways to health careers in social intervention. Social work can lead integrated initiatives for evidence-based workforce development by reviewing practitioner preparation for transdisciplinary social interventions, defining a core curriculum for such initiatives, establishing training standards for advanced practice in specialized areas, and identifying new competence areas for the emerging health system (e.g., prevention science, place- and settings-based research, community engagement, improvement science, health-data analytics, and team methods for collaborative behavioral and physical health care). In addition, we should develop an integrated public health social work curriculum across Master of Social Work programs that goes beyond Master of Social Work–Master of Public Health dual-degree programs.

REDUCING AND PREVENTING ALCOHOL MISUSE AND ITS CONSEQUENCES

Alcohol misuse is a compelling problem for the social work profession, encountered in almost every practice setting, and directly or indirectly relating to every domain of well-being about which the profession is concerned. The biopsychosocial and multisectorial nature of the social work profession makes it uniquely suited to lead a transdisciplinary effort for reducing and preventing the wide range of consequences associated with alcohol misuse. Alcohol issues intersect with multiple other Grand Challenges for Social Work. Among the priority areas that emerged in the Reducing and Preventing Alcohol Misuse and Its Consequences workgroup (Begun et al., 2016) are (1) develop research and scholarship; (2) develop interdisciplinary, multisectorial, and sustainable collaborations; and (3) workforce development.

Priority 8: Develop Research and Scholarship in Alcohol Misuse and Its Consequences

In both the United States and throughout the world, alcohol misuse is associated with high rates of morbidity, mortality, and co-occurring physical, mental health, and social problems. It causes an array of acute and chronic health problems, globally accounting for 3.3 million deaths annually: "The harmful use of alcohol ranks among the top five risk factors for disease, disability and death throughout the world" (WHO, 2014b, p. 2). Alcohol is among the leading risk factors for mortality in the United States and is a recognized contributor to the top 10 causes of death, including heart disease, cancer, stroke, fatal injuries, and suicide (CDC, 2014), as well as maternal–child health complications (e.g., fetal alcohol exposure). In addition to these health consequences, alcohol misuse often accompanies the misuse of other substances, significant cognitive impairments, multiple forms of mental disorder, physical disability, and a host of social problems: intimate partner violence; child maltreatment; human trafficking; sexual assault; problem gambling; school failure; criminal justice system involvement; and insecurity around employment, housing, and safety.

Alcoholic beverages are by far the most commonly used and abused psychoactive substances, and use has increased during the past decade (Dawson, Goldstein, Saha, & Grant, 2015). In the United States, more than 66 million individuals aged 12 years or older engage in binge drinking and 17.3 million in heavy drinking (SAMHSA, 2016). More than 15.7 million persons in this age group met criteria for an alcohol use disorder during the past year, and an additional 2.67 million experienced substance use disorders involving alcohol and other substances as well. There exists a considerable health care gap between the many millions of individuals needing treatment for an alcohol (or other substance) use disorder and the estimated 2.5 million receiving care in specialized alcohol or other drug treatment (SAMHSA, 2014). In the United States, the cost estimate for untreated alcohol misuse is $223.5 billion annually (Research Society on Alcoholism, 2015).

Once depicted as entrenched, unalterable problems, decades of research has proven that evidence-informed strategies can successfully address alcohol misuse and its consequences (Warren & Hewitt, 2010). Alcohol researchers utilize varied methods and designs and include variables ranging from the micro level (e.g., neuroscience, genomics, epigenetics, proteomics, and metabolomics) to the macro level (e.g., population-based epidemiology, "big data, small n" studies, econometrics, health/human services, and policy at local, state, regional, national, and global levels). Contemporary and emerging research approaches to studying alcohol misuse are among many that social work scholars employ and around which we should continue to develop mastery. Social work scholars need to highlight their alcohol research contributions both within the profession and in transdisciplinary ways.

Priority 9: Develop Interdisciplinary, Multisectorial, and Sustainable Collaborations

Partnerships working across disciplines and across the various service delivery sectors that serve individuals, families, communities, and larger social systems can "bring the pieces together" to meet the AGC. For instance, social workers, researchers, and engineers at The Ohio State University are working on systems dynamic approaches to drinking behavior for developing inexpensive, sustainable, "smart" application interventions to prevent acute alcohol problems, such as driving under the influence behavior (Clapp et al., in press; Giraldo, Passino, & Clapp, 2015). A somewhat controversial recommendation presented in the original AGC paper was to collaborate with the alcohol beverage industry to reduce alcohol-related harms. One such project consistent with the AGC is the AB InBev Global Smart Drinking Goals initiative (http://www.ab-inbev.com/better-world/a-healthier-world/global-smart-drinking-goals.html). The collaborative partnership is a decade-long investment of more than $1 billion to reduce alcohol-related harms globally by 10%. AGC progress is also dependent on collaboration with governmental and nongovernmental organizations—locally, nationally, and globally (e.g., state mental health and substance use agencies, the National Institutes of Health, and WHO)—to build the infrastructures and funding for solutions to this challenge.

Priority 10: Develop the Workforce in Social Work to Address Alcohol Misuse

Social work and inter-professional curricula that tap into the evidence base related to alcohol misuse prepare individuals to intervene in ways that reduce or prevent alcohol misuse and its consequences. For example, social work and other curricula are available to train practitioners to deliver evidence-based screening, brief intervention, and referral to treatment (SBIRT) for alcohol misuse. The advent of open-source online training mechanisms offers innovative opportunities for both pre-service and in-service/continuing education related to meeting workforce demands associated with the AGC.

SOCIAL WORK'S ROLES IN LEADING A HEALTH EQUITY GRAND CHALLENGE

Social work is uniquely positioned for a leadership role in addressing health inequities because, as indicated in Jane Addams' speech at the 1930 National Conference of Social Work, "social work's special genius is its closeness to the people it serves" (as quoted in Johnson, 2004, p. 319). Social work's historical social justice mission as well as its commitment to serve the most disenfranchised and health-burdened populations affirm the profession's ability to provide leadership in association with allied health professions. The attributes also speak to the profession's ability to design and develop community-based approaches to eradicate health inequities.

Several factors demonstrate why social work should lead a grand challenge to achieve health equity. First, social workers understand the complex pathways from disadvantage to health risks and outcomes. Those pathways run through the vulnerable communities in which social workers routinely operate. In addition, health risks and outcomes among disadvantaged populations are correlated with structural and sociodemographic disadvantages (e.g., poverty, low levels of education, substandard housing, and poor access to services) as well as with high rates of co-occurring physical health problems (e.g., alcohol misuse, diabetes, and cardiovascular disease). Also, trauma and violence exposure (including intergenerational and historical trauma exposures) are associated with co-occurring psychopathology (e.g., post-traumatic stress disorder and depression; Brand et al., 2010; Matthews & Phillips, 2010; Walters et al., 2011). Addressing these associations will require multitasking across multiple levels of intervention, and such a broad deployment of effort is a hallmark of social work practice. Stated simply, health is not created in a clinic, and we cannot rely on traditional health services alone to heal the wrongs of history and persistent inequality.

Second, social work's leadership is needed to elucidate problems and test solutions. Despite the glaring health disparities, there is a paucity of culturally relevant research on some of the most vulnerable populations. Because of this, the health fields have little data on important risk factors, coping behaviors, and health outcomes. Without a larger body of evidence, it will be difficult to identify the strategies and develop the programs necessary to reduce health inequalities and improve health equity within the United States. Many social work researchers are already at the forefront of research on health disparities and prevention needs among vulnerable populations, particularly among racial and ethnic minorities as well as lesbian, gay, bisexual, and transgender populations (Evans-Campbell, Lincoln, & Takeuchi, 2007; Fredriksen-Goldsen et al., 2014; Marsiglia, Kulis, Yabiku, Nieri, & Coleman, 2011; Wheeler, 2003). Moreover, social work researchers have advanced innovative, community-based, participatory-research approaches as well as conceptual models that include multilevel influences on health (Gehlert & Coleman, 2010; Gehlert, Sohmer, et al., 2008; Spencer et al., 2011; Walters & Simoni, 2002; Walters et al., 2012).

Social work's long-standing commitment to a diverse workforce with full representation of all stakeholders is a third reason for the profession to lead the health equity grand challenge. The ACA and recent national reports, including one from the National Institutes of Health, call for more inclusion of underrepresented ethnic and racial minorities among funded investigators and community-based researchers (Shavers et al., 2005; Sopher et al., 2015). Despite these calls, a very limited number of underrepresented ethnic and racial minorities have served as principal investigators for awards by the National Institutes of Health. Moreover, racial and ethnic minorities remain significantly underrepresented in higher education. In the United States, they account for only 12% of all people with doctorates and less than 3% of medical school professors (Sopher et al., 2015). A broad and dense network of highly trained and productive health science scholars, a network that includes underrepresented ethnic and racial minorities and is dedicated to culturally grounded research, is needed to ameliorate health disparities.

Finally, as suggested previously, the legacy of social work and the roles historically played by social workers should spur the profession to lead the grand challenge of health equity. Throughout history, social workers have played pivotal roles in efforts to increase critical consciousness within competing systems, linked key health system stakeholders, and led in efforts to incorporate social and ecological realities into assessment and treatment. This distinctive legacy enables social work to provide leadership at a time when the ACA is driving promotion of community involvement. The legacy also provides paradigms for creative solutions to problems that extend across systems.

The social work profession is also positioned to facilitate interdisciplinary efforts among applied social and behavioral scientists, educators, and practitioners. As members of interprofessional teams, social workers already contribute in the movement toward patient-centered care. They also are engaged in the implementation of integrated care models to better address physical, mental, and behavioral health issues (e.g., alcohol and substance abuse). The next decade offers an opportunity to develop a strategy for leveraging the momentum of health care reform efforts to create a social determinants-focused agenda for research, practice, and action. Such a strategy would enable social workers to set measureable targets and time frames for alleviating the deep and persistent health inequities in the United States.

Social work is poised and primed to bring our research, education, policy, and practice skills together to adapt and apply what we know for use in national efforts to reduce health disparities; to improve mental and physical health outcomes, particularly among society's most vulnerable and marginalized; and ultimately to promote health equity and well-being for our society as a whole. As our science and profession have matured, we have grown in readiness to tackle the "scale, complexity, and interrelatedness of societal problems—from poverty and dramatic inequality to the sustainability of health and human service infrastructures across the globe—[and to] demand problem-solving skill and collaboration at levels perhaps unprecedented in our history" (Uehara et al., 2013, p. 165). The health of future generations depends on the actions we take in our current generation. Let us be remembered not only for our science and practice but also for our resolve to harness our collective will and intelligence to transform the health of the nation.

REFERENCES

Agency for Healthcare Research and Quality. (2013). *2012 National healthcare disparities report 2012* (AHRQ Publication No. 13-0003). Rockville, MD: US Department of Health and Human Services.

Andrews, C. M. (2014). Unintended consequences: Medicaid expansion and racial inequality in access to health insurance. *Health & Social Work, 39*(3), 131–133. doi:10.1093/hsw/hlu024

Andrews, C. M., Darnell, J. S., McBride, T. D., & Gehlert, S. (2013). Social work and implementation of the Affordable Care Act. *Health & Social Work, 38*(2), 67–71. doi:10 .1093/hsw/hlt002

Andrews, C. M., Guerrero, E. G., Wooten, N. R., & Legnick-Hall, R. (2015). The Medicaid expansion gap and racial and ethnic minorities with substance use disorders. *American Journal of Public Health, 105*(Suppl. 3), S452–S454. doi:10.2105/ AJPH.2015.302560

Arredondo, A., & Orozco, E. (2012). Application of the Ecohealth model to translate knowledge into action in the health sciences. *Environmental Health Perspectives, 120*(3), A104–A105. doi:10.1289/ehp.1104847

Avendano, M., Glymour, M. M., Banks, J., & Mackenbach, J. P. (2009). Health disadvantage in US adults aged 50 to 74 years: A comparison of the health of rich and poor Americans with that of Europeans. *American Journal of Public Health, 99*(3), 540–548. doi:10.2105/AJPH .2008.139469

Babor, T. F., Del Boca, F., & Bray, J. W. (2017). Screening, Brief Intervention and Referral to Treatment: implications of SAMHSA's SBIRT initiative for substance abuse policy and practice. *Addiction, 112*(S2), 110–117.

Begun, A. L., Clapp, J. D., & The Alcohol Misuse Grand Challenge Collective. (2016). *Reducing and preventing alcohol misuse and its consequences: A grand challenge for social work* (Grand Challenges for Social Work Initiative Working Paper No. 17). Cleveland, OH: American Academy of Social Work and Social Welfare. Retrieved from http://aaswsw.org/wp-content/uploads/2015/12/WP14-with-cover.pdf

Brand, S. R., Brennan, P. A., Newport, D. J., Smith, A. K., Weiss, T., & Stowe, Z. N. (2010). The impact of maternal childhood abuse on maternal and infant HPA axis function in the postpartum period. *Psychoneuroendocrinology, 35*(5), 686–693. doi:10.1016/j.psyneuen .2009.10.009

Braveman, P., & Gottlieb, L. (2014). The social determinants of health: It's time to consider the causes of the causes. *Public Health Reports, 129*(Suppl. 2), 19–31.

Brennan Ramirez, L. K., Baker, E. A., & Metzler, M. (2008). *Promoting health equity: A resource to help communities address social determinants of health.* Atlanta, GA: US Department of Health and Human Services, Centers for Disease Control and Prevention.

Buchmueller, T. C., Levinson, Z. M., Levy, H. G., & Wolfe, B. L. (2016). Effect of the Affordable Care Act on racial and ethnic disparities in health insurance coverage. *American Journal of Public Health, 106*(8), 1416–1421.

Carman, K. G., Eibner, C., & Paddock, S. M. (2015, May). Trends in health insurance enrollment, 2013–15. *Health Affairs.* doi:10.1377/hlthaff.2015.0266

Centers for Disease Control and Prevention. (2014). *CDC national health report: Leading causes of morbidity and mortality and associated behavioral risk and protective factors—United States, 2005–2013*. Retrieved from https://stacks.cdc.gov/view/cdc/25809

Clapp, J. D., Madden, D. R., Gonzalez Villasanti, H. J., Giraldo, L. F., Passino, K. M., Reed, M. B., & Fernandez Puentes, I. (in press). A system dynamics model of drinking events: Multi-level ecological approach. *Systems Research and Behavioral Science*.

Commission on Social Determinants of Health. (2008). *Closing the gap in a generation: Health equity through action on the social determinants of health* [Final report]. Retrieved from http://whqlibdoc.who.int/publications/2008/9789241563703_eng.pdf

Dahlgren, G., & Whitehead, M. (1992). *Policies and strategies to promote equity in health*. Copenhagen, Denmark: World Health Organization Regional Office for Europe.

Davison, C. M., Ndumbe-Eyoh, S., & Clement, C. (2015). Critical examination of knowledge to action models and implications for promoting health equity. *International Journal for Equity in Health*, *14*, article 49. doi:10.1186/s12939-015-0178-7

Dawson, D. A., Goldstein, R. B., Saha, T. D., & Grant, B. F. (2015). Changes in alcohol consumption: United States 2001–2002 to 2012–2013. *Drug and Alcohol Dependence*, *148*, 56–61.

DeVore, S., & Champion, R. W. (2011). Driving population health through accountable care organizations. *Health Affairs*, *30*(1), 41–50.

Edgar, L., Herbert, R., Lambert, S., MacDonald, J.-A., Dubois, S., & Latimer, M. (2006). The joint venture model of knowledge utilization: A guide for change in nursing. *Nursing Leadership*, *19*(2), 41–55. doi:10.12927/cjnl.2006.18172

Evans-Campbell, T., Lincoln, K. D., & Takeuchi, D. T. (2007). Race and mental health: Past debates, new opportunities. In W. R. Avison, J. D. McLeod, & B. A. Pescosolido (Eds.), *Mental health, social mirror* (pp. 169–189). New York, NY: Springer.

Farrer, L., Marinetti, C., Cavaco, Y. K., & Costongs, C. (2015). Advocacy for health equity: A synthesis review. *Milbank Quarterly*, *93*(2), 392–437. doi:10.1111/1468-0009.12112

Fisher, E. S., Shortell, S. M., Kreindler, S. A., Van Citters, A. D., & Larson, B. K. (2012). A framework for evaluating the formation, implementation, and performance of accountable care organizations. *Health Affairs*, *31*(11), 2368–2378. doi:10.1377/hlthaff.2012.0544.

Fleming, E. S., Perkins, J., Easa, D., Conde, J. G., Baker, R. S., Southerland, W. M., . . . Norris, K. C. (2008). The role of translational research in addressing health disparities: A conceptual framework. *Ethnicity & Disease*, *18*(Suppl. 2), S2-155–S2-160.

Fredriksen-Goldsen, K. I., Simoni, J. M., Kim, H.-J., Lehavot, K., Walters, K. L., Yang, J., . . . Muraco, A. (2014). The Health Equity Promotion Model: Reconceptualization of lesbian, gay, bisexual, and transgender (LGBT) health disparities. *American Journal of Orthopsychiatry*, *84*(6), 653–663. doi:10.1037/ort0000030

Garfield, R., Damico, A., Cox, C., Claxton, G., & Levitt, L. (2016, January 16). *New estimates of eligibility for ACA coverage among the uninsured*. Retrieved from http://files.kff.org/attachment/data-note-new-estimates-of-eligibility-for-aca-coverage-among-the-uninsured

Gehlert, S., & Coleman, R. (2010). Using community-based participatory research to ameliorate cancer disparities. *Health & Social Work*, *35*(4), 302–309. doi:10.1093/hsw/35.4.302

Gehlert, S., Mininger, C., Sohmer, D., & Berg, K. (2008). (Not so) gently down the stream: Choosing targets to ameliorate health disparities. *Health & Social Work, 33*(3), 163–167. doi:10.1093/hsw/33.3.163

Gehlert, S., Sohmer, D., Sacks, T., Mininger, C., McClintock, M., & Olopade, O. (2008). Targeting health disparities: A model linking upstream determinants to downstream interventions. *Health Affairs, 27*(2), 339–349. doi:10.1377/hlthaff.27.2.339

Giraldo, L. F., Passino, K. M., & Clapp, J. D. (2015). Modeling and analysis of group dynamics in alcohol-consumption environments. *IEEE Transactions on Cybernetics, 99,* 1–12.

Gordon-Larsen, P., Nelson, M. C., Page, P., & Popkin, B. M. (2006). Inequality in the built environment underlies key health disparities in physical activity and obesity. *Pediatrics, 117*(2), 417–424. doi:10.1542/peds.2005-0058

Hood, C. M., Gennuso, K. P., Swain, G. R., & Catlin, B. B. (2016). County health rankings: Relationships between determinant factors and health outcomes. *American Journal of Preventive Medicine, 50*(2), 129–135. doi:10.1016/j.amepre.2015.08.024

Horton, M., Freire, P., Bell, B., Gaventa, J., & Peters, J. (Eds.). (1990). *We make the road by walking: Conversations on education and social change.* Philadelphia, PA: Temple University Press.

Jardine, C., & Furgal, C. (2010). Knowledge translation with northern aboriginal communities: A case study. *Canadian Journal of Nursing Research, 42*(1), 119–127.

Johnson, A. K. (2004). Social work is standing on the legacy of Jane Addams: But are we sitting on the sidelines? *Social Work, 49*(2), 319–322. doi:10.1093/sw/49.2.319

Joseph, T. D. (2016). What health care reform means for immigrants: Comparing the Affordable Care Act and Massachusetts health reforms. *Journal of Health Politics, Policy and Law, 41*(1), 101–116.

Kaplan, G. A., Shema, S. J., & Leite, C. M. A. (2008). Socioeconomic determinants of psychological well-being: The role of income, income change, and income sources during the course of 29 years. *Annals of Epidemiology, 18*(7), 531–537. doi:10.1016/j.annepidem.2008 .03.006

Kathol, R. G., Patel, K., Sacks, L., Sargent, S., & Melek, S. P. (2015). The role of behavioral health services in accountable care organizations. *American Journal of Managed Care, 21*(2), e95–e98.

Krieger, N. (2012). Methods for the scientific study of discrimination and health: An ecosocial approach. *American Journal of Public Health, 102*(5), 936–945. doi:10.2105/AJPH.2011 .300544

Link, B. G., & Phelan, J. C. (1995). Social conditions as fundamental causes of disease. *Journal of Health and Social Behavior, 35*(Extra issue), 80–94. doi:10.2307/2626958

Logie, C., Dimaras, H., Fortin, A., & Ramón-García, S. (2014). Challenges faced by multidisciplinary new investigators on addressing grand challenges in global health. *Globalization and Health, 10,* article 27. doi:10.1186/1744-8603-10-27

Marmot, M. (2005). Social determinants of health inequalities. *Lancet, 365*(9464), 1099–1104. doi:10.1016/S0140-6736(05)71146-6

Marmot, M., & Bell, R. (2012). Fair society, healthy lives. *Public Health, 126*(Suppl. 1), S4–S10. doi:10.1016/j.puhe.2012.05.014

Marsiglia, F. F., Kulis, S., Yabiku, S. T., Nieri, T. A., & Coleman, E. (2011). When to intervene: Elementary school, middle school or both? Effects of Keepin' It REAL on substance use trajectories of Mexican heritage youth. *Prevention Science, 12*(1), 48–62. doi:10.1007 /s11121-010-0189-y

Matthews, S. G., & Phillips, D. I. W. (2010). Minireview: Transgenerational inheritance of the stress response: A new frontier in stress research. *Endocrinology, 151*(1), 7–13. doi:10.1210 /en.2009-0916

McGovern, L., Miller, G., & Hughes-Cromwick, P. (2014, August 21). *The relative contribution of multiple determinants to health outcomes* (Health Policy Brief). Retrieved from http://www.healthaffairs.org/healthpolicybriefs/brief.php?brief_id=123

Mitchell, F. M. (2015). Racial and ethnic health disparities in an era of health care reform. *Health and Social Work, 40*(3), e66–e74. doi:10.1093/hsw/hlv038

National Research Council & Institute of Medicine. (2013, January). *U.S. health in international perspective: Shorter lives, poorer health* (Institute of Medicine Report Brief). Washington, DC: National Academies Press.

Newman, L., Baum, F., Javanparast, S., O'Rourke, K., & Carlon, L. (2015). Addressing social determinants of health inequities through settings: A rapid review. *Health Promotion International, 30*(Suppl. 2), ii126–ii143. doi:10.1093/heapro/dav054

Nieva, V. F., Murphy, R., Ridley, N., Donaldson, N., Combes, J., Mitchell, P., . . . Carpenter, D. (2005). From science to service: A framework for the transfer of patient safety research into practice. In K. Henriksen, J. B. Battles, E. S. Marks, & D. I. Lewin (Eds.), *Advances in patient safety: From research to implementation: Vol. 2. Concepts, and methodology* (pp. 441–453). Rockville, MD: Agency for Healthcare Research and Quality.

Oldham, G., & McLean, R. (1997). *Approaches to knowledge-brokering.* Retrieved from https://www.iisd.org/pdf/2001/networks_knowledge_brokering.pdf

Patient Protection and Affordable Care Act, 42 U.S.C. § 18001 (2010).

Research Society on Alcoholism. (2015). *White paper: Impact of alcoholism and alcohol induced disease and disorders on America.* Retrieved from http://rsoa.org/RSA-2014WhitePaperFinalVersionVH.pdf

Shavers, V. L., Fagan, P., Lawrence D., McCaskill-Stevens, W., McDonald, P., Browne, D., . . . Trimble, E. (2005). Barriers to racial/ethnic minority application and competition for NIH research funding. *Journal of the National Medical Association, 97*(8), 1063–1077.

Smedley, B. D., Stith, A. Y., & Nelson, A. R. (Eds.). (2003). *Unequal treatment: Confronting racial and ethnic disparities in health care.* Washington, DC: National Academies Press.

Sopher, C. J., Adamson, B. J. S., Andrasik, M. P., Flood, D. M., Wakefield, S. F., Stoff, D. M., . . . Fuchs, J. D. (2015). Enhancing diversity in the public health research workforce: The research and mentorship program for future HIV vaccine scientists. *American Journal of Public Health, 105*(4), 823–830. doi:10.2105/AJPH.2014.302076

Spencer, M. S., Rosland, A.-M., Kieffer, E. C., Sinco, B. R., Valerio, M., Palmisano, G., . . . Heisler, M. E. (2011). Effectiveness of a community health worker intervention among African American and Latino adults with type 2 diabetes: A randomized controlled trial. *American Journal of Public Health, 101*(12), 2253–2260. doi:10.2105/AJPH.2010.300106

Stout, J. (2010). *Blessed are the organized: Grassroots democracy in America.* Princeton, NJ: Princeton University Press.

Substance Abuse and Mental Health Administration. (2014). *Results from the 2013 National Survey on Drug Use and Health: Summary of national findings*. Retrieved from https://www.samhsa.gov/data/sites/default/files/NSDUHresultsPDFWHTML2013/Web/NSDUHresults2013.pdf

Substance Abuse and Mental Health Administration. (2016). *Results from the 2015 National Survey on Drug Use and Health: Summary of national findings*. Retrieved from https://www.samhsa.gov/data/sites/default/files/NSDUHresultsPDFWHTML2013/Web/NSDUHresults2013.pdf

Uehara, E., Flynn, M., Fong, R., Brekke, J., Barth, R. P., Coulton, C., . . . Walters, K. (2013). Grand challenges for social work. *Journal of the Society for Social Work and Research, 4*(3), 165–170. doi:10.5243/jsswr.2013.11

US Bureau of Labor Statistics. (2014, January 8). Social workers. In *Occupational outlook handbook* (2014–2015 ed.). Retrieved from http://www.bls.gov/ooh/community-and-social-service/social -workers.htm#tab-6

US Department of Health and Human Services. (n.d.) *Improving data collection to reduce health disparities*. Retrieved from https://minorityhealth.hhs.gov/assets/pdf/checked/1/Fact_Sheet_Section_4302.pdf

US Department of Health and Human Services, Office of Disease Prevention and Health Promotion. (2000). *Healthy people 2020*. Retrieved from https://www.healthypeople.gov

Walters, K. L., LaMarr, J., Levy, R. L., Pearson, C., Maresca, T., Mohammed, S. A., . . . Jobe, J. B. (2012). Project həli? dxw/Healthy Hearts Across Generations: Development and evaluation design of a tribally based cardiovascular disease prevention intervention for American Indian families. *Journal of Primary Prevention, 33*(4), 197–207. doi:10.1007/s10935-012-0274-z

Walters, K. L., Mohammed, S. A., Evans-Campbell, T., Beltrán, R. E., Chae, D. H., & Duran, B. (2011). Bodies don't just tell stories, they tell histories: Embodiment of historical trauma among American Indians and Alaska Natives. *Dubois Review, 8*(1), 179–189. doi:10.1017 /S1742058X1100018X

Walters, K. L., & Simoni, J. M. (2002). Reconceptualizing Native women's health: An "Indigenist" stress-coping model. *American Journal of Public Health, 92*(4), 520–524. doi:10 .2105/AJPH.92.4.520

Warren, K. R., & Hewitt, B. G. (2010). NIAAA: Advancing alcohol research for 40 years. *Alcohol Research & Health, 33*(1–2), 5–17.

Wheeler, D. P. (2003). Methodological issues in conducting community-based health and social services research among urban Black and African American LGBT populations. *Journal of Gay & Lesbian Social Services, 15*(1–2), 65–78. doi:10.1300/J041v15n01_05

Williams, D. R., & Wyatt, R. (2015). Racial bias in health care and health challenges and opportunities. *JAMA, 314*(6), 555–556. doi:10.1001/jama.2015.9260

World Health Organization. (2014a). *Global status report on alcohol and health*. Retrieved from http://www.who.int/substance_abuse/publications/global_alcohol_report/en

World Health Organization. (2014b). *Promoting health and reducing health inequities by addressing the social determinants of health*. Retrieved from http://www.euro.who.int/__data/assets/pdf_file/0016/141226/Brochure_promoting_health.pdf

Grand Challenges
for Social Work
Stop family violence

CHAPTER 4

Stop Family Violence

RICHARD P. BARTH AND REBECCA J. MACY

A FOCUS ON CHILD MALTREATMENT AND INTIMATE PARTNER VIOLENCE

Social work's history has a long, if still incomplete, recognition that family violence is intolerable and that it should be interrupted before it escalates, especially before becoming lethal (Gordon, 1988; Straus, Gelles, & Steinmetz, 1981). Despite ardent and widespread agreement about the need to intervene and prevent family violence, there has been far less agreement among social work practitioners and researchers as to how best to conceptualize and address the overall issue of family violence, which includes specific subtypes of violence, particularly child maltreatment (CM) and intimate partner violence (IPV).

Social workers tend to labor away at the problems of CM and IPV within "siloed" service and research sectors, working to address specific types of family violence without looking above the horizon of siloes—both disciplinary and topical—to find connections and opportunities to intervene with families comprehensively and holistically (Hamby & Grych, 2013). Although there are notable interdisciplinary exceptions (Messing & Campbell, 2016), various IPV interventions have been developed in distinct fields, including social work, as well as criminal justice, law, psychotherapy, and the women's movement (Barner & Carney, 2011). Notably, social work professionals are often found working within these fields. Examples of roles that social workers fill in addressing IPV include leading abuser intervention programs, providing victims' advocacy in court settings, providing cognitive–behavioral therapy to survivors in mental health clinics, and developing domestic violence shelters for adult survivors and their children. In addition, such approaches are grounded in a focus on the safety and well-being of the adult IPV victim and/ or intervention with the perpetrator whether or not the intimate partners have children.

In contrast, intervention approaches for CM are rooted in the early development of the Children's Bureau and formal child protection services, which in turn were subsequently institutionalized through the Child Abuse Protection and Treatment Act as well as various state-interpreted child welfare policies. Accordingly, the focus of CM intervention is the safety of the child or the interaction of the parent and the child, not the separate health and welfare of adult caregivers. Such tailored approaches and attentive efforts to specific forms of family violence have given social workers profound understandings of CM and IPV in focused ways. The inherent tensions in such foci have also led to significant disagreements between those who work in one or the other silo and have only been partially resolved by efforts such as the *Green Book* (http://thegreenbook.info/read.htm). For all these reasons, there is a critical need for social workers to focus on making meaningful connections between the issues of CM and IPV to address the grand challenge of ending family violence successfully. To help address this need, this chapter highlight points of intersection between CM and IPV to inform family-focused preventive and early intervention programs.

A focus on the intersections between CM and IPV, as a way to address this grand challenge, is consistent with a growing call among violence scholars more broadly, as well as the Centers for Disease Control and Prevention (CDC) specifically, to "connect the dots" among various forms of violence in comprehensive, holistic, and person-centered ways (Hamby & Grych, 2013; Wilkins, Tsao, Hertz, Davis, & Klevens, 2014). Mounting and robust evidence shows that diverse forms of violence are both interrelated and share similar etiologies (Abajobir, Kiesely, Williams, Clavarino, & Najman, 2017; Herrenkohl & Jung, 2016; Niolon et al., 2017; Milaniak & Widom, 2015), which means that a targeted focus on shared risk and protective factors may act to simultaneously prevent and end multiple forms of family violence. Likewise, strategies designed to decrease shared risk and protective factors can help extend limited prevention and intervention resources, such as funding, professional capacities, participant time, and organizational support, which are all required to deliver family violence prevention and intervention programs in high-quality ways that ensure fidelity in their implementation. Importantly, these risk and protective factors extend to multiple levels of the social ecology, including individual, relationship, community, and society (Wilkins et al., 2014), suggesting comprehensive prevention strategies must also span multilevel factors.

Thus, the social work grand challenge of stopping family violence can best be accomplished through developing interventions that prevent and respond to both CM and IPV in coordinated ways that build on underlying commonalities. Social work—perhaps more than many other profession—has shown a commitment to making connections across diverse issues and fields. In fact, the history of social work practice and research shows notable efforts to make connections between CM and IPV (Connelly et al., 2006; Edleson, 1999; Herrenkohl, Sousa, Tajima, Herrenkohl, & Moylan, 2008; Schechter & Edleson, 1999). Accordingly, this chapter seeks to build upon and extend this prior work in our field to offer promising, research-based approaches for meeting the grand challenge of ending family violence.

EXTENT, CONSEQUENCES, AND COSTS

Research has repeatedly and robustly shown that family violence overall and particularly CM and IPV are grand challenges for US communities and the nation. Here, we briefly highlight research findings that illustrate the extent and consequences of these problems.

Child Maltreatment

Child maltreatment is defined somewhat differently in each state, but national estimates indicate nearly 6 million annual reports of child abuse and neglect, with most reports given for neglect and less than 20% for physical abuse (US Department of Health and Human Services [US DHHS], 2016). Likewise, 37% of all children in the United States will experience an investigation by a child welfare services (CWS) agency (Kim, Wildeman, Jonson-Reid, & Drake, 2017). As with other statistics that depend on reporting to formal agencies, there may be an undercount for CM, although Kim and colleagues found that this is not the case.

Mounting research also shows that harsh and abusive parenting contributes to toxic stress, which may result in a range of poor outcomes, including adverse changes to brain architecture, abnormal cortisol levels, and numerous health and behavioral health vulnerabilities (Jonson-Reid, Kohl, & Drake, 2012; Shonkoff et al., 2012). Notably, childhood maltreatment of any intensity has been linked to adult stress and can have an adverse impact on physical health more than 30 years after the maltreatment (Widom, Horan, & Brzustowicz, 2015). In addition to such profound consequences for individuals' health and well-being, CM can lead to death. The US DHHS (2016) estimates that 1,670 children died from abuse and neglect in 2012. An estimate from the Fourth National Incidence Study is even higher at 2,400 children (Sedlak et al., 2010).

In addition to consequences for individuals, CM has great societal costs. The CDC (2012) estimated the lifetime cost of child abuse to be more than

$210,000 per victim, with almost all of the cost resulting from the lost economic contribution of child abuse victims rather than from the services they receive or from mortality. Aggregated estimates show that the total cost of child maltreatment is $124 billion per year (Fang, Brown, Florence, & Mercy, 2012). A significant part of that cost is from very serious, nearly fatal assaults such as the violent shaking of babies. Costs related to shaken baby syndrome have been conservatively estimated at approximately $50,000 during the 4 years following the event, excluding costs that do not include the consequences from the fatalities of 7% of the children in the sample (Peterson et al., 2014). The larger point is that CM, in general, leads to significant costs in terms of the lost health and economic opportunities for children.

Intimate Partner Violence

The CDC uses the phrase *intimate partner violence* to describe "physical, sexual, or psychological harm by a current or former partner or spouse" and notes that such violence occurs among both mixed- and same-sex couples and also among dating and relational couples who are not sexually intimate (CDC, n.d.). Estimates of the number of women who report victimization by intimate partners to an authority (e.g., criminal justice, health care, and social services) annually are nearly impossible to discern because there is no centralized federal or state data collection for IPV. Nevertheless, the most recent nationally representative research investigating lifetime IPV determined than one in three women (35.6%) have experienced rape, physical violence, and/or stalking by an intimate partner. Among those affected by IPV, more than one in three women experienced multiple forms of rape, stalking, or physical violence, and approximately one in four women (24.3%) experienced severe physical IPV (Breiding, Chen, & Black, 2014). The same study found that women are disproportionally affected by IPV victimization as well as more likely to experience negative consequences due to IPV, including injury, needing time off from school or work, needing housing services, and needing victim advocate services. This research affirmed the considerable and robust evidence showing that women who experience IPV are also likely to experience serious physical and mental health problems (Breiding et al., 2014).

In addition to such consequences for women's health and well-being, intimate partner femicide remains a significant problem, and it typically follows a history of IPV (Campbell, Glass, Sharps, Laughon, & Bloom, 2007). Some national homicide research shows that although the number of homicide victims killed by intimate partners appears to be in decline, the decline is greater for men (36%) than for women (26%), with women comprising 70% of victims among intimate partner homicides (Catalano, Smith, Snyder, & Rand, 2009).

In addition to the toll of loss of human life, IPV holds serious costs for communities, states, and the country as a whole. One of the studies to estimate the economic cost of IPV against women, which used costs associated with health care, mental health services, lost productivity, and death but not costs incurred through the criminal justice system, determined that IPV cost the nation $5.8 billion in 1995 (Max, Rice, Finkelstein, Bardwell, & Leadbetter, 2004).

Connections Between Child Maltreatment and Intimate Partner Violence

Syntheses of research findings show that there are well-established relationships between IPV and CM, particularly physical CM and IPV (Hamby & Grych, 2013). Likewise, a robust, national research effort determined that 17.3% of children witnessed parental IPV in their lifetimes and that 6.1% of children had witnessed parental IPV in the past year (Finkelhor, Turner, Shattuck, & Hamby, 2013). In addition to the connection with CM, IPV exposure holds detrimental consequences for children's well-being, including academic, behavioral, emotional, health, and social problems (for a summary, see McTavish, MacGregor, Wathen, & MacMillan, 2016). Given such research, it is not surprising that there is a growing call to integrate services and responses for both adult and child victims of family violence (Hamby, Finkelhor, Turner, & Ormrod, 2010). Due to the especially strong connection between these two types of violence, focused practice and research attention to both CM and IPV together can help advance the family violence field in new and important ways.

SHARED RISK FACTORS AND CONTEXTS

As noted previously, violence scholars and policymakers are encouraging both practitioners and researchers to "connect the dots" to prevent and intervene with multiple forms of violence in coordinated, comprehensive, and person-centered ways (Hamby & Grych, 2013; Wilkins et al., 2014). An important step in making such connections is a consideration of the shared risk factors and contexts among various types of violence. The World Health Organization uses the social ecological framework, which conceptualizes the etiology of violence, including CM and IPV, as existing within four nested circles representing the individual, relationship, community, and the social environment (Krug, Dahlberg, Mercy, Zwi, & Lozano, 2002). This framework encourages practitioners and researchers working to prevent and address violence to act at all levels of the social ecology. The CDC monograph on "connecting the dots" among multiple forms of violence provides a detailed cross-walk of these common factors (Wilkins et al., 2014) and some related action strategies (CDC, 2016). Here, we highlight key risk factors and contexts that are especially relevant for both CM and IPV and that may be most actionable for social workers and their allies.

At the individual level, shared risk factors for violence include contemporaneous problems with anger and aggression, emotional reactivity, impulsivity, positive beliefs about aggression, problems with attachment, substance abuse, psychopathology, young age, low education, and low income (Cafferky, Mendez, Anderson, & Stith, 2016; Hamby & Grych, 2013; Jouriles et al., 2008; Wilkins et al., 2014). Also at this level, but in the past and over individuals' lives, experiences of child maltreatment and witnessing family violence are shared risk factors for subsequent CM and IPV (Hamby & Grych, 2013; Wilkins et al., 2014).

At the relational level, shared risk factors for physical abuse include high conflict, low relationship satisfaction, poor parent–child relationships, and social isolation (Hamby & Grych, 2013; Wilkins et al., 2014). Although physical abuse patterns and correlates are different from neglect, the typical CWS records underestimate the overlap and many children are exposed to both (Jonson-Reid, Drake, Chung, & Way, 2003; Kim, Mennen, & Trickett, 2017). It is now also understood that violent or neglectful parenting—even when it is not fatal—creates toxic stress, which may result in a range of poor outcomes. Abused and neglected children, in turn, are more likely as adults, compared to similarly situated adults who did not experience child maltreatment, to be poly-violence perpetrators, perpetrating violence in all three domains of CM, criminal violence, and IPV (Milaniak & Widom, 2015). Notably, such findings expand the cycle of violence literature by combining the distinct literatures on criminal violence, CM, and IPV to call attention to the phenomenon of poly-violence perpetration by maltreated children.

Spanking may be one of the most common precursors of physical abuse and also strongly associated with IPV (Taylor, Lee, Guterman, & Rice, 2010). Research links spanking of young children to greater risk of CWS involvement (Lee, Grogan-Kaylor, & Berger, 2014). Spanking, although often exempted from child abuse laws, has recently been identified as significantly associated with poor outcomes for children and adults (Altschul, Lee, & Gershoff, 2016; Gershoff & Grogan-Kaylor, 2016). Spanking is associated with increased odds of suicide attempts, moderate to heavy drinking, and the use of street drugs in adulthood. In addition to physical abuse or emotional maltreatment, these associations contribute to poor outcomes (Afifi et al., 2017). Admittedly, some of these untoward outcomes may be associated with other problems of parents, and spanking is a marker of those problems as well.

The impact of abusive and neglectful parenting styles can be enduring and broad. Savage, Palmer, and Martin (2014) demonstrated that the impact of physical violence against children has broad and adverse effects on their conduct as young adults, including high rates of violent delinquent behavior. Although this study did not establish a clear or exclusive relationship between hitting children and those children growing up to become violent criminal offenders, its findings did show that physically abused and neglected children, as well as young adults, showed high rates of nonviolent antisocial behavior. Such findings suggest that harsh parenting has an adverse impact on children's and youths' development. Additional research, conducted in a prosperous county near Washington, DC, showed that harsh parenting (including hitting, pushing, grabbing, and shoving of middle school students by their parents) resulted in extreme orientation toward peers (rather than family), delinquency, and poor educational attainment during the subsequent 9 years (Hentges & Wang, 2017).

Shared community and social risk factors for CM and IPV include cultural norms that support violence and promote harmful understandings of gender, exposure to high-risk settings, high alcohol outlet densities within a community, lack of social integration within a community, life stress, media violence, ongoing community stress and disorder, poverty and income inequality, proximity to violent individuals, and unemployment and lack of economic opportunities (Beyer, Wallis, & Hamberger, 2015; Hamby & Grych, 2013; Jouriles et al., 2008; Matjasko, Niolon, & Valle, 2013; Wilkins et al., 2014). Notably, life stress, lack of economic opportunities, low income, unemployment, and poverty contribute to risk at both individual and community levels of the social ecology.

Recognizing the salience of context and the various sources of CM and IPV stressors as well as supports that mitigate risk by promoting protective factors at the individual, family, and societal levels is likely to be critical to successful efforts to combat family violence. The future infrastructure of policies and resources available for preventing and intervening in situations of family violence must adequately attend to the complexity of this social problem to be truly effective in reducing its incidence and outcomes.

CREATING AN EVIDENCE-BASED SERVICE ARRAY

The Institute of Medicine (2015) asserts that only one-third of people with psychosocial problems receive an evidence-based intervention. Although comparable data do not exist for interventions to stop family violence, we argue that evidence-based interventions for CM and IPV have had even less development and dissemination.

The State of the Prevention and Intervention Evidence Base

Child Maltreatment

Interventions to prevent or reduce CM have focused on home visiting programs (to reduce the onset of violence against very young children), parenting programs (to reduce the recurrence of CM), and, recently, community-level interventions. Since the Nurse Family Partnership first began to present results demonstrating an impact on reducing child abuse at the end of the 20th century (Olds et al., 1998), and even child fatality rates two decades later (Olds et al., 2014), home visiting programs that reach women during pregnancy or soon after they give birth have been considered to effectively reduce CM. A federally sponsored review (Sama-Miller et al., 2017) showed that only 19 home visiting models meet the US DHHS criteria for an evidence-based early childhood home visiting service delivery model. Although the programs have a range of favorable effects to reduce parental risks, not all of them have been tested to determine if they reduce CM. Levey and colleagues (2017) completed a systematic review that concluded that home visiting is the only form of child abuse prevention among high-risk families that offers evidence of demonstrated effectiveness. However, these models are not widely available or even replicated for evaluation purposes. Only 7 of these models have been replicated under conditions that showed that the same benefits were achieved each time.

The second major approach to reducing CM is through parenting programs. Child welfare agencies routinely provide parent training to families with substantiated child abuse and neglect in order to prevent recurrence (Barth, 2009). Historically, many of these programs were ad hoc, and few of them included high-fidelity replications of parenting programs that had been tested (Barth et al., 2005). Recently, federal, state, and foundation child welfare leadership has been rallying the field around trying to institute evidence-based parent training programs into child welfare agencies (Akin & Gomi, 2017; Chamberlain, 2017). At least some of this effort is focused on identifying generic, common element solutions to the vexing problem of how to scale up brand-name evidence-based parenting programs (Center for the Study of Social Policy, 2017).

A third approach is community-level strategies to prevent CM (for a review, see Molnar, Beatriz, & Beardslee, 2016). Several models have been developed and show promise, especially Triple P and the Durham Family Initiative, although replication is still needed to ensure that the originally measured benefits can be achieved in other communities. Strong evidence indicates that recurrence of maltreatment, even after services are received, is associated with worse outcomes (Oshima, Jonson-Reid, & Seay, 2014). In-home CWS and mental health services are predictors of reduced recurrence (Jonson-Reid, Emery, Drake, & Stahlschmidt, 2010), although new models for addressing chronically struggling families are needed (National Academies of Sciences, Engineering, and Medicine, 2016). Recent studies showing a strong relationship between access to effective income assistance programs and child maltreatment, are spurring innovative interventions to pair income assistance and social services (Slack, Berger, & Noyes, 2017).

In addition, community-based prevention programs can address factors that serve as precursors of CM, such as physical punishment of children (Klevens & Whitaker, 2007). A report from the CDC called for interventions designed to reduce use of physical punishment as one important strategy for the prevention of child abuse (Fortson, Klevens, Merrick, Gilbert, & Alexander, 2016). There are a number of promising intervention strategies across the social ecological framework to reduce the use of spanking, including parent education in primary care settings and No Hit Zones in hospitals (Gershoff, Lee, & Durrant, 2017).

Although some research addresses interventions with maltreating families, prevention of CM is clearly in need of greater research. This may only occur when the importance of this grand challenge is supported by health care, education, criminal justice, and social services—all of which have a far lessened burden when CM is prevented. Furthermore, evidence is needed to show that the path toward difficult adult outcomes can be interrupted by child abuse prevention programs.

Intimate Partner Violence

In the past several decades, various interventions aimed at addressing IPV to ameliorate recidivism and revictimization have developed within the distinct fields of criminal justice, psychotherapy, counseling and women's studies (Barner & Carney, 2011). As noted previously, social work professionals are often found leading in and working within—and sometimes across—these fields. In general, these distinct strategies have typically aimed to address the needs of individuals within families—that is, adult perpetrators, adult survivors, and child survivors—in targeted ways rather than focusing on the family as a whole. In part, such distinct and tailored approaches were developed to address the concurrent goals of offender accountability and survivors' protection and restoration. Given such worthwhile aims, the reasons for distinct intervention approaches are seemingly sound. Nonetheless, when put into place in community settings, distinct intervention strategies have not always achieved their desired outcomes. Fortunately, there are growing numbers of rigorous intervention research studies, including meta-analyses and systematic reviews, focused on strategies for ameliorating and ending IPV that can help shed light on the ways in which these intervention strategies may work best, as well as the ways in which they may be altered and enhanced to improve their effectiveness (Niolen et al., 2017).

Concerning strategies to address IPV perpetration, results of several meta-analysis studies have shown that abuser intervention programs (AIPs) have little impact on reducing IPV recidivism beyond the effect of being arrested alone (Arias, Arce, & Vilariño, 2013; Babcock, Green, & Robie, 2004; Eckhardt et al., 2013; Feder & Wilson, 2005). Likewise, these studies provide little evidence that either of the major AIP approaches—the Duluth model approach and the cognitive–behavioral therapy approach—is more effective than the other.

Notably, little research has investigated the extent to which AIPs are embedded in coordinated community response (CCR) systems, which was an originally recommended aspect of AIP delivery (Barner & Carney, 2011). A CCR engages multidisciplinary professionals (e.g., child protection, criminal justice, economic empowerment, health care, IPV safety services, mental health care, and substance abuse treatment) in collective efforts to address IPV at the community level. CCRs are encouraged to engage in community awareness and prevention, collective education and training, case reviews and response protocols particularly for high-risk families, and general information sharing. With notable exceptions (Salazar, Emshoff, Baker, & Crowley, 2007), little research has investigated the outcomes of CCRs. Even less research has investigated the pairing of AIPs with CCRs. Accordingly, research investigating whether the addition of CCR systems to AIP delivery improves outcomes compared to those obtained by AIPs that operate as distinct entities is warranted.

Research suggests that the intervention value of AIPs might be enhanced with the addition of motivational readiness of change strategies (Eckhardt et al., 2013) and also strategies that address some of the family violence risk factors highlighted previously, including employment support, housing, and parenting, as well as mental health and substance abuse treatment (Campbell et al., 2007). Although we do not argue here that AIPs move away from their focus on accountability, as well as their emphasis on safety for adult and child survivors, we do acknowledge that the state of the evidence to date urges novel and innovative intervention efforts as well as research to investigate the usefulness of new and augmented approaches to AIPs.

For adult IPV survivors, there is research support for counseling and therapies that help ameliorate the mental health consequences of IPV, particularly depressive and post-traumatic stress disorder symptoms (Eckhardt et al., 2013). Likewise, there is promising, albeit preliminary, evidence for the helpfulness of post-shelter community advocacy for addressing survivors' social support and quality of life (Center for Policy Research [CPR] and National Resource Center on Domestic Violence [NRCDV], 2017; Eckhardt et al., 2013). However, the overall evidence is less clear that advocacy interventions reduce revictimization, particularly compared to arrest for IPV (Eckhardt et al., 2013; Rivas et al., 2015; Stover, Meadows, & Kaufman, 2009). Moreover, the overall body of research investigating interventions for adult IPV survivors is characterized by (1) a relatively low number of rigorous studies (i.e., using randomized designs); (2) small sample sizes; (3) heterogeneity in intervention approaches; and (4) little dedicated focus on survivors from diverse cultural, ethnic, and racial backgrounds as well gender identities and expressions

(Bent-Goodley, 2001; CPR & NRCDV, 2017; Rivas et al., 2015; Tirado-Muñoz, Gilchrist, Farré, Hegarty, & Torrens, 2014).

Concerning services for children living in families with IPV, there is evidence supporting mother–child and child-focused interventions, especially for outcomes related to improvements in children's behavioral and mental health (McTavish et al., 2016; Rizo, Macy, Ermentrout, & Johns, 2011; Stover et al., 2009). Overall, however, this relatively small body of literature is characterized by considerable heterogeneity in intervention targets (i.e., children only, mothers only, or both children and mothers together) and in intervention content and approaches (e.g., individual interventions, group interventions, parenting content, safety planning, and trauma counseling), as well as limitations among the research designs used to investigate these interventions (Rizo et al., 2011). Moreover, Stover and colleagues noted that the studies that investigated such interventions might not translate as well to the "real world" because often women who continued to have relationships with perpetrators and who were using substances were excluded from such research. In addition, research on services for children who have been exposed to IPV recommends that practitioners and scholars be mindful that empirically supported programs for addressing CM solely may not work as well or at all for families affected by IPV (Jouriles et al., 2008).

In summary, the IPV field lacks robustly empirically supported interventions for perpetrators, survivors, and their children (Barner & Carney, 2011; Stover et al., 2009). Many commonly used IPV interventions, such as crisis lines and crisis response services, have not been evaluated (Eckhardt et al., 2013). Furthermore, interventions that help address child safety in the context of current and ongoing IPV are underinvestigated; thus, strategies to help ensure children's safety in the context of IPV are unclear and undetermined (McTavish et al., 2016). In addition, Messing, Ward-Lasher, Thaller, and Bagwell-Gray (2015) encouraged social workers to consider developing novel approaches for empowering IPV survivors that include options for women who do not want to engage in the usual service array that often asks them to end their intimate partnerships.

Accordingly, although various strategies currently in use in many communities show preliminary promise, large and rigorous intervention research studies aimed at understanding the necessary core components of strategies for successfully intervening with IPV, as well as the ways in which these interventions may (or may not) be helpful for families across diverse backgrounds, are urgently needed. Likewise, research is needed to understand the context in which perpetrators, as well as adult survivors and their children, receive such services. Although the current state of the field often entails sanctioning family members to participate in services (e.g., perpetrators required to attend AIPs through arrest and adjudication, and survivors required to attend services by child protection mandates), it is unclear whether such mandates lead to positive outcomes (Barner & Carney, 2011; Hamby & Grych, 2013).

Promoting violence-free relationships requires not only "downstream" crisis responses but also "upstream" prevention efforts. No one effort will end violence in relationships and promote the alternative behaviors of violence-free living. In short, a full array of coordinated efforts—full-stream efforts—is likely to move the needle toward increasing violence-free relationships and decreasing victimization and perpetration. This suggests that an indicator of progress toward achieving more violence-free relationships will be a greater array of service options that better match the typologies of family violence that are emerging (for a review and critique, see Winstok, 2013). This is also likely to require that we change social conditions that foment family violence by reducing extreme economic inequality, building financial capability and assets for all, and achieving equal opportunity and justice—additional grand challenges for social work. Social workers are at the forefront of both downstream and upstream efforts working alongside community activists, legal and criminal justice professionals, health care providers, and others. We have not gone far enough.

Screening, Assessment, and Brief Interventions

A growing body of research suggests that settings in which screening and assessments occur provide an important opportunity for interrupting and addressing family violence, including both CM and IPV. Such research presents a promising strategy for the social work profession because social workers are often placed in various service sectors—including child protection, criminal and juvenile justice, health care, mental health, and substance abuse—in which families affected by IPV are likely to appear. Given this placement, as well as the need to identify families struggling with problems of violence as early as possible, social workers are often well placed to screen for CM and IPV and to subsequently provide further assessments and brief interventions. Notably, many families affected by violence interact with the various service systems noted previously but are unlikely to report CM and IPV. For all these reasons, interventions focused on screening, assessment, and brief intervention offer a valuable way to help address and ameliorate family violence. One noteworthy model is Safe Environment for Every Kid (SEEK), which has shown that pediatricians who invite patients to talk with a social worker to address some of their family risks have been able to markedly reduce CM reports in Baltimore (Dubowitz, 2014; Dubowitz, Feigelman, Lane, & Kim, 2009). SEEK has been recognized by the US Agency for Healthcare Research and Quality on its Innovations website as a promising practice to reduce child abuse and neglect, and it is included in materials of the American Academy of Pediatrics' *Bright Futures* and the California Evidence-Practice for Child Welfare Clearinghouse.

One research review of studies focused on primary, health care-based interventions for IPV showed that brief strategies lead to benefits for individuals (Bair-Merritt et al., 2014). In addition to their brevity, this research showed that successful intervention strategies emphasized community referrals, empowerment, empathetic listening, and safety. Another systematic review concerned with universal IPV screening in health care settings underscored the importance of conceptualizing these screenings as complex processes that require providers' self-efficacy (O'Campo, Kirst, Tsamis, Chambers, & Ahmad, 2011). In turn, findings from this research, as well as other studies, indicate that providers are more likely to have such self-efficacy for screening when they have institutional support via training, effective protocols, and valid screening tools at the ready, as well as immediate referral access to resources and services for women and children who screen positively (Kulkarni, Bell, & Wylie, 2010). Likewise, a systematic review of risk assessment in the criminal justice field determined that although the overall body of studies is relatively small, risk assessment has promise for reducing IPV risk levels while also providing potentially helpful information to professionals, perpetrators, and survivors (Nicholls, Pritchard, Reeves, & Hilterman, 2013).

Readers are encouraged to keep in mind that some of the evidence concerning the value of screening is mixed (Eckhardt et al., 2013; McTavish et al., 2016). In addition, researchers have called for studies to investigate the connections between brief interventions and intensive safety services (Eckhardt et al., 2013). In other words, a brief intervention may be implemented effectively, but if it does not lead families to helpful services with greater intensity, the value of the brief intervention may be lost. Nonetheless, the problems of CM and IPV occur at such a high rate and are also so dangerous that services have to be carefully managed to address the most serious cases with the greatest level of intervention. Given this need, there appears to be promise and value in screening, assessing, and briefly intervening with IPV to ascertain which families need what services and when.

Couples Therapy/Family Work with Lower Risk Families

The risk of recurrence of CM or IPV creates great pressure on service providers. The result has been a long-standing tendency to separate children from their families as well as to exclude partners who use violence from their families. In the CM service world, this has often meant placing children into foster care. In the IPV service array, this has often meant enforcing separation of violent family members through a variety of mechanisms, including restraining orders and arrest (Goodmark, 2012). For approximately the past 30 years,

CWS systems have been moving away from family separation toward family preservation. Specific efforts have been made to try to engage fathers. Family-based interventions are standard for helping determine whether families can remain together and safely care for children and to determine what additional interventions are necessary (LaBrenz & Fong, 2016).

Support for a broader array of interventions to address IPV in settings as varying as health care, education, faith communities, and the military has been mounted (for a broad review of these interventions, see the compendium by Renzetti, Edleson, & Bergen, 2012). Couples therapy with couples engaged in violence has traditionally been discouraged, at least since Susan Schechter's admonition about this approach in the 1980s, but emerging evidence suggests that this approach can be safely used to reduce relationship violence (Stith, McCollum, & Rosen, 2011). Such approaches require attention to the presence of intimidation and fear (O'Leary, 2001). Moreover, couples therapy approaches require considerable safeguards, including specific criteria for exclusion. The potential advantages of these approaches are that they give women more choice and control concerning the goals for the intervention and provide array of possible resolutions (Goodmark, 2012).

George and Stith (2014) argue for a solution-focused approach that empowers women in a range of ways that correspond to the fluctuations in relationships between partners, their cultural and relational bonds, and their ability to engage in a therapeutic intervention to reduce their conflict and violence to acceptable levels. This approach to addressing the wide range of relationships and relationship goals, by crediting the participants as able to engage in relationship development, is part of the emergence of couples treatment—following safety screening—that is likely to help reduce harm and prevent some relationships from spiraling into more dangerous violence (Bradley, Drummey, Gottman, & Gottman, 2014; Karakurt, Whiting, van Esch, Bolen, & Calabrese, 2016). Emerging research from Australia may help determine the limits and value of family mediation for couples with family violence (Cleak, Schofield, & Bickerdike, 2014). The further development and rigorous testing of this approach can be viewed as consistent with social work's historic mission to identify safe family preservation-aligned services (Sherraden et al., 2014).

Violence Prevention Interventions Targeted at New Parents

Child maltreatment prevention can also begin with very early identification of risk and timely interventions. Building on the work of the Grand Challenge to Harness Technology for Social Good, the "Birth Match" initiative has recently gained the interest and support of the Commission to Eliminate Child Abuse and Neglect Fatalities (2016). This innovation relies on identifying risk through matching administrative records from health departments (birth certificates), social service agencies (termination of parental rights), and, in some states, criminal justice bureaus (crimes of violence against children). It is now available in four states: Maryland, Michigan, Minnesota, and Texas. This program enables officials to match the birth records of newborns to information on parents previously found to have harmed their children, and the search for a match is conducted in real time. If a match is found, officials can check on the newborn at an early point and assess whether protective intervention, such as home visiting, is warranted (Shaw, Barth, Mattingly, Ayer, & Berry, 2013). This program is currently undergoing evaluation. Texas has expanded the program to offer voluntary care coordination services to former foster youth who give birth so that they can get the help they need in a timely manner; the uptake by youth who are contacted is reported to be higher than 50% (Clarice Rogers, Texas Department of Family and Protective Services, personal communication, November 12, 2014). Although there is not significant progress on developing family-level preventive interventions in families at high risk of perpetrating IPV, this approach of early identification of vulnerable family situations could certainly be tested for its acceptability, feasibility, and safety for IPV prevention.

Novel Research Strategies to Develop Stronger Research-Driven Interventions

Child Maltreatment

Reducing severe and fatal CM will require coordination of vital records (e.g., birth certificate data), child welfare data (to trigger services for the parents of newborns if the parents have prior histories of child welfare involvement), and other data so that early interventions that strengthen families and protect children can be effectively targeted. All this information is currently largely uncoordinated with CWS providers and planners, but could be developed to improve the proper response to reports of CM. Such information might arise from police departments (e.g., 911 calls), substance abuse treatment programs, hospital emergency departments (King, Farst, Jaeger, Onukwube, & Robbins, 2015), and health departments (e.g., other information gathered during efforts to provide home visiting programs). Certainly, such efforts would require review that weighs the risks of not using this information against the ethics of using the information. Balancing such risks and benefits will be difficult but is most likely to be advantageous when there have been rigorous trials that compare the benefits of voluntary services that reduce harms to children and families.

Testing of predictive analytic models to determine if they improve upon standard ways of serving clients—by helping child welfare workers focus their efforts on those families most likely to experience severe or recurrent abuse—is emerging and badly needed, given that approximately two of three cases of infants substantiated for maltreatment and remaining at home will have a re-report within 5 years (Putnam-Hornstein, Simon, Eastman, & Magruder, 2015).

New measures of CM severity that can be used in practice are critical to understanding the significance of CM reports. All child abuse reports are not equally significant from the standpoint of service planning and evaluation. Some reports are relatively preventive because they occur under conditions of agency surveillance and with a shift to higher risk parenting rather than harmful parenting. Other reports are more harmful, although current reporting systems cannot distinguish these. Longscan and the National Survey of Child and Adolescent Wellbeing I and II have made significant progress in developing severity codes based on the original Child Maltreatment Classification System (Barnett, Manly, & Cicchetti, 1993), but more progress is needed.

Multidisciplinary research is also needed, especially involving the validation of the meaningfulness of CM reports. Two ways to do this are to accelerate our understanding of the way that children and youth cross over from child welfare to juvenile services (Vidal et al., 2017) and to employ records of medical care of children who are maltreated (Stanley & Nigrovic, 2017).

Intimate Partner Violence

Currently in the United States, there are few administrative and social service data systems that consistently, comprehensively, and robustly collect data concerned with IPV (Matjasko et al., 2013). Moreover, programs that serve IPV survivors and their children are prohibited by federal policies from disclosing identifiable information, specifically by the Violence Against Women Act and the Family Violence Prevention and Services Act (CPR & NRCDV, 2017). Such policies exist to safeguard IPV survivors' confidentiality and safety. Nonetheless, such policies can also preclude researchers from using extant services data to investigate the outcomes of community-based IPV interventions for survivors and their families. In addition, researchers cannot readily link IPV services data to other administrative data sets (e.g., child welfare, criminal and civil justice, employment, and health care) to investigate survivors' outcomes after receiving services, as well as the connections between survivors' interactions with IPV services and these other administrative and service sectors.

Along with safeguards on IPV survivor services data, the IPV field also faces significant challenges in building the evidence base, including the following: (1) safety concerns (i.e., research participation should never jeopardize survivors safety), (2) the fact that IPV intervention studies require extensive training for researchers to ensure survivor safety and well-being, (3) building connections between IPV practitioners and researchers so that meaningful research can be conducted, and (4) limited funding dedicated to IPV services and response research (CPR & NRCDV, 2017).

Given these important challenges and considerations for IPV intervention and services research, family violence scholars are encouraged to consider community-based, engaged, and participatory-action study approaches (CPR & NRCDV, 2017). Developing the evidence base for IPV and family violence interventions will require positive, ongoing collaborations between researchers and practitioners in community-based settings. In such efforts, researchers will need to work closely with practitioners to develop ethical, safe, and rigorous research designs. Such research designs should also optimize the available resources and their community-based settings by using cutting-edge design and statistical and research methods. For example, Bayesian analytic approaches might help researchers make the most of small sample sizes (Chen & Fraser, 2017). Likewise, stepped wedge designs and interrupted time-series design may be used with small samples (Fok, Henry, & Allen, 2015). In addition, cross-site randomization designs and adaptive interventions paired with sequential multiple assignment randomized trials (SMARTs) may also be useful for strengthening the rigor and robustness of IPV intervention research (CPR & NRCDV, 2017; Kidwell & Hyde, 2016).

Opportunities for Novel Cross-Sector Involvement

In addition to the promising and emerging strategies noted previously, here we highlight ways in which social workers acting to address family violence can partner with other service sectors and professionals to address family violence in the context of other approaches and intervention efforts. For example, given the strength of low income, unemployment, and poverty as risk factors for family violence, anti-poverty interventions, including economic empowerment (i.e., economic self-sufficiency and financial literacy), microfinance, TANF (when the Family Violence Option is fully implemented), housing support, and workforce development, may hold promise for ameliorating family violence (Matjasko et al., 2013; Peled & Krigel, 2016). Home visiting programs have also been paired with conflict resolution interventions for parents in order to reduce the adverse impact of parental conflict on the entire family. One intervention that added motivational interviewing and training of home visiting professionals on substance abuse, depression, and IPV led to greater retention in the program and fewer referrals for IPV and CM (Silovsky et al., 2011). The next generation of work in this area will build on what we can expect to be the greater impact of a balanced approach to work with families that includes both risk factors (IPV and depression) and protective factors (social support and family resources) (Ridings, Beaseley, & Silovsky, 2017). This approach suggests that social support and family resources are two pivotal protective factors in buffering against CM potential while addressing core risk factors. In addition to these recommendations, we also refer readers to the CDC's recent technical package concerning preventing IPV (available at https://www.cdc.gov/violen-ceprevention/pdf/ipv-technicalpackages.pdf), which highlights a number of cross-sector strategies and approaches (Niolen et al., 2017).

CONCLUSION

Despite the historical and intractable nature of the problem of family violence, progress in accomplishing the grand challenge of stopping family violence is predictable because the problem of family violence is well known and signifi-cant. Important lessons learned can be generated from the growing research on CM and IPV interventions to generate novel and comprehensive strate-gies to end family violence and revictimization, as well as ensure family safety and well-being. In addition to the research and promising strategies discussed here, there are important and innovative efforts in the areas of strategic pre-ventions (i.e., universal, selected, and indicated), historical trauma, protection and resilience, and trauma-informed care that are also related to and relevant for the grand challenge of ending family violence. Although all these topics could not be addressed in this chapter, these are also promising areas for growth and opportunity for social workers.

In closing, we underscore that ending family violence will, in part, require that we break down silos within social work and across disciplines. Moreover, employing a framework such as that offered by the CDC to "connect-the-dots" will help leverage additional research and service opportunities in the general field of violence reduction to address family violence. Furthermore, there are already significant federal, state, local, and foundation investments in reduc-ing family violence. Although additional resources need to be employed to develop and test social work interventions, the promise is significant.

ACKNOWLEDGMENTS

The authors greatly appreciate the helpful reviews by Melissa Jonson-Reid, Shanti Kulkarni, Shawna Lee, Lisa Fedina, and Jill Messing.

REFERENCES

Abajobir, A., Kisely, S., Williams, G., Clavarino, A. M., & Najman, J. (2017). Substantiated childhood maltreatment and intimate partner violence victimization in young adulthood: A birth cohort study. *Journal of Youth & Adolescence, 46*(1), 165. doi:10.1007/s10964-016-0558-3

Afifi, T. O., Ford, D., Gershoff, E. T., Merrick, M., Grogan-Kaylor, A., Ports, K. A., . . . Peters Bennett, R. (2017). Spanking and adult mental health impairment: The case for the designation of spanking as an adverse childhood experience. *Child Abuse & Neglect.* Advance online publication. doi:10.1016/j.chiabu.2017.01.014

Akin, B. A., & Gomi, S. (2017). Noncompletion of evidence-based parent training: An empirical examination among families of children in foster care. *Journal of Social Service Research, 43*(1), 52–68. doi:10.1080/01488376.2016.1226229

Altschul, I., Lee, S. J., & Gershoff, E. T. (2016). Hugs, not hits: Warmth and spanking as predictors of child social competence. *Journal of Marriage and Family, 78*(3), 695–714. doi:10.1111/jomf.12306

Arias, E., Arce, R., & Vilariño, M. (2013). Batterer intervention programmes: A meta-analytic review of effectiveness. *Psychosocial Intervention, 22*(2), 153–160. doi:10.5093/in2013a18

Babcock, J. C., Green, C. E., & Robie, C. (2004). Does batterers' treatment work? A meta-analytic review of domestic violence treatment. *Clinical Psychology Review, 23*(8), 1023–1053. doi:10.1016/j.cpr.2002.07.001

Bair-Merritt, M. H., Lewis-O'Connor, A., Goel, S., Amato, P., Ismailji, T., Jelley, M., . . . Cronholm, P. (2014). Primary care-based interventions for intimate partner violence: A systematic review. *American Journal of Preventive Medicine, 46*(2), 188–194. doi:10.1016/j.amepre.2013.10.001

Barner, J. R., & Carney, M. M. (2011). Interventions for intimate partner violence: A historical review. *Journal of Family Violence, 26*(3), 235–244. doi:10.1007/s10896-011-9359-3

Barnett, D., Manly, J. T., & Cicchetti, D. (1993). Defining child maltreatment: The interface between policy and research. In D. Cicchetti & S. L. Toth (Eds.), *Advances in Applied Developmental Psychology: Child Abuse, Child Development and Social Policy* (pp. 7–73). Norwood, NJ: Ablex.

Barth, R. P. (2009). Preventing child abuse and neglect with parent training: Evidence and opportunities. *Future of Children, 19*(2), 95–118.

Barth, R. P., Landsverk, J., Chamberlain, P., Reid, J., Rolls, J., Hurlburt, M., & Kohl, P. L. (2005). Parent training in child welfare services: Planning for a more evidence based approach to serving biological parents. *Research on Social Work Practice, 15*, 353–371.

Bent-Goodley, T. B. (2001). Eradicating domestic violence in the African American community: A literature review and action agenda. *Trauma, Violence, & Abuse, 2*(4), 316–330. doi:10.1177/1524838001002004003

Beyer, K., Wallis, A. B., & Hamberger, L. K. (2015). Neighborhood environment and intimate partner violence: A systematic review. *Trauma, Violence, & Abuse, 16*(1), 16–47. doi:10.1177/1524838013515758

Bradley, R. P. C., Drummey, K., Gottman, J. M., & Gottman, J. S. (2014). Treating couples who mutually exhibit violence or aggression: Reducing behaviors that show a susceptibility for violence. *Journal of Family Violence, 29*, 549–558. doi:10.1007/s10896-014-9615-4

Breiding, M. J., Chen, J., & Black, M. C. (2014). *Intimate partner violence in the United States—2010.* Atlanta, GA: National Center for Injury Prevention and Control, Centers for Disease Control and Prevention. Retrieved from https://www.cdc.gov/violenceprevention/pdf/cdc_nisvs_ipv_report_2013_v17_single_a.pdf

Cafferky, B. M., Mendez, M., Anderson, J. R., & Stith, S. M. (2016). Substance use and intimate partner violence: A meta-analytic review. *Psychology of Violence.* Advance online publication. doi:10.1037/vio0000074

Campbell, J. C., Glass, N., Sharps, P. W., Laughon, K., & Bloom, T. (2007). Intimate partner homicide: Review and implications of research and policy. *Trauma, Violence, & Abuse, 8*(3), 246–269. doi:10.1177/1524838007303505

Catalano, S., Smith, E., Snyder, H., & Rand, R. (2009). *Female victims of violence* (NCJ 228356). Washington, DC: US Department of Justice, Office of Justice Programs.

Center for Policy Research and National Resource Center on Domestic Violence. (2017). *Building evidence for domestic violence services and interventions.* Washington, DC: Office of the Assistant Secretary for Planning and Evaluation. Retrieved from https://aspe.hhs.gov/pdf-report/building-evidence-domestic-violence-services-interventions-framing-paper

Center for the Study of Social Policy. (2017). *Better evidence for decision-makers.* Washington, DC: Author.

Centers for Disease Control and Prevention. (n.d.). *Intimate partner violence.* Retrieved from https://www.cdc.gov/violenceprevention/intimatepartnerviolence

Centers for Disease Control and Prevention. (2012). *Child abuse and neglect cost the United States $124 Billion: Rivals cost of other high profile public health problems.* Retrieved from https://www.cdc.gov/media/releases/2012/p0201_child_abuse.html

Centers for Disease Control and Prevention. (2016). *Preventing multiple forms of violence: A strategic vision for connecting the dots.* Atlanta, GA: Division of Violence Prevention, National Center for Injury Prevention and Control, Centers for Disease Control and Prevention.

Chamberlain, P. (2017). Toward creating synergy among policy, procedures, and implementation of evidence-based models in child welfare systems: Two case examples. *Clinical Child and Family Psychology Review, 20*(1), 78–86. doi:10.1007/s10567-017-0226-5

Chen, D. G., & Fraser, M. W. (2017). *Introduction to Bayesian modeling in intervention research.* Paper presented at the annual conference of the Society for Social Work & Research, New Orleans, LA.

Cleak, H., Schofield, M., & Bickerdike, A. (2014). Efficacy of family mediation and the role of family violence: Study protocol. *BMC Public Health, 14,* 57. doi:10.1186/1471-2458-14-57

Commission to Eliminate Child Abuse and Neglect Fatalities. (2016). *Within our reach: A national strategy to eliminate child abuse and neglect fatalities.* Washington, DC: Government Printing Office. Retrieved from https://www.acf.hhs.gov/programs/cb/resource/cecanf-final-report

Connelly, C. D., Hazen, A. L., Coben, J. H., Kelleher, K. J., Barth, R. P., & Landsverk, J. A. (2006). Persistence of intimate partner violence among families referred to child welfare. *Journal of Interpersonal Violence, 21*(6), 774–797. doi:10.1177/0886260506287316

Dubowitz, H. (2014). The Safe Environment for Every Kid (SEEK) model: Helping promote children's health, development, and safety. *Child Abuse & Neglect, 38*(11), 1725–1733. doi:10.1016/j.chiabu.2014.07.011

Dubowitz, H., Feigelman, S., Lane, W., & Kim, J. (2009). Pediatric primary care to help prevent child maltreatment: The Safe Environment for Every Kid (SEEK) model. *Pediatrics, 123*(3), 858–864. doi:10.1542/peds.2008-1376

Eckhardt, C. I., Murphy, C. M., Whitaker, D. J., Sprunger, J., Dykstra, R., & Woodard, K. (2013). The effectiveness of intervention programs for perpetrators and victims of intimate partner violence. *Partner Abuse, 4*(2), 196–231. doi:10.1891/1946-6560.4.2.196

Edleson, J. L. (1999). Children's witnessing of adult domestic violence. *Journal of Interpersonal Violence, 14*(8), 839–870. doi:10.1177/088626099014008004

Fang, X. M., Brown, D. S., Florence, C. S., & Mercy, J. A. (2012). The economic burden of child maltreatment in the United States and implications for prevention. *Child Abuse & Neglect, 36*(2), 156–165. doi:10.1016/j.chiabu.2011.10.006

Feder, L., & Wilson, D. B. (2005). A meta-analytic review of court-mandated batterer intervention programs: Can courts affect abusers' behavior? *Journal of Experimental Criminology, 1*(2), 239–262. doi:10.1007/s11292-005-1179-0

Finkelhor, D., Turner, H. A., Shattuck, A., & Hamby, S. L. (2013). Violence, crime, and abuse exposure in a national sample of children and youth: An update. *JAMA Pediatrics, 167*(7), 614–621. doi:10.1001/jamapediatrics.2013.42

Fok, C. C. T., Henry, D., & Allen, J. (2015). Research designs for intervention research with small samples II: Stepped wedge and interrupted time-series designs. *Prevention Science, 16*(7), 967–977. doi:10.1007/s11121-015-0569-4

Fortson, B. L., Klevens, J., Merrick, M. T., Gilbert, L. K., & Alexander, S. P. (2016). *Preventing child abuse and neglect: A technical package for policy, norm, and programmatic activities.* Atlanta, GA: National Center for Injury Prevention and Control, Centers for Disease Control and Prevention. Retrieved from https://www.cdc.gov/violenceprevention/pdf/can-prevention-technical-package.pdf

George, J., & Stith, S. M. (2014). An updated feminist view of intimate partner violence. *Family Process, 53*(2), 179–193.

Gershoff, E. T., & Grogan-Kaylor, A. (2016). Spanking and child outcomes: Old controversies and new meta-analyses. *Journal of Family Psychology, 30*(4), 453–469. doi:10.1037/fam0000191

Gershoff, E. T., Lee, S. J., & Durrant, J. E. (2017). Promising intervention strategies to reduce parents' use of physical punishment. *Child Abuse & Neglect.* Advance online publication. doi:10.1016/j.chiabu.2017.01.017

Goodmark, L. (2012). *A troubled marriage: Domestic violence and the legal system.* New York, NY: NYU Press.

Gordon, L. (1988). *Heroes of their own lives.* New York, NY: Penguin.

Hamby, S., Finkelhor, D., Turner, H., & Ormrod, R. (2010). The overlap of witnessing partner violence with child maltreatment and other victimizations in a nationally representative survey of youth. *Child Abuse & Neglect, 34*(10), 734–741.

Hamby, S., & Grych, J. (2013). *The web of violence: Exploring connections among different forms of interpersonal violence and abuse.* New York, NY: Springer.

Hentges, R. F., & Wang, M.-T. (2017). Gender differences in the developmental cascade from harsh parenting to educational attainment: An evolutionary perspective. *Child Development.* Advance online publication. doi:10.1111/cdev.12719

Herrenkohl, T. I., & Jung, H. (2016). Effects of child abuse, adolescent violence, peer approval and pro-violence attitudes on intimate partner violence in adulthood. *Criminal Behavior & Mental Health, 26*(4), 304–314. doi:10.1002/cbm.2014

Herrenkohl, T. I., Sousa, C., Tajima, E. A., Herrenkohl, R. C., & Moylan, C. A. (2008). Intersection of child abuse and children's exposure to domestic violence. *Trauma, Violence, & Abuse, 9*(2), 84–99. doi:10.1177/1524838008314797

Institute of Medicine. (2015). *Psychosocial interventions for mental and substance use disorders: A framework for establishing evidence-based standards.* Washington, DC: National Academies Press.

Jonson-Reid, M., Drake, B., Chung, S., & Way, I. (2003). Cross-type recidivism among child maltreatment victims and perpetrators. *Child Abuse & Neglect, 27*(8), 899–917. doi:10.1016/s0145-2134(03)00138-8

Jonson-Reid, M., Emery, C. R., Drake, B., & Stahlschmidt, M. J. (2010). Understanding chronically reported families. *Child Maltreatment, 15*(4), 271–281. doi:10.1177/1077559510380738

Jonson-Reid, M., Kohl, P. L., & Drake, B. (2012). Child and adult outcomes of chronic child maltreatment. *Pediatrics, 129*(5), 839–845. doi:10.1542/peds.2011-2529

Jouriles, E. N., McDonald, R., Smith Slep, A. M., Heyman, R. E., & Garrido, E. (2008). Child abuse in the context of domestic violence: Prevalence, explanations, and practice implications. *Violence and Victims, 23*(2), 221–235. doi:10.1891/0886-6708.23.2.221

Karakurt, G., Whiting, K., van Esch, C., Bolen, S. D., & Calabrese, J. R. (2016). Couples therapy for intimate partner violence: A systematic review and meta-analysis. *Journal of Marital and Family Therapy, 42,* 567–583. doi:10.1111/jmft.12178

Kidwell, K. M., & Hyde, L. W. (2016). Adaptive interventions and SMART designs: Application to child behavior research in a community setting. *American Journal of Evaluation, 37*(3), 344–363. http://dx.doi.org/10.1177%2F1098214015617013

Kim, H., Wildeman, C., Jonson-Reid, M., & Drake, B. (2017). Lifetime prevalence of investigating child maltreatment among US children. *American Journal of Public Health, 107*(2), 274–280.

Kim, K., Mennen, F. E., & Trickett, P. K. (2017). Patterns and correlates of co-occurrence among multiple types of child maltreatment. *Child & Family Social Work, 22*(1), 492–502. doi:10.1111/cfs.12268

King, A. J., Farst, K. J., Jaeger, M. W., Onukwube, J. I., & Robbins, J. M. (2015). Maltreatment-related emergency department visits among children 0 to 3 years old in the United States. *Child Maltreatment, 20*(3), 151–161. doi:10.1177/1077559514567176

Klevens, J., & Whitaker, D. J. (2007). Primary prevention of child physical abuse and neglect: Gaps and promising directions. *Child Maltreatment, 12*(4), 364–377.

Kulkarni, S. J., Bell, H., & Wylie, L. (2010). Why don't they follow through? Intimate partner survivors' challenges in accessing health and social services. *Family & Community Health, 33*(2), 94–105.

Krug, E. G., Dahlberg, L. L., Mercy, J. A., Zwi, A. B., & Lozano, R. (2002). *World report on violence and health.* Geneva, Switzerland: World Health Organization. Retrieved from www.who.int/violence_injury_prevention/violence/world_report/en/introduction.pdf

LaBrenz, C. A., & Fong, R. (2016). Outcomes of family centered meetings for families referred to child protective services. *Children and Youth Services Review, 71,* 93–102. doi:10.1016/j.childyouth.2016.10.032

Lee, S. J., Grogan-Kaylor, A., & Berger, L. M. (2014). Parental spanking of 1-year-old children and subsequent child protective services involvement. *Child Abuse & Neglect, 38,* 875–883. doi:10.1016/j.chiabu.2014.01.018

Levey, E. J., Gelaye, B., Bain, P., Rondon, M. B., Borba, C. P., Henderson, D. C., & Williams, M. A. (2017). A systematic review of randomized controlled trials of interventions designed to decrease child abuse in high-risk families. *Child Abuse & Neglect, 6548*–6557. doi:10.1016/j.chiabu.2017.01.004

Matjasko, J. L., Niolon, P. H., & Valle, L. A. (2013). The role of economic factors and economic support in preventing and escaping from intimate partner violence. *Journal of Policy Analysis & Management, 32*(1), 122–128. doi:10.1002/pam.21666

Max, W., Rice, D. P., Finkelstein, E., Bardwell, R. A., & Leadbetter, S. (2004). The economic toll of intimate partner violence against women in the United States. *Violence and Victims, 19*(3), 259–272. doi:10.1891/vivi.19.3.259.65767

McTavish, J. R., MacGregor, J. D., Wathen, C. N., & MacMillan, H. L. (2016). Children's exposure to intimate partner violence: An overview. *International Review of Psychiatry, 28*(5), 504–518.

Messing, J. T., & Campbell, J. C. (2016). Informing collaborative interventions: Intimate partner violence risk assessment for front line police officers. *Policing, 10*(4), 328–340.

Messing, J. T., Ward-Lasher, A., Thaller, J., & Bagwell-Gray, M. (2015). The state of intimate partner violence intervention: Progress and continuing challenges. *Social Work, 60*(4), 305–313.

Milaniak, I., & Widom, C. S. (2015). Does child abuse and neglect increase risk for perpetration of violence inside and outside the home? *Psychology of Violence, 5*(3), 246–255. doi:10.1037/a0037956

Molnar, B. E., Beatriz, E. D., & Beardslee, W. R. (2016). Community-level approaches to child maltreatment prevention. *Trauma, Violence, & Abuse, 17*(4), 387–397. doi:10.1177/1524838016658879

National Academies of Sciences, Engineering, and Medicine. (2016). *Parenting matters: Supporting Parents of children ages 0–8.* Washington, DC: National Academies Press. https://doi.org/10.17226/21868

Nicholls, T. L., Pritchard, M. M., Reeves, K. A., & Hilterman, E. (2013). Risk assessment in intimate partner violence: A systematic review of contemporary approaches. *Partner Abuse, 4*(1), 76–168. doi:10.1891/1946-6560.4.1.76

Niolon, P. H., Kearns, M., Dills, J., Rambo, K., Irving, S., Armstead, T., & Gilbert, L. (2017). *Preventing intimate partner violence across the lifespan: A technical package of programs, policies, and practices.* Atlanta, GA: National Center for Injury Prevention and Control, Centers for Disease Control and Prevention.

O'Campo, P., Kirst, M., Tsamis, C., Chambers, C., & Ahmad, F. (2011). Implementing successful intimate partner violence screening programs in health care settings: Evidence generated from a realist-informed systematic review. *Social Science & Medicine, 72*(6), 855–866. doi:10.1016/j.socscimed.2010.12.019

Olds, D. L., Henderson, C., Kitzman, H., Eckenrode, J., Cole, R., & Tatelbaum, R. (1998). The promise of home visitation: Results of two randomized trials. *Journal of Community Psychology, 26*(1), 5–21.

Olds, D. L., Kitzman, H., Knudtson, M. D., Anson, E., Smith, J. A., & Cole, R. (2014). Effect of home visiting by nurses on maternal and child mortality: Results of a 2-decade follow-up of a randomized clinical trial. *JAMA Pediatrics, 168*(9), 800–806. doi:10.1001/jamapediatrics.2014.472.

O'Leary, K. D. (2001). Conjoint therapy for partners who engage in physically aggressive behavior. *Journal of Aggression, Maltreatment & Trauma, 5*(2), 145–164.

Oshima, K. M. M., Jonson-Reid, M., & Seay, K. D. (2014). The influence of childhood sexual abuse on adolescent outcomes: The roles of gender, poverty, and revictimization. *Journal of Child Sexual Abuse, 23*(4), 367–386. doi:10.1080/10538712.2014.896845

Peled, E., & Krigel, K. (2016). The path to economic independence among survivors of intimate partner violence: A critical review of the literature and courses for action. *Aggression and Violent Behavior, 31,* 127–135. doi:10.1016/j.avb.2016.08.005

Peterson, C., Xu, L. K., Florence, C., Parks, S. E., Miller, T. R., Barr, R. G., . . . Steinbeigle, R. (2014). The medical cost of abusive head trauma in the United States. *Pediatrics, 134*(1), 91–99. doi:10.1542/peds.2014-0117

Putnam-Hornstein, E., Simon, J. D., Eastman, A. L., & Magruder, J. (2015). Risk of re-reporting among infants who remain at home following alleged maltreatment. *Child Maltreatment, 20*(2), 92–103. doi:10.1177/1077559514558586

Renzettti, C. M., Edleson, J. L., & Bergen, R. K. (2012). *Sourcebook on violence against women* (2nd ed.). Thousand Oaks, CA: Sage.

Ridings, L. E., Beasley, L. O., & Silovsky, J. F. (2017). Consideration of risk and protective factors for families at risk for child maltreatment: An intervention approach. *Journal of Family Violence, 32*(2), 179–188. doi:10.1007/s10896-016-9826-y

Rivas, C., Ramsay, J., Sadowski, L., Davidson, L. L., Dunne, D., Eldridge, S., . . . Feder, G. (2015). Advocacy interventions to reduce or eliminate violence and promote the physical and psychosocial well-being of women who experience intimate partner abuse. *Cochrane Database of Systematic Reviews, 2015*(12), CD005043. doi:10.1002/14651858.CD005043.pub3

Rizo, C. F., Macy, R. J., Ermentrout, D. M., & Johns, N. B. (2011). A review of family interventions for intimate partner violence with a child focus or child component. *Aggression and Violent Behavior, 16*(2), 144–166. doi:10.1016/j.avb.2011.02.004

Salazar, L. F., Emshoff, J. G., Baker, C. K., & Crowley, T. (2007). Examining the behavior of a system: An outcome evaluation of a coordinated community response to domestic violence. *Journal of Family Violence, 22*(7), 631–641. doi:10.1007/s10896-007-9116-9

Sama-Miller, E., Akers, L., Mraz-Esposito, A., Zukiewicz, M., Avellar, S., Paulsell, D., & Del Grosso, P. (2017). *Home visiting programs: Reviewing evidence of effectiveness* [Brief]. Washington, DC: US Department of Health and Human Services, Administration for Children and Families, Office of Planning, Research and Evaluation. Retrieved from https://www.mathematica-mpr.com/our-publications-and-findings/publications/home-visiting-programs-reviewing-evidence-of-effectiveness-brief-april-2017

Savage, J., Palmer, J. E., & Martin, A. B. (2014). Intergenerational transmission: Physical abuse and violent vs. nonviolent criminal outcomes. *Journal of Family Violence, 29*(7), 739–748. doi:10.1007/s10896-014-9629-y

Schechter, S., & Edleson, J. L. (1999). *Effective intervention in domestic violence & child maltreatment cases: Guidelines for policy and practice: Recommendations.* Retrieved from https://www.rcdvcpc.org/the-greenbook.html

Sedlak, A. J., Mettenburg, J., Basena, M., Petta, I., McPherson, K., Greene, A., & Li, S. (2010). *Fourth National Incidence Study of Child Abuse and Neglect (NIS–4): Report to Congress, executive summary.* Washington, DC: US Department of Health and Human Services, Administration for Children and Families.

Shaw, T. V., Barth, R. P., Mattingly, J., Ayer, D., & Berry, S. (2013). Child welfare birth match: The timely use of child welfare administrative data to protect newborns. *Journal of Public Child Welfare, 7,* 217–234.

Sherraden, M., Stuart, P., Barth, R. P., Kemp, S., Lubben, J., Hawkins, J. D., . . . Catalano, R. (2014). *Grand accomplishments in social work* (Grand Challenges for Social Work Initiative Working Paper No. 2). Baltimore, MD: American Academy of Social Work and Social Welfare.

Shonkoff, J. P., Garner, A. S.; Committee on Psychosocial Aspects of Child and Family Health, Committee on Early Childhood, Adoption, Dependent Care, & Section on Developmental and Behavioral Pediatrics. (2012). The lifelong effects of early childhood adversity and toxic stress. *Pediatrics*, *129*(1), E232–E246. doi:10.1542/peds.2011-2663

Silovsky, J. F., Bard, D., Chaffin, M., Hecht, D., Burris, L., Owora, A., . . . Lutzker, J. (2011). Prevention of child maltreatment in high-risk rural families: A randomized clinical trial with child welfare outcomes. *Children and Youth Services Review*, *33*(8), 1435–1444. doi:10.1016/j.childyouth.2011.04.023

Slack, K. S., Berger, L. M., & Noyes, J. L. (2017). Introduction to the special issue on the economic causes and consequences of child maltreatment. *Children & Youth Services Review*, *72*, 1–4. doi:10.1016/j.childyouth.2016.11.013

Stanley, R. M., & Nigrovic, L. E. (2017). Research priorities for a multi-center child abuse network: Lessons learned from pediatric emergency medicine networks. *Child Abuse & Neglect*, *65*, 152–157. https://doi.org/10.1016/j.chiabu.2017.03.020

Stith, S. M., McCollum, E. E., & Rosen, K. H. (2011). *Couples therapy for domestic violence: Finding safe solutions*. Washington, DC: American Psychological Association.

Straus, M. A., Gelles, R. J., & Steinmetz, S. K. (1981). Violence in the home. In *Behind closed doors: Violence in the American family* (pp. 4–28). London, UK: Routledge.

Stover, C. S., Meadows, A. L., & Kaufman, J. (2009). Interventions for intimate partner violence: Review and implications for evidence-based practice. *Professional Psychology: Research and Practice*, *40*(3), 223–233. doi:10.1037/a0012718

Taylor, C., Lee, S., Guterman, N., & Rice, J. (2010). Use of spanking for 3-year-old children and associated intimate partner aggression or violence. *Pediatrics*, *126*(3), 415–424. doi:10.1542/peds.2010-0314

Tirado-Muñoz, J., Gilchrist, G., Farré, M., Hegarty, K., & Torrens, M. (2014). The efficacy of cognitive behavioural therapy and advocacy interventions for women who have experienced intimate partner violence: A systematic review and meta-analysis. *Annals of Medicine*, *46*(8), 567–586. doi:10.3109/07853890.2014.941918

US Department of Health and Human Services, Administration on Children Youth and Families. (2016). *Child maltreatment 2015*. Washington, DC: Government Printing Office.

Vidal, S., Prince, D., Connell, C. M., Caron, C. M., Kaufman, J. S., & Tebes, J. K. (2017). Maltreatment, family environment, and social risk factors: Determinants of the child welfare to juvenile justice transition among maltreated children and adolescents. *Child Abuse & Neglect*, *63*, 7–18. https://doi.org/10.1016/j.chiabu.2016.11.013

Widom, C. S., Horan, J., & Brzustowicz, L. (2015). Childhood maltreatment predicts allostatic load in adulthood. *Child Abuse & Neglect*, *47*, 59–69. doi:10.1016/j.chiabu.2015.01.016

Wilkins, N., Tsao, B., Hertz, M., Davis, R., & Klevens, J. (2014). *Connecting the dots: An overview of the links among multiple forms of violence*. Atlanta, GA: National Center for Injury Prevention and Control, Centers for Disease Control and Prevention.

Winstok, Z. (2013). From a static to a dynamic approach to the study of partner violence. *Sex Roles*, *69*(3–4), 193–204. doi:10.1007/s11199-013-0278-z

Grand Challenges
for Social Work
Advance long and productive lives

CHAPTER 5

Advance Long and Productive Lives

NANCY MORROW-HOWELL, ERNEST GONZALES,
JACQUELYN B. JAMES, CHRISTINA MATZ-COSTA,
AND MICHELLE PUTNAM

THE CHALLENGE

The age distribution of societies throughout the world is changing rapidly. In the United States and most other countries with advanced economies, lower birth rates and increasing life expectancy are shifting populations toward "top-heavy" societies, in which there are more people older than age 60 years than there are people younger than age 15 years (He, Goodkind, & Kowal, 2016). In the United States, the population older than age 65 years increased from 36.6 million in 2005 to 47.8 million in 2015 (a 30% increase), and it is projected to more than double to 98 million by 2060 (Administration on Aging, 2013). Throughout the world, 8% of the population was age 65 years or older in 2010, and this will increase to 16% by 2050 (National Institute on Aging, 2011). The growing number and proportion of older adults in these nations present aging-related challenges to families, communities, and countries as a whole—challenges that are unprecedented because never before in human history have so many people lived into the eighth and ninth decades of life. The success of this new longevity has often been overshadowed in public discourse by the daunting issues of economic security and health care, especially long-term care, in these extended years of life.

The press of these challenges has made it more difficult to focus on the opportunities that come with population aging. Of principal note is the reality that as the health, education, and economic security of older adults have become better over time, so too has the interest of individuals to initiate and continue productive activities longer into the life course, as evidenced by greater numbers of older adults engaging in paid work, volunteering, caregiving, and other activities. Thus, another challenge that nations face is increased demand for older adults to continue in and/or take on these roles. Provision of more productive aging opportunities requires a social development response to shape social policies and programs to engage the growing human capital of the aging population and to ensure the inclusion of all segments of the older adult population, especially among those who are more likely to be excluded. In short, *productive aging* asserts the fundamental view that aging societies will do better when they make better use of older adults' capacity to make economic contributions through employment, volunteering, and caregiving (Morrow-Howell & Greenfield, 2015).

Multiple positive societal outcomes can be achieved through optimizing the productive engagement of older adults. First, the paid labor force has potential to benefit from the infusion of experienced workers at the same time as the supply of younger workers shrinks; and longer working lives can extend the time that people rely on earned income rather than public pensions and savings (Munnell & Sass, 2008). Second, public and nonprofit agencies would greatly benefit from higher levels of volunteering by older adults (Bridgeland, McNaught, Reed, & Dunkelman, 2009), particularly those with relevant technical and professional skills, but also by those with lesser skills but great enthusiasm. Third, there will be an increasing demand for caregivers as the number of people older than age 85 years increases. This demand for caregivers (National Alliance for Caregiving & AARP, 2009) can be met at least in part by the growing number of older adults with time, energy, and ability to provide care for those in their families and social networks who need assistance.

Productive engagement can benefit individuals as well. As societies age, living 25 years beyond the normal retirement age of 65 years will be common. Maintaining economic security, social ties, health, and sense of purpose in later life have been shown to be important for quality of life (James, Matz-Costa, & Smyer, 2016). At the individual level, productive engagement can contribute to these important outcomes. Thus, national attention to advancing productive engagement opportunities for older adults at both the society level and the individual level is a crucial investment in maximizing positive outcomes for aging societies.

ANALYSIS OF THE PROBLEM AND OPPORTUNITY FOR IMPROVEMENT

Although societal aging is often viewed as a "problem," the trends toward lower birth rates and longer life expectancy have resulted from significant positive economic and social developments in the United States and other advanced economies (Morrow-Howell, Hinterlong, & Sherraden, 2001; Sherraden, et al., 2014). However, as noted previously, these demographic shifts put pressure on various sectors of societies, ranging from publicly funded social welfare programs to private family budgets, from employment markets to individual business owners in search of skilled labor, and from demands for formal long-term care services from nonprofit and public service sectors to demands for informal care from families and friends. Part of the problem is that although we have known for many decades that the population is aging, we have done little to prepare for it. Our institutions, infrastructures, and policies and programs were designed when human lives were much shorter and roles were more singular and sequential rather than multiple and less age-specific. For example, we created pathways that were segmented by age—young people go to school, adults work and raise families, and older adults step back and engage in leisure for their retirement years. Arguably, this pathway was never universal, but with much larger numbers of people living 20–30 years past their 60th birthday, the lack of fit of this presumed life course pattern becomes much more obvious, as have the barriers for productive engagement.

It is not just our physical and social infrastructures that are out of step with the current demographic shifts; our expectations and attitudes about later life and older adults also limit the potential of a productive aging society. Stereotypes of the frail, cognitively impaired elder ignore the demographic reality, highlighting how pervasive ageism still is in our society.

Institutional and societal barriers to productive engagement among older adults must be confronted and changed. In part, this can be done by working to shift public discourse away from the idea that population aging is a social problem and toward the view that the growing number of older adults represents a new resource for families, communities, and society at large. Creating more productive engagement opportunities will require institutional change, which is difficult but possible. Specifically, we must improve work environments and employment policies to enable people to work longer; restructure educational institutions so individuals can develop new knowledge and skills across the life course; create more diverse opportunities to enable older adults to engage in volunteer work while helping organizations more fully utilize this talent pool; and improve the way we support caregiving and other forms of care work in later life to facilitate positive individual outcomes, such as life satisfaction and social purpose, and reduce negative ones, such as stress and reduced health.

Dr. Robert Butler, a pioneer in the field of gerontology who coined the term *productive aging* in 1983, warned that society cannot afford to dismiss the human capital of the older population. Butler described older adults' productive engagement as a necessity, not a luxury (Butler, 1997). However, we must view this societal necessity within a paradigm that privileges choice to engage in productive activities rather than a mandate to do so. Not all individuals have achieved the same longevity gains, nor do all have the ability to perform or interest in activities such as paid work, volunteering, and caregiving compared to other activity choices or responsibilities. In addition, we must be keenly aware of larger social factors, such as racism, sexism, gender discrimination, and disability discrimination, that reduce opportunities for individuals to participate in their communities. As we seek to transform societal norms, programs, and policies to facilitate productive engagement, we must be guided by principles of choice, opportunity, and inclusion instead of by coercion, obligation, or elitism. Holstein and Minkler (2007) express concern that certain older adults will be marginalized, or continue to be marginalized, if certain expectations for productive engagement are not met. Therefore, we propose that efforts to advance productive engagement include the following: (1) ample opportunities for continued engagement for those older adults who choose this route, (2) identification and removal of barriers that artificially reduce productive engagement by older adults, and (3) support for caregivers to participate in and/or transition to other forms of productive engagement and for those engaged in work and volunteering to transition to caregiving roles. The grand challenge is to reimagine a lifetime filled with opportunities to acquire new knowledge and skills and to utilize talents and resources in a variety of paid and unpaid roles that foster economic security, provide purpose in life, and enrich families and communities. The trend of societal aging presents an open window for moving a productive engagement agenda forward as a means of meeting the challenge of an aging society and improving health, social, and economic outcomes for older individuals.

POTENTIAL OUTCOMES OF PRODUCTIVE ENGAGEMENT

Productive engagement is a potentially powerful mechanism with influence on numerous well-being outcomes. Scholars have conceptualized the effects of engagement in productive roles at the level of the individual, the family, the organization, the community, and society as a whole. Box 5.1 lists the outcomes that might be achieved.

The rates and levels of participation of older adults as workers, volunteers, and caregivers have been captured, and we can continue to track these metrics over time. These benchmarks can be attained from several large nationally representative data sets that track older adults and their engagement in productive activities longitudinally. Furthermore, dollar values of these time commitments can be assigned. Johnson and Schaner (2005) estimated that older adults provide $100 billion worth of care to parents, spouses, and grandchildren as well as $44.3 billion of formal volunteer service a year. Emerging evidence also suggests older workers contribute to a large portion of gross domestic product (Cohen, 2014).

Box 5.1: POTENTIAL OUTCOMES OF THE PRODUCTIVE
ENGAGEMENT OF OLDER ADULTS

INDIVIDUAL
- Physical health/function
- Mental health
- Self-efficacy
- Purpose in life
- Economic well-being

FAMILY
- Engaged grandparents and caregivers
- Transfer of income and assets from older to younger
- Healthier/happier older relatives

ORGANIZATIONS/COMMUNITY
- Experienced workers/volunteers
- Loyal/dependable workers/volunteers
- Age/generational diversity
- Mentors for younger workers

SOCIETY
- Less reliance on public pensions and savings
- More intergenerational exchange
- Less demand for long-term care due to postponement of disability

The physical, psychological, and financial effects of productive engagement on the individual have received the most scholarly attention because there are straightforward methods to estimate them. Evidence suggests that working can increase economic security while also leading to decreased mortality and better mental health and cognitive function (Calvo, 2006; Rohwedder & Willis, 2010). Volunteering also has been associated with positive health and psychological outcomes as well as higher odds of employment (Kim & Ferraro, 2013; Hong & Morrow-Howell, 2010; Spera, Ghertner, Nerino, & DiTommaso, 2013). Reduced mortality as well as caregiver report of benefits have been associated with caregiving (Roth, Fredman, & Haley, 2015). Outcomes are not always positive: Working longer in certain employment conditions can reduce health and mental health. In addition, the negative effects of caregiving on older adults are widely documented (Coughlin, 2010; Feinberg, Reinhard, Houser, & Choula, 2011).

Assessing the societal outcomes of the productive engagement of older adults may be more challenging than measuring its impact at the individual level. Theoretically, the increased productive engagement of older adults could lead to less reliance on public and private post-retirement income support programs, stronger civic society through increased involvement in volunteering and political engagement, increased intergenerational reciprocity, and higher levels of health among the older population. Indeed, Alvor Svanborg (2001) suggested that the major dividend of productive engagement would come at the society level from postponing decline associated with aging.

CURRENT REALITIES AND INNOVATIONS

Working

The number of people age 65 years or older who remain in the US workforce is growing as the average age of retirement has risen in the past two decades (US Department of Labor, Bureau of Labor Statistics [US BLS], 2016a). According to a 2014 AARP survey, a clear majority of workers older than age 50 years plan to work past the age of 65 years, including a sizable 18% who indicate that they never intend to retire (Skufca, 2014). There are several noteworthy elements in this overall trend toward working longer. First, more women are working in their later years than ever before. The labor force participation rates of women aged 55–65 years increased from 53.2% in 2000 to 59.2% in 2015 (Brown, Rhee, Saad-Lessler, & Oakley, 2016). The number of working women older than age 65 years also increased from 17% in 1990 to 27% in 2010, a trend that is expected to continue for some time (Poterba, 2014). Although labor force participation rates for older women have risen, women older than age 65 years are 80% more likely than men to live in poverty. Many of these women like their work and want to continue (Kerman & Keenan, 2017); however, many older women need to work in order to make ends meet.

A second later life trend is toward more full-time than part-time work (fewer than 35 hours/week). Since 2000, the number of adults older than age 65 years working full-time rather than part-time more than doubled from approximately 4 million people (approximately 13%) to 9 million (approximately 20%) (DeSilver, 2016). An important factor in this trend may be the recent evidence that increasingly fewer people are "very confident" that they have enough money for a comfortable retirement—only 18% of respondents in a recent survey (Greenwald, Copeland, & VanDerhei, 2017). Finally, there is a trend toward self-employment in later life (Halvorsen & Morrow-Howell, 2016). According to a 2016 analysis of US BLS data, the rate of self-employment among workers older than age 65 years was the highest (at 15.5%) of any age group (Hipple & Hammond, 2016). Indeed, analyses of the Health and Retirement Study reveal that 1 in 10 career wage and salary workers transition into self-employment before full retirement (Cahill, Giandrea, & Kovacs, 2014).

Clearly, federal and state work policies influence tenure in the workforce, as exemplified by raising the full retirement age from 65 to 67 years for Social Security benefits and eliminating the earnings test for workers older than the normal retirement age (Coile & Gruber, 2003; Olshansky, Goldman, & Rowe, 2015). Organizational policies also play a major role in retirement decisions. Specifically, the need for increased flexible work options has been well documented for employees of all ages. More than 90% of non-retirees who plan to work in retirement would like some kind of reduced work arrangement. However, in the face of this demand, only approximately one-third of employed retirees have such arrangements (Bankers Center for a Secure Retirement, 2015). McGuire, Kenney, and Brashler (2010) report that flexible work options include flexibility in the scheduling of hours worked (e.g., compressed work weeks), the number of hours worked (e.g., part-time and/or job-sharing), and the place of work (e.g., working off site or at home) (Cahill, James, & Pitt-Catsouphes, 2015). Although many employers indicate that such options are established policies, few employees take advantage of them for a host of reasons, the most important of which is lack of managerial support and encouragement (Sweet, Pitt-Catsouphes, & James, 2017).

There are innovative employment programs, including career counseling and job search websites, geared toward older adults. Private and nonprofit organizations have supported programming at community colleges to guide older workers in career decision-making and training curriculums (Halvorsen & Emerman, 2013–2014). The federal investment in workforce development for older adults remains low, but for more than 40 years, Title V of the Older American's Act has supported a job training program for low-income older workers. A nonprofit organization, Senior Entrepreneurship Works, provides training and support to individuals aged 50 years or older to start new businesses.

In summary, there has been program and policy attention at the employer level to support the older worker. However, employers have been slow to innovate while age discrimination, job insecurity, and changing technology continue to affect the employment options of older adults (Roscigno, 2010).

Volunteering

Approximately one-fourth of the US population older than age 65 years volunteers (US BLS, 2016b), a rate lower than that of younger adults. The fact is that retired older adults volunteer less than working adults, despite an increase in discretionary time. Decreases in rates of volunteering can be explained by disconnection from work and educational organizations, the major avenues through which people are asked to volunteer (Musick & Wilson, 2008; Opportunity Nation, 2014). There is evidence that older adults are more likely to volunteer when asked and contribute more hours per year than younger adults (90 vs. 32 hours per year, respectively). Furthermore, older adults provide informal volunteer hours assisting neighbors and friends that are not captured in volunteer metrics (Taniguchi, 2012; Zedlewski & Schaner, 2006).

The gap between the actual and potential volunteer time among older adults has increased interest in encouraging greater civic involvement among the older population. Service programs geared toward engaging older volunteers have received attention in the past decade. Examples include intergenerational tutoring programs (i.e., OASIS Intergenerational Tutoring; Experience Corps), coaching/mentoring programs (i.e., Wisdom of Age–National Mentoring Partnership), and friendly visitor programs (i.e., Village Model's Neighbors Helping Neighbors). Federal programs, including Senior Companions, Foster Grandparents, and Retired and Senior Volunteer Program (RSVP), continue to place older adults in service roles in their local communities. Online websites have reached out to older adults to match them with community needs (see http://comingofage.org and https://www.volunteermatch.org). The Serve America Act of 2009 recognized the potential of late-life volunteering and prompted AmeriCorps to increase the number of older adults involved in this national service program. The Peace Corps has a Fifty-Plus program to increase the number of older volunteers.

In summary, programs and policies have acknowledged the growing number of older adults and facilitated involvement in volunteering. However, efforts have not been commensurate with the growing potential of the aging population.

Caregiving

Currently, approximately 35% of caregivers are 50–64 years old, 9% are 65–74 years old, and 4% are older than age 75 years. Also, the average age of caregivers is increasing as members of the Baby Boom generation provide assistance to their parents, other relatives, and adult children with disabilities (National Alliance for Caregiving & AARP, 2009). Furthermore, the rate of custodial grandparenting is growing, with 1.6 million or 2.2% of all children in the United States being raised by a custodial grandparent—a number three times greater than the number of children in foster care (US Census, 2011). Clearly, caregiving is becoming a normative experience in which three- and four-generation families are becoming more common.

Nonprofit and public agencies have offered psychoeducational support programs and respite programs for caregivers for many years, and a large number of evidence-based interventions aimed at supporting caregiving have been developed. For example, the Rosslyn Carter Institute lists more than 70 evidence-based programs, such as REACH, NYU's Caregiving Counseling and Support Intervention, and Skills2Care. Furthermore, to promote the implementation of the strongest programs, the Institute sorts the interventions into two levels of evidence: those tested in randomized controlled trials, demonstrating positive outcomes for caregivers and published in peer-reviewed journals, and those without these characteristics. There is also indication of whether the intervention is "implementation ready," in that there are adequate materials for training.

The current challenge is that most caregivers are not reached by these programs. Dissemination and implementation of these programs is limited, and resources are not available within aging network services (Gitlin & Czaja, 2012). Online resources and support groups are being developed to eliminate access barriers. Some of these efforts are directed toward subpopulations of caregivers, such as custodial grandparents and parents of adult children with developmental disabilities. Financial support for caregivers is being made possible by public consumer-directed care programs, in which relatives and friends can be paid to provide assistance (Mahoney, Simon-Rusinowitz, Simone, & Zgoda, 2006).

In summary, there are promising practices and interesting innovations to support older caregivers, but reach is limited.

NEXT STEPS

As reviewed previously, research and demonstrations have supported the development of interventions to facilitate the productive engagement of older adults as workers, volunteers, and caregivers. Despite this promise, efforts are not widespread enough, not institutionalized enough, and not commensurate with the present demographic revolution. There are immediate next steps to be taken.

Increase Financial Support to Caregivers

Most caregivers are employed, and the challenges of working and caregiving concurrently can cause significant financial strains and conflict (Rainville, Skufca, & Mehegan, 2016). Although federal law allows workers to take up to 6 weeks of leave to take care of a relative, this time is typically unpaid. Nearly half of caregivers who take time away from work to fulfill their elder-care responsibilities report losing income (Aumann, Galinsky, Sakai, Brown, & Bond, 2010). Of this group, more than half stated they had to leave their jobs because their employers did not allow the flexibility needed to work and provide eldercare (Matos, 2014). The average caregiver older than age 50 years who leaves the workforce to care for a parent loses more than $300,000 in wages and retirement income (MetLife Mature Market Institute, 2011). Thus, there is legislation under consideration to amend the federal Family and Medical Leave Act to provide paid leave when caregivers must temporarily leave the workforce to care for family members.

Evidence from the implementation of paid leave policies at the state level reveals that families benefit and that productivity is not negatively affected (National Partnership for Women and Families, 2016). The Society for Human Resource Management, one of the chief opponents of paid family leave in California, issued a report finding that the law had created "relatively few" new burdens for employers and that employers' concerns about the program "have so far not been realized" (Redmond & Fkiaras, 2010). Similarly, a survey of New Jersey employers found that a majority did not experience negative effects on profitability or increased paperwork, and no employer was aware of a single instance of the program being abused (Lerner & Appelbaum, 2014).

We can also expand participant-directed programs within the long-term service and support system, particularly those funded through Medicaid that permit beneficiaries to pay caregivers of their choice, including family members. Evidence from participant direction programs, such as the Cash and Counseling random control trial, has demonstrated that consumers and caregivers have high rates of satisfaction, low rates of unmet need, and that this type of service delivery model offers flexibility that cannot be achieved through traditional case management (Mahoney et al., 2006). This flexibility permits both individuals and caregivers to exercise choice and preference that supports them in better meeting their care needs (San Antonio et al., 2010) and in adapting to change over time (Harry et al., 2016).

Expand Federal Recognition and Local Support for Older Adults Who Volunteer

The Corporation for National and Community Service (CNCS) operates several model programs under SeniorCorps, including RSVP, the Foster Grandparents Program, and the Senior Companion Program, which together link more than 243,000 older adults to service opportunities annually (CNCS, 2017). However, SeniorCorps is currently threatened by federal budget cuts or elimination altogether, despite its success in engaging low-income adults in stipended service aimed at children or older adults who need assistance (Tan et al., 2016). Instead of cutting or eliminating funding to these programs, there are compelling arguments for expansion. Not only do these national service programs have a history of broad bipartisan support but also the entire CNCS budget represents only 0.03% of federal spending (Mulhere,

2017). SeniorCorps programs provided almost 75 million hours of national service in fiscal year 2017, and more than 1.2 million elderly, children, and veterans in need were served (CNCS, 2017). According to Belfield (2013), the social benefits are almost four times as large as the costs of these programs, and the taxpayer benefits are twice the taxpayer costs. Wacker and Roberto (2013) estimate a 26.1-fold return on the federal dollar for RSVP in 2011. However, these programs are currently only able to reach a small portion of the older adults who could benefit from them because most older adults do not know about these programs and racial and ethnic minorities, immigrants, low-income older adults, non-college-educated individuals, and the disabled continue to be underrepresented in these programs and also service programs in general (Foster-Bey, 2008; Wacker & Roberto, 2013).

Similarly, the promise of the Edward M. Kennedy Serve America Act of 2009 has yet to be fully realized in its potential as a tool for promoting productive engagement. This Act was significant in that it includes several provisions specifically targeting older adults and contains language that promotes service for older adults of all socioeconomic backgrounds by stipulating that organizations specifically target, recruit, and leverage the resources of seniors (Cutler, Hendricks, & O'Neill, 2011). However, the authorized ramp-up of AmeriCorps positions from 75,000 to 250,000 by 2017—10% of which were for those age 55 years or older—has not yet occurred because funding levels have not kept pace.

Finally, we can develop innovative ways to incentivize volunteering at the local level. Many municipalities throughout the country offer property tax work-off programs. For example, the town of Littleton, Massachusetts, offers property owners older than age 60 years the opportunity to provide volunteer services to the town in exchange for a reduction of up to $1,000 on the amount paid on their property taxes via a minimum wage hourly rate (Town of Littleton, Massachusetts, n.d.). Some local communities have implemented programs that facilitate the exchange of non-cash incentives (e.g., "time banking"). In Montpelier, Vermont, the Administration on Aging has invested in a form of time banks called "Carebanks," in which older adults can get informal care and support if they or their families pay regular premiums—in "time dollars"—earned helping to build community or helping other seniors in various ways (Cahn, 2011).

Encourage Employers to Support Older Workers

The federal and state governments and research institutions can be more active in influencing employing organizations to support longer working lives. According to a recent Transamerica retirement survey, almost 80% of employers agree that they are supportive of their employees working past age

65 years. However, workers are less likely to assess that their employers are indeed supportive (Collinson, 2016). There needs to be more research and dissemination of evidence that older workers and flexible arrangements create positive outcomes for all involved. In a randomized controlled trial, Cahill, James, and Pitt-Catsouphes (2015) found that older workers who perceived increased organizational support for flexible work options (the intervention) increased their expected retirement age over the course of 2 years. A second analysis of these same data revealed that having a greater sense of schedule control makes a difference for employee satisfaction with work–family balance even under conditions of high work unit pressure (James, Pitt-Catsouphes, McNamara, Snow, & Johnson, 2015).

There needs to be more education and advice to employers about options for recruiting and supporting older workers. Practices such as adding age diversity to the interviewing team, publicizing an "age-friendly" image, partnering with external organizations that connect employers with older job seekers, and implementing such innovations as "returnships" (an unpaid internship for a specified time) might help employers move beyond the current status quo with regard to hiring practices (Boston College Center on Aging & Work & AARP, 2015).

In addition to support from employers, there are policy options that can enhance the productive engagement of older adults. Berkman, Boersch-Supan, and Avendano (2015) suggest policies that invest in human capital throughout individuals' lives that enable them to work longer, including early childhood education, poverty reduction, and health care access. Similarly, government can offer incentives for reinvesting in skill development, especially for blue-collar workers (Zissimopoulos, Goldman, Olshansky, Rother, & Rowe, 2015).

Support Transitions Between Working, Volunteering, and Caregiving

Research confirms that older adults who volunteer while still employed are more likely to volunteer after retirement (Tang, 2016). Furthermore, retirement planning can lay the foundation for later-life volunteering. As such, it would be useful for organizations to develop employee volunteer programs geared toward offering continuity after retirement. For example, Intel's Encore Fellows program places retiring employees at a local nonprofit for an assignment that typically lasts 6–12 months, half- or full-time, and involves a commitment to work (on average) 1,000 hours; Fellows are paid a set annual stipend of $25,000 (Encore.org, n.d.). Such an experience can facilitate the transition from the private sector to the nonprofit sector, in either paid or unpaid work.

We can financially support caregivers who transition in and out of caregiving and the workforce by acknowledging this important work via the Social

Security system. Legislation has been proposed that would not jeopardize caregivers' future retirement income from Social Security. This legislation (Social Security Caregiver Credit Act of 2014) would count time dedicated to caregiving toward employment history, with a formula assigning a paid wage to Social Security work history records during each month in which a caregiver provided at least 80 hours of assistance without financial compensation.

Transform Physical and Social Environments to Promote Productive Engagement

Aging-friendly community initiatives show promise to improve physical and social environments to support productive engagement. Many local governments and community organizations are focusing on ways to reduce barriers and facilitate participation of older adults, improve the possibilities to age in place, and increase age inclusiveness (e.g., see AARP and the World Health Organization's [2007] age-friendly community initiatives). These efforts include increasing walkability and accessibility, improving public transportation, providing affordable housing options, promoting respect and inclusion, and ensuring essential health and social services. Although working, volunteering, and caregiving are all supported through any of these transformations in community infrastructure, many initiatives have specific goals in regard to these productive activities. For example, Age-Friendly NYC (2009) calls for action include the following: provide job training and search assistance to older New Yorkers, increase the number of paid job opportunities for older New Yorkers, promote intergenerational volunteering and learning through partnerships with schools and nonprofit organizations, provide new volunteer opportunities, provide counseling and support services to grandparents raising grandchildren, expand educational materials and supports available to family caregivers, explore policies that would allow more New Yorkers to take family leave when needed, conduct outreach and workshops on long-term care and caregiving resources for employers in New York City, and expand training opportunities and other supports for paid caregivers.

End Discrimination and Bias

The negative effects of discrimination and bias in any form and at any age have been documented. The aging population is very diverse, and there is evidence linking perceived discrimination on basic features of an individual—age, sex, race, ethnicity, sexual orientation, physical ability, weight, and appearance—with deleterious physical, cognitive, and emotional health, as well as negative economic outcomes (Allen, 2016; Marchiondo, Gonzales, & Ran, 2016; Sutin,

Stephen, Carretta, & Terracciano, 2015). Individuals who perceive discrimination within the workplace are at greater risk of turnover and early retirement (Brooke & Taylor, 2005; Lim, Cortina, & Magley, 2008), as well as job dissatisfaction (Judge, Thoresen, Bono, & Patton, 2001), which can affect performance, organizational climate, and productively (Barsade, 2002). Older adults with multiple vulnerable identities are susceptible to ageism and other biases (Sutin, Stephen, Carretta, & Terracciano, 2015), which underscores the importance of social workers to advocate for populations that have been historically discriminated at any age for any reason. The research on structural or institutional discrimination based on race is quite sophisticated (Delgado & Stephancic, 2012; Miller & Garran, 2008), and more can be done to link it with age discrimination, health, and productive engagement. We must see beyond stereotypes, whether negative or positive, and match the capacity of individuals with the employment, volunteering, or caregiving role—as opposed to current stereotypes of incompetent, useless, and "greedy geezers" (Gendron, Welleford, Inker, & White, 2016). Future research is needed to identify the prevalence and consequences of discrimination in various contexts (e.g., workplace, volunteer and community settings, and home), as well as the individual and institutional protective mechanisms that buffer health and social engagement across the lifespan.

Current legislation seeks to strengthen protection against age discrimination. The Protect Older Workers Against Discrimination Act (POWADA) will reinstate Congress' original intent for age to be a factor in an age discrimination claim, as opposed to the primary factor. The Fair Employment Protection Act of 2014 (H.R. 4227) will also protect employees from covert discriminatory practices based on age and other vulnerable identities. Employers and volunteer sites that foster inclusion can also benefit financially with a healthier workforce and stronger commitment of diverse employees.

CALLS FOR INNOVATION

Several specific issues warrant innovative, indeed transformative, solutions. First, there are not many examples of interventions to change attitudes and social expectations about later life or to confront ageism. Perhaps these changes will emerge as programs and policies further re-create the social roles of older adults. However, there may be interventions to accelerate these changes. It is necessary to seek creative solutions to reduce the widespread age discrimination and stereotyping that currently exist and fundamentally limit the participation of older adults in productive roles.

Second, solutions that directly address gender, ethnic, and racial diversity are essential, especially given society's history of discrimination in the educational and employment sector. For example, older racial minorities are underrepresented and underrecognized in the paid and volunteer labor force, and women provide the bulk of unpaid caregiving. American society has a long history of paid and unpaid roles that are tied to gender and race, and Butler (1980) drew parallels between ageism, racism, and sexism. Intervention development to facilitate productive engagement in later life will require innovative solutions that confront the exclusion of less advantaged older adults; otherwise, disparities in later life could increase.

Third, solutions must be developed from a life course perspective. Early and midlife health, education, work, volunteering, and caregiving experiences shape subsequent abilities to engage successfully in paid and unpaid work in later life (Hirshorn & Settersten, 2013). Attitudes and motivations for involvement in family and community are not formed when one reaches older adulthood but, rather, are shaped over decades. Significant innovation will be necessary for solutions that address how attitudes, expectations, programs, and policies can be shaped across the life course to ensure a productive old age.

CHARGE TO THE SOCIAL WORK PROFESSION

Social work education traditionally includes curriculum on older adults, aging policies, and aging network services. However, the topic of the productive engagement of older adults requires a new perspective for social work because we have largely focused on human problems. Indeed, the roots of gerontological social work are helping with the inability to take care of oneself financially or because of disability or dementia. We must confront our own professional expectations and practices because social workers are as vulnerable to age bias and age stereotyping as anyone else. In fact, social work's important commitment to individuals who face challenging psychosocial life situations makes us more vulnerable to distorted views of the aging population. That is, we focus on problems older adults face, including dementia, disabling health conditions, mental disorder, isolation, and neglect, rather than focusing on the whole person and the strengths of each older adult. It is easy to forget that most older adults are living well, and those who face challenges still may be quite interested and capable of participating in productive activities—and often are—despite our misperceptions.

Correspondingly, our educational curriculums skew toward the problems commonly experienced in later life and fail to adequately capture the reality of normal human development throughout the life course. We use language, examples, and experiences that support age stereotyping. For example, discussions of later life in foundation social work courses are often relegated to a single class or reading, whereas discussion of issues related to youth and middle adulthood are well represented throughout the curriculum. Furthermore, these discussions often conflate older adulthood with disability, with little focus on an assets-based orientation in later life, intergenerational equity approaches, or understanding that disability does not preclude engagement. Clearly, these are critical topics for social workers, and all social workers need to be equipped to mediate the great social transformation signaled by the growing proportion of older adults in society. Yet we fail to include content that portrays the reality of the capacity, desire, and strength of older adults and the potential to improve their lives and the lives of others via productive engagement. These issues could be incorporated into the curriculum in innovative and seamless ways, ranging from an exercise in which students are asked to reflect on maintaining or creating meaningful roles and identities across the lifespan, and particularly in later life, to staging a debate focused on intergenerational tensions/equity/fairness in different contexts and how these issues might be resolved with the goal of an age-inclusive society.

Infusion of productive aging perspectives into social work curriculum is facilitated by the reality that the productive aging framework is highly compatible with social work's person–environment fit perspective. The productive aging perspective focuses on programs, policies, and social contexts to leverage the growing capital of the older population. Interventions to promote working, volunteering, and caregiving focus on supports and opportunities, not on changing the individual older adults themselves. This person–environment fit approach positions social work to lead initiatives and partner with many disciplines to work toward maximizing the productive engagement of older adults. Colleagues from medical and allied professions, psychology, sociology, economics, architecture, business, and public health must be involved to make significant progress toward achieving an aging society that can be characterized, in part, by older adults' productive activity. Social work scholars are also leaders of research that examines productive engagement in later life with particular attention to issues concerning social and economic justice. The Productive Aging Interest Group, associated with the Hartford Geriatric Social Work Leadership Initiative and the Gerontological Society of America, is further evidence of social work's leadership on productive aging within gerontology as a whole.

CONCLUSION

Population aging is transforming societies throughout the world. The demographic shift is creating significant challenges but also presents great opportunity. To complement long-standing problem-oriented approaches, such as fixing Social Security and reforming health care, we must take a more strengths-based perspective by focusing on increasing the productive engagement of a growing natural human resource: the older population (Freedman,

2011). To do this requires applied research and innovations in policy and programs across multiple disciplines and changes in assumptions about older adults and aging populations. Social work can help lead the productive engagement agenda with an emphasis on creating equity in opportunity for all older adults who desire to participate in productive activities.

REFERENCES

Administration on Aging. (2016). *Profile of older Americans: 2016*. Washington, DC: Administration on Aging, Administration for Community Living, US Department of Health and Human Service. Retrieved from https://www.acl. gov/sites/default/files/Aging%20and%20Disability%20in%20America/2016-Profile.pdf

Age-Friendly NYC. (2009). *Enhancing our city's livability for older New Yorkers*. Retrieved from http://www.nyc.gov/html/dfta/downloads/pdf/age_friendly/agefriend-lynyc.pdf

Allen, J. O. (2016). Ageism as a risk factor for chronic disease. *The Gerontologist, 56*(4), 610–614. doi:10.1093/geront/gnu158

Aumann, K., Galinsky, E., Sakai, K., Brown, M., & Bond, J. T. (2010). *The elder care study: Everyday realities and wishes for change*. Retrieved from http://familiesand-work.org/site/research/reports/elder_care.pdf

Bankers Center for a Secure Retirement. (2015). *New expectations, new rewards: Work in retirement for middle-income boomers*. Chicago, IL: Bankers Life. Retrieved from http://www.centerforasecureretirement.com/media/65648/work-in-retirement-report-may-2015.pdf

Barsade, S. G. (2002). The ripple effect: Emotional contagion and its influence on group behavior. *Administrative Science Quarterly, 47*(4), 644–675.

Belfield, C. (2013). *The economic value of national service*. New York, NY: Center for Benefit–Cost Studies in Education. Retrieved from http://voicesforservice.org/wp-content/uploads/2016/03/Sep19_Econ_Value_National_Service-2.pdf

Berkman, L. F., Boersch-Supan, A., & Avendano, M. (2015). Labor-force participation, policies, & practices in an aging America: Adaptation essential for a healthy & resilient population. *Dædalus, 144*(2), 41–54. doi:10.1162/DAED_a_00329

Boston College Center on Aging & Work & AARP. (2015). *Workforce benchmarking tool*. Retrieved April 12, 2017, from http://virgo.bc.edu/employerbenchmarking

Bridgeland, J. M., McNaught, M., Reed, B., & Dunkelman, M. (2009). The Quiet Crisis: The Impact of the Economic Downturn on the Nonprofit Sector. *Civic Enterprises*.

Brooke, L., & Taylor, P. (2005). Older workers and employment: Managing age relations. *Ageing and Society, 25*(3), 415–429.

Brown, J. E., Rhee, N., Saad-Lessler, J., & Oakley, D. (2016). *Shortchanges in retirement: Continuing challenges to women's financial future*. Washington, DC: National Institute on Retirement. Retrieved from http://laborcenter.berkeley.edu/pdf/2016/NIRS-Women-In-Retirement.pdf

Butler, R. N. (1980). Ageism: A foreword. *Journal of Social Issues, 36*(2), 8–11. doi:10.1111/j.1540-4560.1980.tb02018.x

Butler, R. N. (1997). Living longer, contributing longer. *Journal of the American Medical Association, 278*(16), 1372–1374. doi:10.1001/jama.1997.03550160092044

Cahill, K. E., Giandrea, M. D., & Kovacs, G. J. (2014). Self-employment: The answer for an aging workforce and a sluggish economy? Retrieved from http://agingandwork.bc.edu/blog/self-employment-the-answer-for-an-aging-workforce-and-a-sluggish-economy

Cahill, K. E., James, J. B., & Pitt-Catsouphes, M. (2015). The impact of a randomly assigned time and place management initiative on work and retirement expectations. *Work, Aging and Retirement, 1*(4), 350–368. doi:10.1093/workar/wav012

Cahn, E. (2011, November 17). Time banking: An idea whose time has come? *Yes! Magazine.* Retrieved from http://www.yesmagazine.org/new-economy/time-banking-an-idea-whose-time-has-come

Calvo, E. (2006). *Does working longer make people healthier and happier?* (Work Opportunities for Older Americans Brief, Series 2). Chestnut Hill, MA: Center for Retirement Research, Boston College.

Cohen, N. (2014, January 28). Rise in number of older workers set to drive UK economy. *Financial Times.* Retrieved from http://www.ft.com/cms/s/0/c562a032-881f-11e3-a926-00144feab7de.html#axzz362YhGvxr

Coile, C. C., & Gruber, J. (2003). *Fiscal effects of social security reform in the United States.* Retrieved from http://crr.bc.edu/working-papers/fiscal-effects-of-social-security-reform-in-the-united-states

Collinson, S. (2016). *The current state of 401(k)s: The employer's perspective. 16th annual Transamerica retirement survey.* Los Angeles, CA: Transamerica Center for Retirement Studies. Retrieved from https://www.transamericacenter.org/docs/default-source/employer-research/tcrs2016_sr_the_current_state_of_401ks_the_employer_perspective.pdf

Corporation for National and Community Service. (2017). *Corporation for National and Community Service Fact Sheet: SeniorCorps.* Retrieved from https://www.nationalservice.gov/sites/default/files/documents/CNCS-Fact-Sheet-2017-SeniorCorps_0.pdf

Coughlin, J. (2010). Estimating the impact of caregiving and employment on well-being. *Outcomes & Insights in Health Management, 2*(1), 1–7.

Cutler, S. J., Hendricks, J., & O'Neill, G. (2011). Civic engagement and aging. In B. H. Binstock & L. George (Eds.), *Handbook of aging & the social sciences* (7th ed.). New York, NY: Academic Press.

Delgado, R., & Stephancic, C. (2012). *Critical race theory: An introduction* (2nd ed.). New York, NY: New York University Press.

DeSilver, D. (2016). *More older Americans are working than in recent years.* Washington, DC: Pew Research Center. Retrieved from http://www.pewresearch.org/fact-tank/2016/06/20/more-older-americans-are-working-and-working-more-than-they-used-to

Encore.org. (n.d.). *Intel Encore Fellows: A pathway to a new stage of work and contribution.* Retrieved from http://encore.org/fellowships/intel

Feinberg, L., Reinhard, S. C., Houser, A., & Choula, R. (2011). *Valuing the invaluable: 2011 update, the growing contributions and costs of family caregiving.* Retrieved from https://assets.aarp.org/rgcenter/ppi/ltc/i51-caregiving.pdf

Foster-Bey, J. (2008). *Do race, ethnicity, citizenship and socioeconomic status determine civic engagement?* Retrieved from http://www.civicyouth.org/PopUps/WorkingPapers/WP62_Foster.Bey.pdf

Freedman, M. (2011). *The big shift: Navigating midlife and beyond.* New York, NY: Perseus.

Gendron, T. L., Welleford, A., Inker, J., & White, J. T. (2016). The language of ageism: Why we need to use words carefully. *The Gerontologist, 56*(6), 997–1006. doi:10.1093/geront/gnv066

Gitlin, L. N., & Czaja, S. (2012). *Pre-conference workshop: Current and future challenges in designing behavioral interventions—From randomized trials to community implementations.* Paper presented at the annual conference of the Gerontological Society of American, San Diego, CA.

Greenwald, L., Copeland, C., & VanDerhei, J. (2017). *The 2017 retirement confidence survey—Many workers lack retirement confidence and feel stressed about retirement preparations* (Issue Brief, No. 431). Washington, DC: Employee Benefit Research Institute.

Halvorsen, C., & Emerman, J. (2013–2014). The encore movement: Baby boomers and older adults building community. *Generations, 37*(4), 33–39.

Halvorsen, C., & Morrow-Howell, N. (2016). A conceptual framework on self-employment in later life: Toward a research agenda. *Work, Aging and Retirement.* doi:10.1093/workar/waw031

Harry, M. L., Kong, J., MacDonald, L. M., McLuckie, A., Battista, C., & Mahoney, K. J. (2016). The long-term effects of participant direction of supports and services for people with disabilities. *Care Management Journals, 17*(1), 2–12. doi:10.1891/1521-0987.17.1.2

He, W., Goodkind, D., & Kowal, P. (2016). *U.S. Census Bureau, International Population Reports, P95/16-1, An aging world: 2015.* Washington, DC: US Government Publishing Office.

Hipple, S. F., & Hammond, L. A. (2016). *Self-employment in the United States: Spotlight on statistics* (p. 5). Washington, DC: Bureau of Labor Statistics. Retrieved from http://www.bls.gov/spotlight/2016/self-employment-in-the-united-states/home.htm

Hirshorn, B. A., & Settersten, R. A., Jr. (2013). Civic involvement across the life course: Moving beyond age-based assumptions. *Advances in Life Course Research, 18*(3), 199–211. doi:10.1016/j.alcr.2013.05.001

Holstein, M. B., & Minkler, M. (2007). Critical gerontology: Reflections for the 21st century. In M. Bernard & T. Scharf (Eds.), *Critical perspectives on ageing societies* (pp. 12–26). Buckingham, UK: Open University Press.

Hong, S. I., & Morrow-Howell, N. (2010). Health outcomes of Experience Corps: A high-commitment volunteer program. *Social Science & Medicine, 71*(2), 414–420. doi:10.1016/j.socscimed.2010.04.009

James, J. B., Matz-Costa, C., & Smyer, M. (2016). Retirement security: It's not just about the money. *American Psychologist, 7*(4), 334–344. doi:10.1037/a0040220

James, J. B., Pitt-Catsouphes, M., McNamara, T. K., Snow, D. L., & Johnson, P. (2015). The relationship of work unit pressure to satisfaction with work–family balance: A new twist on negative spillover? In S. Ammons & E. Kelly (Eds.), *Research in the sociology of work: Work and family in the new economy* (pp. 219–247). Bingley, UK: Emerald Group. doi:10.1108/S0277-283320150000026015

Johnson, R. W., & Schaner, S. G. (2005). *Value of unpaid activities by older Americans tops $160 billion per year.* Washington, DC: Urban Institute.

Judge, T. A., Thoresen, C. J., Bono, J. E., & Patton, G. K. (2001). The job satisfaction–job performance relationship: A qualitative and quantitative review. *Psychological Bulletin, 127*(3), 376–407.

Kerman, S. C., & Keenan, T. A. (2017). *The multi-generational labor force: Perceptions of jobs among Millennials, Gen-xers, and Boomers.* Washington, DC: AARP. Retrieved from http://www.aarp.org/content/dam/aarp/research/surveys_statistics/econ/2016/multi-gen-labor-force-report-res-econ.pdf

Kim, S., & Ferraro, K. F. (2013). Do productive activities reduce inflammation in later life? Multiple roles, frequency of activities, and C-reactive protein. *The Gerontologist, 54*(5), 830–839. doi:10.1093/geront/gnt090

Lerner, S., & Appelbaum, E. (2014). *Business as usual: New Jersey employers' experiences with family leave insurance*. Retrieved from http://www.cepr.net/documents/nj-fli-2014-06.pdf

Lim, S., Cortina, L. M., & Magley, V. J. (2008). Personal and workgroup incivility: Impact on work and health outcomes. *Journal of Applied Psychology, 9*(1), 95–107.

Mahoney, K. J., Simon-Rusinowitz, L., Simone, K., & Zgoda, K. (2006). Cash and counseling: A promising option for consumer direction of home- and community-based services and supports. *Care Management Journals, 7*(4), 199–204.

Marchiondo, L., Gonzales, E., & Ran, S. (2016). Development and validation of the Workplace Age Discrimination Scale (WADS). *Journal of Business and Psychology, 31*(4), 493–513. doi:10.1007/s10869-015-9425-6

Matos, K. (2014). *Highlights from the 2014 older adult caregiver study*. Retrieved from http://www.familiesandwork.org/downloads/2014-Older-Adult-Caregiver-Study.pdf

McGuire, J. F., Kenney, K., & Brashler, P. (2010). Flexible work arrangements: The fact sheet. *Workplace Flexibility 2010*, 1–10.

MetLife Mature Market Institute. (2011). The MetLife study of caregiving costs to working caregivers: Double jeopardy for baby boomers caring for their parents. Retrieved from https://www.metlife.com/assets/cao/mmi/publications/studies/2011/Caregiving-Costs-to-Working-Caregivers.pdf

Miller, J., & Garran, A. M. (2008). *Racism in the United States: Implications for the helping professions*. Belmont, CA: Brooks/Cole.

Morrow-Howell, N., & Greenfield, E. (2015). Productive engagement in later life. In L. George & K. Ferraro (Eds.), *Handbook of aging and the social sciences* (pp. 293–314). London, UK: Elsevier.

Morrow-Howell, N., Hinterlong, J., & Sherraden, M. (2001). *Productive aging: Concepts and challenges*. Baltimore, MD: Johns Hopkins University Press.

Mulhere, K. (2017, March 16). Trump's budget would kill the beloved volunteer program AmeriCorps. *Money*. Retrieved from http://time.com/money/4703924/trump-budget-americorps-college-funding-cut

Munnell, A., & Sass, S. A. (2008). *Working longer: The solution to the retirement income challenge*. Washington, DC: Brookings Institute Press.

Musick, M. A., & Wilson, J. (2008). *Volunteers: A social profile*. Bloomington, IN: Indiana University Press.

National Alliance for Caregiving & AARP. (2009). *Caregiving in the U.S. 2009*. Retrieved from http://www.caregiving.org/data/Caregiving_in_the_US_2009_full_report.pdf

National Institute on Aging. (2011). *Global health and aging* (NIH Publication No. 11-7737). Washington, DC: National Institutes of Health.

National Partnership for Women and Families. (2016). *Paid leave works in California, New Jersey and Rhode Island*. Retrieved from http://www.nationalpartnership.org/research-library/work-family/paid-leave/paid-leave-works-in-california-new-jersey-and-rhode-island.pdf

Olshansky, S. J., Goldman, D. P., & Rowe, J. W. (2015). Resetting Social Security. *Dædalus, 144*(2), 68–79. doi:10.1162/DAED_a_00331

Opportunity Nation. (2014). *Connecting youth and strengthening communities: The data behind civic engagement and economic opportunity*. Retrieved from http://www.pointsoflight.org/sites/default/files/resources/files/opportunity_nation_civic_engagement_report_2014.pdf

Poterba, J. M. (2014). Retirement security in an aging population. *American Economic Review*, 104(5), 1–30. doi:10.1257/aer.104.5.1

Rainville, C., Skufca, L., & Mehegan, L. (2016). *Family caregiving and out-of-pocket costs: 2016 report*. Washington, DC: AARP. Retrieved from http://www.aarp.org/content/dam/aarp/research/surveys_statistics/ltc/2016/family-caregiving-cost-survey-res-ltc.pdf

Redmond, J., & Fkiaras, E. (2010). *Legal report: California's Paid Family Leave Act is less onerous than predicted*. Retrieved from https://www.sheppardmullin.com/media/article/809_CA%20Paid%20Family%20Leave%20Act%20Is%20Less%20Onerous%20Than%20Predicted.pdf

Rohwedder, S., & Willis, R. J. (2010). Mental retirement. *Journal of Economic Perspectives*, 24(1), 119–138. doi:10.1257/jep.24.1.119

Roscigno, V. (2010). Ageism in the American workplace. *Contexts*, 9(1), 16–21.

Roth, D., Fredman, L., & Haley, W. (2015). Informal caregiving and its impact on health: A reappraisal from population-based studies. *The Gerontologist*, 55(2), 309–319. doi:10.1093/geront/gnu177

San Antonio, P., Simon-Rusinowitz, L., Loughlin, D., Eckert, J. K., Mahoney, K. J., & Ruben, K. A. D. (2010). Lessons from the Arkansas cash and counseling program: How the experiences of diverse older consumers and their caregivers address family policy concerns. *Journal of Aging & Social Policy*, 22(1), 1–17.

Sherraden, M., Stuart, P., Barth, R. P., Kemp, S., Lubben, J., Hawkins, J. D., . . . Catalano, R. (2014). *Grand accomplishments in social work* (Grand Challenges for Social Work Initiative Working Paper No. 2). Baltimore, MD: American Academy of Social Work and Social Welfare.

Skufca, L. (2014). *Planning for health care costs in retirement: A 2014 survey of 50+ workers*. Washington, DC: AARP. Retrieved from http://www.aarp.org/content/dam/aarp/research/surveys_statistics/econ/2014/Planning-for-Health-Care-Costs-in-Retirement-A-2014-Survey-of-50-Plus-Workers-AARP-econ.pdf

Spera, C., Ghertner, R., Nerino, A., & DiTommaso, A. (2013). *Volunteering as a pathway to employment: Does volunteering increase odds of finding a job for the out of work?* Washington, DC: Corporation for National & Community Service, Office of Research & Evaluation. Retrieved from https://www.nationalservice.gov/sites/default/files/upload/employment_research_report.pdf

Sutin, A. R., Stephen, Y., Carretta, H., & Terracciano, A. (2015). Perceived discrimination and physical, cognitive, and emotional health in older adulthood. *American Journal of Geriatric Psychiatry*, 23(2), 171–179. doi:10.1016/j.jagp.2014.03.007

Svanborg, A. (2001). Biomedical perspectives on productive aging. In N. Morrow-Howell, J. Hinterlong, & M. Sherraden (Eds.), *Productive aging: Concepts and challenges* (pp. 81–101). Baltimore, MD: Johns Hopkins University Press.

Sweet, S., Pitt-Catsouphes, M., & James, J. (2017). Manager attitudes concerning flexible work arrangements: Fixed or changeable? *Community, Work & Family*, 20(1), 50–71. doi:10.1080/13668803.2016.1271311

Tan, E. J., Georges, A., Gabbard, S. M., Pratt, D. J., Nerino, A., Roberts, A. S., . . . Hyde, M. (2016). The 2013–2014 Senior Corps study: Foster grandparents and senior companions. *Public Policy & Aging Report*, 26(3), 88–95. doi:10.1093/ppar/prw016

Tang, F. (2016). Retirement patterns and their relationship to volunteering. *Nonprofit and Voluntary Sector Quarterly*, 45(5), 910–930. doi:10.1177/0899764015602128

Taniguchi, H. (2012). The determinants of formal and informal volunteering: Evidence from the American Time Use Survey. *Voluntas, 23,* 920–939. doi:10.1007/s11266-011-9236-y

Town of Littleton, Massachusetts. (n.d.). *Senior citizen property tax work-off program.* Retrieved from http://www.littletonma.org/filestorage/19479/28346/20201/20312/Senior_Tax__Work-off_Program.pdf

US Census. (2011). *Facts for features: Grandparents Day 2011: Sept. 11.* Retrieved from https://www.census.gov/newsroom/releases/archives/facts_for_features_special_editions/cb11-ff17.html

US Department of Labor, Bureau of Labor Statistics. (2016a). *Household data annual averages: Employment status of the civilian noninstitutional population by age, sex, and race.* Retrieved from https://www.bls.gov/cps/cpsaat03.pdf

US Department of Labor, Bureau of Labor Statistics. (2016b). *Volunteering in the United States—2015.* Retrieved from https://www.bls.gov/news.release/pdf/volun.pdf

Wacker, R. R., & Roberto, K. A. (2013). *Community resources for older adults: Programs and services in an era of change* (4th ed.). Thousand Oaks, CA: Sage.

World Health Organization. (2007). *Active ageing: A policy framework.* Retrieved from http://whqlibdoc.who.int/hq/2002/WHO_NMH_NPH_02.8.pdf

Zedlewski, S. R., & Schaner, S. G. (2006). Older adults engaged as volunteers. *The Retirement Project—Perspectives on Productive Aging, 5,* 1–8. Retrieved from http://www.urban.org/sites/default/files/publication/50556/311325-Older-Adults-Engaged-as-Volunteers.PDF

Zissimopoulos, J., Goldman, D., Olshansky, S., Rother, J., & Rowe, J. (2015). Individual & social strategies to mitigate the risks & expand opportunities of an aging America. *Dædalus, 144*(2), 93–102. doi:10.1162/DAED_a_00333

Grand Challenges
for Social Work
Eradicate social isolation

CHAPTER 6

Eradicate Social Isolation

JAMES E. LUBBEN, ELIZABETH M. TRACY,
SANDRA EDMONDS CREWE, ERIKA L. SABBATH,
MELANIE GIRONDA, CARRIE JOHNSON,
JOOYOUNG KONG, MICHELLE R. MUNSON,
AND SUZANNE BROWN

Social isolation is a potent killer. Public health experts (House, 2001; Pantell et al., 2013) posit that the association between social isolation and health is as strong as the epidemiological evidence that linked smoking and health at the time US Surgeon General C. Everett Koop issued his now-famous warning. Some health researchers report that social isolation is as detrimental to one's health as smoking 15 cigarettes a day (Holt-Lunstad, Smith, & Layton, 2010; Holt-Lunstad, Smith, Baker, Harris, & Stephenson, 2015).

The health risks of social isolation are often studied in adult populations, but isolation can also be deadly for young people (e.g., school shootings perpetrated by individuals described as socially withdrawn). Thus, it is appropriate for social work to strategically address the challenge of social isolation across the lifespan. Working in tandem with other key professions, social workers possess unique expertise to partner in working to greatly reduce the risk and consequences of social isolation.

Americans may be more socially isolated now than ever before. McPherson, Smith-Lovin, and Brashears (2006) compared network structures from 1985 to those of 2004 and found that the number of people in the study who reported not having anyone with whom to discuss important matters nearly tripled. Americans were connected far less tightly. The mean network size decreased from an average of 2.94 to 2.08 people per person, and individuals reported fewer contacts with network members that existed through voluntary associations and neighborhoods. In addition, approximately 10% of elementary school-age children, a developmental period typically expected to be characterized by peer friendships, report perceived social isolation (or loneliness) some or all of the time (Asher & Paquette, 2003). Developmental changes of autonomy and individuation during adolescence may tend to increase the risk of and pose special vulnerabilities for social isolation during this developmental period (Laursen & Hartl, 2013). Indeed, with the advent of numerous social media platforms, studies are reporting increases in cyberbullying and what pediatricians and researchers alike are calling "Facebook depression" (O'Keeffe, Clarke-Pearson, and Council on Communications and Media, 2011).

Among both young and older adult populations, social isolation has been linked with a wide array of health problems ranging from susceptibility to the common cold (Cohen, 2001) to the ability to survive a natural disaster (Pekovic, Seff, & Rothman, 2007; Semenza et al., 1996). A number of health researchers have demonstrated that limited social support networks are associated with increases in both morbidity and mortality (Berkman, 1986; Bosworth & Schaie, 1997; Ceria et al., 2001). Other scholars have reported a significant association between limited social ties and poor overall health and well-being (Chappell, 1991; Krause, Herzog, & Baker, 1992; Lubben, Weiler, & Chi, 1989; Stuck et al., 1999). Still others have documented a connection between social support networks and adherence to desired health practices (Pescosolido, 2011; Pescosolido, Gardner, & Lubell, 1998; Umberson & Montez, 2010). Social isolation has been associated with increased symptoms of psychological distress or loneliness, which may be risk factors for future disease and disability (Lin, Ye, & Ensel, 1999; Thoits, 1995; Wenger, Davies, Shahtahmasebi, & Scott, 1996). Chronic isolation in childhood has been associated with dropping out of school, depression, substance use, and medical problems (Asher & Paquette, 2003). Among marginalized youth and young adults, research has documented that the presence of a supportive adult, such as a mentor, natural mentor, or extended relative, can improve psychological and social outcomes (Thompson, Greeson, & Brunsink, 2016).

Isolation is also associated with an array of social problems. Stigmatization and labeling are linked to social isolation across the lifespan (Crewe & Guyot-Diagnone, 2016; Kranke, Floersch, Kranke, & Munson, 2011). Victor, Scambler, Bond, and Bowling (2000) note that loneliness itself is a stigma. Race, class, and neighborhood effects have been associated with increased isolation, thereby constraining social resources (Tigges, Browne, & Green, 1998).

EVIDENCE INDICATES THAT SOCIAL ISOLATION CAN BE REDUCED

As a result of the overwhelming body of evidence, a special committee at the National Institutes of Health (National Research Council [NRC], 2001) issued a report in 2001 that identifies a domain of behavioral and social sciences research questions whose resolution could lead to major improvements in the health of the US population. The NRC report lists *personal ties* as one of the top 10 priority areas for research investment that could lead to major health improvements. It summarizes a growing body of epidemiological findings that link social relationships with mental and physical health outcomes, including mortality. Furthermore, the report explores how disruption of personal ties, loneliness, and conflictual interactions produce stress, and it discusses how supportive social ties are vital sources of emotional well-being.

Since the publication of the NRC report, evidence regarding the impact of social isolation on various measures of morbidity and mortality has grown even stronger (Berkman, 2009; Eng, Rimm, Fitzmaurice, & Kawachi, 2002; Giles, Glonek, Luszcz, & Andres, 2005; Holt-Lunstad et al., 2010; Lubben et al., 2006; Pantell et al., 2013; Schnittger, Wherton, Prendergast, & Lawlor, 2012; Zhang, Norris, Gregg, & Beckles, 2007). Similarly, researchers have further documented the negative consequences of social isolation on mental health (Adams, Sanders, & Auth, 2004; Alspach, 2013; Esgalhado, Reis, Pereira, & Afonso, 2010). There has also been increased evidence of the impact of social isolation on self-reported health and well-being (Chan, Malhotra, Malhotra, & Ostbye, 2011; Kimura, Yamazaki, Haga, & Yasumura, 2013; McHugh & Lawlor, 2012; Schnittger et al., 2012).

Social Isolation in Children and Youth

Attachment and social functioning that are formed early in life have profound impacts on the ways that individuals interface with the social world throughout their lives (Bowlby, 1969). Early attachments inform one's ability to form and maintain strong relationships. Research suggests that the sensitive period in which social connections can most benefit health and well-being may occur at younger ages than was once hypothesized (Berkman, 2009). For example, strong social support networks are particularly important to mental health and preventing behavioral problems (McPherson et al., 2014). Social connections can help parents cope with stress and also influence parent–child relationships (Quittner, Glueckauf, & Jackson, 1990). Caregivers who know people on whom they can rely for child care advice and assistance have been found to be more sensitive to their infant's needs and able to have higher quality interactions with their infants (Green, Furrer, & McAllister, 2007). The infants, in turn, are less avoidant of interactions. Social connections of the caregivers, then, have direct and indirect effects on child development.

In particular, social isolation has been associated with increased risk of depressive symptoms, suicide attempts, and low self-esteem in young people (Hall-Lande, Eisenberg, Christenson, & Neumark-Sztainer, 2007). In fact, the

Centers for Disease Control and Prevention has focused on increasing "connectedness" among youth as an orienting framework due to its fundamental understanding about the importance of social relationships on overall health and well-being, including decreasing suicide (Whitlock, Wyman, & Moore, 2014). In a large national child development study in the United Kingdom, researchers found that social isolation in childhood is associated with higher levels of C-reactive protein (an indicator of coronary heart disease) in midlife (Lacey, Jumari, & Bartley, 2014). Finally, social isolation in younger people may ultimately threaten the safety and well-being of others when negative emotions are externalized. This has been documented in the cases of many adolescent mass murderers who were retrospectively described as socially isolated or ostracized from peers (Levin & Madfis, 2009).

There are many groups of children who are at heighted risk for social isolation during critical periods of their development. Overweight adolescents, for example, are more likely to be socially isolated and on the periphery of social networks (Strauss & Pollack, 2003). Research has documented the degree to which youth with an autism spectrum disorder are vulnerable both to social isolation and to bullying (Bauminger, Shulman, & Agam, 2003; Rowley et al., 2012). Research on the friendship patterns of children with autism spectrum disorders also reveals the intersection of race, disability, and grade; one study of friendship patterns among children with autism spectrum disorder found that children who were African American and Latino received the fewest friendship nominations and also that Latino children in upper grades were at the highest risk for social isolation (Azad, Locke, Kasari, & Mandell, 2017).

The estimated 5.5 million children and adolescents raised by unauthorized immigrants are at increased risk of social isolation because fear of detainment leads families to not take advantage of social services and to not encourage or allow their children to be involved with after-school or community activities (Chavez, Lopez, Englebrecht, & Viramontez Anguiano, 2012). In one Canadian study, 1 in 10 immigrant children were socially isolated (Oxman-Martinez et al., 2012), and this social isolation combined with ethnic discrimination was associated with children's self-esteem, sense of academic competence, and actual academic performance. Many immigrant parents are not aware that their US-born children are eligible for benefits (Yoshikawa & Kalil, 2011). The result is that the 1 in 5 American children who have a foreign-born parent have restricted access to contexts that support development—child care, preschool, school, work, and so on (Suarez-Orozco, Yoshikawa, Teranishi, & Suarez-Orozco, 2011). Another group of children and youth at risk of social isolation due to discrimination and social exclusion are lesbian, gay, bisexual, and transgender (LGBT) youth. Johnson and Amella (2014) identified the following dimensions of social isolation common among LGBT youth: emotional isolation, cognitive isolation, concealment of identify, and recognition of self as different. Transgender youth may be particularly isolated from family support due to transphobic attitudes within social networks that lead to less social support availability (Mizock & Lewis, 2008).

Young people who are considered "marginalized" and who are involved in the child welfare system are also at tremendous risk for high levels of social isolation because they are often removed from their homes and experience high levels of transience during their child and adolescent years. Initial loss, complicated by repeated losses that can cause trauma and challenges with emotion regulation, can create challenges for these young people in forming healthy relationships (Cummings & Cicchetti, 1990).

Social Isolation in Older Adults

Social isolation among older adults is becoming increasingly recognized as a critical issue worthy of more attention. The AARP Foundation (2016) reported that social isolation is a growing epidemic in America, affecting more than 8 million older adults.

Recent research has demonstrated that social isolation is a significant risk factor for cognitive impairment and dementia (Crooks, Lubben, Petitti, Little, & Chiu, 2008; Ertel, Glymour, & Berkman, 2008; Maki et al., 2012; Seeman, Lusignolo, Albert, & Berkman, 2001). Acierno et al. (2010) found that low social support increased the likelihood of elder mistreatment, which, in addition to the human costs of such abuse, carries financial costs of approximately $12 million dollars annually (Dong & Simon, 2011). Victims of elder abuse are three times more likely to be admitted to a hospital (Dong & Simon, 2013).

Two specific isolating factors tied to the increasing risk of elder mistreatment are loss of friends and perceived social alienation from the community (Von Heydrich, Schiamberg, & Chee, 2012). For some vulnerable older adults, living with a caregiver, particularly with a spouse, is also associated with an increased risk of abuse (Beach et al., 2005; Cooney, Howard, & Lawlor, 2006; Paveza et al., 1992), suggesting that an isolated dyad, outside of a larger support structure, especially places people at risk for being either the victim or the potential perpetrator of mistreatment. In addition to physical or mental abuse, socially isolated older adults are also highly vulnerable to financial scams and manipulations.

A relatively recent AARP report synthesized research findings about social isolation in older populations (AARP Foundation, 2012). The report identified key risk factors for social isolation: physical or functional impairments, particularly for older adults who lack instrumental support (e.g., transportation); low socioeconomic status; and poor mental health status (e.g., depression and cognitive impairments). As a result, AARP initiated a campaign to raise awareness about social isolation and stimulate more intervention research on the topic (AARP Foundation, 2012). In 2016, the AARP Foundation announced the Connect2Affect campaign to draw more attention to social isolation.

Historical Progress of Research on Social Isolation

The research on social isolation has made remarkable progress since Lisa Berkman and Leonard Syme published their seminal article in the *American Journal of Epidemiology* in 1979. Their research examined the connection between social networks and mortality among a general adult population (Berkman & Syme, 1979). They constructed the Berkman–Syme Social Network Index (SNI) for this research by summing up whether or not a respondent (1) was married, (2) belonged to a church or temple, (3) participated in clubs or organized groups, and (4) had social contact with family or friends. Remarkably, this relatively simple SNI measure was significantly correlated with mortality rates in this 9-year follow-up epidemiological study.

Soon thereafter, health researchers across the board scrambled to replicate these results using various proxies for social networks. Some of the selected proxies (e.g., marital status and living alone) failed to capture important nuances of social connections, so health researchers spent the 1980s and 1990s refining measures for social networks and supports. The central goal of this process was to determine which aspects of an individual's social connections should be measured and which dimensions or perceptions of those relationships are particularly relevant for predicting subsequent morbidity and mortality.

One distinction is related to the sources of social support. *Primary social groups* (e.g., family, friends, and neighbors) are the foundation of social ties across the lifespan, particularly in youth and old age. Family is generally considered the most central primary group to which an individual belongs. However, close or intimate friends can also be as vital as family ties, especially when family relations are geographically unavailable, strained, or deficient for other reasons. Alternative family arrangements and the formation of non-married couples—especially as social norms and practices of family formation change—impart new complexity to quantifying social connections. *Secondary social groups* include membership organizations such as recreational or culture clubs, professional societies, and various political and religious organizations. The workplace is an important forum for social relationships, and for individuals who are otherwise isolated, it can serve as a regular form of social contact and connection. There is evidence that those who maintain contact with colleagues from their workplace after retirement are less depressed.

The distinction between primary and secondary social groups is relevant to understand major approaches to measuring social isolation. For example, many social researchers tend to examine social networks through a lens that measures participation in social activities and organizations, whereas clinical researchers have largely focused on primary social groups. The SNI (Berkman & Syme, 1979; Pantell et al., 2013), a common instrument in public health research, is a classic example of a measure that emphasizes secondary social groups. The Lubben Social Network Scale (Lubben, 1988; Lubben & Gironda, 2003; Lubben et al., 2006; Rubenstein, Lubben, & Mintzer, 1994) is an example of a measure of social isolation that focuses on primary group membership, so it has particularly found favor with social workers, health practitioners, and clinical researchers.

Although there are differences in focus, researchers can now draw from a wide array of social network measures with excellent psychometric properties (Berkman, Kawachi, & Glymour, 2014). A number of sociometric surveys are used to study social isolation in children by mapping peer interactions as well as peer acceptance in social settings, such as in the classroom. There is also a growing body of social network analysis techniques to study the composition, functioning, and structure of social networks (Rice & Yoshioka-Maxwell, 2015; Tracy & Brown, 2011; Tracy & Whittaker, 2015). Remarkably, the connection between social isolation and health remains quite consistent despite the lack of consistency in measuring both social support networks and health outcomes. Such diversity of studies adds significance to the convergence of their findings.

Research Efforts to Overcome Social Isolation

In 2001, House concluded that social isolation kills, but how and why it does damage were very much unknown. The developmental period in which isolation may disproportionately affect later disease risk was also very much unknown. In addition, the extent to which social isolation's health effects are reversible if isolation is successfully reduced remained unknown (House, 2001).

Since 2001, researchers have made progress in understanding these basic questions. Nicholson (2012) reported a systematic review of 70 studies that examined the negative impact of isolation on a wide array of outcome measures. He concluded that social isolation is an important but underassessed condition, as well as a risk factor for other conditions. Dickens, Richards, Greaves, and Campbell (2011) performed a systematic review of 32 intervention studies that targeted isolation among older adults. Although some intervention trials failed to modify desired behaviors or downstream health outcomes (e.g., ENRICHD Investigators, 2001), other clinical interventions reported success (e.g., Nicholson, 2009). Overall in their systematic review, Dickens et al. found that 79% of group-based interventions and 55% of one-on-one interventions reported at least one improved participant outcome.

Berkman and associates (Berkman, Glass, Brissette, & Seeman, 2000; Berkman et al., 2014) proposed four key pathways to explain apparent links between social isolation and health: (1) provision of social support, (2) social influence, (3) social engagement and attachment, and (4) access to resources. For example, social networks may provide essential support needed during times of illness, thereby contributing to better adaptation and quicker recovery time. Social ties can be instrumental in adherence to good health practices and the cessation of bad ones (Umberson & Montez, 2010). The role of social networks in helping persons with substance use disorders maintain sobriety has been well documented (Stone, Jason, Light, & Stevens, 2016). Strong social bonds may offer a stress-buffering effect that reduces the susceptibility of an individual to stress-related illnesses (Cassel, 1976; Cobb, 1976; Krause et al., 1992; Thoits, 1995). Social connections might also provide improved access to important resources such as relevant health knowledge, timely care, or transportation to and from health care appointments. Relatively recent research explored possible biological effects of social ties on human physiology, perhaps by stimulating the immune system to ward off illnesses more effectively (Seeman, Singer, Ryff, Dienberg Love, & Levy-Storms, 2002). There is also evidence from neuroimaging studies that social exclusion "hurts" in a similar way in the brain as physical pain (Eisenberger, Lieberman, & Williams, 2003).

Social Isolation in Health Care Settings

Although there is extensive evidence that links social ties to health and well-being, this body of research is only beginning to change social work practice (Gironda & Lubben, 2002). In health care settings, minimal attention is given to social health status compared to that given to other attributes people present when seeking care. Specifically, the health care system shows much more regard for the physical and mental health dimensions of patients while giving only minor attention to the social health dimensions of patients.

As identified in *Introduction and Context for Grand Challenges in Social Work* (Sherraden et al., 2015), when comparing social and health expenditures, the ratio averages 2:1 among the Organization for Economic Co-operation and Development (OECD) countries; however, it is only 0.8:1 in the United States, indicating that health spending is crowding out social and educational spending (Kaplan, 2013). This marginal concern for social health is demonstrated in many health care encounters. For example, geriatric assessment has been called the "heart and soul" of geriatric practice (Solomon, 2000, p. ix). However, geriatric assessment instruments seldom deal with social health matters, suggesting that they are not perceived to be central to geriatric practice. Although health care providers have made great strides in getting patients to understand that their mental health is as important as physical health, health professionals have yet to devote sufficient attention to getting people to value the importance of their social health.

Therefore, indicators of a person's social health should be a part of assessment protocols along with mental and physical health markers (Lubben & Gironda, 2003; Pantell et al., 2013). In an era that stresses community-based delivery of health care, members of a person's social support network are often more responsible for successful execution of treatment plans than are members of the formal health care team. For isolated older adults, social supports often end up being the in-home care managers who monitor compliance with treatment regimens and provide early detection of new problems that require intervention. Accordingly, in-depth quality assistance from close supportive relationships should be facilitated and encouraged throughout the health care process.

Increased sensitivity to the importance of social support networks might help identify those individuals in need of a more comprehensive assessment from a social worker or another health or mental health care practitioner. As community health nurses are being urged to screen home health clients and assisted living residents for social isolation (Tremethick, 2001), other practitioners should be encouraged to similarly adopt such practice protocols. A practitioner's focus on the importance of social connections can also increase the patient's or client's attention to his or her own social health. Similarly, those working with families can assess the extent to which the family has supports and resources for parenting. In addition, attention to the growing racial/ethnic differences between the care providers and the residents of assisted living is important in addressing social isolation. Cultural and linguistic differences can contribute to isolation, and cultural competence training can maximize positive encounters.

MEANINGFUL AND MEASURABLE PROGRESS TO ADDRESS SOCIAL ISOLATION CAN BE MADE IN THE NEXT DECADE

The coming decade provides an opportunity to develop and test specific interventions that rebuild the fabric of frayed social connections in both older adults and younger people. With a Grand Challenge focus on social isolation, social workers could better consolidate the existing knowledge about social isolation and initiate a paradigm shift in the practice community. The possibilities of such a concerted effort are suggested in a website launched by AARP that provides practical hints regarding what can be done to address social isolation (AARP Foundation, 2012). Another approach for aging populations can be found in the WHO Age-Friendly Communities movement (WHO, 2007). In the United States, the Village models of age-friendly communities attempt to fabricate new social ties to replace those lost or frayed among older adults wishing to remain in their long-term communities as they age (Scharlach, Davitt, Lehning, Greenfield, & Graham, 2014).

Another example is a community-based intervention called Eliciting Change in At-Risk Elders (ECARE), which is aimed at building resilience in response to extreme stressors and lowering the risk of elder abuse. This program assists suspected victims of elder abuse and self-neglect with building connections with family members and support services in their communities (Mariam, McClure, Robinson, & Yang, 2015). In an evaluation of the program, results showed that risk factors of elder abuse, including isolation, decreased over the course of the intervention.

Another example of efforts to modify social work practice can be gleaned from an open access social isolation module developed by the Institute on Aging at Boston College (2017) in conjunction with the Hartford Center of Excellence at the Boston College School of Social Work. This online module includes YouTube videos and links to other references that inform both lay and professional people about the importance of addressing social isolation, and it offers suggestions for interventions. The online module has been used by local and national health and social agencies to train their staff and is available to the general public.

Examples of innovative approaches to address isolation among younger populations also exist. Social isolation in children and youth differs from that in adults because children and youth have certain mandates for social participation, namely enrollment in educational programs that offer some degree of social inclusion. Young people differ from adults in terms of how and where they develop social connections (Morgan, 2010). Strong school connectedness has been shown to reduce the risk of depressive symptoms, suicide attempts, and low self-esteem among youth (Hall-Lande et al., 2007). Building connections to enable all students to feel less isolated through school-based universal support programs has also been proposed as one way to address bullying in school (Newman, Holden, & Delville, 2005). Furthermore, youth mentoring, both formal and informal, is an approach that is increasingly illustrating efficacy among varying groups of youth in improving health outcomes and psychosocial outcomes (Ahrens, DuBois, Richardson, Fan, & Lozano, 2008; Munson & McMillen, 2009; Thompson et al., 2016).

Researchers have also demonstrated a link between childhood trauma and health effects of social isolation in later life. In a study that examined whether perceived social isolation moderates the relationship between early trauma and pulse pressure (a marker for cardiovascular health), it was found that those with higher levels of perceived social isolation showed a significant positive association between childhood trauma and pulse pressure (Norman, Hawkley, Ball, Berntson, & Cacioppo, 2013). Accordingly, more attention is required to assess for social isolation among the victims of child abuse and neglect. Violence, including bullying among children and youth, also has a social isolation component. The Centers for Disease Control and Prevention launched a program to reduce youth violence that includes a component that attempts to build positive relationships between youth and adults and peers (David-Ferdon & Simon, 2012). Peer support is also increasingly being integrated into psychosocial interventions for youth who are often socially marginalized, such as youth with serious mental health challenges (Gopalan, Lee, Harris, Acri, & Munson, 2017) and those aging out of foster care (Geenen et al., 2013).

MEETING THE CHALLENGE OF SOCIAL ISOLATION WILL REQUIRE INTERDISCIPLINARY AND CROSS-SECTOR COLLABORATION

The approach to solve social isolation needs to be more inclusive and incorporate diverse populations. Studies of social isolation tend to focus on older populations, but social isolation is an important issue for all ages. The impact of "otherness" and stigma are important considerations when addressing social isolation. In addition, researchers should pay more attention to socially marginalized groups, especially those exposed to generational poverty. This will require an interdisciplinary, multisystem approach that considers social isolation not only at the individual level but also at the familial, community, and societal levels. For example, enhancing social inclusion for older adults has to be a part of creating aging-friendly community environments, which will provide more sustainable and comprehensive solutions for the population (Scharlach et al., 2014).

Similarly, there will need to be more interdisciplinary cooperation to address the complexity of social isolation. Much of the scholarship to date has been conducted in disciplinary silos, but cross-sector and interdisciplinary approaches are crucial for moving to the next level of understanding. A preliminary taxonomy of these disciplinary silos includes (1) epidemiologists focused on identifying at-risk populations and subpopulations, (2) health service researchers focused on "controlling for" social isolation in their models rather than seeking to understand the phenomena, (3) biologists and neuroscientists examining biological pathways that account for the linkage between isolation and health consequences, and (4) clinical researchers focused on developing and testing interventions with limited capacity to digest all of the new information from the other disciplinary silos. Adopting social isolation as a Grand Challenge will motivate and empower social workers to take the lead on this enterprise and to break down these disciplinary barriers to improve the flow of knowledge and innovation across groups.

The Role of Social Work

Social work is well positioned for interdisciplinary research on social isolation. Most schools of social work are housed at universities with easy access to other disciplines and professions, making them conducive to networking and collaboration. Given their community-based practice orientation, social workers are generally well integrated in communities. Social workers have been doing community-based and person-centered research for many years. It has now become mandatory in clinical effectiveness research funded by the Patient-Centered Outcomes Research Institute (PCORI) through the Patient Protection and Affordable Care Act of 2010. Specifically, key users of study information (e.g., patients, caregivers, clinicians, community members, and policymakers) are now expected to be active members of the research "team" (Selby, Beal, & Frank, 2012), putting social workers in a pivotal role of bringing key stakeholders to the table.

Although this may be a new approach for some disciplines, social work researchers have a long history of community-based participatory research with an interdisciplinary approach. Sabir et al. (2009) suggested community-based research on transportation barriers, psychiatric disabilities, varying types of communities, and multicomponent and person-centered interventions. Recommended future research priority areas include (1) the need to understand use of service (or, more to the point, non-use), (2) measures to identify isolated adults during a community crisis (e.g., disaster relief), (3) evaluation of direct or indirect contact interventions, (4) efficacy of multicomponent interventions, and (5) research that reflects respect for continuing self-determination in older adulthood. These are all areas of research in which social work has been involved that can accommodate an interdisciplinary focus.

OVERCOMING SOCIAL ISOLATION REQUIRES SIGNIFICANT INNOVATION

Reducing the incidence of social isolation will require innovation to develop and test individual- and societal-level interventions. For example, social workers can explore new social media technologies to test innovative interventions that reweave frayed networks and provide lifelines to vulnerable isolated individuals. As stated in *Context for Grand Challenges*, "It is not overstating to say that we live in a time of emergence of new social worlds of social media, social networks, and other social engagements via internet technology" (Sherraden et al., 2015, p. 5).

In addition, there is a critical need for innovative approaches that make use of new mobile technologies. For example, a Pew Research Center 2012 survey reported that fully 85% of adults in the United States own a cell phone. Of those, 53% own smartphones. Approximately one-third of cell phone owners (31%) have used their phones to search for health information, which is almost double the rate (17%) reported in a Pew survey conducted just 2 years earlier. Every major demographic group experienced significant year-to-year growth in smartphone ownership. This changing means of communication and information-seeking requires new approaches to reducing isolation that are nimble to our quickly evolving technological landscape.

Currently, there is a multitude of mobile device health apps created for a variety of health issues. The challenge is to understand how information technology can be used to enhance social connections among vulnerable populations. The use of newer information and communication technologies (e.g., Internet social networking services) can be particularly beneficial for some groups to address social isolation. For example, several studies have found that adults with physical and functional health decline combat loneliness and increase a sense of connectedness by using computers (Clark, 2002; Gatto & Tak, 2008; Sayago & Blat, 2010). In a review of literature that examines the potential for social networks and support to enhance tele-health interventions for people with a diagnosis of schizophrenia, most studies focused on improving medical adherence, providing medical information, and monitoring symptoms. However, the benefits of technology for mobilizing resources for self-management and peer support were evident but more peripheral (Daker-White & Rogers, 2013). In a meta-analysis of the effect of Internet group support for family caregivers, 10 peer-reviewed studies were identified showing that Internet support groups have a positive effect on social support and self-efficacy (Oliver et al., 2017).

Social isolation is inextricably linked to social and environmental justice. Conditions that breed poverty and economic insecurity also contribute to social isolation. Interventions aimed at eradicating social isolation should be mindful of how to address social stigmas, such as mental health, HIV/AIDS, poverty, and otherness, that can result in social isolation. Accordingly, strategies to eradicate social isolation must also include advocacy to address a range of social justice issues, including poverty and racism, that present barriers to access to services. The Grand Challenges for Social Work aimed at reducing extreme economic insecurity, achieving equal opportunity and justice, and ending homelessness offer additional valuable context for addressing critically important structural dimensions that are associated with social isolation.

CONCLUSION

In 1979, the World Health Organization (WHO) noted that social isolation needed to be addressed as a major health risk factor. Twenty-two years later,

WHO reaffirmed the importance of addressing social isolation in a report on active aging (WHO, 2002), and it did so again in its Age Friendly Communities initiative (WHO, 2007). The importance of social ties—the inverse of social isolation—has been affirmed as a top 10 area for future National Institutes of Health research investment (NRC, 2001). AARP has recently adopted it as one of its top 5 new initiatives (AARP Foundation, 2012). It is fitting and timely for social work to adopt social isolation as one of its grand challenges. Social work has the unique capacity to work with complex systems and generate research that can bridge disciplinary silos that currently impede a complete understanding of social isolation.

The American Academy of Social Work and Social Welfare's adoption of social isolation as a grand challenge will undoubtedly elevate this domain among practitioners and their clients and patients. Indeed, the social element of social work is essential for solving the grand challenge of reducing the risk of social isolation among all populations.

REFERENCES

AARP Foundation. (2012). *Framework for isolation in adults over 50*. Retrieved from http://www.aarp.org/content/dam/aarp/aarp_foundation/2012_PDFs/AARP-Foundation-Isolation-Framework-Report.pdf

AARP Foundation. (2016). Connect2Affect campaign. Retrieved from https://www.aarp.org/about-aarp/press-center/info-12-2016/aarp-foundation-draws-attention-social-isolation-with-launch-connect2affect.html and https://connect2affect.org

Acierno, R., Hernandez, M. A., Amstadter, A. B., Resnick, H. S., Steve, K., Muzzy, W., & Kilpatrick, D. G. (2010). Prevalence and correlates of emotional, physical, sexual, and financial abuse and potential neglect in the United States: The National Elder Mistreatment Study. *American Journal of Public Health, 100*(2), 292–297. doi:10.2105/AJPH.2009.163089

Adams, K., Sanders, S., & Auth, E. (2004). Loneliness and depression in independent living retirement communities: Risk and resilience factors. *Aging & Mental Health, 8*(6), 475–485.

Ahrens, K. R., DuBois, D. L., Richardson, L. P., Fan, M. Y., & Lozano, P. (2008). Youth in foster care with adult mentors during adolescence have improved adult outcomes. *Pediatrics, 121*, e246–e252.

Alspach, J. (2013). Loneliness and social isolation: Risk factors long overdue for surveillance. *Critical Care Nurse, 33*(6), 8–13. doi:10.4037/ccn2013377

Asher, S. R., & Paquette, J. A. (2003). Loneliness and peer relations in childhood. *Current Directions in Psychological Science, 12*(3), 75–78. doi:10.1111/1467-8721.01233

Azad, G. F., Locke, J., Kasari, C., & Mandell, D. S. (2017). Race, disability, and grade: Social relationships in children with autism spectrum disorders. *Autism, 21*(1), 92–99. doi:10.1177/1362361315627792

Bauminger, N., Shulman, C., & Agam, G. (2003). Peer interaction and loneliness in high-functioning children with autism. *Journal of Autism and Developmental Disorders, 33*(5), 489–507. doi:10.1023/A:1025827427901

Beach, S. R., Schulz, R., Williamson, G. M., Miller, L. S., Weiner, M. F., & Lance, C. E. (2005). Risk factors for potentially harmful informal caregiver behavior. *Journal of the American Geriatrics Society*, 53(2), 255–261. doi:10.1111/j.1532-5415.2005.53111.x

Berkman, L. F. (1986). Social networks, support and health: Taking the next step forward. *American Journal of Epidemiology*, 123, 559–562.

Berkman, L. F. (2009). Social epidemiology: Social determinants of health in the United States: Are we losing ground? *Annual Review of Public Health*, 30, 27–41.

Berkman, L. F., Glass, T., Brissette, I., & Seeman, T. E. (2000). From social integration to health: Durkheim in the new millennium. *Social Science and Medicine*, 51(6), 843–857.

Berkman, L. F., Kawachi, I., & Glymour, M. (2014). *Social epidemiology* (2nd ed.). New York, NY: Oxford University Press.

Berkman, L. F., & Syme, S. L. (1979). Social networks, host resistance, and mortality: A nine-year follow-up study of Alameda County residents. *American Journal of Epidemiology*, 109, 186–204.

Bosworth, H. B., & Schaie, K. W. (1997). The relationship of social environment, social networks, and health outcomes in the Seattle Longitudinal Study: Two analytical approaches. *Journal of Gerontology: Psychological Sciences*, 52B, P197–P205.

Bowlby, J. (1969). *Attachment and loss volume 1: Attachment*. London, UK: Hogarth.

Cassel, J. (1976). The contribution of the social environment to host resistance. *American Journal of Epidemiology*, 104(2), 107–123.

Ceria, C. D., Masaki, K. H., Rodriguez, B. L., Chen, R., Yano, K., & Curb, J. D. (2001). The relationship of psychosocial factors to total mortality among older Japanese American men: The Honolulu Heart Program. *Journal of the American Geriatrics Society*, 49, 725–731.

Chan, A., Malhotra, C., Malhotra, R., & Ostbye, T. (2011). Living arrangements, social networks and depressive symptoms among older men and women in Singapore. *International Journal of Geriatric Psychiatry*, 26, 630–639. doi:10.1002/gps.2574

Chappell, N. L. (1991). Living arrangements and sources of caregiving. *Journal of Gerontology: Social Sciences*, 46, S1–S8.

Chavez, J. M., Lopez, A., Englebrecht, C. M., & Viramontez Anguiano, R. P. (2012). Sufren los niños: Exploring the impact of unauthorized immigration status on children's well-being. *Family Court Review*, 50(4), 638–649. doi:10.1111/j.1744-1617.2012.01482.x

Clark, D. J. (2002). Older adults living through and with their computers. *CIN: Computers, Informatics, Nursing*, 20, 117–124.

Cobb, S. (1976). Social support as a moderator of life stress. *Psychosomatic Medicine*, 38(5), 300–313.

Cohen, S. (2001). Social relationships and susceptibility to the common cold. In C. D. Ryff & B. S. Singer (Eds.), *Emotion, social relationships and health* (pp. 221–232). New York, NY: Oxford University Press.

Cooney, C., Howard, R., & Lawlor, B. (2006). Abuse of vulnerable people with dementia by their carers: Can we identify those most at risk? *International Journal of Geriatric Psychiatry*, 21(6), 564–571. doi:10.1002/gps.1525

Crewe, S. E., & Guyot-Diagnone, J. (2016). Stigmatization and labelling. In *Encyclopedia of social work* [Online publication]. Washington, DC/New York, NY: National Association of Social Workers Press/Oxford University Press. doi:10.1093/acrefore/9780199975839.013.1043

Crooks, V., Lubben, J., Petitti, D., Little, D., & Chiu, V. (2008). Social network, cognitive function, and dementia incidence among elderly women. *American Journal of Public Health, 98*(7), 1221–1227. doi:10.2105/AJPH.2007.115923

Cummings, E. M., & Cicchetti, D. (1990). Toward a transactional model of relations between attachment and depression. In M. T. Greenberg, D. Cicchetti, & E. M. Cummings (Eds.), *Attachment in the preschool years* (pp. 339–374). Chicago, IL: University of Chicago.

Daker-White, G., & Rogers, A. (2013). What is the potential for social networks and support to enhance future telehealth interventions for people with a diagnosis of schizophrenia: A critical interpretive synthesis. *BMC Psychiatry, 13*(1), 279.

David-Ferdon, C., & Simon, T. R. (2012). *Striving to Reduce Youth Violence Everywhere (STRYVE): The Centers for Disease Control and Prevention's national initiative to prevent youth violence foundational resource.* Atlanta, GA: Centers for Disease Control and Prevention.

Dickens, A. P., Richards, S. H., Greaves, C. J., & Campbell, J. L. (2011). Interventions targeting social isolation in older people: A systematic review. *BMC Public Health, 11*, 647. doi:10.1186/1471-2458-11-647

Dong, X. Q., & Simon, M. A. (2011). Enhancing national policy and programs to address elder abuse. *JAMA, 305*(23), 2460–2461.

Dong, X. Q., & Simon, M. A. (2013). Elder abuse as a risk factor for hospitalization in older persons. *JAMA Internal Medicine, 173*(10), 911–917. doi:10.1001/jamainternmed.2013.238

Eisenberger, N. I., Lieberman, M. D., & Williams, K. D. (2003). Does rejection hurt? An fMRI study of social exclusion. *Science, 302*(5643), 290–292. doi:10.1126/science.1089134

Eng, P., Rimm, E., Fitzmaurice, G., & Kawachi, I. (2002). Social ties and change in social ties in relation to subsequent total and cause-specific mortality and coronary heart disease incidence in men. *American Journal of Epidemiology, 155*(8), 700–709.

ENRICHD Investigators. (2001). Enhancing Recovery in Coronary Heart Disease (ENRICHD) study intervention. *Psychosomatic Medicine, 63*, 747–755.

Ertel, K. A., Glymour, M. M., & Berkman, L. F. (2008). Effects of social integration on preserving memory function in a nationally representative US elderly population. *American Journal of Public Health, 98*(7), 1215–1220. doi:10.2105/AJPH.2007.113654

Esgalhado, M., Reis, M., Pereira, H., & Afonso, R. (2010). Influence of social support on the psychological well-being and mental health of older adults living in assisted-living residences. *International Journal of Developmental and Educational Psychology, 1*, 267–278.

Gatto, S. L., & Tak, S. H. (2008). Computer, Internet, and e-mail use among older adults: Benefits and barriers. *Educational Gerontology, 34*, 800–811.

Geenen, S., Powers, L. E., Powers, J., Cunningham, M., McMahon, L., Nelson, M., . . . Fullerton, A. (2013). Experimental study of a self-determination intervention for youth in foster care. *Career Development and Transition for Exceptional Individuals, 36*(2), 84–95.

Giles, L., Glonek, G., Luszcz, M., & Andres, G. (2005). Effect of social networks on 10-year survival in very old Australians: The Australian Longitudinal Study of Aging. *Journal of Epidemiology & Community Health, 59*(7), 574–579.

Gironda, M., & Lubben, J. (2002). Preventing loneliness and isolation in older adulthood. In T. Gullotta & M. Bloom (Eds.), *Encyclopedia of primary prevention and health promotion* (pp. 20–34). New York, NY: Kluwer /Plenum.

Gopalan, G., Lee, S. J., Harris R., Acri, M. C., & Munson, M. R. (2017). Utilization of peers in services for youth with emotional and behavioral challenges: A scoping review. *Journal of Adolescence, 55*, 88–115.

Green, B. L., Furrer, C., & McAllister, C. (2007). How do relationships support parenting? Effects of attachment style and social support on parenting behavior in an at-risk population. *American Journal of Community Psychology, 40*(1–2), 96–108. doi:10.1007/s10464-007-9127-y

Hall-Lande, J. A., Eisenberg, M. E., Christenson, L. S., & Neumark-Sztainer, D. (2007). Social isolation, psychological health, and protective factors in adolescence. *Adolescence, 42*(166), 265–286.

Holt-Lunstad, J., Smith, T., Baker, M., Harris, T., & Stephenson, D. (2015). Loneliness and social isolation as risk factors for mortality: A meta-analytic review. *Perspectives on Psychological Science, 10*(2), 227–237. doi:10.1177/1745691614568352

Holt-Lunstad, J., Smith, T., & Layton, B. (2010). Social relationships and mortality risk: A meta-analytic review. *PLOS Medicine, 7*(7), e1000316. doi:10.1371/journal.pmed.1000316

House, J. S. (2001). Social isolation kills, but how and why? *Psychosomatic Medicine, 63*, 273–274.

Institute on Aging at Boston College. (2017, June 6). *Module 1: Social isolation.* Retrieved from http://www.bc.edu/centers/ioa/videos/social-isolation.html

Johnson, M. J., & Amella, E. J. (2014). Isolation of lesbian, gay, bisexual and transgender youth: A dimensional concept analysis. *Journal of Advanced Nursing, 70*(3), 523–532. doi:10.1111/jan.12212

Kaplan, R. (2013, January). *Stimulating the science of social work thinking.* Paper presented at the annual conference of the Society for Social Work and Research, San Diego, CA.

Kimura, M., Yamazaki, S., Haga, H., & Yasumura, S. (2013). The prevalence of social engagement in the disabled elderly and related factors. *ISRN Geriatrics*, Article ID 709823. doi:10.1155/2013/709823

Kranke, D., Floersch, J. E., Kranke, B., & Munson, M. R. (2011). A qualitative investigation of self-stigma among adolescents taking psychiatric medications. *Psychiatric Services, 62*(8), 893–899.

Krause, N., Herzog, A. R., & Baker, E. (1992). Providing support to others and well-being in later life. *Journal of Gerontology: Psychological Sciences, 47*, P300–P311.

Lacey, R. E., Jumari, M., & Bartley M. (2014). Social isolation in childhood and adult inflammation: Evidence from the National Child Development Study. *Psychoneuroendocrinology, 50*, 85–94.

Laursen, B., & Hartl, A. (2013). Understanding loneliness during adolescence: Developmental changes that increase the risk of perceived social isolation. *Journal of Adolescence, 36*(6), 1261–1268. doi:10.1016/j.adolescence.2013.06.003

Levin, J., & Madfis, E. (2009). Mass murder at school and cumulative strain: A sequential model. *American Behavioral Scientist, 52*(9), 1227–1245.

Lubben, J. E. (1988). Assessing social networks among elderly populations. *Family and Community Health, 11*, 42–52.

Lubben, J. E., Blozik, E., Gillmann, G., Iliffe, S., von Renteln Kruse, W., Beck, J., & Stuck, A. (2006). Performance of an abbreviated version of the Lubben Social Network Scale among three European community-dwelling older adult populations. *The Gerontologist, 46*(4), 503–513. doi.org/10.1093/geront/46.4.503

Lubben, J. E., & Gironda, M. (2003). Centrality of social ties to the health and well-being of older adults. In B. Berkman & L. K. Harooytoan (Eds.), *Social work and health care in an aging world* (pp. 319–350). New York, NY: Springer.

Lubben, J. E., Weiler, P. G., & Chi, I. (1989). Health practices of the elderly poor. *American Journal of Public Health, 79*, 731–734. doi:10.2105/AJPH.79.6.731

Lin, N., Ye, X., & Ensel, W. (1999). Social support and depressed mood: A structural analysis. *Journal of Health and Social Behavior, 40*(4), 344–359.

Maki, Y., Ura, C., Yamaguchi, T., Murai, T., Isahai, M., Kaiho, A., ... Yamaguchi, H. (2012). Effects of intervention using a community-based walking program for prevention of mental decline: A randomized controlled trial. *Journal of the American Geriatrics Society, 60*, 505–510. doi:10.1111/j.1532-5415.2011.03838.x

Mariam, L. M., McClure, R., Robinson, J. B., & Yang, J. A. (2015). Eliciting Change in At-Risk Elders (ECARE): Evaluation of an elder abuse intervention program. *Journal of Elder Abuse and Neglect, 27*(1), 19–33. doi:10.1080/08946566.2013.86724

McHugh, J., & Lawlor, B. (2012). Social support differentially moderates the impact of neuroticism and extraversion on mental well-being among community-dwelling older adults. *Journal of Mental Health, 21*(5), 448–458. doi:10.3109/09638237.2012.689436

McPherson, K. E., Kerr, S., McGee, E., Morgan, A., Cheater, F. M., Mclean J., & Egan J. (2014). The association between social capital and mental health and behavioral problems in children and adolescents: An integrative systematic review. *BMC Psychology, 2*, 7. doi:10.1186/2050-7283-2-7

McPherson, M., Smith-Lovin, L., & Brashears, M. E. (2006). Social isolation in America: Changes in core discussion networks over two decades. *American Sociological Review, 71*, 353–375.

Mizock, L., & Lewis, T. K. (2008). Trauma in transgender populations: Risk, resilience, and clinical care. *Journal of Emotional Abuse, 8*(3), 335–354. doi:10.1080/10926790802262523

Morgan, A. (2010). Social capital as a health asset for young people's health and wellbeing. *Journal of Child and Adolescent Psychology, S2*, 19–42.

Munson, M. R., & McMillen, J. C. (2009). Natural mentoring and psychosocial outcomes among older youth transitioning from foster care. *Children and Youth Services Review, 31*(1), 104–111.

National Research Council. (2001). *New horizons in health: An integrative approach.* Washington, DC: National Academy Press.

Newman, M. L., Holden, G. W., & Delville, Y. (2005). Isolation and the stress of being bullied. *Journal of Adolescence, 28*(3), 343–357. doi:10.1016/j.adolescence.2004.08.002

Nicholson, N. R., Jr. (2009). Social isolation in older adults: An evolutionary concept analysis. *Journal of Advanced Nursing, 65*(6), 1342–1352. doi:10.1111/j.1365-2648.2008.04959.x

Nicholson, N. R., Jr. (2012). A review of social isolation: An important but underassessed condition in older adults. *Journal of Primary Prevention, 33*(2–3), 137–152.

Norman, G. J., Hawkley, L., Ball, A., Berntson, G. G., & Cacioppo, J. T. (2013). Perceived social isolation moderates the relationship between early childhood trauma and pulse pressure in older adults. *International Journal of Psychophysiology, 88*(3): 334–338.

O'Keeffe, G. S., Clarke-Pearson, K., & Council on Communications and Media (2011). The impact of social media on children, adolescents, and families. *Pediatrics, 127*(4), 800–804.

Oliver, P. D., Patil, S., Benson, J. J., Gage, A., Washington, K., Kruse, R. L., & Demiris, G. (2017). The effect of Internet group support for caregivers on social support, self-efficacy, and caregiver burden: A meta-analysis. *Telemed Journal of Electronic Health*. Advance online publication. doi:10.1089/tmj.2016.0183.

Oxman-Martinez, J., Rummens, A. J., Moreau, J., Choi, Y. R., Beiser, M., Ogilvie, L., & Armstrong, R. (2012). Perceived ethnic discrimination and social exclusion: Newcomer immigrant children in Canada. *American Journal of Orthopsychiatry*, 82(3), 376–388. doi:10.1111/j.1939-0025.2012.01161.x

Pantell, M., Rehkopf, D., Jutte, D., Syme, S. L., Balmes, J., & Adler, N. (2013). Social isolation: A predictor of mortality comparable to traditional clinical risk factors. *American Journal of Public Health*, 103, 2056–2062. doi:10.2105/AJPH.2013.301261

Paveza, G. J., Cohen, D., Eisdorfer, C., Freels, S., Semla, T., Ashford, J. W., . . . Levy, P. (1992). Severe family violence and Alzheimer's disease: Prevalence and risk factors. *Gerontologist*, 32(4), 493–497.

Pekovic, V., Seff, L., & Rothman, M. D. (2007). Planning for and responding to special needs of elders in natural disasters. *Generations*, 31(4), 37–41.

Pescosolido, B. A. (2011). Organizing the sociological landscape for the next decades of health and health care research: The network episode model III-R as cartographic subfield guide. In B. A. Pescosolido, J. K. Martin, J. D. McLeod, & A. Rogers (Eds.), *Handbook of the sociology of health, illness, and healing* (pp. 39–66). New York, NY: Springer.

Pescosolido, B. A., Gardner, C. B., & Lubell, K. M. (1998). How people get into mental health services: Stories of choice, coercion and "muddling through" from "first-timers." *Social Science and Medicine*, 46(2), 275–286.

Pew Research Center, Internet & American Life Project. (2012, November 8). *Mobile health 2012*. Retrieved from http://pewinternet.org/Reports/2012/Mobile-Health.aspx

Quittner, A. L., Glueckauf, R. L., & Jackson, D. N. (1990). Chronic parenting stress: Moderating versus mediating effects of social support. *Journal of Personality and Social Psychology*, 59(6), 1266–1278. doi:10.1037/0022-3514.59.6.1266

Rice, E., & Yoshioka-Maxwell, A. (2015). Social network analysis as a toolkit for the science of social work. *Journal of the Society for Social Work and Research*, 6, 369–383. http://dx.doi.org/10.1086/682723

Rowley, E., Chandler, S., Baird, G., Simonoff, E., Pickles, A., Loucas, T., & Charman, T. (2012). The experience of friendship, victimization and bullying in children with an autism spectrum disorder: Associations with child characteristics and school placement. *Research in Autism Spectrum Disorders*, 6(3), 1126–1134. doi:10.1016/j.rasd.2012.03.00

Rubenstein, R. L., Lubben, J. E., & Mintzer, J. E. (1994). Social isolation and social support: An applied perspective. *Journal of Applied Gerontology*, 13, 58–72.

Sabir, M., Wethington, E., Breckman, R., Meador, R., Reid, M. C., & Pillemer, K. A. (2009). Community-based participatory critique of social isolation intervention research for community-dwelling older adults. *Journal of Applied Gerontology*, 28(2), 218–234.

Sayago, S., & Blat, J. (2010). Telling the story of older people e-mailing: An ethnographical study. *International Journal of Human–Computer Studies*, 68, 105–120. doi:10.1016/ j.ijhcs.2009.10.004

Scharlach, J. K., Davitt, A. J., Lehning, E. A., Greenfield, C. L., & Graham, C. L. (2014). Does the Village model help to foster age-friendly communities? *Journal of Aging & Social Policy*, 26(1–2), 181–196. doi:10.1080/08959420.2014.854664

Schnittger, R., Wherton, J., Prendergast, D., & Lawlor, B. (2012). Risk factors and mediating pathways of loneliness and social support in community-dwelling older adults. *Aging & Mental Health*, *16*(3), 335–346. doi:10.1080/13607863.2011.629092

Seeman, T. E., Lusignolo, T. M., Albert, M., & Berkman, L. (2001). Social relationships, social support, and patterns of cognitive aging in healthy, high-functioning older adults: MacArthur Studies of Successful Aging. *Health Psychology*, *20*, 243–255.

Seeman, T. E., Singer, B. H., Ryff, C. D., Dienberg Love, G., & Levy-Storms, L. (2002). Social relationships, gender, and allostatic load across two age cohorts. *Psychosomatic Medicine*, *64*, 395–406.

Selby, J. V., Beal, A. C., & Frank, L. (2012). The Patient-Centered Outcomes Research Institute (PCORI) national priorities for research and initial research agenda. *JAMA*, *307*(15), 1583–1584.

Semenza, J. C., Rubin, C. H., Falter, K. H., Selanikio, J. D., Flanders, W. D., Howe, H. L., & Wilhelm, J. L. (1996). Heat-related deaths during the July 1995 heat wave in Chicago. *New England Journal of Medicine*, *335*, 84–90.

Sherraden, M., Barth, R. P., Brekke, J., Fraser, M., Madershied, R., & Padgett, D. (2015). *Social is fundamental: Introduction and context for Grand Challenges for Social Work* (Grand Challenges for Social Work Initiative, Working Paper No. 1). Baltimore, MD: American Academy of Social Work and Social Welfare.

Solomon, D. H. (2000). Foreword. In D. Osterweil, K. Brummel-Smith, & J. C. Beck (Eds.), *Comprehensive geriatric assessment* (pp. ix–xii). New York, NY: McGraw-Hill.

Stone, A., Jason, L. A., Light, J. M., & Stevens, E. B. (2016). The role of ego networks in studies of substance use disorder recovery. *Alcoholism Treatment Quarterly*, *34*(3), 315–328.

Strauss, R. S., & Pollack, H. A. (2003). Social marginalization of overweight children. *Archives of Pediatrics & Adolescent Medicine*, *157*(8), 746–752.

Stuck, A. E., Walthert, J. M., Nikolaus, T., Bula, C. J., Hohmann, C., & Beck, J. C. (1999). Risk factors for functional status decline in community-living elderly people: A systematic literature review. *Social Science and Medicine*, *48*, 445–469.

Suarez-Orozco, C., Yoshikawa, H., Teranishi, R., & Suarez-Orozco, M. (2011). Growing up in the shadows: The developmental implications of unauthorized status. *Harvard Educational Review*, *81*(3), 438–472.

Thoits, P. A. (1995). Stress, coping and social support processes: Where are we? What next? *Journal of Health and Social Behavior*, *35*, 53–79.

Thompson, A. E., Greeson, J. K. P., & Brunsink, A. M. (2016). Natural mentoring among older youth in and aging out of foster care: A systematic review. *Children and Youth Services Review*, *61*, 40–50.

Tigges, L. M., Browne, I., & Green, G. P. (1998). Social isolation of the urban poor: Race, class and neighborhood effects on social resources. *Sociological Quarterly*, *39*(1), 53–77.

Tracy, E. M., & Brown, S. (2011). Social networks and social work practice. In F. Turner (Ed.), *Social work treatment* (5th ed., pp. 447–459). New York, NY: Oxford University Press.

Tracy, E. M., & Whittaker, J. K. (2015). Commentary: Social network analysis and the social work profession. *Journal of the Society for Social Work and Research*, *6*(4), 643–654.

Tremethick, M. J. (2001). Alone in a crowd. A study of social networks in home health and assisted living. *Journal of Gerontological Nursing*, *27*, 42–47.

Umberson, D., & Montez, J. K. (2010). Social relationships and health: A flashpoint for health policy. *Journal of Health and Social Behavior, 51*(Suppl.), S54–S66. http://doi.org/10.1177/0022146510383501

Victor, C. R., Scambler, S. J., Bond, J., & Bowling, A. (2000). Being alone in later life: Loneliness, isolation and living alone in later life. *Reviews in Clinical Gerontology, 10,* 407–417. doi:10.1017/S0959259800104101

Von Heydrich, L., Schiamberg, L. B., & Chee, G. (2012). Social-relational risk factors for predicting elder physical abuse: An ecological bi-focal model. *International Journal of Aging & Human Development, 75*(1), 71–94. doi:10.2190/Ag.75.1.F

Wenger, C., Davies, R., Shahtahmasebi, S., & Scott, A. (1996). Social isolation and loneliness in old age: Review and model refinement. *Ageing & Society, 16,* 333–358.

Whitlock, J., Wyman, P. A., & Moore, S. R. (2014). Connectedness and suicide prevention in adolescents: Pathways and implications. *Suicide and Life-Threatening Behavior, 44*(3), 246–272.

World Health Organization. (1979). *Psychogeriatric care in the community: Public health in Europe* (No. 10). Copenhagen, Denmark: World Health Organization Regional Office for Europe.

World Health Organization. (2002). *Active ageing: A policy framework.* Geneva, Switzerland: Author. Retrieved from http://whqlibdoc.who.int/hq/2002/WHO_NMH_NPH_02.8.pdf?ua=1

World Health Organization. (2007). *Global age-friendly cities: A guide.* Geneva, Switzerland: Author. Retrieved from http://www.who.int/ageing/publications/Global_age_friendly_cities_Guide_English.pdf

Yoshikawa, H., & Kalil, A. (2011). The effects of parental undocumented status on the developmental contexts of young children in immigrant families: Undocumented status in immigrant families. *Child Development Perspectives, 5*(4), 291–297. doi:10.1111/j.1750-8606.2011.00204.x

Zhang, X., Norris, S., Gregg, E., & Beckles, G. (2007). Social support and mortality among older persons with diabetes. *The Diabetes Educator, 33*(2), 273–281.

Grand Challenges
for Social Work
End homelessness

CHAPTER 7

End Homelessness

DEBORAH K. PADGETT AND BENJAMIN F. HENWOOD

ENDING HOMELESSNESS: A MAJOR AND COMPELLING CHALLENGE

The United Nations proclaimed the right to adequate housing in 1991 (Office of the United Nations High Commissioner for Human Rights, 2009), but the actualization of this human right remains stubbornly elusive for millions of people who live in slums, substandard dwellings, and public spaces. Housing—specifically having a place to call home—is essential for physical, social, and emotional well-being (Fenelon et al., 2017). The extent of housing insecurity and literal homelessness attests to the deep-rooted nature of global poverty and income inequality (Piketty & Saez, 2014).

In the United States, the upstream causes of the dramatic rise in homelessness that began in the 1980s can be found in a shrinking supply of affordable housing vis-à-vis growing demand (Dolbeare & Crowley, 2002), reduced employment opportunities and living wages, and inadequate social and health care safety net programs (Padgett, Henwood, & Tsemberis, 2016). However, downstream or individual causes have received more attention in the national discourse on what causes homelessness and how to end it—that is, serious mental illness, addiction, and family violence, among others. Added to these individualist attributions are lingering perceptions that some homeless people prefer the lure of the streets (Hopper, 2003). Whatever the particular combination of factors that lead an individual or family to a shelter or the streets, there are few worse fates in life. Without the security of a home, health and well-being are under constant threat and death is far more likely (Henwood, Byrne, & Scriber, 2015; Padgett, 2007).

Once deemed a temporary crisis, homelessness in the United States has become an intransigent part of the urban landscape. Efforts to address this problem have been motivated as much by reducing the economic costs of homelessness as by concern for those who experience it. Economic interests also drive the use of housing as a commodity rather than a public good (Madden & Marcuse, 2016), and impoverished Americans are much more likely to be evicted than they are to receive homelessness prevention services (Desmond, 2016).

In this chapter, we describe the state of homelessness in the United States; give an overview of progress made thus far, including promising practices and policies; and discuss efforts being made as part of the Grand Challenge to End Homelessness (Henwood, Wenzel, et al., 2015). Along with the other Grand Challenges, this endeavor represents a bold agenda for the social work profession.

ANALYSIS OF THE PROBLEM AND OPPORTUNITIES FOR IMPROVEMENT

Few social problems affect as many institutional sectors as homelessness, and a lack of coordination impedes efforts to help homeless persons find and remain in permanent housing. The burgeoning homelessness services sector is largely funded to operate in crisis mode, focusing on shelters rather than permanent housing. Exiting homelessness is also made difficult by a shortage of low-income housing commonly found in many cities. Consequently, other institutional sectors become involved, from criminal justice (jails, prisons, and court-mandated treatment) to education and child welfare (schools and child protection authorities) and health care (Medicaid funding covering the costs of support services and health care).

Notwithstanding such daunting conditions, recent efforts have been significant in reducing the number of unsheltered homeless persons—a 20% decrease during the past 5 years (US Department of Housing and Urban Development [HUD], 2016). In addition, the much-heralded ending of veterans' homelessness in many localities has provided a rare example of the successful alignment of political will and increased resources (Montgomery, Fargo, & Byrne, 2015).

These promising trends are countered by unforeseen recent increases in homelessness in cities such as Los Angeles and New York (National Alliance to End Homelessness, 2016). In addition to an increase in family homelessness, demographic data point to substantial growth among two vulnerable populations at either end of the age spectrum: older adults aged 55 years or older and younger adults between ages 18 and 24 years (Culhane, Metraux, Byrne, Stino, & Bainbridge, 2013). Without a coordinated and targeted strategy to provide housing and clinical services for these two groups, older homeless adults are likely to place serious strains on health care resources, and young homeless adults are at risk of poor economic and social outcomes that will affect their life course.

According to HUD's *2016 Annual Homeless Assessment Report to Congress*, the point-in-time (PIT) count was an estimated 549,928 people experiencing homelessness on a single night, with 32% unsheltered or "sleeping rough." Of this population, almost 121,000 were children (22%), 35,686 were unaccompanied youths aged 18–24 years (7%), and more than one-third were experiencing homelessness as part of a family (HUD, 2016). Although there is reasonable concern about the accuracy of such numbers, they are more likely to be under- rather than overestimates of the number of homeless persons.

Given increasing housing insecurity and rates of eviction affecting broad swaths of the US population living near or below the poverty line (Desmond, 2016), meaningfully addressing homelessness requires attention to prevention and early intervention (Gaetz & Dej, 2017). Whereas the demand for affordable housing has increased over time with the growth of the US population alongside increasing income disparities, the supply of such housing has shrunk in recent decades as public housing construction stagnated and urban gentrification raised the cost of rent beyond the means of poor and working-class Americans (Dolbeare & Crowley, 2002).

Perhaps not surprisingly, the descent into homelessness is more likely for some groups than others. In addition to single-parent families, subpopulations of the homeless include older adults with health problems, youths (runaway; lesbian, gay, bisexual, and transgender; and former foster care youths), victims of domestic violence, veterans, and single adults with serious mental illness and substance abuse problems. Beyond providing access to housing, the need for additional support services varies considerably across these groups, and interventions need not be one-size-fits-all.

Since 2005, federal government policies have been concentrated on prioritizing chronically homeless single adults using an innovative evidence-based approach known as Housing First (HF; Padgett et al., 2016). This trend was expanded in the federal plan announced in 2010 titled *Opening Doors: A Federal Strategic Plan to Prevent and End Homelessness* (HUD, 2010). Building on successes in reducing chronic homelessness (particularly among veterans), HUD has promoted national adoption of HF along with rapid rehousing, an approach targeting prevention and early intervention for families and other non-chronic homeless subpopulations.

Such changes have been influenced by accumulating research evidence showing cost savings and positive outcomes associated with HF (Tsemberis, Gulcur, & Nakae, 2004). In addition, strong leadership at the federal and local levels and popular media reports (Gladwell, 2006) have made innovation more readily accepted. Facilitating this willingness to change was a growing consensus that existing services were contributing to a costly institutional circuit of homeless persons' movement among shelters, streets, hospitals, and jails (Hopper, Jost, Hay, Welber, & Haugland, 1997). Homelessness incurs great economic costs to society—costs that are not always factored in when addressing solutions to the problem.

Studies that documented the high costs of health care, behavioral health, criminal justice, and other services incurred by homeless persons make it clear that the continued existence of homelessness is staggeringly expensive to taxpayers (Culhane, Metraux, & Hadley, 2002; Larimer et al., 2009; Poulin, Maguire, Metraux, & Culhane, 2010). In the United States, the annual cost to maintain a person on the streets or in shelters, which often involves health care settings and law enforcement agencies, ranges from $35,000 to $150,000 per person. By comparison, it costs $13,000 to $25,000 annually to end chronic homelessness through use of existing permanent supportive housing.

The growing consensus that homelessness in the United States can be ended rather than managed and that workable evidence-based solutions are less costly represents a fundamental shift in expectations since the crisis began in the 1980s (Gladwell, 2006; Padgett et al., 2016). Beginning in the early 2000s, a reimagined approach took hold among policymakers, advocates, and service providers based on accumulating research evidence and national leadership. Following this trend, many US cities adopted 10-year plans to end homelessness (National Alliance to End Homelessness, 2006). As a result, great strides have been made in ending homelessness for thousands of individuals and families, but much more work is needed at multiple levels.

Ending homelessness cannot be accomplished simply by resolving individual needs; it will require ongoing efforts to address the structural factors of entrenched poverty and income inequality. In this regard, the policy shift from emergency shelters to more permanent solutions is necessary but not sufficient. Indeed, broader shifts are needed on several fronts encompassing prevention and early intervention (Gaetz & Dej, 2017). Prevention can be fostered by increasing the stock of affordable housing, expanding access to housing choice vouchers, raising the minimum wage, and increasing disability benefits. Early interventions centering on adaptations of HF and rapid rehousing afford the ability to address housing-plus-services needs for the minority of homeless persons who require additional support once housed. In addition to delivering evidence-based interventions, social work can help meet the Grand Challenge of eradicating homelessness through community organizing and advocacy, educating new generations of professionals working to help those most in need, and leveraging the field's strength of working across micro, mezzo, and macro levels.

SUMMARY OF SIGNIFICANT INNOVATIONS NEEDING
DEVELOPMENT OR DISSEMINATION

Ending homelessness requires a comprehensive prevention framework. Without stopping the inflow into homelessness (primary prevention), secondary and tertiary prevention efforts to assist those in short- or long-term phases of homelessness will continue to fall short. Thus far, the most sweeping innovation to affect homelessness services has been the rise of a form of tertiary prevention mentioned previously in this chapter—HF. An evidence-based approach originating in New York City in 1992, HF has since been embraced as the dominant policy in the United States, Canada, and many Western European nations (Padgett et al., 2016).

HF reverses the usual staircase approach requiring homeless persons to demonstrate "housing worthiness" through sobriety and rules compliance as they ascend from shelters through transitional to permanent housing—an ascent that can takes years and typically results in "falling off" the staircase and returning to the institutional circuit. Instead, HF operates with a philosophy that values consumer choice and empowerment over coercion and harm reduction over abstinence. Originally focused on providing scatter-site housing in the private rental market for homeless persons with a serious mental illness, HF has since been adapted for use in single-site programs for individuals with substance abuse problems (Larimer et al., 2009).

An extensive body of research in the United States and abroad has shown HF to produce robust positive outcomes, including housing stability, cost savings, and reductions in use of drugs and alcohol (Padgett et al., 2016). HF is strongly endorsed by HUD in its funding directives to local jurisdictions seeking federal funding, and it has been the linchpin of Canada's Homelessness Partnering Strategy since 2014 (Aubry et al., 2016). Although less is known about HF's effectiveness with subpopulations such as homeless families and youths, a small but growing evidence base supports its use with these groups and survivors of partner violence (Einbinder & Tull, 2007). The model's central tenets of consumer choice, harm reduction, and immediate access to housing are considered essential to its adaptations to other settings and populations.

If HF can be viewed as a tertiary prevention response to chronic homelessness, Critical Time Intervention (CTI) and rapid rehousing are two approaches intended to help persons on the verge or in the earliest stages of homelessness, thus corresponding to primary and secondary prevention. CTI was developed to help prevent homelessness among psychiatric and other high-risk patients leaving institutions (Herman, Conover, Felix, Nakagawa, & Mills, 2007). Rapid rehousing has its origins in New York City in 2005 as the Housing Stability Plus (later renamed Advantage) program. Rapid rehousing helps homeless individuals and families find housing without depending on access to public housing or housing vouchers (National Alliance to End Homelessness, 2017).

Rapid rehousing fills an important gap in the service system because it is designed for the majority of homeless persons who do not have psychiatric or other disabilities and can benefit from a one-time infusion of cash or resources to prevent becoming homeless or exit early from the shelter system. Rapid rehousing may also include short-term or partial rental subsidies (sometimes termed shallow subsidies).

Primary prevention of homelessness can be addressed through increasing the stock and availability of affordable housing and access to rental vouchers for eligible individuals and families. Legal representation in housing court is another form of primary prevention. The maxim "90% of landlords have attorneys and 99% of tenants do not" in eviction proceedings demonstrates the extraordinary challenge confronting individuals who fall behind in rent or are deemed a nuisance by a property owner. Also referred to as civil Gideon (recalling the 1963 Supreme Court decision in *Gideon v. Wainwright* that affirmed the rights of criminal defendants to legal counsel at no cost), such assistance would save shelter costs and reduce the number of unlawful evictions pursued by unscrupulous landlords. In February 2017, the New York City Council announced the approval of a legal right-to-counsel program, the first of its kind in the United States. Funded by an initial budget of $93 million, the program provides free legal representation in court for individuals in households earning less than $50,000 per year and free legal counseling for those in households earning more (City of New York, 2017a). City officials estimate 400,000 families will benefit from the program annually.

Specific to the needs of at-risk adolescents are prevention and early intervention programs designed to facilitate stable housing and a smooth transition to young adulthood and independence. Host homes—in which trained community volunteers open their homes to homeless youths—have been used successfully in Minneapolis and promoted by the National Alliance to End Homelessness (Avenues for Homeless Youth, n.d.). In response to growing awareness that many foster care youths face homelessness once emancipated at age 18 years, 25 states have instituted extended foster care programs that subsidize education, job training, and housing until age 21 years (some states have extended funding until age 24 years).

The 20% decline in unsheltered homelessness mentioned previously in this chapter is a sign of progress, particularly because the number of shelter-dwelling homeless persons remained stable during the same 5-year period (HUD, 2016). The increased adoption of HF and policies favoring permanent rather than temporary housing is likely responsible. Although still relatively untested by empirical research, rapid rehousing has generated improved outcomes when used in combination with Support Services for Veteran Families (Byrne, Treglia, Culhane, Kuhn, & Kane, 2016).

In the HUD-sponsored Family Options Study, a 36-month national experiment testing the effects of rapid rehousing compared to rental subsidies, supportive transitional housing, and usual care (a family emergency shelter), rapid rehousing showed modest improvement in homelessness prevention compared to usual care and at a reduced cost. However, the study concluded that provision of permanent rental subsidies (even without support services) was substantially more successful in improving all study outcomes (Gubits et al., 2016).

In summary, proven and promising innovations are available, including HF, rapid rehousing, legal counsel to prevent eviction, and youth-oriented programs such as host homes and extended foster care. Last but not least are the benefits of subsidies without time limits for low-need homeless families.

PLANS FOR METRICS AND MOVEMENT TOWARD MEASURABLE PROGRESS

A metric for assessing an end to homelessness depends on a reliable census or count conducted over time. A regular PIT count is required by HUD of any jurisdiction seeking McKinney–Vento funding for homelessness services. Typically conducted on a single night in late January or early February, the PIT count depends on trained volunteers who seek out unsheltered persons sleeping in doorways, cars, abandoned buildings, and other places not fit for human habitation. Adding the number of individuals living in shelters provides a full, unduplicated enumeration of the extent of homelessness in a city or county.

Annual PIT counts are criticized by homelessness advocates and researchers who assert that they are woefully inadequate to achieve the task. A tendency to undercount is understandable given the limits of any method intended to locate persons who wish to remain undisturbed and hidden. In this context, using the same PIT methods annually at least ensures that comparisons can be made across years. Flawed as they can be, PIT counts have few, if any, viable alternatives with regard to estimating prevalence and tracking trends.

Regarding information on homelessness in families, the US Department of Education collects data on schoolchildren who live in doubled-up, sheltered, or unsheltered conditions each year. This more expansive definition of homelessness offers different estimates that can be compared to PIT counts for families with school-aged children (US Department of Education, 2016). Other metrics are used to track homelessness services users, thus excluding those who do not access services. For example, HUD requires local authorities to maintain homeless management information systems, which include demographic and other data to coordinate service provision.

A broader approach or metric draws on estimating the number of at-risk households based on income and housing affordability. According to HUD, households with incomes 30% or more below the local area median are considered extremely low income (ELI). In 2016, 3.2 million affordable housing units were available for the 10.4 million ELI households in the United States. Without access to affordable housing, 75% of ELI households are at risk of homelessness, paying 50% or more of their income toward housing costs (National Low Income Housing Coalition, 2016).

The success of the HUD–Veterans Affairs Supportive Housing program brought to the fore the need to define what it actually means to end homelessness and the difficulty of declaring such an ending given the fluid nature of the phenomenon in any given locality. In response, the term *functional zero* was devised by the nonprofit organization Community Solutions (2016) and defined as follows: "At any point in time, the number of people experiencing sheltered or unsheltered homelessness will be no greater than the current monthly housing placement rate for people experiencing homelessness" (para. 4). In New Orleans, for example, 227 veterans were permanently housed between July 2014 and January 2015, but 9 veterans declined housing (Kegel, 2014). Notwithstanding those 9 individuals, the city of New Orleans declared that veterans' homelessness had reached zero.

Critics of functional zero argue that definitions should not be created to fit circumstances and that doing so deflects attention from the structural or upstream factors that produce the seemingly constant downstream flow of persons into shelters and street living (Erlenbusch, 2015). A preference to announce zero homelessness when in fact dozens (or even hundreds) of persons remain unhoused is expedient but not entirely satisfactory.

The persistence of the problem received a candid public acknowledgment in a February 2017 announcement by New York City Mayor Bill de Blasio regarding the city's efforts to address the recent increase in homelessness, especially among families (City of New York, 2017b). Taking a major departure from the usual announcement of a multiyear campaign to eliminate homelessness, de Blasio announced a modest goal: a 4% reduction in the shelter population over 5 years (Stewart & Neuman, 2017). His plan to open 90 new shelters and refurbish 30 existing shelters, at a cost of $300 million, was greeted with favor by homelessness service providers, wary approval by homelessness advocates, and consternation by neighborhood groups contemplating a new shelter in their midst. Whether this portends a national trend toward more moderate (but achievable) goals in ending homelessness remains to be seen.

OPPORTUNITIES FOR NEW INTERDISCIPLINARY AND CROSS-SECTOR INITIATIVES

Homelessness involves a highly diverse group of stakeholders and institutional sectors beyond shelters and support services. These include city and county housing authorities and nonprofit groups engaged in charitable giving (food pantries, soup kitchens, coat drives, etc.). Health and mental health care facilities—hospitals, emergency departments, and outpatient clinics—frequently interact with homeless persons. Homeless persons are often entangled in the criminal justice system (police officers, judges, and incarceration facilities). Other affected institutional sectors include schools, child welfare authorities, public libraries, public transportation (buses and subways), and parks departments.

Partnerships among universities (particularly schools of social work), nonprofit groups, and government entities offer new opportunities to address homelessness (Flynn, 2017). In Los Angeles, a targeted focus on the city's burgeoning homeless population brought together the University of Southern California (USC) and local community partners in 2016 to address "the most intractable, difficult, multifaceted problems of our time" (University of Southern California, n.d., para. 1). Led by the USC Suzanne Dworak-Peck School of Social Work, addressing homelessness became a hallmark of university-wide efforts beginning in 2016.

In 2014, the Institute of Global Homelessness was established at DePaul University in Chicago. Funded by DePaul International (a Catholic philanthropic organization headquartered in Great Britain), the institute in 2016 announced its Countdown 2030: A Place to Call Home Initiative, a coordinated international endeavor to gradually scale-up a true and sustainable end to homelessness in 120 cities worldwide (Institute of Global Homelessness, 2016). The institute sponsors training and technical assistance and supports conferences intended to bring together homelessness advocates from throughout the world.

The health care professions—medicine, nursing, and public health—have played a key role in assisting homeless persons with health and mental health problems. Street medicine outreach and dedicated clinics funded under the Health Care for the Homeless program are currently supported by McKinney–Vento funds. In a novel approach to extend such efforts into housing access, a Hawaii state legislator introduced a bill in March 2017 that would permit physicians to prescribe housing as the cure for homelessness (Barney, 2017). The realization by physicians that many of their recurring (and high-need) patients are homeless renders a medical solution as a plausible response for patients with medical disabilities. Ostensibly, Medicaid funding could be diverted for such a purpose, although Congress has thus far not approved such use. Taking an advocacy stance, the American Public Health Association created an active homelessness caucus that has produced reports intended to prod changes in policies to improve the health and well-being of homeless persons (Elder & King, 2016).

The Grand Challenges Initiative begun by the American Academy of Social Work and Social Welfare represents a cross-sector effort in the social work profession, with presentations at major social conferences such as the Council on Social Work Education's Annual Program Meeting and the Society for Social Work and Research's annual conference. The latter also hosts a special interest group dedicated to homelessness that has proven to be a meeting ground for researchers.

Cross-sector coordination in social work was advanced in 2013 when two faculty members at the School of Social Welfare at the University at Albany—former dean Katharine Briar-Lawson and Heather Larkin Holloway—received a grant from the New York Community Trust to establish the National Homelessness Social Work Initiative and the National Center for Excellence in Homeless Services (University at Albany, 2017). These initiatives are dedicated to expanding content on homelessness in social work education and forging partnerships across social work schools and between those schools and homeless providers to improve services and policies.

In summary, a number of professional and institutional sponsors have become involved in projects to address and end homelessness. Although relatively recent, the promise of greater involvement, particularly in social work, has never been better.

PROGRESS AND FUTURE DIRECTIONS IN EDUCATION, PRACTICE, AND POLICY

As noted previously, substantial progress has been made in reducing the number of unsheltered chronically homeless adults, especially veterans. The profound shift in thinking toward favoring permanent housing over emergency shelters and temporary housing is an important first step in enacting systems change.

Structural remedies to expand access to housing—building more affordable housing, opening public housing to homeless individuals and families, and expanding the number of housing choice vouchers—can help close the gap. In addition, increasing economic opportunities through a higher minimum wage, health insurance access, and an increase in disability income would help prevent homelessness.

The motivations for change are diverse, whether rooted in human rights, political will, or economic calculations. The human right to housing is a powerful moral argument for ending homelessness put forth by advocacy groups and the United Nations. It is also consonant with social work's values as a profession. Attitudes toward homelessness and how it should be addressed vary considerably throughout the United States, with more conservative jurisdictions emphasizing stricter enforcement and shelters over permanent housing and support services. However, growing awareness that the status quo has not worked in the past 30 years, along with changes in federal government funding priorities, has gradually shifted local attitudes and political responses toward greater receptivity to permanent solutions.

More pragmatic have been cost-savings arguments citing robust evidence that chronically homeless adults with high rates of service use can be stably housed at substantial savings in public funds. This has been a powerful motivator for policy changes as public officials confront the need to apportion scarce resources. However, we note that the prospect of cost-offset savings is not a guarantee nor is it a requirement for other types of public spending in health and social services. A recent editorial in the *New England Journal of Medicine* cautioned against using cost savings as the primary driver of homelessness services, noting the "incongruity of persistent homelessness in one of the wealthiest countries in the world" (Kertesz, Baggett, O'Connell, Buck, & Kushel, 2016, p. 2117).

In response to shortages of funding for new initiatives, it could be argued that summoning the political will to shift existing funds could in itself constitute a major change. For example, if the approximate budget of $2.4 billion allotted for 2017 McKinney–Vento funding was diverted to housing choice vouchers, each voucher (roughly $12,000 per year) would enable 200,000 persons or families to receive a rental subsidy. Of course, a challenge emerges when diverting resources from emergency shelter services to more permanent solutions without displacing or disrupting those in need. There is also the problem of a decreasing number of landlords willing to accept such vouchers (Semuels, 2015), although a proactive stance can ameliorate landlords' qualms.

Nevertheless, the alternative—building and expanding shelters and skimping on the support services needed by a vulnerable minority of homeless persons—is profoundly expensive both in terms of real dollars and in terms of the loss of individual lives and futures. Feasibility is also problematic as vociferous NIMBY (not in my backyard) resistance has emerged in neighborhoods asked to cooperate with siting such shelters in their environs. Shelters and congregate living arrangements—with the accompanying need for 24-hour security and on-site staff—are one of the most costly alternatives in homelessness services.

Although the future contours of homelessness services—and the success or failure of various attempts to end homelessness—cannot be foretold, progress has been considerable. The paradigm shift favoring permanent housing has attained substantial momentum with the support of HUD and other funding sources. Of course, the pace of change can hasten or slow depending on political will and popular support. The engagement of many public and private sectors in homelessness amplifies the bureaucratic complexity of coordinating such efforts (Padgett et al., 2016).

The Grand Challenge to End Homelessness has been a leading part of several promising endeavors in the social work profession, as described in the following:

> *Education*: Both baccalaureate and master's-level social work students have field learning placements in homelessness services agencies in which they may assist individuals and families in applying for housing, enrolling in entitlement programs such as Medicaid, or making referrals for medical and mental health treatment. Although working with homeless individuals remains a challenge for the profession— low salaries, job turnover, and unstable funding create disincentives for many—increasing awareness of best practices can attract greater interest. Under the leadership of the National Center for Excellence in Homeless Services (mentioned previously), attention to homelessness in social work education has been increasing.
>
> *Practice*: Evidence-based practices such as assertive community treatment (ACT) and CTI feature social workers as providers of services to persons at immediate risk of homelessness (CTI) or who are newly housed (ACT). ACT was a key component of HF in its original form because a diagnosis of serious mental illness was a key part of program eligibility (Tsemberis et al., 2004); later, intensive case management was added for clients with less intense service needs. Originally developed for psychiatric hospital patients facing discharge, CTI has been adapted for use with ex-prisoners and patients leaving residential treatment for substance abuse (Lako et al., 2013).

Variable support services based on need rather than a one-size-fits-all approach highlight the importance of social work practitioners as leading the way in developing and implementing needs assessments, providing direct services and targeted referrals, and ensuring that formerly homeless persons can remain stably housed. Although homelessness service providers tend to rely on paraprofessional case managers, professional social workers can be involved in supportive supervision of frontline workers and administrative oversight and advocacy on behalf of homelessness services organizations (Henwood, Shinn, Tsemberis, & Padgett, 2013).

THE POLITICAL LANDSCAPE

With significantly more conservative policies affecting the United States since the 2016 national election, the possibilities for new initiatives and new funding are uncertain; maintaining the status quo could be considered the best hoped-for outcome. The US Interagency Council on Homelessness is scheduled to sunset, or cease existence, in 2017, which adds to the uncertainty.

At the same time, reinvigorated local efforts have begun to appear and will likely intensify in the event of reduced national funding. In 2016, for example, Los Angeles County residents by a two-thirds majority voted to increase taxes to fund a $1.2 billion bond to build additional supportive housing. Voters also approved an annual sales tax to provide almost $500 million annually for support services for homeless populations.

The societal benefits of ending homelessness go well beyond the obvious improvements in the lives of those who have experienced one of life's most catastrophic events. They include greater social inclusion, economic self-sufficiency, improved health, and psychological well-being. Freeing up public funds currently spent on managing homelessness could also lead to expanded funding for early childhood education and health care. Moreover, ending homelessness would have positive reverberations in multiple sectors—childhood education, foster care, criminal justice, and health care. It is an investment in the futures of millions of children whose lives are marred by instability, deprivation, and stigma. Whether affecting young or old, homelessness is a "grand challenge" for which solutions are available.

REFERENCES

Aubry, T., Goering, P., Veldhuizen, S., Adair, C. E., Bourque, J., Distasio, J., . . . Tsemberis, S. (2016). A multiple-RCT of Housing First with Assertive Community Treatment for homeless Canadians with serious mental illness. *Psychiatric Services*, *67*, 275–281. doi:10.1176/appi.ps.201400587

Avenues for Homeless Youth. (n.d.). *Minneapolis & Suburban Host Home Program*. Retrieved from http://avenuesforyouth.org/minneapolis-host-home-program

Barney, L. (2017, February 28). Doctors could prescribe houses to the homeless under radical Hawaii bill. *The Guardian*. Retrieved from https://www.theguardian.com/us-news/2017/feb/28/hawaii-homeless-housing-bill-healthcare-costs

Byrne, T., Treglia, D., Culhane, D. P., Kuhn, J., & Kane, V. (2016). Predictors of homelessness among families and single adults following exit from homelessness prevention and rapid re-housing programs: Evidence for the Department of Veterans Affairs Supportive Services for Veteran Families program. *Housing Policy Debate*, *26*, 252–275.

City of New York. (2017a, February 12). *State of the city: Mayor de Blasio and Speaker Mark Viverito rally around universal access to free legal services for tenants facing eviction in housing court*. Retrieved from http://www1.nyc.gov/office-of-the-mayor/news/079-17/state-the-city-mayor-de-blasio-speaker-mark-viverito-rally-universal-access-free

City of New York, Mayor Bill De Blasio. (2017b, February 28). *De Blasio administration announces plan to turn the tide on homelessness with borough-based approach; Plan will reduce shelter facilities by forty five percent*. Retrieved from http://www1.nyc.gov/office-of-the-mayor/news/118-17/de-blasio-administration-plan-turn-tide-homelessness-borough-based

Community Solutions. (2016). *Zero 2016 glossary*. Retrieved from https://www.community.solutions/sites/default/files/zero2016glossary.pdf

Culhane, D. P., Metraux, S., Byrne, T., Stino, M., & Bainbridge, J. (2013). The age structure of contemporary homelessness: Evidence and implications for public policy. *Analyses of Social Issues and Public Policy, 13*, 228–244. doi:10.1111/asap.12004

Culhane, D. P., Metraux, S., & Hadley, T. (2002). Public service reductions associated with placement of homeless persons with severe mental illness in supportive housing. *Housing Policy Debate, 13*, 107–163. doi:10.1080/10511482.2002.9521437

Desmond, M. (2016). *Evicted: Poverty and profit in the American city*. New York, NY: Crown.

Dolbeare, C. N., & Crowley, S. (2002). *Changing priorities: The federal budget and housing assistance 1976–2007*. Retrieved from http://nlihc.org/sites/default/files/Changing-Priorities-Report_August-2002.pdf

Einbinder, S. D., & Tull, T. (2007). *The Housing First program for homeless families: Empirical evidence of long-term efficacy to end and prevent family homelessness*. Washington, DC: National Alliance to End Homelessness.

Elder, J., & King, B. (2016). *Housing and homelessness as a public health issue*. Unpublished manuscript, Homelessness Caucus, American Public Health Association, Washington, DC.

Erlenbusch, B. (2015). *Homelessness & "functional zero": A critique*. Sacramento, CA: Sacramento Regional Coalition to End Homelessness.

Fenelon, A., Mayne, P., Simon, A. E., Rossen, L. M., Helms, V., Lloyd, P., . . . Steffen, B. L. (2017). Housing assistance programs and adult health in the United States. *American Journal of Public Health, 107*, 571–578. doi:10.2105/AJPH.2016.303649

Flynn, M. L. (2017). The Grand Challenges concept: Campus strategies for implementation. *Journal of the Society for Social Work and Research, 8*, 87–98. doi:10.1086/690564

Gaetz, S., & Dej, E. (2017). *A new direction: A framework for homelessness prevention*. Toronto, Ontario, Canada: Canadian Observatory on Homelessness Press.

Gideon v. Wainwright, 372 U.S. 335 (1963).

Gladwell, M. (2006). Million-dollar Murray. *The New Yorker*. Retrieved from http://gladwell.com/million-dollar-murray

Gubits, D., Shinn, M., Wood, M., Bell, S., Dastrup, S., Solari, C. D., . . . Kattel, U. (2016). *Family Options Study: 3-year impacts of housing and services interventions for homeless families*. Washington, DC: US Department of Housing and Urban Development.

Henwood, B. F., Byrne, T., & Scriber, B. (2015). Examining mortality among formerly homeless adults enrolled in Housing First: An observational study. *BMC Public Health, 15*, 1209. doi:10.1186/s12889-015-2552-1

Henwood, B. F., Shinn, M., Tsemberis, S., & Padgett, D. K. (2013). Examining provider perspectives within Housing First and traditional programs. *American Journal of Psychiatric Rehabilitation, 62*, 262–274.

Henwood, B. F., Wenzel, S. L., Mangano, P. F., Hombs, M., Padgett, D. K., Byrne, T., . . . Uretsky, M. C. (2015). *The grand challenge of ending homelessness* (Grand Challenges for Social Work Initiative Working Paper No. 9). Cleveland, OH: American Academy of Social Work and Social Welfare.

Herman, D., Conover, S., Felix, A., Nakagawa, A., & Mills, D. (2007). Critical time intervention: An empirically supported model for preventing homelessness in high risk groups. *Journal of Primary Prevention*, *28*, 295–312. doi:10.1007/s10935-007-0099-3

Hopper, K. (2003). *Reckoning with homelessness*. Ithaca, NY: Cornell University Press.

Hopper, K., Jost, J., Hay, T., Welber, S., & Haugland, G. (1997). Homelessness, severe mental illness, and the institutional circuit. *Psychiatric Services*, *48*, 659–665. doi:10.1176/ps.48.5.659

Institute of Global Homelessness. (2016). *Countdown 2030: A Place to Call Home Initiative*. Retrieved from http://www.ighomelessness.org/countdown-2030

Kegel, M. J. (2014, July 16). *A functional zero in veteran homelessness: What does it mean and how do you achieve it?* Paper presented at the National Conference to End Homelessness, New Orleans, LA.

Kertesz, S. G., Baggett, T. P., O'Connell, J. J., Buck, D. S., & Kushel, M. B. (2016). Permanent supportive housing for homeless people—Reframing the debate. *New England Journal of Medicine*, *375*, 2115–2117. doi:10.1056/NEJMp1608326

Lako, D. A. M., de Vet, R., Beijersbergen, M. D., Herman, D. B., van Hemert, A. M., & Wolf, J. R. L. M. (2013). The effectiveness of critical time intervention for abused women and homeless people leaving Dutch shelters: Study protocol of two randomised controlled trials. *BMC Public Health*, *13*, 555. doi:10.1186/1471-2458-13-555

Larimer, M. E., Malone, D. K., Garner, M. D., Atkins, D. C., Burlingham, B., Lonczak, H. S., . . . Marlatt, G. A. (2009). Health care and public service use and costs before and after provision of housing for chronically homeless persons with severe alcohol problems. *JAMA*, *301*, 1349–1357. doi:10.1001/jama.2009.414

Madden, D., & Marcuse, P. (2016). *In defense of housing: The politics of crisis*. London, UK: Verso.

Montgomery, A. E., Fargo, J. D., & Byrne, T. H. (2015). Impact of community investment in safety net services on rates of unsheltered homelessness among veterans. *Journal of Sociology & Social Welfare*, *42*(4), 23–36.

National Alliance to End Homelessness. (2006). *A plan, not a dream: How to end homelessness in ten years*. Retrieved from http://www.endhomelessness.org/page/-/files/585_file_TYP_pdf

National Alliance to End Homelessness. (2016). *The state of homelessness in America 2016*. Retrieved from https://www.endhomelessness.org/library/entry/SOH2016

National Alliance to End Homelessness. (2017). *Rapid re-housing*. Retrieved from https://www.endhomelessness.org/pages/rapid-re-housing

National Low Income Housing Coalition. (2016). *Out of reach 2016*. Retrieved from http://nlihc.org/oor

Office of the United Nations High Commissioner for Human Rights. (2009). *The right to adequate housing* (Fact Sheet No. 21, Rev. 1). Geneva, Switzerland: Author. Retrieved from http://www.ohchr.org/Documents/Publications/FS21_rev_1_Housing_en.pdf

Padgett, D. K. (2007). There's no place like (a) home: Ontological security among persons with serious mental illness in the United States. *Social Science & Medicine*, *64*, 1925–1936. doi:10.1016/j.socscimed.2007.02.011

Padgett, D. K., Henwood, B. F., & Tsemberis, S. J. (2016). *Housing First: Ending homelessness, transforming systems, and changing lives*. New York, NY: Oxford University Press.

Piketty, T., & Saez, E. (2014). Inequality in the long run. *Science, 344,* 838–843. doi:10.1126/science.1251936

Poulin, S. R., Maguire, M., Metraux, S., & Culhane, D. P. (2010). Service use and costs for persons experiencing chronic homelessness in Philadelphia: A population-based study. *Psychiatric Services, 61,* 1093–1098. doi:10.1176/ps.2010.61.11.1093

Semuels, A. (2015, June 24). How housing policy is failing America's poor. *The Atlantic.* Retrieved from https://www.theatlantic.com/business/archive/2015/06/section-8-is-failing/396650

Stewart, N., & Neuman, W. (2017, March 1). De Blasio's modest goal on homelessness: 4% out of shelters in 5 years. *The New York Times,* p. A24.

Tsemberis, S., Gulcur, L., & Nakae, M. (2004). Housing First, consumer choice, and harm reduction for homeless individuals with a dual diagnosis. *American Journal of Public Health, 94,* 651–656. doi:10.2105/AJPH.94.4.651

US Department of Education. (2016, July 27). *Education department releases guidance on homeless children and youth.* Retrieved from https://www.ed.gov/news/press-releases/education-department-releases-guidance-homeless-children-and-youth

US Department of Housing and Urban Development. (2010). *Opening doors: A federal strategic plan to prevent and end homelessness.* Washington, DC: Author.

US Department of Housing and Urban Development. (2016). *The 2016 Annual Homeless Assessment Report (AHAR) to Congress: Part 1. Point-in-time estimates of homelessness.* Washington, DC: Author. Retrieved from https://www.hudexchange.info/resources/documents/2016-AHAR-Part-1.pdf

University at Albany. (2017). *National Center for Excellence in Homeless Services.* Retrieved from http://www.albany.edu/excellencehomelessservices

University of Southern California. (n.d.). *A vision for USC: Wicked problems.* Retrieved from https://avisionfor.usc.edu/wicked-problems

Grand Challenges
for Social Work
*Create social responses to a
changing environment*

CHAPTER 8

Create Social Responses to a Changing Environment

SUSAN P. KEMP, LAWRENCE A. PALINKAS,
AND LISA REYES MASON

Environmental challenges facing contemporary societies pose significant risks to human health and well-being, particularly for the world's most marginalized communities. Not only was 2016 the hottest year on record (National Aeronautics and Space Administration, 2017) but also extreme weather events such as floods, storms, tornados, heatwaves, droughts, and wildfires are expected to increase in both severity and number (US Environmental Protection Agency, 2016). Between 1995 and 2015, an average of 205 million people per year were affected by climate-related disasters globally and this figure is likely to rise as weather-related events escalate (Centre for Research on the Epidemiology of Disasters and United Nations Office for Disaster Risk Reduction, 2015). Evidence is also growing regarding the increasing numbers of migrants displaced by climate-related environmental factors such as sea level rise, prolonged drought, agricultural disruption, and food shortages (Rechkemmer et al., 2016). Human-driven factors, including man-made disasters, political conflict (e.g., in South Sudan and Syria), and infrastructure neglect and failure (as with Hurricane Katrina), frequently interact with environmental events to significantly increase human vulnerability, particularly for already marginalized populations.

At the same time, the rates at which cities are growing throughout the world will place enormous strains on equity and sustainability (United Nations, 2014; United Nations Human Settlements Programme, 2016). Urban growth increases environmental risks such as air and water pollution and heat concentration. It also strains infrastructure, service systems, and urban ecologies; and frequently deepens social and economic inequities. Furthermore, many of the world's largest cities are highly vulnerable to environmental threats associated with climate change, including sea level rise and extreme weather events. The context of urbanization climate change is a threat multiplier. Accordingly the 2015 United Nations Sustainable Development Goals (United Nations, 2015) stress the importance of action to develop inclusive, resilient, and sustainable cities (Goal No. 11) in concert with efforts to strengthen adaptive capacity to climate-related hazards and natural disasters (Goal No. 13).

Both acute environmental hazards and slow-onset threats such as droughts are inescapably *social* as well as environmental challenges. They threaten physical and mental health. They destabilize coping capacities and response infrastructures;. They exacerbate existing social, economic, and environmental inequities. Further, they pose distinct risks to safety, security, and human rights (Intergovernmental Panel on Climate Change [IPCC], 2014). Children, the poor, older adults, members of racial or ethnic minority groups, and people with a history of mental health problems are especially vulnerable. Disproportionate impacts include food insufficiency, heat exhaustion, exposure to environmental toxins, health and mental health concerns, and disaster-related trauma and displacement.

As the risks to human well-being of global environmental changes become increasingly apparent, social and behavioral interventions—to strengthen individual, family, and community resilience, build adaptive and sustainable socioecological systems, enhance disaster preparedness and responses, and reduce social and economic inequalities—are increasingly recognized as central to the capacity to respond and adapt to current and forthcoming challenges (Hackmann, Moser, & St. Clair, 2014; Weaver et al., 2014). Social work has much to contribute to these efforts, including deep experience with people-in-context; a robust, multilevel portfolio of tested interventions; and a thoroughgoing commitment to social justice, equity, and the protection of human rights. Historically, however, the profession has lacked a robust presence in environmental research, practice, and policymaking.

Enhancing the field's socioenvironmental impact is central to the Grand Challenge for Social Work, Create Social Responses to a Changing Environment. At the heart of this grand challenge is the belief that the social work profession is "uniquely positioned to catalyze, facilitate, and propel social innovation at the human–environment nexus, promoting justice, equity, and human and social development through person-in-environment oriented policies and practices" (Kemp & Palinkas, 2015). If successful, it will lead to social responses that strengthen individual and community capacities for anticipating and adapting to environmental changes, particularly for vulnerable groups, and reduce inequities in exposure to environmental risks.

ANALYSIS OF THE SOCIAL PROBLEM AND
OPPORTUNITIES FOR IMPROVEMENT

The concept paper developed by the Grand Challenge coordinating group (Kemp & Palinkas, 2015) proposes a multi-tier approach to advancing social responses to environmental changes, including *mitigation* (actions to limit the rate or magnitude of environmental effects), *adaptation* (actions to build capacity in advance of environmental events), and *treatment* (post-event actions to alleviate the health and mental health impacts). It also recognizes the importance of transformative as well as adaptive responses to environmental challenges. An ensuing policy brief identifies the following as priority areas (Kemp, Mason, Palinkas, Rechkemmer, & Teixeira, 2016):

1. Disaster risk reduction
2. Environmentally displaced populations
3. Community adaptation and resilience to environmental change

Disaster Risk Reduction

Adequate preparation for and response to extreme weather events as well as other natural hazards requires initiatives in five key areas. First, an evidence-based approach to disaster risk reduction should be adopted and implemented, targeting three categories or tiers of disaster impact: biopsychosocial, interpersonal, and intrapersonal or behavioral health. Second, in all three tiers, evidence-based and evidence-informed interventions should become the standard in preparing for and responding to disaster impacts. Priority should be given to developing, evaluating, and scaling up interventions designed to build community resilience, address human insecurity, and manage social conflict before and after disasters. Third, social workers should be trained in the use of these evidence-based interventions. For instance, funding should be made available to create and deliver trauma-informed programs for training disaster-relief and recovery personnel in such interventions as psychological first aid (Forbes et al., 2011) and Cognitive–Behavioral Intervention for Trauma in Schools (CBITS; Jaycox, 2004). Fourth, all masters-level social work curricula in the United States should include courses in disaster preparedness and response as well as in evidence-based interventions targeting post-traumatic stress. Fifth, specifically trained social workers should be added to interdisciplinary teams and programs for disaster management and response at local, state, and national levels.

Environmentally Displaced Populations

The profession's deep experience with serving immigrants and refugees and its commitment to human rights and social justice position it for leadership in crafting policy and practice responses to the growing numbers of people globally who are being displaced by climate change, environmental degradation, extreme weather events, and disasters (Drolet, Sampson, Jebaraj, & Richard, 2014). We recommend that social workers mobilize efforts to (1) raise awareness, in the profession and among communities, policymakers, and decision-makers, of the numerous challenges posed by global environmental migration; (2) advocate at all governance levels for new and enhanced policies to protect environmentally displaced persons (Sears, Kemp, & Palinkas, 2017), providing legal, political, and material resources as well as human and social services; (3) push policymakers in the United States to negotiate an amendment to the 1951 Geneva Convention, granting refugee status to environmental migrants, and push federal and state legislators to grant adequate legal status in the meantime; (4) reduce vulnerability to displacement, decrease unplanned displacement, and strengthen community resilience (e.g., through investments to reduce dependence on climate-dependent livelihoods); (5) develop strategies for planned, long-term relocation of environmental migrants; and (6) engage affected communities in planning and decision-making.

Community Adaptation and Resilience to Environmental Change

Cities increasingly are recognized as important sites for policies and interventions aimed at supporting and strengthening the ability of local communities to sustain, reorganize, and renew themselves through adaptive and transformative responses to stressors and shocks (Aldrich & Meyer, 2015; IPCC, 2014). Emerging emphases on urban community adaptation align closely with the profession's long investment in research and interventions aimed at strengthening community resilience and reducing disparities (Appleby, Bell, & Boetto, 2017; Drolet, 2012). Adaptation-oriented policies and initiatives frequently overlook sociostructural factors—such as housing affordability, access to employment, and historical and contemporary patterns of racism and discrimination—that compound the vulnerability of marginalized groups, particularly in the context of rising social and economic inequality (Archer & Dodman, 2015; Shi et al., 2016). We therefore recommend social work efforts to

- ensure that policies and interventions aimed at fostering urban resilience routinely focus on the social equity and environmental justice implications of adaptation efforts (e.g., equitable land use; safe, secure, and affordable housing; nontoxic built and natural environments; and equitable access to services, resources, and jobs);

- broaden the participation of marginalized and vulnerable communities in resilience and adaptation planning; and
- strengthen policy and planning attention to the social dimensions of climate change adaptation and advocate for the inclusion of social agencies, social workers, and community development practitioners in adaptation planning teams. These professionals have deep social–ecological expertise; are highly skilled in participatory community engagement; can serve as bridges among communities, disciplines, and sectors; and espouse values of participation, social justice, and self-determination.

OPPORTUNITIES FOR INTERDISCIPLINARY AND CROSS-SECTOR INVOLVEMENT

Engaging socioenvironmental challenges in innovative and equitable ways will necessarily involve social work scholars and practitioners in collaborations with a diverse array of partners. Broad-based collaborations are becoming the norm in global environmental change efforts, spanning diverse disciplines and also tapping the valuable knowledge and expertise of key stakeholders (IPCC, 2014; Moser, 2016). Fields such as sustainability science and urban science, for example, increasingly span the social sciences and humanities along with the biophysical sciences; spatial disciplines and professions; engineering; technology; professions such as law, public health, and public policy; and stakeholders such as residents, community organizations, local governments, and tribes.

FUTURE DIRECTIONS IN RESEARCH, PRACTICE, POLICY, AND EDUCATION

Realizing social work's potential for significant impact on the social and human dimensions of global environmental changes will require strategic, interlocking investments in several key areas, including research capacity building, interdisciplinary research and new partnerships, and educational transformation and practice innovation. Investments in building social work's socioenvironmental research capacity will be particularly critical to achieving the multidimensional agenda envisioned by this Grand Challenge (Kemp & Palinkas, 2015). Although the International Federation of Social Workers' *Global Agenda for Social Work and Social Development* (2012) called on the profession to "encourage and facilitate research into the social work role in relation to disasters and environmental challenges," socioenvironmental issues remain a relatively low priority on social work's research agenda (Bexell & Rechkemmer, 2016). In addition, although scholarship in this area has recently increased, there is a critical need for more rigorous study design and intervention research by social work scholars examining global environmental change (Mason, Shires, Arwood, & Borst, in press).

Recognizing that significant investments in closing this gap are unlikely unless the profession places higher priority on environmental research, the Grand Challenge aims to (1) bring socioenvironmental issues to the foreground of social work's research agenda and (2) strengthen the capacity of social work researchers to engage in socioenvironmental and sustainability research. Investments in social work's emerging and early career scholars will be particularly important to ensure that going forward they can confidently participate in and contribute to innovative, cross-sector socioenvironmental research programs (Gehlert, Hall, & Palinkas, 2017) that pursue innovative, equity-oriented policies and interventions; better understanding of the implications of current interventions, particularly for vulnerable and marginalized populations; and development of a robust, multilevel evidence base.

This agenda, in turn, has significant implications for both research capacity building and partnership development. Tackling the complex socioenvironmental issues confronting contemporary societies requires a capacity to frame innovative questions, diverse research discipline and practice partnerships, and theoretical frameworks and research methods with the potential to stimulate and undergird new perspectives and approaches. A diverse array of analytics and methods (both quantitative and qualitative) now characterize fields such as sustainability science, urban science, and environmental science, including spatial analytics (e.g., geographic information systems [GIS], technological innovations (e.g., digital and visual methods, social media, and mobile technologies), data-intensive science, complex systems science, community-based participatory research, and innovative mixed methods approaches (e.g., qualitative GIS). Opportunities for exposure to these methods through interdisciplinary coursework and training opportunities such as institutes and workshops, as well as hands-on experience in interdisciplinary research projects, will add significantly to the profession's capacity for capable involvement in environmental research teams. Training in the skill sets required for participatory and collaborative research will also be essential (Moser, 2016).

To be not just effective but also transformative in how social responses to a changing environment are achieved, social work's impact-oriented interdisciplinary research efforts and new partnerships must span community, disciplinary, and sectoral boundaries. Several synergies exist, for example, between this grand challenge and those of the National Academy of Engineering (http://www.engineeringchallenges.org). New partnerships among social work and engineering scholars, which also involve practitioners in the human services, urban planning, and civil and environmental engineering fields—as just one example—could transform how cities prepare for and adapt to environmental change.

Preparing social work scientists and practitioners for effective engagement with the very complex societal issues entailed in this and other societal grand challenges also requires a willingness by the profession to step back, appraise, and rethink its prevailing educational paradigms and practices (Miller & Hayward, 2014; O'Brien et al., 2013). Although the profession's long history of boundary-spanning activities gives it a "natural ability to draw together and integrate knowledge from a variety of disciplines" (Gehlert, 2016, p. 222), relatively few social work practitioners and researchers are fully prepared for effective participation in the diverse teams that increasingly are the norm in global environmental change and sustainability science, policymaking, and practice (Moore, Martinson, Nurius, & Kemp, in press). Efforts to more fully partner with community stakeholders only intensify these challenges. Systematic investments in preparing social work scholars for transdisciplinary and team science research (Gehlert, Hall, & Palinkas, 2017; Nurius, Kemp, Köngeter, & Gehlert, 2017) and translational research (Palinkas & Soydan, 2012) will thus be essential, as will similar investments in interprofessional and interdisciplinary preparation for social work professional degree students (Nurius, Coffey, Fong, Korr, & McRoy, 2017). Efforts to bring active, collaborative learning strategies (e.g., problem-based learning, studio learning, design thinking, and place-based learning) to the center of social work's educational paradigm will also be vital. Through these educational advancements, social work practitioners will be prepared for adaptation and scaling up of environmentally oriented social work roles and interventions, at multiple ecological levels, including evidence-based psychosocial interventions, community engagement and mobilization, and policy advocacy.

ASSESSMENT OF PROGRESS

Developing metrics for assessing measureable progress toward achieving the grand challenge to create social responses to a changing environment faces several obstacles. Among the greatest of these is convincing the public in general and social workers in particular of the need for action. According to the Pew Research Center (2016),

> Nearly half of US adults say climate change is due to human activity and a similar share says either that the Earth's warming stems from natural causes or that there is no evidence of warming. The disputes extend to differing views about

the likely impact of climate change and the possible remedies, both at the policy level and the level of personal behavior.

A recent report by the Yale Program on Climate Change Communication (2016) found that although most Americans (70%) think global warming is happening, only 40% believe that it will affect them personally). Anecdotally—and despite the reality that this grand challenge aligns closely with the profession's historic commitment to addressing "the environmental forces that create, contribute to, and address problems in living" (National Association of Social Workers [NASW], 2008)—efforts to mobilize a response to climate change among social workers have met with reports that other problems such as poverty, violence, and racism are more pressing and affect larger numbers of people.

We propose to assess progress in achieving our three priority areas (Kemp, Mason, Palinkas, Rechkemmer, & Teixeira, 2016)—disaster risk reduction, environmentally displaced populations, and community adaptation and resilience to environmental change—in addition to the area of mitigation of environment effects, using the RE-AIM framework, which is often used to understand and monitor the feasibility and success of intervention effectiveness, dissemination, and implementation in real-life settings. The acronym RE-AIM stands for reach, efficacy/effectiveness, adoption, implementation, and maintenance (http://re-aim.org). Reach refers to the absolute number, proportion, and representativeness of individuals who are willing to participate in a given initiative, intervention, or program. Efficacy refers to the impact of an intervention on important outcomes, including potential negative effects, quality of life, and economic outcomes. Adoption refers to the absolute number, proportion, and representativeness of settings and intervention agents (people who deliver the program) who are willing to initiate a program. Implementation refers to the intervention agents' fidelity to the various elements of an intervention's protocol, including consistency of delivery as intended and the time and cost of the intervention at the setting level, and to clients' use of the intervention strategies at the individual level. Maintenance refers to the extent to which a program or policy becomes institutionalized or part of the routine organizational practices and policies. Within the RE-AIM framework, maintenance also applies at the individual level.

The outcomes associated with achieving our priorities are listed in Table 8.1. Progress toward achieving these priorities will be assessed as shown in Table 8.2.

DISSEMINATION ACTIVITIES

We have been active in raising awareness about the relevance and urgency of this grand challenge, underscoring the importance of moving a focus on

Table 8.1. SOCIAL WORK ACCOMPLISHMENTS FOR THE NEXT DECADE

Priority Area	Type of Response	Domains Addressed	Outcome
Disaster risk reduction	• Mitigation • Treatment • Prevention	• Basic needs (e.g., food, water, and shelter) • Safety • Health	• Implement a nationwide program for training teachers to recognize trauma symptoms and make appropriate referrals for treatment of child disaster survivors. • Contribute to the evidence base for interventions, such as Psychological First Aid. • Evaluate the effectiveness of web-based technology in delivering mental health services to disaster survivors. • Develop an EBP for preventing and mitigating community-level conflicts, reducing community uncertainty, and building social capital post-disaster. • Adapt evidence-based approaches to community empowerment in preparing for and responding to disasters. • Develop a CSWE-approved training model in disaster preparedness and response for use in schools of social work. • Develop an evidence-based strategy for scaling up use of EBPs post-disaster that will have the following aims: • Fewer disaster victims per event • Fewer victims with trauma per event • Quicker disaster response • Increased recovery time
Environmentally displaced populations	• Resettlement • Integration	• Basic needs • Safety • Health • Social connectedness • Self-actualization	• Implement a collaborative care model for management of mental and behavioral health impacts of involuntary relocation because of environmental changes in primary care settings. • Adapt, evaluate, and implement EBPs for treatment and prevention of mental and behavioral health problems associated with involuntary migration.

Table 8.1. CONTINUED

Priority Area	Type of Response	Domains Addressed	Outcome
			• Collaborate with the UNHCR in developing a plan for implementing an ERRP, a three-tier plan for environmental refugee assistance and resettlement. • Coordinate with international, national, and local agencies to implement the ERRP, which will have the following aims: • Fewer refugees living in camps and other temporary shelters • Reduced time spent in transitional living arrangements • More refugees employed in host communities • Increased access to health and social services • Fewer physical and mental health problems related to migration stress and acculturation • Develop a CSWE-approved training model in refugee resettlement and community integration for use in schools of social work.
Community adaptation and resilience to environmental change	• Advocacy • Community empowerment • Community capacity building • Prevention	• Basic needs • Safety • Health • Social connectedness • Self-actualization	• Develop, tailor, and implement participatory interventions for enhancing community-based adaptation to current and future environmental challenges, with the following aims: • Identification of urban communities most vulnerable to negative environmental impacts • More communities demonstrating positive changes in measures of community adaptation and resilience (e.g., social capital, social cohesion, network density, civic engagement, community participation [e.g., in grassroots sustainability and urban rejuvenation projects], and financial asset accumulation)

(continued)

Table 8.1. CONTINUED

Priority Area	Type of Response	Domains Addressed	Outcome
			• More governments (e.g., municipal, regional, and national) implementing adaptation policies and programs developed with community input
• More interdisciplinary partnerships between social work and other urban professions (e.g., urban planning, architecture, and public health)
• Develop a guidebook for international field placements and student exchanges in planning, implementation, and sustainability.
• Develop measures of social sustainability inclusive of indices of social equity and inclusion.
Mitigation of environmental effects	• Advocacy
• Community empowerment
• Community education	• Basic needs
• Safety
• Health	• Develop a CSWE-approved training module on mitigation of environmental degradation associated with increasing urbanization/enhancement of community adaptive capacity for use in schools of social work.
• Develop, evaluate, and implement EBPs for reducing exposure to environmental degradation in low-income poor neighborhoods and low-income nations that will have the following aims:
• Fewer low-income individuals exposed to environmental contaminants
• Reduced incidence of environment-related chronic diseases
• Reduced impact on low-income communities of chronic and acute extreme weather events

CSWE, Council on Social Work Education; EBP, evidence-based practice; ERRP, environmental refugee resettlement plan; UNHCR, United Nations High Commissioner for Refugees.
Source: Adapted from Kemp and Palinkas (2015).

RE-AIM	Disaster Risk Reduction	Environmentally Displaced Populations	Community Adaptation and Resilience to Environmental Change	Mitigation of Environmental Effects
Reach	• Number and proportion of disaster victims who received evidence-based services after a natural disaster • Number and proportion of teachers and first responders trained in EBPs • Number and proportion of schools of social work using CSWE-approved training module in disaster preparedness and response	• Number and proportion of climate refugees receiving evidence-based services • Number and proportion of refugee resettlement workers trained in climate-related refugee EBPs • Number and proportion of schools of social work using CSWE-approved training module in refugee resettlement and community integration	• Number and proportion of schools of social work using CSWE-approved training module in building community sustainability and resilience	• Number and proportion of schools of social work using CSWE-approved training module in mitigation of urbanization-related environmental degradation
Efficacy/ effectiveness	• Fewer disaster victims per event • Fewer victims with trauma per event • Quicker disaster response • Faster recovery	• Significant reductions in mental health symptoms related to migration	• Significant improvements in measures of community adaptation and resilience (e.g., social capital, social cohesion, network density, civic engagement, community participation, and financial asset accumulation) • More governments (e.g., municipal, regional, and national) implementing adaptation policies and programs developed with community input	• Fewer individuals exposed to environmental contaminants • Reduced incidence of environment-related chronic diseases • Reduced impact on low-income communities of chronic and acute extreme weather events

(continued)

Table 8.2. CONTINUED

RE-AIM	Disaster Risk Reduction	Environmentally Displaced Populations	Community Adaptation and Resilience to Environmental Change	Mitigation of Environmental Effects
Adoption	• Number and proportion of first responders and agencies using EBPs	• Number and proportion of resettlement workers and agencies using EBPs • Number of communities with ERRP	• More interdisciplinary partnerships between social work and other urban professions • Number and proportion of community urban redevelopment boards with representation	• Number and proportion of low-income communities in which mitigation is being addressed
Implementation	• Fidelity assessments of EBPs • Effective strategies identified for scale-up	• Fidelity assessments of ERRP • Effective strategies identified for scale-up	• Fidelity assessments of social sustainability • Effective strategies identified for scale-up	• Fidelity assessments of EBPs designed to reduce exposure to environmental contaminants • Effective strategies identified for scale-up
Maintenance	• Number of EBP services available 1 year after implementation	• Number of EBP services available 1 year after implementation • Number of communities delivering ERRP-based services 1 year after implementation	• Number of sustainability partnerships 1 year after creation • Number of interdisciplinary partnerships 1 year after creation	• Number of mitigation partnerships 1 year after creation

CSWE, Council on Social Work Education; EBP, evidence-based practice; ERRP, environmental refugee resettlement plan.
Source: Adapted from Kemp and Palinkas (2015).

environmental change and sustainable development from the margins to the center of the profession's discourse and attention, and articulating a preliminary vision for goals and potential impacts. In addition to the initial position paper (Kemp & Palinkas, 2015), we developed a policy brief making recommendations in three priority areas: disaster risk reduction, environmentally displaced populations, and community adaptation and resilience (Kemp, Mason, Palinkas, Rechkemmer, & Teixeira, 2016). We elaborated on the second recommendation in a policy action statement (Sears, Kemp, & Palinkas, 2017). Members of the coordinating group also have presented on the Grand Challenge at a series of major conferences in the United States, Europe, and Asia.

In November 2016, Dr. Lisa Reyes Mason co-convened an interdisciplinary symposium, People and Climate Change: Vulnerability, Adaptation, Social Justice, at Washington University in St. Louis, and at the University of Washington in Seattle, Dr. Susan Kemp collaborated with colleagues to convene a symposium, Urban Environmental Justice in a Time of Climate Change (http://urban.uw.edu/index.php/events/details/urban-environmental-justice-in-a-time-of-climate-change). We have produced journal articles and chapters on moving the grand challenges forward (Gehlert, Hall, & Palinkas, 2017; Kemp & Palinkas, in press; Palinkas & Wong, in press); provided background for articles produced by our universities and by NASW (2017); and are participating consultatively in institution-level efforts to bring the Grand Challenges to the center of social work curricula and research programs (including a recent meeting at the University of Southern California). In addition, the Grand Challenges successfully advocated for the development of a new research cluster within the Society for Social Work and Research—Sustainable Development, Urbanization, and Environmental Justice.

Social work faculty involved in the Grand Challenge have been actively involved in conducting research and developing new initiatives in the following areas:

- Disaster preparedness and response: Marleen Wong and Vivien Villaverde (University of Southern California) have been engaged in training teachers and first responders in the Philippines and South Korea using the three-tiered framework developed by Palinkas (2015). Wong and Villaverde are also developing trauma-informed schools as a tool for coping with inner-city violence and responding to natural disasters. Lisa Reyes Mason is collaborating with engineers and geographers in examining socially responsible storm water management in the face of climate change uncertainty. This team is also funded by the National Oceanic and Atmospheric Administration to examine tornado warning response in Tennessee. Andreas Rechkemmer (University of Denver) is part of a team of researchers exploring the dynamics of fear-related behaviors related to environmental disasters and emerging infectious diseases such as Ebola.

- Climate-related migration: Andreas Rechkemmer has been examining the social, political, and legal ramifications of climate-related forced migration.
- Food and water insecurity: Michelle Kaiser (The Ohio State University) has been examining food insecurity, social worker roles in community food strategies, and use of food pantries (Kaiser, 2017; Kaiser & Hermsen, 2015; Kaiser, Usher, & Spees, 2015). Water insecurity has been studied in the Philippines by Lisa Reyes Mason (2015) and in Kenya by Jennifer Willett (2015b).
- Older adults: Tam Perry (Wayne State University) has been conducting research on older adults' experiences and understandings of the Flint, Michigan, water crisis as part of a larger effort to identify the problems that environmental degradation and climate change can yield for older adults and families and to develop research that can strengthen multisystemic responses to prevent and mitigate such negative effects.
- Low- and middle-income countries: Jennifer Willett (University of Nevada, Reno) has conducted research on experiences of environmental degradation in poor communities in Kenya, including the occurrence of micro disasters, formal aid responses, and community support through social networks (Willett, 2015a, 2015b, 2017). Andreas Rechkemmer has been examining the social, political, and legal ramifications of climate-related forced migration in low- and middle-income countries.
- Environmental justice: Amy Krings (Loyola University, Chicago) has studied environmental justice issues in Detroit and Flint, Michigan (Teixeira & Krings, 2015). A chapter on social work and environmental justice has been authored by Powers, Willett, Mathias, and Hayward (in press).
- Indigenous communities: Shanondora Billiot (Washington University, St Louis), Felicia Mitchell (Arizona State University), and Angela Fernandez (University of Washington, Seattle) are among a growing group of indigenous doctoral and early career researchers focusing on the intersections among environmental changes, historical inequities, and the health and well-being of indigenous peoples.
- Urbanization and climate: In collaboration with colleagues from the Department of Geography and School of Engineering at the University of Tennessee–Knoxville, Lisa Reyes Mason has examined spatiotemporal variability of urban heat islands and its impact on quality of life for low-income neighborhoods (Mason, Ellis, & Hathaway, 2017; Mason, Hathaway, Ellis, & Harrison, 2017).
- Youth: Samantha Teixeira (Boston College) focuses on how neighborhood environmental conditions affect youth and how youth can be engaged in creating solutions to environmental problems in their communities (Teixeira & Zuberi, 2016). Russell Vergara (University of Southern California) is the founder and director of CYPHER, a nonprofit organization dedicated

to developing socially responsible technology entrepreneurs through tech-enabled innovation at the nexus of food, energy, and water systems. CYPHER targets students with little or no background in engineering and youth from "developing and least developed places" with little or no infrastructure for CleanTech ideation and innovation.

FUTURE DIRECTIONS: MOVING THE GRAND CHALLENGE FORWARD

Given the significant complexities inherent in addressing "wicked" problems, moving Grand Challenge initiatives from initial launch to full implementation requires careful attention to the mechanisms necessary to "link strategy and action to achieve specific grand challenges goals" (Uehara, Barth, Coffey, Padilla, & McClain, 2017, p. 77). A range of such mechanisms will be needed to put lift under this Grand Challenge, many of which we have referred to in this chapter. In closing, we summarize two that we view as key.

Visibility and Outreach

If social work is to be viewed as a value-added contributor in interdisciplinary socioenvironmental research and policymaking contexts, it is essential that we raise the profession's profile and reach in these domains. This task has at least three central dimensions. First, the profession needs effective mechanisms for communicating with others about the socioenvironmental needs it identifies and the knowledge it can contribute to crafting robust solutions. Second (and related to the first), as a profession and a science, social work needs to be able to clearly and confidently articulate what it distinctively brings to the table. Third, the field needs to both leverage and create mechanisms for building stronger connections with research and policy organizations and collaborations working at the social–ecological interface. Some of these relationships already exist, but in general, the profession is still treated as an afterthought in environmental and sustainability circles. The Grand Challenge also provides an opportunity to inventory and build on the various connections that individual social work scholars and practitioners have forged with national and global sustainability efforts.

Networks and Collaborations

In addition to cross-disciplinary and transdisciplinary partnerships, robust networks within the profession—both nationally and cross-nationally—will be critical to elevating social work's environmental research capacity and reach. Although some key connective mechanisms are already in place, such as the Green-EcoSocial Work Network listserve (Green-EcoSocial-Work-Network-l@uncg.edu), the Grand Challenge provides an opportunity for a more intentional focus on the development of research-oriented environmental social work collaborations, from research clusters organized around topical issues (e.g., water, which emerged as a shared interest among several scholars attending the Society for Social Work and Research conference) to broader national and cross-national networks focused on shaping and coordinating social work's socioenvironmental research agenda, strengthening the profession's environmental research capacity, solidifying connections with scholars in other disciplines, and elevating social work's access to national and cross-national funding opportunities.

CONCLUSION

During its long history of contextually oriented practice, social work has developed a robust, multilevel portfolio of interventions that in various ways address the relationship between human challenges and impinging environments. In recent years, the profession has buttressed this practice portfolio with a growing body of expertise in intervention research (Jenson, 2014) and implementation science, which is centrally concerned with the challenging but essential task of taking evidence-based interventions to scale in complex, turbulent, frequently underresourced, culturally diverse contexts (Palinkas & Soydan, 2012) and also with the vital importance of building robust partnerships with diverse stakeholders, including practitioners, community residents and organizations, local and state governments, and tribes (Palinkas, He, Choy-Brown, & Hertel, 2017). In concert with the profession's social justice mission and person–environment orientation, these strengths position social work for a larger role in global environmental change science and practice. Realizing this potential, however, will require intentional investments aimed at building the profession's capacity for engaging as a peer in sustainability and environmental science, policymaking, programming, and practice.

REFERENCES

Aldrich, D. P., & Meyer, M. A. (2015). Social capital and community resilience. *American Behavioral Scientist, 59*, 254–269.

Appleby, K., Bell, K., & Boetto, H. (2017). Climate change adaptation: Community action, disadvantaged groups and practice implications for social work. *Australian Social Work, 70*(1), 78–91. http://dx.doi.org/10.1080/0312407X.2015.1088558

Archer, D., & Dodman, D. (2015). Making capacity building critical: Power and justice in building urban climate resilience in Indonesia and Thailand. *Urban Climate*, *14*, 68–78.

Bexell, S. M., & Rechkemmer, A. (2016). *A critical analysis of inclusion gaps in directly relevant sustainable development themes, facts and findings in recent social work research.* Retrieved from http://sswr.confex.com/sswr/2016/webprogram/Paper26054.html

Centre for Research on the Epidemiology of Disasters and United Nations Office for Disaster Risk Reduction. (2015). *The human cost of weather-related disasters, 1995–2015.* Retrieved from https://www.unisdr.org/we/inform/publications/46796

Drolet, J. (2012). Climate change, food security, and sustainable development: A study in community-based responses and adaptations in British Columbia, Canada. *Community Development*, *43*, 630–644.

Drolet, J., Sampson, T., Jebaraj, D. P., & Richard, L. (2014). Social work and environmentally induced displacement: A commentary. *Refuge: Canada's Journal on Refugees*, *29*, 55–62.

Forbes, D., Lewis, V., Varker, T., Phelps, A., O'Donnell, M., Wade, D. J., . . . Creamer, M. (2011). Psychological first aid following trauma: Implementation and evaluation framework for high-risk organizations. *Psychiatry*, *74*(3), 224–239. doi:10.1521/psyc.2011.74.3.224

Gehlert, S. (2016). Social work and science. *Research on Social Work Practice*, *26*, 219–224.

Gehlert, S., Hall, K. I., & Palinkas, L. A. (2017). Preparing our next-generation scientific workforce to address the Grand Challenges for Social Work. *Journal of the Society for Social Work and Research*, *8*, 119–136.

Hackmann, H., Moser, S. C., & St. Clair, A. L. (2014). The social heart of global environmental change. *Nature Climate Change*, *4*, 653–655.

Intergovernmental Panel on Climate Change. (2014). *Climate change 2014—Impacts, adaptation, and vulnerability: Part A. Global and sectoral aspects.* New York, NY: Cambridge University Press.

International Federation of Social Workers. (2012). *The global agenda for social work and social development: Commitment to action.* Retrieved from http://ifsw.org/get-involved/agenda-for-social-work

Jaycox, L. (2004). *Cognitive Behavioral Intervention for Trauma in Schools (CBITS).* Longmont, CO: Lopris West.

Jenson, J. M. (2014). Science, social work, and intervention research: The case of Critical Time Intervention. *Research on Social Work Practice*, *24*, 564–570.

Kaiser, M. L. (2017). Redefining food security in a community context: An exploration of community food security indicators and social worker roles in community food strategies. *Journal of Community Practice*, *25*(2), 213–234. doi:10.1080/10705422.2017.1308897

Kaiser, M. L., & Hermsen, J. (2015). Food acquisition strategies, food security, and health status among families with children using food pantries. *Families in Society: The Journal of Contemporary Social Services*, *96*(2), 83–90. doi:10.1606/1044-3894.2015.96.16

Kaiser, M. L., Usher, K., & Spees, C. K. (2015). Community food security strategies: An exploratory study of their potential for food insecure households with children. *Journal of Applied Research on Children: Informing Policy for Children at Risk*, *6*(2), Article 2. Retrieved from http://digitalcommons.library.tmc.edu/childrenatrisk/vol6/iss2/2

Kemp, S. P., Mason, L. R., Palinkas, L. A., Rechkemmer, A., & Teixeira, S. (2016). *Policy recommendations for meeting the Grand Challenge to Create Social Responses to a Changing Environment* (Grand Challenges for Social Work: Policy Brief No.7). Baltimore, MD: American Academy of Social Work and Social Welfare. Retrieved from https://csd.wustl.edu/Publications/Documents/PB7.pdf

Kemp, S. P., & Palinkas, L. A. (2015). *Create social responses to the human impacts of environmental change.* Retrieved from http://aaswsw.org/grand-challenges-initiative/12-challenges/create-social-responses-to-a-changing-environment

Kemp, S. P., & Palinkas, L. A. (in press). Responding to global environmental change: A grand challenge for social work. In *Welfare, citizenship and human rights: Rethinking social work in the XXI century.* Proceedings of the 2016 Il Congreso Internacional de Trabajo Social, University of Rioja, Logrono, Spain.

Mason, L. R. (2015). Beyond improved access: Seasonal and multidimensional water security in urban Philippines. *Global Social Welfare, 2*(3), 119–128.

Mason, L. R., Ellis, K. N., & Hathaway, J. M. (2017). Experiences of urban environmental conditions in socially and economically diverse neighborhoods. *Journal of Community Practice, 25*(1), 48–67.

Mason, L. R., Hathaway, J. M., Ellis, K. N., & Harrison, T. (2017). Public interest in microclimate data in Knoxville, Tennessee, USA. *Sustainability, 9,* 23. doi:10.3390/su9010023

Mason, L. R., Shires, M. K., Arwood, C., & Borst, A. (in press). Social work research and global environmental change: A scoping review. *Journal of the Society for Social Work and Research.*

Miller, S. E., & Hayward, R. A. (2014). Social work education's role in addressing people and a planet at risk. *Social Work Education, 33,* 280–295.

Moore, M., Martinson, M. I., Nurius, P. S., & Kemp, S. P. (in press). Transdisciplinarity in research: Perspectives of early career faculty. *Research on Social Work Practice.*

Moser, S. C. (2016). Transformations and co-design: Co-designing research projects on social transformations to sustainability. *Current Opinion in Environmental Sustainability, 20,* v–viii.

National Aeronautics and Space Administration. (2017). *NASA–NOAA data show 2016 warmest year on record globally.* Retrieved from https://www.nasa.gov/press-release/nasa-noaa-data-show-2016-warmest-year-on-record-globally

National Association of Social Workers. (2008). *Code of ethics of the National Association of Social Workers.* Retrieved from https://www.socialworkers.org/pubs/code/code.asp

National Association of Social Workers. (2017). *Climate change, natural disasters affect well-being. NASW News, 62.* Retrieved from http://www.socialworkers.org/pubs/news/2017/2/Climate%20change.asp

Nurius, P. S., Coffey, D. S., Fong, R., Korr, W. S., & McRoy, R. (2017). Preparing professional degree students to tackle grand challenges: A framework for aligning social work curricula. *Journal of the Society for Social Work and Research, 8*(1), 99–118.

Nurius, P. S., Kemp, S. P., Köngeter, S., & Gehlert, S. (2017). Next generation social work research education: Fostering transdisciplinary readiness. *European Journal of Social Work.* Advance online publication. doi:10.1080/13691457.2017.1320530

O'Brien, K., Reams, J., Caspari, A., Dugmore, A., Faghihimani, M., Fazey, I., . . . Winiwarter, V. (2013). You say you want a revolution? Transforming education and capacity building in response to global change. *Environmental Science & Policy, 28,* 48–59.

Palinkas, L. A. (2015). Behavioral health and disasters: Looking to the future. *Journal of Behavioral Health Services & Research, 42*, 86–95.

Palinkas, L. A., He, A. S., Choy-Brown, M., & Hertel, A. L. (2017). Operationalizing social work science through research–practice partnerships: Lessons from implementation science. *Research on Social Work Practice, 21*, 181–188.

Palinkas, L. A., & Soydan, H. (2012). *Translation and implementation of evidence-based practice.* New York, NY: Oxford University Press.

Palinkas, L. A., & Wong, M. (in press). Social sustainability and global climate change: A new challenge for social work. In A. Chong & I. Chi (Eds.), *Social and environmental sustainability in Asia and the Pacific Rim: Implications to social work.* London, UK: Routledge.

Pew Research Center. (2016). *The politics of climate.* Retrieved from http://www.pewinternet.org/2016/10/04/the-politics-of-climate

Powers, M. C. F, Willett, J., Mathias, J. & Hayward, A. (forthcoming). Green Social Work for Environmental Justice: Implications for International Social Workers. In L. Dominelli, H. B. Ku, & B. R. Nikku (Eds.), *Green Social Work Handbook.* London, England: Routledge.

Rechkemmer, A., O'Connor, A., Rai, A., Decker Sparks, J. L., Mudliar, P., & Shultz, J. M. (2016). A complex social–ecological disaster: Environmentally induced forced migration. *Disaster Health, 3*, 112–120.

Sears, J., Kemp, S. P., & Palinkas, L. A. (2017). *Develop policies targeting environmentally induced displacement in the United States.* Retrieved from http://aaswsw.org/wp-content/uploads/2017/03/PAS.7.1.pdf

Shi, L., Chu, E, M.,Anguelovski, I., Aylett, A., Debats, J., Goh, K., . . . VanDeveer, S. D. (2016). Roadmap towards justice in urban climate adaptation research. *Nature Climate Change, 6*, 131–137.

Teixeira, S., & Krings, A. (2015). Sustainable social work: An environmental justice framework for social work education. *Social Work Education, 35*, 513–527.

Teixeira, S., & Zuberi, A. (2016). Mapping the racial inequality in place: Using youth perceptions to identify unequal exposure to neighborhood environmental hazards. *International Journal of Environmental Research and Public Health, 13*(9), 844. doi:10.3390/ijerph13090844

Uehara, E. S., Barth, R. P., Coffey, D., Padilla, Y., & McClain, A. (2017). An introduction to the special section on Grand Challenges for Social Work. *Journal of the Society for Social Work and Research, 8*, 75–85.

United Nations. (2015). *Sustainable development goals.* Retrieved from http://www.un.org/sustainabledevelopment/sustainable-development-goals

United Nations, Department of Economic and Social Affairs, Population Division. (2014). *World urbanization prospects: The 2014 revision—Highlights* (ST/ESA/SER.A/352). Retrieved from https://esa.un.org/unpd/wup/publications/files/wup2014-highlights.Pdf

United Nations Human Settlements Programme. (2016). *World cities report 2016: Urbanization and development.* Retrieved from http://wcr.unhabitat.org/main-report

US Environmental Protection Agency. (2016). *National climate assessment: Extreme weather.* Retrieved from http://nca2014.globalchange.gov/highlights/report-findings/extreme-weather

Weaver, C. P., Mooney, S., Allen, D., Beller-Simmons, N., Fish, T., Grambsch, A. E., . . . Winthrop, R. (2014). From global change science to action with social sciences. *Nature Climate Change, 4*, 656–659.

Willett, J. (2015a). Exploring the intersection of environmental degradation and poverty: Environmental injustice in Nairobi, Kenya. *Social Work Education, 35*(5), 558–572.

Willett, J. (2015b). The slow violence of climate change in poor rural Kenyan communities: "Water is life. Water is everything." *Contemporary Rural Social Work, 7*(1), 39–55.

Willett, J. (2017). Micro disasters: Expanding the social work conceptualization of disasters. *International Social Work.* Article first published online: July 7, 2017. doi:https://doi.org/10.1177/0020872817712565

Yale Program on Climate Change Communication. (2016). *Yale climate opinion maps—U.S. 2016.* Retrieved from http://climatecommunication.yale.edu/visualizations-data/ycom-us-2016

Grand Challenges
for Social Work
Harness technology for social good

CHAPTER 9

Harness Technology for Social Good

STEPHANIE COSNER BERZIN AND CLAUDIA J. COULTON

Information and communication technology (ICT) is transformational in its power to connect, create access to, and embolden new opportunities to rethink social work practice. We live in a digital society in which vast quantities of data are produced, but much of these data remain untapped for social work. Although selected examples of practice and policy innovation through digital technologies have been documented (Barak & Grohol, 2011), social work practitioners and scholars remain hesitant to fully embrace and take leadership in this movement. Moreover, despite existing troves of data and promising analytic technology, the social and human services sector lags behind in using data-driven strategies in designing programs and policies. As the world becomes increasingly reliant on technology, a grand challenge for social work is to harness technological and digital advancements for social good.

Compared to the business sector, social work has been slow to adopt technology (Zorn, Flanagin, & Shoham, 2011). Many established companies now have chief information and technology officers to ensure that technology is optimally applied to business operations. Businesses in the technology sector are experiencing unprecedented growth, and some of them are developing products for the social welfare sector. Engineers are developing software and hardware being adapted by the social work field, often without the input of social work professionals. Although these fields show considerable progress in technology as it applies to social impact, limited resources, ethical and legal considerations, lack of training, and social work's historical reliance on face-to-face communications have prevented significant progress in the field. Despite the slow start, ICT is beginning to permeate social work structures. Social workers use technology for administration in human service agencies and for communication in practice. However, these basic uses represent a fraction of technology's capacity to enhance practice and to reshape social context (Goldkind & Wolf, 2015). Social work has an important role to play in not only harnessing the power of ICT to improve practice but also ensuring that ICT is developed to support social good.

Social programs have also not benefitted fully from the technological advances that enable the applications of big data. For example, businesses glean a great deal about consumers' behaviors and tastes from big data and customize products to match, whereas human service organizations have yet to fully implement these types of practices to improve the effectiveness of their programs at scale.

Disadvantaged communities have arguably faced barriers to accessing information and analytic tools that could individually or collectively advance their quality of life and economic opportunities. However, innovative technologies, if made affordable and available, can connect populations previously marginalized by geography, disability, or economics. Although currently there is great unevenness on the part of government agencies in providing open access to public data, technology used well could provide diverse communities information that they can use to better their own circumstances (Goldsmith & Crawford, 2014).

If social work does not invest in building the capacity to fully make use of technology to benefit society, and particularly vulnerable groups and communities, the promise of these innovations will not be universally achieved. Moreover, the risks and burdens emanating from technological advances may disproportionately fall on those who are not equipped to smartly engage with them.

The compelling nature of this challenge stems from not only the magnitude of use but also the possibility of solutions. Digital and technology-based solutions have the power to create massive change and radical transformation in who is served and how. Technology has fundamentally shifted the way humans communicate with each other and their environment (Mishna, Bogo, Root, Sawyer, & Khoury-Kassabri, 2012), made disruptive shifts in philanthropy (Arrillaga-Andreessen, 2015), and created transformational opportunities for new interventions in social work practice (Barak & Grohol, 2011; Chan & Holosko, 2016).

Meeting this challenge would result in a broader and more equitable distribution of the benefits of technology in society. Enhanced by innovative integration of ICT into practice, social work would expand its reach and impact. Social services would be available to people who traditionally have been excluded because of geography, transportation, and scheduling barriers. Powerful data analytics would enable more customized, timelier, and better targeted services. Technology would support the design of more effective assessment tools, intervention modalities, and real-time feedback mechanisms. Populations currently victimized by the digital divide would be able to participate on an equal footing.

OPPORTUNITIES FOR IMPROVEMENT

Failure to incorporate technological advances into social work and social welfare means that large portions of the population fail to benefit fully and scarce resources are not optimally deployed. Progress on many fronts will be hindered if promising technologies are not incorporated into social work interventions, service delivery systems, organizational decision-making, program and policy evaluation, and social innovation. Opportunities exist for integration of technology through the use of social media, mobile technology, wearable technology and sensors, robotics and artificial intelligence, gaming, geospatial technology, big data, and data analytics.

Although this robust set of opportunities for technology integration exists, several limitations prevent the intentional use of technology into practice (Mishna et al., 2012). Limited education and training prevent many practitioners from knowing how to incorporate technology effectively (Mishna, Bogo, & Sawyer, 2015). Limited exposure to innovative applications of technology to therapeutic work creates misperceptions that also prevent their widespread adoption. A recent systematic review of social work interventions using technology found that of 17 studies that met criteria for good validity and high intervention fidelity, only 3 evaluated the role that technology played in the intervention (Chan & Holosko, 2016).

The implication is that there are very few social work interventions that use ICT, and there is even less empirical information about the role that the technology plays in the interventions. Limited financial resources hinder the adoption and testing of technologies in the field. Although the availability of mobile technology, wireless services, and low-cost apps has removed several barriers, social workers are adapting and modifying technologies developed for non-social work purposes. In addition, although many sectors are developing technologies that will improve the emotional, behavioral, and cognitive well-being of people, the promise of innovating and integrating technology into social work practice has yet to be realized.

At the policy and systems level, technological advances in data science and analytics are not being taken up as quickly as they could. Massive amounts of valuable social data remain locked up in legacy data systems and agency silos, where the data cannot readily be used to improve performance or optimally respond to changing needs. Shrinking resources for social programs make leveraging data to drive programming even more vital. Although there is a growing demand to prove what works, human service systems often lack the data management and analysis infrastructure necessary to efficiently evaluate programs. Moreover, such systems lack interoperability and standardization, making it challenging to integrate data across sectors to examine the long-term costs and benefits of social programs.

At the same time, expectations to use data and predictive analytics to make sound decisions are increasing. These expectations are migrating from the corporate sector to the boards of nonprofit organizations and influential foundation funders. Agency executives and managers are now expected to have data at the ready to support their operational decisions and long-term strategies. They are increasingly required to provide metrics to show what is working and to ensure that quality standards and outcomes are meeting the mark.

In addition, the general public is beginning to call for more civic engagement with socially relevant data. Open government and civic hacking movements provide vehicles for mining data and generating information for communal use. The term *open data* describes the idea that certain kinds of data should be disseminated freely so that they can be reused, analyzed, published, and transformed into new and useful products (Bertot, Gorham, Jaeger, Sarin, & Choi, 2014). Furthermore, community coalitions that work to improve outcomes for target populations (e.g., vulnerable youth, homeless veterans, and children growing up in deep poverty) require access to cross-system data as a way to keep all the partners on track and working toward common goals (Kania & Kramer, 2011).

Despite the push toward data applications, the social sector needs to address numerous obstacles to benefit from its data resources. Data security breaches and privacy are a central concern, especially with respect to human service, educational, and health records (Hoffman & Podgurski, 2013; Strandburg, 2014). Although the law permits many of these records to be used for research, evaluation, and quality improvement purposes, agencies are often reluctant to share the records for analysis. Moreover, the social sector must consider the ethical matter of using digital material for purposes of which individuals may not have been aware when providing personal information. A related difficulty concerns data ownership and control, especially when data from various sources are combined to create applications beyond the scope of the original intent. Although such "mash-ups" often yield information of very high value, exemplifying the power of big data, they require agencies to cede individual control to achieve a larger societal benefit. Such agreements often encounter legal and practical complications.

Curation of big data is another enormous challenge because the data are a byproduct of numerous processes, not generated specifically for the purpose to which they are eventually applied. Understanding how these processes shape the data is crucial to producing valid information and correct interpretation. The data require careful cleaning and validation by specialists with a deep understanding of the data-generation processes. A related issue is determining how to allow other analysts to replicate the results from big data. Unlike the fixed data sets associated with traditional research projects, big data platforms are typically refreshed by a continuous flow of new information. It may be difficult to exactly reproduce results if the data have shifted between the original and validation analysis. Before fully adopting big data applications, social work professionals need to develop, vet, and document rigorous quality assurance, versioning, and archiving techniques and ensure awareness of the factors that affect the data-generation process (Lazer, Kennedy, King, & Vespignani, 2014).

INNOVATIONS AND THEIR IMPORTANCE

Recent accomplishments across a range of technologies suggest that they can be successfully applied in social work and social welfare. Action can be taken in a number of areas during the next decade to ensure that available technology is effectively applied in social work and social welfare to maximize attainment of social good.

Considering the range of ICT services, ample opportunities exist for expanding social work practice by geography, availability, access to providers, and lowering cost. Populations that have been difficult to reach through traditional services might find new opportunities for engagement in social work services through technology (Best, Manktelow, & Taylor, 2014; Craig, McInroy, McCready, Di Cesare, & Pettaway, 2015). Services provided across a range of Internet and technology-enabled platforms also potentially transform access for those with disabilities, who lack transportation, are homebound, or need specific communication strategies (Barak & Grohol, 2011; Brownlee, Graham, Doucette, Hotson, & Halverson, 2010). ICT also enhances the speed and flexibility of services, and it provides the ability for individual pacing (Proudfoot, 2013). Data mining tools and integrated data systems provide the potential for directing policy and programs more effectively. In the area of technology, there has been a huge range of innovations and demonstrated effectiveness (Barak, Hen, Boniel-Nissim, & Shapira, 2008). Specific innovations are discussed next.

Social Media and the Internet

The Internet and social media have changed the way people communicate in the 21st century. These tools have opened new forms of communication, closed gaps based on geography, allowed new access to information, and expanded interactivity and collaboration. Approximately 50% of the world's population uses the Internet, and more than one-third (37%) use social media (Hootsuite, 2017). With this level of penetration, the opportunities for incorporation into social work are limitless. Internet and social media have been applied to social work clinical and macro practice through online help-seeking (Best et al., 2014), advocacy (Guo & Saxton, 2013; Sitter & Curnew, 2016), peer support and self-care (Gandy-Guedes, Vance, Bridgewater, Montgomery, & Taylor, 2016), and health promotion and education (Korda & Itani, 2011). In addition, data applications include the use of social media to identify emerging social movements (Tinati, Halford, Carr, & Pope, 2014) and to track trends related to social issues (Stephens-Davidowitz, 2013).

Mobile Technology

The promise of mobile technology allows for accessing information and services where and when they are needed. With 66% of the world's population using mobile technology, it also provides access across populations and geography (Hootsuite, 2017). Used in the health care field, mobile technology allows for the delivery of interventions with access to information, tracking, and monitoring on a constant basis (Klasnja & Pratt, 2012). In social work practice, this might include access to intervention components, model fidelity checks, real-time assessment, and connection to mental health professionals. Supplementing with global positioning systems (GPS) and sensors allows for more specified tracking and notification systems. Cognitive interventions making use of these technologies (Griffiths, Farrer, & Christensen, 2010; Lintvedt et al., 2013) have obtained positive outcomes related to services delivered in real time. Mobile technology that provides ongoing information and support has also been shown to improve practice (Lee & Walsh, 2015).

Wearable Technology and Sensors

Whereas mobile technology provides some access to ongoing data collection and real-time intervention, wearable technology and sensors provide another avenue for monitoring. In one example, combining mobile technology with wearables blends self-report questionnaires with physiological data to collecting mental health information (Gaggioli et al., 2013). In other studies relying on wearable technology, eye tracking sensors were used to successfully monitor mental health in daily life (Vidal, Turner, Bulling, & Gellersen, 2012), and wrist sensors were used to gauge stress (Sano & Picard, 2013). A T-shirt with embedded sensors has been used effectively to monitor electrocardiogram-heart rate variability, respiration activity, and activity recognition in the treatment of patients with serious mental illness (Lanata, Valenza, Nardelli, Gentili, & Scilingo, 2015). Wearable sensors can track noise, body metrics, ingestion, and location as a supplement to existing data (Goldkind & Wolf, 2015).

Physiological tracking allows self-report and retrospective data to be supplemented with real-time and continuous data. Social work assessment and intervention can make use of these new sources of data to create more personalized feedback (Barak & Grohol, 2011) and enhance client self-management (Craig & Calleja Lorenzo, 2014). Feedback that goes directly to clinicians can also help direct treatment and support clinical decision-making (Lanata et al., 2015).

Robotics and Artificial Intelligence

Another innovation that supports real-time assessment, intervention, and feedback derives from the promise of robotics and artificial intelligence (Kumar et al., 2013). Integrating artificial intelligence into screening and intake might support detection of particular response patterns or support clinical decision-making. Although only in a nascent stage of development in mental health, the field of social robotics seeks to blend robotics, computer science, engineering, and psychology to create robots that are able to engage in human interaction (Hegel, Muhl, Wrede, Hielscher-Fastabend, & Sagerer, 2009). Used in the treatment of depression in older adults (Banks, Wiloughby, & Banks, 2008) and autism spectrum disorder (Giullian et al., 2010), robots may play an expanded role in social work research and practice.

Gaming and Gamification

Although not directly an ICT, gaming and gamification represent avenues of innovation that come out of the ICT landscape. Video games have become ubiquitous in modern life, and exploiting them and their mechanisms has potential for social work practice. Gamification, which includes the use of gamelike mechanisms in nongaming environments, such as badging and recognition systems, supports learning specific behaviors (Langlois, 2013). Already being used in the treatment of depression (Rao, 2013), anxiety (Dennis & O'Toole, 2014), substance abuse, and violence prevention (Schoech, Boyas, Black, & Elias-Lambert, 2013), gamification represents a potential avenue for future social work practice. Related to gamification, gaming uses actual games in the intervention. The prevalence of technology-based gaming has led video games to be incorporated in the treatment of post-traumatic stress disorder (Holmes, James, Coode-Bate, & Deeprose, 2009), schizophrenia (Han & colleagues, 2008), and phobias (Walshe, Lewis, Kim, O'Sullivan, & Wiederhold, 2004). Virtual reality has been shown to be effective in therapeutic treatment, particularly for anxiety and pediatric disorders (Mohr, Burns, Schueller, Clarke, & Klinkman, 2013).

Geospatial Technology

Geographically referenced information is now ubiquitous coming from GPS-enabled devices, sensors, images, geo-coded records, and other sources. Geographic information systems (GIS) integrate spatial data and information and also incorporate tools that enable displays, mapping, visualization, and spatial analysis. Geospatial technology is already being incorporated into social work practice and research, but it has the potential to be more valuable in a very broad range of applications (Mandayam & Joosten, 2016). One area in which it has found immediate relevance is in community practice. For example, youth have been engaged in exploring their community and the issues that affect them using spatial data and mapping tools (Teixeira & Zuberi, 2016). Also, these technologies are used extensively in planning the locations and needs for services, evaluating service accessibility, and identifying clusters of social need or risk (Daley et al., 2016; Freisthler & Weiss, 2008; Thurston et al., 2017).

Big Data and Integrated Data Systems

There is a growing interest in how to take advantage of big data in social work. Social agencies are the holders of massive data systems that can be turned into generators of actionable information. Agencies are beginning to automate performance metrics, progress dashboards, and assessment tools that support practice and policy.

Another significant development using big data is the movement to build and maintain multiagency integrated data systems (IDS) as a permanent utility for the social sector. In most IDS, administrative records from many agencies are retrieved on an ongoing basis, linked at the individual level, cleaned and organized, and made available for analysis. Although these systems are under development, they have great potential to deliver high-quality big data with almost unlimited possibilities to yield vital information to transform social policy and practice. For example, such systems are already making it possible to estimate the scope of multiple system use and the associated costs, suggesting starting points for overall improvements in the social service sector (Goerge, Smithgall, Seshadri, & Ballard, 2010). They are also foundational for data-driven social innovations such as community-wide, collaborative impact projects (London & McLaughlin, 2014) and social impact financing (Butler, Bloom, & Rudd, 2013; Stoesz, 2014). A series of case studies of selected IDS affirm the technical and practical feasibility of building these systems and generating actionable information for policy (Fantuzzo & Culhane, 2015).

Social services IDS are not the only innovative type of integrated data platform emerging in the social sector. Community revitalization work is benefiting from "mash-ups" of property, housing, and neighborhood data using GIS technology (Kingsley, Coulton, & Pettit, 2014). For example, community partners in some cities have been enabled to fight blight and disinvestment using open data portals that link numerous transactional records (e.g., foreclosure filings, deed transfers, evictions, and complaints) in real time and make them available through a user-friendly interface for action on the ground (Nelson, 2014). Among other things, the data have been instrumental in alerting foreclosure prevention counselors and mitigation specialists to reach out to specific housing units and their occupants based on predictive models of risk found from mining the data and to fight predatory lending with data-based evidence (Coulton, Schramm, & Hirsh, 2010).

Advanced Data Analytics

To get the most out of massive amounts of social data, it is necessary to move beyond standard statistical models (Hindman, 2015). Big data allows many more variables to be taken into account in predicting what interventions will work for individuals with a unique social profile or in evaluating risk potential within populations. For example, predictive analytics have been applied to linked birth and child welfare records to identify young children at high risk of child maltreatment (Vaithianathan, Maloney, Putnam-Hornstein, & Jiang, 2013) and households that are highly likely to become homeless (Greer, Shinn, Kwan, & Zuiderveen, 2016). Validation with holdout samples and various calibration techniques enable these prediction models to be refined so that they can be incorporated into practice and further evaluated for their impact.

Machine learning algorithms are increasingly being applied in efforts to increase the accuracy of predictions and improve decisions. For example, risk scoring algorithms derived from machine learning have been used to assess risk of flight and crime among pretrial defendants (Kleinberg, Lakkaraju, Leskovec, Ludwig, & Mullainathan, 2017). Text mining methods are evolving rapidly and are now being applied to unstructured notes to gain a more complete picture of behaviors—for example, in child welfare cases—that could not be ascertained by simply tabulating structured data fields (Goerge, Ozik, & Collier, 2012). Similarly, the application of a hybrid text mining approach to massive numbers of text records in the Veterans Administration's data warehouse yielded an innovative method to calibrate suicide risk in that population (Hammond & Laundry, 2014).

Microsimulation models are also proving useful for evaluating how policy or practice changes might play out over entire human service systems (Goldhaber-Fiebert et al., 2012). In addition, applying predictive analytics from numerous digital touch points to detailed data on individuals and their social settings might eventually lead to policy or practice interventions that could modify elements of behavior (Moore, Sacks, Manlove, & Sawhill, 2014). Such types of analyses consider the sequential nature of the elements and the potential for nonlinear and reciprocal relationships and the complex system dynamics that may evolve over various layers of social organization. Therefore, they hold great promise for eventually customizing social interventions with precision. Such discoveries could ultimately be the basis for social interventions that are finely tuned to the person in the situation—ones that will work with relatively higher levels of certainty.

Randomized controlled trials (RCTs) can be implemented frequently and at low cost when they are embedded in a data-rich environment and carried out with the help of automated systems. Just like the for-profit sector that engages experiment-driven innovation (Manzi, 2012), human service organizations can fruitfully use RCTs to test the impact of changes in practices or procedures and observe results through data in their automated systems. With the advent of IDS described previously, they can also look beyond their own programs to track longer term effects of innovative practices through rigorous designs. If outcomes for experimental and control subjects can be tracked through IDS, findings can be produced quicker and at lower cost compared to those obtained from conventional experiments, which require expensive follow-up studies (Coalition for Evidence-Based Policy, 2012). For example, an randomized trial of a new case management model with disabled Medicaid beneficiaries relied on linked individual records from several social service agencies to show positive impact on emergency hospital readmissions, homelessness, and receipt of substance abuse treatment but no discernable cost savings (Bell et al., 2015). This type of information can be directly pertinent to government decisions.

METRICS AND MOVEMENT TOWARD MEASURABLE PROGRESS

The innovations discussed previously, although not exhaustive, represent some of the most promising avenues for social work research, policy, and practice. Moving forward in these areas will take coordinated efforts and investment. In addition, it will be crucial to guard against potential negative consequences of technology, such as disproportionate impact on disadvantaged groups, violations of privacy and human rights, and cyber victimization. Table 9.1 summarizes some of the outcomes that we anticipate can be accomplished and steps that are needed to achieve measurable progress. Although developing specific metrics is difficult due to the evolving nature of technology, we expect considerable progress in these areas during the next decade.

Table 9.1. TECHNOLOGY INNOVATION FOR SOCIAL WORK:
PROMISE AND PROGRESS

Technology	Promise	Moving Forward
Social media	1. Social media will be flexible and on-demand services, in that billons of people will be able to easily access it (e.g., Facebook). 2. Social media will be a protective tool to help people at risk. (e.g., for people having indicated risk for suicide, send message or connect to a suicide helpline). 3. Social media will enable to leverage the collective crowd to engage in problem-solving. 4. Blog will enhance treatment fidelity through standardized instructions and algorithms. 5. Social media (e.g., Twitter) will identify emerging social movement and issues.	1. Partnership with social media companies to leverage potential. 2. Training for social workers to utilize social media effectively.
Mobile devices	1. Mobile apps will enable people to get the services they need at their pace and when they want them. 2. Combining global positioning system (GPS) technology, mobile apps will allow behavior tracking when people are in a no-go zone (e.g., a bar or casino). 3. Interventions, particularly cognitive–behavioral interventions, with mobile devices including GPS and self-paced Internet modules will create positive outcomes and increase effectiveness.	1. Understand when, where, and how to work with self-paced mobile technologies to improve outcomes for people. 2. Collaboration with computer software engineers to develop mobile apps with consideration for social justice.
Wearable technology and sensors	1. Using wearable sensors will enable clients to gather constant data for assessment and intervention. 2. Real-time tracking will enhance opportunities for client self-management.	1. Partnership with companies developing wearable technology is warranted. 2. Research examining the connection between physiological indicators and mental health outcomes. 3. Training in the integration of physiological markers with other sources of data.

(*continued*)

Table 9.1. CONTINUED

Technology	Promise	Moving Forward
Robotics and artificial intelligence	1. Robotics will provide alternatives to human interaction for assessment, monitoring, and intervention. 2. Integrating artificial intelligence into intake phone calls will improve client satisfaction and client–therapist match by using algorithms to detect optimal response patterns.	1. Collaboration with engineers and computer scientists to develop appropriate social robots. 2. Training prepares social workers for integration with this new technology. 3. Increased automation of service delivery increases efficiency and effectiveness.
Gamification and gaming	1. Gamification will promote positive in-game behaviors to be used in other environments. 2. The use of gaming will reduce clients' symptoms and improve functioning, for example, through simulation or role playing (e.g., using video games to treat post-traumatic stress disorder).	1. Promote development and responsible games that support mental health. 2. Develop social workers with skills to integrate gaming and gamification into practice.
Geospatial technology	1. GIS-enabled applications allow location-based work, monitoring, and community engagement.	1. Social workers trained in geospatial technology. 2. Mobile record and data collection systems are GIS enabled. 3. Programs and resources improve geographic accessibility.
Integrated data system)	1. IDS will deliver high-quality big data to yield vital information to transform social policy and practice, considering the scope of multiple systems and costs. 2. IDS will enable data-driven social innovations such as community-wide, collaborative impact projects. 3. IDS will allow many more variables to be taken into account in predicting what interventions will work for individuals with unique social profiles. 4. Open data portals will enhance IDS, making a user-friendly interface for action on the ground.	1. Standardize policies and practices in order to expand data access and use. 2. Form and maintain relationships with numerous data providers to access big data beyond open data portals. 3. Implement advanced data management, security, and analysis. 4. Prepare data-savvy social workers by providing advanced curriculum. 5. Promote data-driven social policy and practice.

Table 9.1. CONTINUED

Technology	Promise	Moving Forward
Advanced data analytics	1. Predictive models inform prevention or early intervention. 2. Machine learning supports decision-making. 3. Text mining and visualization reveals previously hidden patterns. 4. Rapid experimentation improves service design.	1. Social workers trained in data science. 2. Predictive analytics refined and evaluated. 3. Visualization tools and data mining built into electronic records systems. 4. Social workers incorporate analytics into practice and program operations.
Digital privacy, ethics, and equity	1. Security and privacy tools are uniform and effective. 2. Disadvantaged groups have full digital access. 3. Ethical applications of digital capability.	1. Develop standards and best practices for data security and privacy. 2. Achieve equity in high-speed Internet access and digital literacy. 3. Develop methods for tracking adverse events and potential harms to individuals and groups from technology.

GIS, geographic information system; GPS, global positioning system; IDS, integrated data system.

OPPORTUNITIES FOR NEW INITIATIVES IN INTERDISCIPLINARY AND CROSS-SECTOR INVOLVEMENT

As indicated at many points in Table 9.1, leveraging the promise of technology toward social good requires not only the investment of social work but also the collaboration of social work with other disciplines. Together with computer science, engineering, statistics, social science, and business, we must create interdisciplinary partnerships to support this work. Working with computer scientists, technologists, and software engineers, we can build the technology that will support social service delivery (Aguirre, McCoy, & Roan, 2013). Transforming big data into useful information for social work requires computational science and data expertise. Teams of specialists that blend substantive knowledge with analytic and technological expertise allow us to realize the promise of ICT innovations. In addition, collaboration with government supports access to data that can be used in the social sector and application of technology in government-run or government-funded programs. Because technology has significant commercial applications, the business sector is another potential partner.

Technology has the power to transform our response to social problems and the structures of the social sector. Disruptive paradigms that marry new partners, blend scholarship across disciplines, and create integrated training models will be required to realize this potential. The field of social work requires significant investment and restructuring to leverage new discoveries and new technologies as they emerge. Social workers with a new understanding of and enhanced appreciation for technologies and the promise of big data will advance the field at a pace that allows us to realize the benefits of this progress. As the sector becomes more adept at integrating these advances, our ability to respond to novel problems becomes enhanced. Shifting social work to respond to these challenges and lead these conversations is imperative for our continued ability to meet the demands of complex social problems.

PROGRESS AND FUTURE DIRECTIONS

Harnessing technology for social good calls for the field's engagement with existing technologies and readiness for new technologies that emerge. Technology changes at a rapid pace, with new developments occurring on a constant basis. Full involvement is required to ensure that the fruits of technology are equitably distributed and that social programs and services reach optimal effectiveness. To realize these aims and make significant progress requires transformations in social work education, research programs, and human services systems.

Social work education programs require shifts in pedagogy and curriculum to support the adoption of technology innovations (Craig & Calleja Lorenzo, 2014; Hitchcock & Battista, 2013). Accreditation bodies throughout the world have begun to consider technology, but these standards mostly note the value of technology and do not suggest concrete curricular arrangement. Further progress will be achieved only with significant changes to social work training and pedagogy that supports technology infusion across courses and across schools (Craig & Calleja Lorenzo, 2014; Hitchcock & Battista, 2013). It will be important that the field develop measures to evaluate the development of digital literacy among social work students and practitioners. Development of an accessible repository of technology-related assignments, syllabi, and teaching materials that meet accreditation standards and also freely accessible webinars and podcasts for social work faculty on current trends in technology and practice would help accelerate the pace of incorporation of technology into the overall curriculum.

In addition to a focus on technology for practice, the field needs to attract, train, and retain a generation of social workers who are passionate about data and able to work in teams to manage, curate, analyze, interpret, and apply big data for social good. Some social workers will choose to specialize, but it will also be important to prepare all social workers to appreciate their role in data generation and become adept at applying data in their practice (Naccarato, 2010; Shaw, Lee, & Wulczyn, 2012). These individuals need to have skills in working with large and complex data sets, and they need to become trained in data science. Schools of social work should consider developing joint programs with computer science departments to train some social workers in both fields. This is already occurring in selected public policy and social science departments, suggesting that social work can also move in this direction. Such programs would attract a new type of student to the field and give those already committed to social work an opportunity to employ technology and data science to their practice, analysis, and research. The availability of such opportunities, when widely promoted, will bring in a number of talented individuals who want to be part of the digital revolution but are also interested in having an impact in their communities.

Investment in research around social work practice and technology is critical to harnessing this potential. The field of social work has the opportunity to develop, test, and refine interventions that use technology. A lack of empirical research on technology-based interventions has inhibited practitioners (Ceranoglu, 2010). Funding significant research in this area and testing its use would remove this barrier to full implementation. Research on the integration of technology into practice will shed light on what technologies are best incorporated in social work. A research agenda should be built that includes evaluating existing programs, developing technology-based interventions while collecting empirical data on the impact of the technology (Chan & Holosko, 2016), and researching technology-assisted and hybrid interventions (Eack, 2012). In addition, research that makes use of large administrative data sets (Putnam-Hornstein & King, 2014; Wulczyn, Chen, & Hislop, 2007) helps us realize the potential uses of technology to support social work outcomes.

Technology raises or brings into focus various ethical and human rights issues that must be addressed. Although principles of protecting confidentiality, privacy, and self-determination are not new to social work, technology raises the risk of such breaches that are immeasurably greater. The amount of information that is amassed on unsuspecting individual is growing and could disadvantage them. Issues around social worker–client boundaries, client safety, and cross-jurisdictional practice arise with the inclusion of technology in social work practice (Barsky, 2017). Social workers must join with other professions to evaluate the potential harms and risks that will emerge as technologies are increasingly employed.

As we consider potential progress, we must remain steadfast in our commitment to the value of social justice. Technological innovation continuously alters the landscape of human possibility, but it does not guarantee the momentum toward this value. Social work is both uniquely positioned and ethically obligated to ensure that the drive of technological evolution is a project open to all, that it does not replicate or amplify existing inequalities, and that negative effects of technology on individuals and groups are minimized as much as possible (Goldkind & Wolf, 2015, p. 85). As we measure progress, this remains a most important consideration.

REFERENCES

Aguirre, R. T. P., McCoy, M. K., & Roan, M. (2013). Development guidelines from a study of suicide prevention mobile applications (apps). *Journal of Technology in Human Services, 31*(3), 269–293. doi:10.1080/15228835.2013.814750

Arrillaga-Andreessen, L. (2015, Spring). Disruption for good. *Stanford Social Innovation Review*, 34–39.

Banks, M. R., Willoughby, L. M., & Banks, W. A. (2008). Animal-assisted therapy and loneliness in nursing homes: Use of robotic versus living dogs. *Journal of the American Medical Directors Association, 9*, 173–177.

Barak, A., & Grohol, J. A. (2011). Current and future trends in Internet-supported mental health interventions. *Journal of Technology in Human Services, 29*, 155–196.

Barak, A., Hen, L., Boniel-Nissim, M., & Shapira, N. (2008). A comprehensive review and a meta-analysis of the effectiveness of Internet-based psychotherapeutic interventions. *Journal of Technology in Human Services, 26*(2–4), 109–160. doi:10.1080/15228830802094429

Barsky, A. E. (2017). Social work practice and technology: Ethical issues and policy responses. *Journal of Technology in Human Services, 1*, 8–29.

Bell, J. F., Krupski, A., Joesch, J. M., West, I. I., Atkins, D. C., Court, B., & Roy-Byrne, P. (2015). A randomized controlled trial of intensive care management for disabled Medicaid beneficiaries with high health care costs. *Health Services Research, 50*(3), 663–689. doi:10.1111/1475-6773.12258

Bertot, J. C., Gorham, U., Jaeger, P. T., Sarin, L. C., & Choi, H. (2014). Big data, open government and e-government: Issues, policies and recommendations. *Information Polity, 19*(1), 5–16.

Best, P., Manktelow, R., & Taylor, B. J. (2014). Social work and social media: Online help-seeking and the mental well-being of adolescent males. *British Journal of Social Work, 51*, S54–S86. doi:10.1093/bjsw/bcu130

Brownlee, K., Graham, J. R., Doucette, E., Hotson, N., & Halverson, G. (2010). Have communication technologies influenced rural social work practice? *British Journal of Social Work, 40*, 622–637.

Butler, D., Bloom, D., & Rudd, T. (2013). Using social impact bonds to spur innovation, knowledge-building, and accountability. In *Community Development Investment Review*. San Francisco, CA: Federal Reserve Bank of San Francisco.

Ceranoglu, T. A. (2010). Video games in psychotherapy. *Review of General Psychology, 14*, 141–146.

Chan, C., & Holosko, M. J. (2016). A review of information and communication technology enhanced social work interventions. *Research on Social Work Practice, 26*(1), 88–100. doi:10.1177/1049731515578884

Coalition for Evidence-Based Policy. (2012). *Rigorous program evaluations on a budget: How low-cost randomized controlled trials are possible in many areas of social policy*. Washington, DC: Author.

Coulton, C. J., Schramm, M., & Hirsh, A. (2010). REO and beyond: The aftermath of the foreclosure crisis in Cuyahoga County, Ohio. In E. Rosengren & S. Pianalto (Eds.), *REO & vacant properties: Strategies for neighborhood stabilization* (pp. 47–54). Boston, MA/Cleveland, OH: Federal Reserve Banks of Boston and Cleveland.

Craig, S. L., & Calleja Lorenzo, M. V. (2014). Can information and communication technologies support patient engagement? A review of opportunities and challenges in health social work. *Social Work in Health Care, 53*(9), 845–864. doi:10.1080/00981389.2014.936991

Craig, S. L., McInroy, L., McCready, L., Di Cesare, D., & Pettaway, L. (2015). Connecting without fear: Clinical implications of the consumption of information and communication technologies by sexual minority youth and young adults. *Clinical Social Work Journal, 43*(2), 159–168. doi:10.1007/s10615-014-0505-2

Daley, D., Bachmann, M., Bachmann, B. A., Pedigo, C., Bui, M. T., & Coffman, J. (2016). Risk terrain modeling predicts child maltreatment. *Child Abuse & Neglect, 62*, 29–38.

Dennis, T. A., & O'Toole, L. J. (2014). Mental health on the go: Effects of a gamified attention-bias modification mobile application in trait-anxious adults. *Clinical Psychological Science, 2*(5), 576–590. https://doi.org/10.1177/2167702614522228

Eack, S. M. (2012). Cognitive remediation: A new generation of psychosocial interventions for people with schizophrenia. *Social Work, 57*(3), 235–246.

Fantuzzo, J., & Culhane, D. (2015). *Actionable intelligence: Using integrated data systems to achieve more effective and efficient government*. New York: Palgrave/MacMillian.

Freisthler, B., & Weiss, R. E. (2008). Using Bayesian space–time models to understand the substance use environment and risk for being referred to Child Protective Services. *Substance Use & Misuse Special Issue, 43*(2), 239–251.

Gaggioli, A., Pioggia, G., Tartarisco, G., Baldus, G., Corda, D., Cipresso, P., & Riva, G. (2013). A mobile data collection platform for mental health research. *Personal and Ubiquitous Computing, 17*, 241. doi:10.1007/s00779-011-0465-2

Greer, A. L., Shinn, M., Kwon, J., & Zuiderveen, S. (2016). Targeting services to individuals most likely to enter shelter: Evaluating the efficiency of homelessness prevention. *Social Service Review, 90*(1), 130–155.

Gandy-Guedes, M. E., Vance, M., Bridgewater, E. A., Montgomery, T., & Taylor, K. (2016). Using Facebook as a tool for informal peer support: A case example. *Social Work Education, 35*(3), 323–332. doi:10.1080/02615479.2016.1154937

Giullian, N., Ricks, D., Atherton, A., Colton, M., Goodrich, M., & Brinton, B. (2010). Detailed requirements for robots in autism therapy. *IEEExplore*. Retrieved from http://ieeexplore.ieee.org/document/5641908

Goerge, R., Ozik, J., & Collier, N. (2012). *Bringing big data into public policy research: Text mining to acquire richer data on program participants, their behavior and services*. Paper presented at the Association of Public Policy and Management, Baltimore. Retrieved from http://www.appam.org/assets/1/7/Goerge_20text_20mining_20final_2012_20pt.pdf

Goerge, R., Smithgall, C., Seshadri, R., & Ballard, P. (2010). *Illinois families and their use of multiple service systems*. Chicago, IL: Chapin Hall at the University of Chicago.

Goldhaber-Fiebert, J. D., Bailey, S. L., Hurlburt, M. S., Zhang, J., Snowden, L. R., Wulczyn, F., & Horwitz, S. M. (2012). Evaluating child welfare policies with decision-analytic simulation models. *Administration and Policy in Mental Health and Mental Health Services Research, 39*(6), 466–477.

Goldkind, L., & Wolf, L. (2015). A digital environment approach: Four technologies that will disrupt social work practice. *Social Work, 60*(1), 85–87. doi:10.1093/sw/swu045

Goldsmith, S., & Crawford, S. (2014). *The responsive city: Engaging communities through data-smart governance.* Hoboken, NJ: Wiley.

Griffiths, K. M., Farrer, L., & Christensen, H. (2010) The efficacy of Internet interventions for depression and anxiety disorders: A review of randomised controlled trials. *Medical Journal of Australia, 192*, S4–S11.

Guo, C., & Saxton, G. D. (2013). Tweeting social change: How social media are changing nonprofit advocacy. *Nonprofit and Voluntary Sector Quarterly, 43*, 57–79. doi:10.1177/0899764012471585

Hammond, K. W., & Laundry, R. J. (2014, January). *Application of a hybrid text mining approach to the study of suicidal behavior in a large population.* Paper presented at System Sciences (HICSS) 2014 47th Hawaii International Conference, Waikoloa, HI.

Han, D. H., Sim, M. E., Kim, J. I., Arenella, L. S., Lyoo, I. K., & Renshaw, P. F. (2008). The effect of internet video game play on clinical and extrapyramidal symptoms in patients with schizophrenia. *Schizophrenia Research, 103*(1-3), 338–340. doi:10.1016/j.schres.2008.01.026

Hegel, F., Muhl, C., Wrede, B., Hielscher-Fastabend, M., & Sagerer, G. (2009, February). *Understanding social robots.* Paper presented at the Second International Conferences on Advances in Computer–Human Interactions, 2009, Cancun, Mexico. doi:10.1109/ACHI.2009.51

Hindman, M. (2015). Building better models: Prediction, replication, and machine learning in the social sciences. *Annals of the American Academy of Political and Social Science, 659*(1), 48–62.

Hitchcock, L. I., & Battista, A. (2013). Social media for professional practice: Integrating Twitter with social work pedagogy. *Journal of Baccalaureate Social Work, 18*(1), 43–54.

Hoffman, S., & Podgurski, A. (2013). Big bad data: Law, public health, and biomedical databases. *Journal of Law, Medicine & Ethics, 41*(Suppl. 1), 56–60.

Holmes, E. A., James, E. L., Coode-Bate, T., & Deeprose, C. (2009). Can playing the computer game "Tetris" reduce the build-up of flashbacks for trauma? A proposal from cognitive science. *PLoS One, 4*(1), e415.

Hootsuite. (2017). *Digital in 2017 global overview.* Retrieved from https://www.slideshare.net/wearesocialsg/digital-in-2017-global-overview.

Kania, J., & Kramer, M. (2011). Collective impact. *Stanford Social Innovation Review, 9*(1), 36–41.

Kingsley, G. T., Coulton, C. J., & Pettit, K. L. (2014). *Strengthening communities with neighborhood data.* Washington, DC: Urban Institute.

Klasnja, P., & Pratt, W. (2012). Methodological review: Healthcare in the pocket: Mapping the space of mobile-phone health interventions. *Journal of Biomedical Informatics, 45*(1), 184–198. doi:10.1016/j.jbi.2011.08.017

Kleinberg, J., Lakkaraju, H., Leskovec, J., Ludwig, J., & Mullainathan, S. (2017). *Human decisions and machine predictions* (No. w23180). National Bureau of Economic Research. http://www.nber.org/papers/w23180

Korda, H., & Itani, Z. (2011). Harnessing social media for health promotion and behavior change. *Health Promotion Practice, 14*, 15–23.

Kumar, S., Nilsen, W. J., Abernethy, A., Atienza, A., Patrick, K., Pavel, M., . . . Swendeman, D. (2013). Mobile health technology evaluation: The mHealth evidence workshop. *American Journal of Preventive Medicine, 45*(2), 228–236. doi:10.1016/j.amepre.2013.03.017

Lanata, A., Valenza, G., Nardelli, M., Gentili, C., & Scilingo, E. P. (2015). Complexity index from a personalized wearable monitoring system for assessing remission in mental health. *IEEE Journal of Biomedical and Health Informatics, 19*(1), 132–139. doi:10.1109/JBHI.2014.2360711

Langlois, M. (2013). *Reset: Video games & psychotherapy (2nd Edition).* Cambridge, MA: Online Therapy Institute.

Lazer, D. M., Kennedy, R., King, G., & Vespignani, A. (2014). The parable of Google Flu: Traps in big data analysis. *Science, 343,* 1203–1205.

Lee, S. J., & Walsh, T. B. (2015). Using technology in social work practice: The mDad (Mobile Device Assisted Dad) case study, *Advances in Social Work, 16*(1), 107–124.

Lintvedt, O. K., Griffiths, K. M., Sorensen, K., Ostvik, A. R., Wang, C. E., Eisemann, M., & Waterloo, K. (2013). Evaluating the effectiveness and efficacy of unguided Internet-based self-help intervention for the prevention of depression: A randomized controlled trial. *Clinical Psychology Psychotherapy, 20*(1), 10–27.

London, R. A., & McLaughlin, M. (2014). *The youth sector: Supporting cross-institutional community collaboration through shared data.* San Francisco, CA/Washington, DC: Federal Reserve Bank of San Francisco/Urban Institute.

Mandayam, G., & Joosten, D. (2016). Understanding client communities spatially for developing effective interventions: Application of geographic information systems (GIS) technology for program planning in health and human services agencies. *Journal of Technology in Human Services, 34*(2), 171–182.

Manzi, J. (2012). *Uncontrolled: The surprising payoff of trial and error for business, politics, and society.* New York, NY: Basic Books.

Mishna, F., Bogo, M., Root, J., Sawyer, J.-L., & Khoury-Kassabri, M. (2012). "It just crept in": The digital age and implications for social work practice. *Clinical Social Work Journal, 40*(3), 277–286. doi:10.1007/s10615-012-0383-4

Mishna, F., Bogo, M., & Sawyer, J.-L. (2015). Cyber counseling: Illuminating benefits and challenges. *Clinical Social Work Journal, 43*(2), 169–178.

Mohr, D. C., Burns, M. N., Schueller, S. M., Clarke, G., & Klinkman, M. (2013). Behavioral intervention technologies: Evidence review and recommendations for future research in mental health. *General Hospital Psychiatry, 35*(4), 332–338.

Moore, K. A., Sacks, V. H., Manlove, J., & Sawhill, I. (2014). *"What if" you earned a diploma and delayed parenthood?* (Research Brief Publication No. 2014-27). Bethesda, MD: Child Trends.

Naccarato, T. (2010). Child welfare informatics: A proposed subspecialty for social work. *Children and Youth Services Review, 32*(12), 1729–1734.

Nelson, L. (2014). Cutting through the fog. In G. T. Kingsley, C. J. Coulton, & K. L. Pettit (Eds.), *Strengthening communities with neighborhood data* (pp. 205–218). Washington, DC: Urban Institute.

Proudfoot, J. (2013). The future is in our hands: The role of mobile phones in the prevention and management of mental disorders. *Australian & New Zealand Journal of Psychiatry, 47*(2), 111–113. doi:10.1177/0004867412471441

Putnam-Hornstein, E., & King, B. (2014). Cumulative teen birth rates among girls in foster care at age 17: An analysis of linked birth and child protection records from California. *Child Abuse & Neglect, 38*(4), 698–705.

Rao, V. (2013, April). Challenges of implementing gamification for behavior change: Lessons learned from the design of Blues Buddies. In *Proceedings of CHI 2013 workshop "designing gamification"* (pp. 61–64). Alpha, NJ: Sheridan Communications.

Sano, A., & Picard, R. W. (2013, September). *Stress recognition using wearable sensors and mobile phones.* Paper presented at the 2013 Humane Association Conference on Affective Computing and Intelligent Interaction. doi:10.1109/ACII.2013.117

Schoech, D., Boyas, J. F., Black, B. M., & Elias-Lambert, N. (2013). Gamification for behavior change: Lessons from developing a social, multiuser, Web-tablet based prevention game for youths. *Journal of Technology in Human Services, 31*(3), 197–217.

Shaw, T. V., Lee, B. R., & Wulczyn, F. (2012). "I thought I hated data": Preparing MSW students for data-driven practice. *Journal of Teaching in Social Work, 32*(1), 78–89.

Sitter, K. C., & Curnew, A. H. (2016). The application of social media in social work community RudinPractice. *Social Work Education, 35*, 271–283. doi:10.1080/02615479.2015

Stephens-Davidowitz, S. (2013). *Unreported victims of an economic downtown.* Retrieved from http://static1.squarespace.com/static/51d894bee4b01caf88ccb4f3/t/51e22f38e4b0502fe211fab7/1373777720363/childabusepaper13.pdf

Stoesz, D. (2014). Evidence-based policy reorganizing social services through accountable care organizations and social impact bonds. *Research on Social Work Practice, 24*(2), 181–185.

Strandburg, K. J. (2014). Monitoring, datafication and consent: Legal approaches to privacy in a big data context. In J. Lane, V. Stodden, S. Bender, & H. Nissenbaum (Eds.), *Privacy, big data, and the public good: Frameworks for engagement* (pp. 5–43). New York, NY: Cambridge University Press.

Teixeira, S., & Zuberi, A. (2016). Mapping the racial inequality in place: Using youth perceptions to identify unequal exposure to neighborhood environmental hazards. *International Journal of Environmental Research and Public Health, 13*(9), 844.

Thurston, H., Freisthler, B., Bell, J., Tancredi, D., Romano, P., Miyamoto, S., & Joseph, J. G. (2017). The temporal–spatial distribution of seriously maltreated children. *Spatial and Spatio-temporal Epidemiology, 20*, 1–8.

Tinati, R., Halford, S., Carr, L., & Pope, C. (2014). Big data: Methodological challenges and approaches for sociological analysis. *Sociology, 48*(4), 663–681.

Vaithianathan, R., Maloney, T., Putnam-Hornstein, E., & Jiang, N. (2013). Children in the public benefit system at risk of maltreatment: Identification via predictive modeling. *American Journal of Preventive Medicine, 45*(3), 354–359.

Vidal, M., Turner, J., Bulling, A., & Gellersen, H., (2012). Wearable eye tracking for mental health monitoring. *Computer Communications, 35*(11), 1306–1311. http://doi.org/10.1016/j.comcom.2011.11.002

Walshe, D. G., Lewis, E. J., Kim, S. I., O'Sullivan, K., & Wiederhold, B. K. (2004). Exploring the use of computer games and virtual reality in exposure therapy for fear of driving following a motor vehicle accident. *CyberPsychology & Behavior, 6*(3), 329–334. doi:10.1089/109493103322011641

Wulczyn, F., Chen, L., & Hislop, K. B. (2007). *Foster care dynamics, 2000–2005: A report from the Multistate Foster Care Data Archive.* Chicago, IL: Chapin Hall Center for Children at the University of Chicago.

Zorn, T. E., Flanagin, A. J., & Shoham, M. D. (2011). Institutional and noninstitutional influences on information and communication technology adoption and use among nonprofit organizations. *Human Communication Research, 37*(1), 1–33. doi:10.1111=j.1468-2958.2010.01387.x

Grand Challenges
for Social Work
Promote smart decarceration

CHAPTER 10

Promote Smart Decarceration

MATTHEW W. EPPERSON, CARRIE PETTUS-DAVIS,
ANNIE GRIER, AND LEON SAWH

As 2020 nears, the United States is entering into an era of *decarceration*, a systematic reduction in the use of incarceration. This era promises to provide a new understanding of how society defines crime, responds to other undesirable behaviors, and performs criminal justice. The forming social movement for decarceration comes almost 45 years after the rise of mass incarceration in America, which led to the United States being the world leader in incarceration. On any given day, nearly 1.5 million individuals reside in state or federal prisons, and more than 728,000 are confined in a local jail; in addition, approximately 13 million people cycle in and out of American prisons and jails each year (Minton & Zeng, 2015; Pew Center on the States, 2008; Subramanian, Delaney, Roberts, Fishman, & McGarry, 2015). Moreover, incarceration disproportionately affects society's most vulnerable, marginalized, and oppressed communities. Stated simply, mass incarceration has become ground zero for social injustice in the United States.

The United States has hit its tipping point with incarceration—it no longer has the fiscal ability or moral will to continue expanding incarceration rates. In fact, an unprecedented and growing number of local and state leaders throughout the country are pushing for paradigm-shifting reforms (Obama, 2017; Rosenberg, 2017; Zorn, 2015). Although this momentum is encouraging, the reality is that no other developed country has grappled with decarceration at this magnitude. As a result, Americans are faced with this grand social challenge with few guideposts to reference. Factors contributing to mass incarceration are many and varied, and efforts to drive the era of decarceration will require comprehensive, well-planned innovations.

Although substantial resources were allocated to criminal justice during the era of mass incarceration, few have been invested in generating evidence for alternative responses to incarceration or how to ensure the success of those re-entering society from incarceration. Existing evidence is not routinely incorporated into re-entry practice (Johnson & Cullen, 2015). Understanding how to adapt and implement evidence-based practices in the US criminal justice system has emerged as a high priority within the National Institute of Justice and the National Institutes of Health. The complexities of the criminal justice system and its perceived inability to respond to multiple needs of clients make identifying and moving treatments into practice all the more challenging. Therefore, as the country moves into the era of decarceration, there is a pressing need for not only a paradigm shift regarding the use of incarceration but also a surge of evidence and application of science to help usher in a more socially just and safe society.

More so than most, the profession of social work is positioned to lead in this far-reaching social justice challenge. Social work is uniquely qualified because of its history of reform efforts, an ethical commitment to social justice, and emerging leadership in structural and behavioral interventions addressing complex social problems (Abramovitz, 1998; Brekke, Ell, & Palinkas, 2007; Fraser, 2004). Social work can bring siloed social sectors and diverse academic disciplines together to create a rational and effective response as prisons and jails devolve.

Several complex racial, economic, and political histories led to mass incarceration; therefore, the smart decarceration approach must not employ quick and simplistic methods to cut incarceration rates (Epperson & Pettus-Davis, 2015a). There must also be an intentional effort to assess whether and how emerging decarceration policies improve or exacerbate the disparities of the criminal justice system as it currently exists. Reductions in racial, economic, and behavioral–health disparities should be reconceptualized as key outcomes in federal, state, and local smart decarceration policies. Therefore, we define *smart decarceration* as effective, sustainable, and socially just decarceration with three simultaneous outcomes: (1) The incarcerated population in US jails and prisons is substantially decreased, (2) existing racial and economic disparities in the criminal justice system are redressed, and (3) public safety and public well-being are maximized. To achieve these interrelated outcomes, smart decarceration strategies must be proactive, transdisciplinary, and empirically driven. Ultimately, smart decarceration aims to build social capacity and provide a more robust and community-driven response to local issues that does not resort to the default incarceration approach.

In the remainder of this chapter, we provide a more in-depth description of the problem of mass incarceration and the opportunities for promoting smart decarceration through the building of social capacity. We present conceptual innovations that are proliferating as the nation enters a new era of transformation. We describe promising and evidence-driven alternatives to incarceration that are gaining momentum in the 21st century. We conclude by offering definitions and strategies for building social capacity to support smart decarceration approaches, paving the way for a more socially just and thriving society for all.

THE PROBLEM OF MASS INCARCERATION

Mass incarceration refers to the period in the United States beginning in the 1970s and extending into the early 21st century in which incarceration rates increased nearly sevenfold, resulting in nearly 2.2 million persons held daily in adult prisons or jails in 2015 (Kaeble & Glaze, 2016). The United States has the largest incarcerated population in the world and by far the highest rate of imprisonment (Human Rights Watch, 2013; Pew Center on the States, 2008). Although comprising only 5% of the world's population, the United States holds nearly 25% of the world's prisoners. In addition, with more than 4.6 million adults currently under community correctional supervision, which can often lead to incarceration (Kaeble & Bonczar, 2016), it is apparent that incarceration's reach is, in many communities, ubiquitous and overwhelming.

Complicated and intersecting societal circumstances contributed to the phenomenon. The era of mass incarceration in the United States was due largely to a concentration of poverty and unemployment in US cities (Travis, Western, & Redburn, 2014). Sentencing policy changes developed during the 1960s and, lasting throughout the early 1990s, led to a more punitive political and social climate nationally. A rise in violent crime rates in the 1960s and 1970s and the crack cocaine epidemic of the 1980s were responded to with President Nixon's campaign for a War on Drugs and President Reagan's Tough on Crime approach in America. The rhetoric of these two presidential administrations led to a lengthy political era in which a successful political campaign was a tough-on-crime campaign. President Clinton's administration solidified the political momentum for punishment by passing the harshest criminal legislation in the history of the country, the 1994 Crime Control Act. This legislation included federally driven financial incentives to states for incarcerating individuals for longer lengths of times and on less serious criminal convictions. Mandatory minimum sentences and "three strikes you're out" legislation were adopted throughout the country in federal and state jurisdictions. These sentencing approaches took discretion away from judges to incorporate mitigating circumstances of offenses (e.g., the presence of serious mental illness) and required individuals to be incarcerated for life after a third criminal conviction. As incarceration rates were rising, increasingly, public schools were failing, and the criminalization of adolescent behavior became commonplace.

Disparities in the Criminal Justice System

Mass incarceration in the United States is a problem not only because of the large volume of individuals incarcerated but also because of who it affects most—the poor and disadvantaged. For example, disparities of race, age, and gender have led to exorbitant rates of incarceration among young African American males (Western & Pettit, 2010). As of 2016, 60% of incarcerated individuals were people of color: 35% identified as Black, 34% as White, 22% as Latino, and 9% as another race or ethnicity (Carson & Anderson, 2016). Black men are six times and Latino men 2.3 times more likely to be incarcerated than are White men (Pew Research Center, 2013). However, people of color and individuals who identify as White engage in illegal behavior at relatively similar rates (Brame, Bushway, Paternoster, & Turner, 2014). Despite similar behaviors, people of color, particularly African Americans, are much more likely to come into contact with law enforcement (Nellis, 2016; Rojek, Rosenfeld, & Decker, 2012) and significantly more likely to be charged with a crime (Wooldredge, Frank, Goulette, & Travis, 2015). Once charged, they are sentenced more harshly (Johnson, 2003); once sentenced, they are at greater risk of a subsequent incarceration (Berg & Huebner, 2011). Meaningful reform to the criminal justice system cannot be accomplished without acknowledgment of these racial and ethnic disparities in the prison system and without focused attention on the reduction of these disparities (Sered, 2017).

In addition to disparities of race, mass incarceration also disproportionately affects people with substance use and mental health disorders (Clear, 2007; Roberts, 2004; Sampson & Loeffler, 2010). Nearly 1.5 million prison and jail inmates meet the criteria for a substance use disorder (National Center on Addiction and Substance Abuse at Columbia University, 2010), and more than 375,000 people with serious mental illnesses are incarcerated on any given day. Because of defunded community systems of care for those suffering from mental health and substance use disorders and the criminalization of public health issues, jails and prisons have become the de facto treatment locations for those with behavioral health impairments. Rates of mental illnesses are three to six times higher among the incarcerated population compared to the general population (Fazel & Danesh, 2002; Steadman, Osher, Robbins, Case, & Samuels, 2009). More than two-thirds of incarcerated persons have histories of substance use disorders, and less than 10% receive evidence-based treatments (National Center on Addiction and Substance Abuse, 2010). Complicating matters, a striking 72% of incarcerated individuals with mental illnesses have a reported co-occurring substance use disorder (Abram & Teplin, 1991); almost none of these individuals receive adequate treatments (Taxman, Perdoni, & Harrison, 2007).

Similarly, many studies report that approximately 90% of people in jails and prisons have high rates of lifetime traumatic experiences (Pettus-Davis,

2014; Teplin, Abram, & McClelland, 1996; Weeks & Spatz Widom,1998; Wolff & Shi, 2012). Because imprisonment is a traumatic experience, incarceration can amplify the negative psychological symptoms of trauma and cause problems during and after incarceration. Few people receive adequate supports for health, substance abuse, and mental health problems during or after incarceration. This is exacerbated by poor access to treatment within many of the communities to which large numbers of inmates eventually return (Mallik-Kane & Visher, 2008).

The Failures of Mass Incarceration

Mass incarceration has been deemed ineffective on multiple fronts. Nearly 77% of individuals released from prisons are rearrested for a new crime within 5 years (Durose, Cooper, & Snyder, 2014). Moreover, the social intervention of "incarceration" has failed to reach its intended goals of deterrence and rehabilitation. Researchers of the deterrence theory of incarceration have found there to be limited or no deterrent effects (Travis et al., 2014). On the contrary, incarceration is criminogenic (i.e., crime producing): People who experience incarceration are 30–45 times more likely to be arrested for another crime compared to the general population (Rosenfeld, Wallman, & Fornango, 2005). Even short-term incarceration in jail is associated with increased rates of criminal activity: Low-risk defendants held 2 or 3 days during the pretrial phase are approximately 40% more likely to commit new crimes before trial compared to defendants held less than 24 hours (Lowenkamp, VanNostrand, & Holsinger, 2013).

Successful re-entry to the community remains a great challenge for those returning home from incarceration. Upon release from prison, most individuals have poor access to the conventional means of citizenry that promote desistance from crime (Hagan & Dinovitzer, 1999; Pettus-Davis, 2012). For example, more than half of prisoners were in poverty the year before their arrest and have little chance of rising out of poverty after incarceration (Wheelock & Uggen, 2005). Having a history of incarceration reduces men's annual income by 40% (Western, 2002; Western & Pettit, 2010), and two-thirds of state prisoners do not have a high school diploma upon entering prison (Harlow, 2003). Furthermore, homelessness among formerly incarcerated individuals is four to six times the rate of the general population (Greenberg & Rosenheck, 2008).

Stated mildly, having a history of incarceration also creates a lifetime of collateral consequences that include limited or nonexistent employment opportunities, housing instability, family problems, stigma, trauma, and disenfranchisement (Nellis, 2016). Rather than reforming incarcerated individuals, mass incarceration has caused a number of trickle-down consequences that affect not only the incarcerated individuals over the course of their own lives but also their families and communities (Clear, 2007; Travis & Waul, 2003). Incarceration negatively affects the prospects of US children. Before they became incarcerated, more than two-thirds of men and women were actively involved in their children's lives (The Pew Charitable Trusts, 2010). Losing a parent to incarceration is a traumatic event for children, and it can push those left behind into financial crises, placing the mobility of their children at increased risk. Some research has found that children of incarcerated parents have heightened rates of emotional problems, poor academic performance, behavioral problems, and future engagement in criminal behavior (Pew Charitable Trusts, 2010). Thus, incarceration does not merely affect the individual who is imprisoned; it also shapes the lives of people who have never engaged in crime. The failed effects of incarceration ripple out to communities; nearly $1 trillion dollars in social costs are borne mostly from incarceration in urban and impoverished rural communities (McLaughlin, Pettus-Davis, Brown, Veeh, & Renn, 2016). Therefore, it is imperative to identify strategies that will better align public policies and rehabilitative practices to ensure people with criminal convictions have the greatest possible chance of success.

The Future of Mass Incarceration

Mass incarceration may seem to be an intractable issue, but it is in fact a relatively recent phenomenon. Current trends indicate that the incarceration bubble is bursting. For the first time since the 1980s, the incarcerated population declined slightly in 2009 after several years of plateau, continuing to decline for 6 consecutive years (Carson, 2015; Minton & Zeng, 2015). Many rationalized the first year or two of incarceration declines by citing the effects of the Great Recession and subsequent budget crises, which prompted many states to reduce all levels of expenditure, including corrections (Gottschalk, 2009; Kyckelhahn, 2012; Spelman, 2009). However, recent declines occurred in the midst of a growing skepticism about the effectiveness and use of incarceration in the United States (Bosworth, 2011). The War on Drugs and other forms of severe sentencing are increasingly being questioned on both societal and policy levels. Media exposés regularly illuminate the ripple effects of mass incarceration (Gopnik, 2012; Rubin & Turner, 2014). On both sides of the political aisle, there is growing consensus that reducing the incarcerated population makes sense for both financial and policy reasons. After nearly two decades of declining crime rates nationwide, political will driving the tough-on-crime approach, which fueled mass incarceration, is today largely dissipated (Petersilia & Cullen, 2014).

Incarceration declines, accumulating evidence of ineffectiveness, and mounting weariness of the morality of mass incarceration may signal a "perfect storm" in which decarceration becomes a reality. Lessons from deinstitutionalization (e.g., poor houses, orphanages, and psychiatric institutions) demonstrate that the major problem is not in getting institutions to devolve but, rather, in how society responds to decarceration and in the systems that decarceration efforts create to reintegrate those who are set free to live as ordinary citizens (Draine & Muñoz-Laboy, 2014). If decarceration is not carried out thoughtfully, humanely, and justly, the United States could easily revert back to mass incarceration policies and practices.

Building Social Capacity

In many ways, the era of mass incarceration led to a major expansion and transformation of the criminal justice system into one that would support the overuse of incarceration. This growth came at a high financial and social cost and the neglect of developing alternative structures. To move forward in an era of decarceration will require a different approach, one grounded in the building of *social capacity*—a community's ability to work together to build and sustain its own solutions rather than give responsibility primarily to one set of actors. We define *community* as individuals, families, formal and informal institutions, and public and private sector actors grouped locally and interacting within larger structures.

As applied to the grand challenge of smart decarceration, building social capacity suggests that communities have interest and expertise in responding to many "crimes" and undesired behaviors, but they may lack the resources, legal means, or facilitating structures (i.e., social capacity) to provide such responses. A smart approach to decarceration calls for investment in behavioral health services, public education, economic infrastructure, and other forms of community supports. Also, it calls for alternatives to and early exit points from the traditional criminal justice system to reduce undue harm from justice system contact and promote rehabilitation through minimal disruption to community connections. Such an approach would strengthen community vitality and provide a range of opportunities for communities to prevent and respond to neighborhood crime. In short, promoting smart decarceration means creating a different balance and collaborative relationship between the formal criminal justice system and the communities in which it operates, particularly those communities that have been heavily affected by incarceration. Building social capacity is the primary mechanism to fuel that collaboration and develop innovative, localized decarceration solutions.

CONCEPTS TO GUIDE SMART DECARCERATION

Although there is considerable motivation on multiple fronts to reduce incarceration, a comprehensive approach to decarceration has not yet been developed. Smart decarceration requires recognizing that altering the overreliance on incarceration is a multifaceted endeavor. To build social capacity to achieve smart decarceration, we offer three guiding concepts: (1) changing the narrative on incarceration and the incarcerated, (2) making criminal justice system-wide innovations, and (3) implementing transdisciplinary policy and practice interventions using evidence-driven strategies (Epperson & Pettus-Davis, 2015a).

Changing the Narrative on Incarceration and the Incarcerated

In the United States' current system, incarceration is typically the default response to crime. There are many assumptions embedded in this incarceration-first approach, with the primary assumption being that incarceration serves the public good by achieving public safety. There is little evidence for this assumption, however. The majority of individuals incarcerated in US jails and prisons do not pose an imminent risk to public safety (Minton & Zeng, 2015; Snyder, 2012). Moreover, incarceration does not reduce future offending for most, and in many cases, it increases the risk for recidivism (Durose, Cooper, & Snyder, 2014; Lowenkamp, VanNostrand, & Holsinger, 2013). Changing the narrative on incarceration means first recognizing that incarceration is primarily effective at incapacitation, or removing a person who is an imminent threat to public safety from the community.

For the United States to move from a moment in which decarceration is plausible to a *movement* of sustained decarceration, individuals who are directly affected by incarceration must play a leading role. In many instances, however, individuals who have experienced incarceration have been systematically disenfranchised from efforts to reform the criminal justice system. A key component of an overall strategy to build social capacity is to prioritize the social and financial investment in individuals and communities most affected by incarceration. People with histories of incarceration have expert knowledge about the various factors that contributed to their criminal justice involvement, and leaders with incarceration histories are therefore positioned to bring a much-needed perspective to the table (Epperson & Pettus-Davis, 2015b).

Changing narratives on incarceration and the incarcerated can be accomplished through multiple means, including public awareness campaigns in which the realities of incarceration and its ineffectiveness are made clear. These sober appraisals of incarceration must be incorporated into an array of criminal justice policies, particularly sentencing policies. Decarceration-driven policymaking should include legislative provisions with the input of individuals, families, and communities most affected by incarceration. Policies will be shaped by asking the following difficult questions: "What would the use of incarceration look like if it were used to incapacitate only the most dangerous?" and "What if incarceration were *not* an option for certain types of offenses?" Public forums at the local, state, and national level are needed to develop genuine and critical dialogues and construct new narratives. In many settings, these conversations are beginning to take place. It is imperative that these forums include formerly incarcerated leaders as key planners and facilitators. Formerly incarcerated individuals could also be incorporated as peer mentors in interventions targeting people with criminal records (Pettus-Davis, Epperson, & Grier, 2017).

Making Criminal Justice System-Wide Innovations

Discourse about reversing mass incarceration often focuses on the physical structures of incarceration, namely jails and prisons. However, each sector of the criminal justice system (e.g., law enforcement, courts, jails, prisons, and community supervision) has contributed to the phenomenon of mass incarceration and must be engaged to achieve smart decarceration. A critical first step will be to determine the parts of the current siloed criminal justice system that could benefit from less baton passing and more integration. In developing innovations across the criminal justice system, priority should be given to efforts that create or expand exit points from incarceration and from the criminal justice system altogether. When paired with an overall approach to building social capacity, expanding exit points from the criminal justice system creates an environment in which local communities are better resourced and empowered to respond to local issues without excessive and ineffective use of incarceration.

As one looks across the entirety of the criminal justice system, examples of potential innovations to achieve smart decarceration abound (Epperson & Pettus-Davis, 2017). The path to incarceration begins with encounters with law enforcement and police decisions to make an arrest or to provide alternative and diversionary approaches. The range and feasibility of diversionary approaches, such as community crisis centers, hospitals, and family-based diversion, will help provide police with better alternatives to arrest, and accountability measures can be employed to ensure diversion is occurring in an equitable manner. Prosecutorial innovations, such as deferred prosecution, have tremendous potential to create new exit points from criminal justice entrenchment and incarceration (Boggess & McGregor, 2013; Campana, 2013; Dembo et al., 2008; George et al., 2015). Problem-solving courts, such as drug courts, mental health courts, and veterans' treatment courts, represent a court-based alternative to incarceration with promising effects on reducing recidivism (Rossman, 2011; Sarteschi, Vaughn, & Kim, 2011). A range of behavioral rehabilitative interventions have been developed to reduce future offending among people involved in the criminal justice system, and these interventions could be deployed beyond prison and jail settings to non-incarceration efforts (Aos, Miller, & Drake, 2006; Lipsey & Cullen, 2007). Also, evidence-based community supervision that emphasizes rehabilitative supports and services, combined with expanded social capacity, can help create community-based interventions that will reduce the use of incarceration.

Implementing Transdisciplinary Interventions Using Evidence-Driven Strategies

The policies and practices that fueled mass incarceration represent an extremely costly experiment. During the era of mass incarceration, few coherent and effective policy or practice interventions have been developed to address the needs of the expanding incarcerated population or to prevent incarceration. To develop a transformative era of smart decarceration, considerable fiscal, political, human capital, and community investment is required. Building a field of decarceration will mean incorporating the perspectives of experts from multiple disciplines and sectors, both within and outside of the criminal justice system.

One need not look far into our nation's history to discover the problems of building less than comprehensive policy and practice innovations. The deinstitutionalization movement that occurred in the latter half of the 20th century sought to transfer people with serious mental illnesses out of state-run psychiatric hospitals. By some measure, deinstitutionalization was effective at moving people from long-term institutional care into the community. However, the aftermath of deinstitutionalization shows that the movement was not necessarily successful. Although the intentions of deinstitutionalization were noble, the movement lacked the community resources and capacity to provide proper support, leading to high levels of homelessness and incarceration among people with mental illnesses. In fact, people with mental illnesses are now more likely to be found in jails and prisons than in psychiatric hospitals (Torrey, Kennard, Eslinger, Lamb, & Pavle, 2010). Similarly, if efforts fail to build the social capacity necessary to support decarceration using cross-sector innovations and employing evidence-driven strategies, the process could mirror the turbulent history of deinstitutionalization.

Much of what led to mass incarceration was the proliferation of policies and practices based on political ideology, reactive impulses, and immediate, ungrounded attempts at solutions. Many of these policies and practices were implemented without evaluation, and their expansion often occurred despite any meaningful evidence on effectiveness or, worse, decades of poor outcomes. By contrast, addressing the grand challenge of smart decarceration must employ an evaluative approach—one that continuously assesses the effects of interventions at multiple levels and responds to emerging evidence. Gaps in knowledge must be addressed through research on the drivers of incarceration, including social determinants, and how decarceration innovations can have an impact on the social and individual drivers of crime (Pettus-Davis et al., 2017).

SMART DECARCERATION GOALS AND OUTCOMES

What does success look like in the context of the grand challenge to promote smart decarceration? The three key outcomes identified previously, and the simultaneous advancement of these three outcomes, will mark sustained progress toward meeting the grand challenge. In this section, we further describe each outcome and offer suggestions on how progress for each could be measured.

Substantially Reduce the Incarcerated Population in Jails and Prisons

A major indicator of successful decarceration is the number of people being held in both jails and prisons (Epperson & Pettus-Davis, 2017). Building on the small but meaningful declines since 2009, smart decarceration approaches have the potential to reduce the prison and jail population by 25% in the next 10 years. Doing so requires cohesive strategies that both reduce the flow of individuals into the front end of the system and also reduce lengths of stay for those who are incarcerated (Jacobson, 2005; Subramanian et al., 2015). Connecticut's recent success at reducing incarceration by 50% for people who violate probation provides evidence that even relatively minor structural interventions can lead to dramatic reductions in the incarcerated population (Clement, Schwarzfeld, & Thompson, 2011).

Periods of extreme decline in incarceration may be likely during an era of decarceration. However, consistent decreases over time are far more preferable. For example, one potential target for long-term decarceration efforts could be a return to the pre-mass incarceration rate of roughly fewer than 200 per 100,000 people. Working toward this target would ultimately result in a reduction in the total incarcerated population by 1 million individuals. However, it must be carefully considered whether 200 per 100,000 people incarcerated would be an acceptable rate or whether it would be possible to downsize incarceration even further with the appropriately based supports in place.

Redress Existing Social Disparities in the Criminal Justice System

As discussed previously, the phenomenon of mass incarceration has unevenly affected people of color, people with various forms of social disadvantage, and people with behavioral health disorders. The overrepresentation of social disparities in the criminal justice system stems from numerous causes, including systemic bias in court case processing (Kingsnorth, MacIntosh, & Sutherland, 2002); uneven policing in poor minority neighborhoods (Brunson & Miller, 2006); irregular sentencing practices (Bushway & Piehl, 2001); and, for some crimes, differential offending patterns (Sampson, Morenoff, & Raudenbush, 2005). In a post-decarceration era, the way in which a person experiences the criminal justice system will not depend on the color of one's skin or on how much money a person can access. Nor should a person be more likely to be incarcerated because he or she suffers from drug or alcohol dependence or a mental illness. Building social capacity as a means to reduce disparities is critical to ensuring that decarceration is achieved in a way that is just while maximizing public safety and well-being.

Maximize Public Safety and Well-Being

Although there is considerable political and social will to undo mass incarceration, decarceration efforts must continue to uphold public safety. Reductions in the overall number of incarcerated people, as well as reduced racial and behavioral health disparities in incarceration, will especially benefit communities hardest hit by the past four decades of mass incarceration. Reversing the ripple effects of mass incarceration on individuals and communities will ultimately improve public well-being by reducing the likelihood that individuals' and families' lives will be disrupted by incarceration. In those cases in which a person does become involved in the criminal justice system, evidence-driven and effective exit strategies will assist with reinstating access to pro-social life and ensure the likelihood of social participation and social mobility for a large segment of society.

INTERDISCIPLINARY AND CROSS-SECTOR INNOVATIONS

Mass incarceration has proliferated for four decades, and it may take decades more to reverse. As it stands, if decarceration were to take place, the large numbers of people who would be released from prison would be likely to fare poorly in the absence of a cogent, deliberate, and smart decarceration approach. To create new initiatives for justice system reform, decarceration efforts must build social capacity in ways that are effective, sustainable, and socially just. Meaningful innovations in the criminal justice system will be reliant on the interdisciplinary work of various community entities. Cross-sector practice and policy solutions are emerging at a number of touchpoints in the justice system from prosecution to defense and from courts to community.

Early Stage Criminal Justice Interventions

Interdisciplinary interventions in law enforcement provide the earliest exit point for people at risk of incarceration. Cross-sector innovations in policing include specialized response teams in which trained officers are partnered with mental health clinicians (stationed within the police department) so that they may "co-respond" in crisis situations (Pinals, 2017). In addition, "restoration centers" such as those in San Antonio, Texas, and Chicago provide a community-based alternative to which police officers may take individuals in a mental health crisis instead of jail (Pinals, 2017).

Given the anchor of power in prosecutors' offices, decarcerative shifts in policy and practice within prosecution may potentially affect the greatest number of individuals. Prosecutors throughout the country are employing strategies that reduce the level of early system contact while seeking justice and maximizing public safety. These efforts simultaneously reduce the overall burden on their offices while focusing resources on more serious cases and immediate threats to public safety. One such initiative is deferred prosecution. Deferred prosecution programs divert people charged with certain criminal offenses from traditional court proceedings if they agree to participate in pre-adjudication requirements in return for dismissal or expungement of their charge(s). Whereas typical diversion and probation programs divert offenders from incarceration, deferred prosecution programs provide an innovative opportunity to avoid both deeper involvement in the criminal justice system and the many consequences of having a criminal record. They also help reduce the volume and cost of cases handled by overburdened court systems, enabling prosecutorial and judicial efforts to focus on cases deemed urgent for public safety.

Other "front-end" interventions require coordination between multiple entities, such as police departments, prosecutors, defense attorneys, judges, and community-based social service agencies (Stevenson & Mayson, 2017). Examples include (1) therapeutic policing models (which require coordination between police and clinicians such as social workers), (2) police issuing citations instead of arrests as well as release from the station based on risk (requires agreement between police and prosecutors), (3) extending the length of bail hearings to ensure that defense counsel is present (requires agreement between prosecutors and judges and timely notification to defense attorneys), (4) using a court reminder system through mail, phone, or text (which may be coordinated by prosecutors, defense attorneys, courts, or a community service agency), and (5) community courts (which involve a partnership between police officers, prosecutors, defense attorneys, and the neighborhoods and communities affected by crime) (Stevenson & Mayson, 2017).

Many early stage interventions in the criminal justice system vary widely in program configuration, length, eligibility criteria, and key program elements that may contribute to achieving primary outcomes. The uniqueness of each criminal justice jurisdiction creates an ideal environment for innovation in a specific context, making such innovation relevant and thus more feasible and acceptable to each jurisdiction's target population and the various community actors. However, jurisdictional variance also presents multiple challenges, such as determining the efficacy of new interventions; implementing models with fidelity; and creating acceptable and sustainable solutions for all community members within a jurisdiction. In otherwords, an intervention that was successful in one jurisdiction, is at risk of not being successful of another jurisdiction. Another challenge of sustaining jurisdiction-specific innovations is that interventions or policies may not survive changes in political power or elected offices. Ultimately, the grand challenge of implementing smart decarceration strategies is to generate evidence to develop models with core elements that are transferrable and able to be implemented with fidelity but flexible enough to account for the processes and policies of varying jurisdictions.

Community-Led Interventions

Cross-sector innovations are also being implemented by community members often left out of reform discussions. Participatory defense is an example of an innovation that brings community members, particularly loved ones of those with justice system contact, into the criminal justice system process in a way that provides meaningful engagement between multiple actors and seeks to improve client legal outcomes (Gray, Staff, Gest, & News, 2017; Jayadev, 2014; Moore, Sandys, & Jayadev, 2015). Participatory defense empowers family members through training that includes an overview of the criminal justice system; how to access critical documents; and strategies for aiding in defense, such as identifying potential witnesses and mounting evidence for mitigation reports (Gray et al., 2017; Jayadev, 2014; Moore et al., 2015).

Another avenue toward community-led initiatives is the deep engagement and leadership of formerly incarcerated individuals in the generation of innovations at each intervention point in the criminal justice system. Expanding opportunities for leadership for those with the lived experience of justice system contact is a way to ensure that innovations are not only amenable to criminal justice actors but also reflective of the needs and strengths of those likely to experience them. Supporting the formation of policy advocacy groups such as JustLeadershipUSA and Families Against Mandatory Minimums is a critical first step toward creating a decarceration movement that builds social capacity for all community actors.

Research–Practice–Policy Integration

To maintain the momentum of the decarceration movement, it is imperative that practice and policy innovators design interventions that are evidence driven and supported by multiple stakeholders. During a span of 2 years, the Smart Decarceration Initiative conducted concept mapping activities and focus groups with research, practice, education, policymaking, and formerly incarcerated stakeholders to identify action steps that crossed sectors in an effort to justly reduce incarceration rates through four guiding concepts. These concepts fostered more than 60 guideposts along the road to decarceration (Pettus-Davis et al., 2017). Development of comprehensive and integrated initiatives is necessary to facilitate decarceration-focused policies and practices at the local, state, and national level.

For example, boundary spanning is an innovative practice that has seen success in other fields but is new in the criminal justice realm (Pettus & Severson, 2006). Boundary spanners forge interdisciplinary relationships, leverage connections, and catalyze sustainable system-wide transformation within a jurisdiction through scalable policy changes and programs. Boundary spanners may be used to research decarcerative policy initiatives from jurisdictions throughout the country or propose potential policy changes based on emerging evidence. In addition, boundary spanners may be instrumental in developing policy simulation models to test practice and policy feasibility, acceptability, and scalability.

The proliferation of research–practice–policy partnerships (RPPPs) is a way in which new interdisciplinary initiatives may arise. Successful RPPPs ensure the implementation of evidence-based interventions and shorten the translation period from research into practice. They use the differing roles of the contributors to generate cross-sector solutions that are informed by evidence and seek to influence policy. Harvard University's Center for Research in Policy and Practice provides a model for RPPPs that can be adapted specifically and effectively to the criminal justice field.

In all these opportunities for new initiatives, social workers can and should take a leadership role. The social work discipline is rooted in relationship building, whether the relationships are interpersonal, familial, organizational, or systemic. Social workers are equipped to bridge relationships across disciplines integral to the criminal justice system, such as law, health, and education, and can bring these entities together not only to develop transdisciplinary solutions but also to allow each discipline to operate in its designed capacity. Powered by science, social workers can vet reforms to ensure that they are designed and implemented to reduce disparities and promote social justice.

FUTURE DIRECTIONS IN EDUCATION, PRACTICE, AND POLICY

Developments in social work research, education, practice, and policy are moving the field closer to the forefront of smart decarceration. Since the turn of the century, there has been an increase in social work coursework focused on the criminal justice system as well as increases in social work practicum opportunities in the criminal justice field (Epperson, Roberts, Ivanoff, Tripodi, & Gilmer, 2013; Scheyett, Pettus-Davis, McCarter, & Bringham, 2012). Both the Council on Social Work Education and the Society for Social Work and Research maintain special interest groups related to social work in the criminal justice field, demonstrating a sustained interest in social work's presence in the justice system and its reformation. In addition, organizations such as the National Association of Forensic Social Workers hold robust yearly conferences and routinely engage social workers throughout the country who directly engage in the criminal justice system. Schools of social work are also dedicating significant resources to equip their student bodies and engage their faculty in developing the field in relation to criminal justice reform. For example, the University of Pennsylvania School of Social Policy and Practice instituted the Goldring Reentry Initiative, which aims to equip its Master's of Social Work students with the knowledge and skills necessary to work in the criminal justice field to reduce mass incarceration (University of Pennsylvania, 2017).

In light of advancements in social work education, research, practice, and policy, greater opportunities exist to expand the reach of social work into the justice system and decarceration overall. For example, widespread efforts to develop a training pipeline in the social work field could better equip social workers for decarcerative work. Expanding criminal justice coursework at the bachelor's, master's, and doctoral levels is one way to increase the knowledge and application of social work principles in a criminal justice context. In addition, the field of social work should create more internships, research assistantships, practicum opportunities, and mentorships to develop tools and sharpen skills in criminal justice settings. For continued development, the field should increase postdoctoral fellowships, continuing education credits, and professional development training for social workers who engage with individuals, families, organizations, and communities that touch the criminal justice system.

Likewise, there are ways in which social work research can guide the development and implementation of effective practice and policy. For example, organizations such as Society for Social Work and Research can take the lead in identifying and promoting evidence-based practices for adoption as well as ineffective practices and policies that should be de-adopted in the field. This leadership may manifest in training for its members, presentations at its national conferences, and practice and policy briefs for distribution throughout the field.

Finally, policy is another arena in which many opportunities for progress exist. Organizations such as the Congressional Research Institute for Social Work and Policy (CRISP) can equip social workers to inform policy and advocate for social justice in the criminal justice field. CRISP and other such entities can provide advocacy training, templates for policymaking, and sample policy packets for distribution to decision-making stakeholders.

To move this grand challenge forward, the social work field must address key questions with respect to social work research, practice (both micro and macro), and education. Social work researchers should ask, "What are the gaps in knowledge in social work's understanding of the criminal justice field?" "How do we effectively adapt evidence-based models to the criminal justice context?" and "How do we measure intervention effectiveness within jurisdiction variance?" Questions for social work practitioners include the following: "What are the evidence-based models that should be adopted?" "Which models should be discontinued?" "Which policies facilitate successful intervention adoption?" "Which policies present barriers?" and "How do we best educate policy- and decision-makers on evidence-driven strategies for decarceration?" Finally, social work educators need to discover how to equip social workers to best deliver evidence-based interventions in context: "How do we (re)design social work curriculum to prepare bachelor's, master's, doctoral, and continuing education-level social workers for decarceration?" and "In what ways can social work cross-train with other fields in order to create transdisciplinary solutions?"

Answering these key questions in the social work field will pinpoint future directions for social workers as agents in and leaders of decarceration efforts. These answers will lead us to solutions that build social capacity—reducing the overall incarcerated population in ways that redress social disparities and maximize public safety and well-being.

Now is the time to end mass incarceration. A range of scalable and transformative interventions are necessary for decarceration's success. Although many of these social innovations have yet to be identified, the characteristics are clear. The Unites States is at a unique historic moment in which decarceration is desired on multiple levels: fiscally, politically, and societally. Perhaps more important, the social work profession stands at the crossroads of decarceration because of the profound negative effects that mass incarceration has had on disadvantaged, marginalized, and vulnerable groups—it is the ethical obligation of social workers to alter such injustice. At this critical junction in American history, there is a compelling opportunity for social work to engage other professions and disciplines in developing the resources, legal means, and infrastructure necessary to usher in an era of decarceration. With a value compass and solid evidence to successfully affect the reduction of incarceration in the United States, social work can improve community conditions and opportunities to support those who have been incarcerated to live productive and safe lives. Although smart decarceration will likely entail navigating uncertain and even risky terrain, it is imperative to use the tools of social work to build social capacity, catalyzing an era of smart decarceration.

REFERENCES

Abram, K. M., & Teplin, L. A. (1991). Co-occurring disorders among mentally ill jail detainees: Implications for public policy. *American Psychologist, 46*(10), 1036–1045.

Abramovitz, M. (1998). Social work and social reform: An arena of struggle. *Social Work, 43*(6), 512–526.

Aos, S., Miller, M. G., & Drake, E. (2006). *Evidence-based adult corrections programs: What works and what does not.* Retrieved from http://www.wsipp.wa.gov/ReportFile/924

Berg, M. T., & Huebner, B. M. (2011). Reentry and the ties that bind: An examination of social ties, employment, and recidivism. *Justice Quarterly, 28*(2), 382–410.

Boggess, P., & McGregor, C. (2013). Tarrant County's deferred prosecution program. *The Prosecutor, 43*(3). Retrieved from http://www.tdcaa.com/journal/tarrant-county%E2%80%99s-deferred-prosecution-program-dpp

Bosworth, M. (2011). Penal moderation in the United States? *Criminology & Public Policy, 10*(2), 335–343.

Brame, R., Bushway, S. D., Paternoster, R., & Turner, M. G. (2014). Demographic patterns of cumulative arrest prevalence by ages 18 and 23. *Crime & Delinquency, 60*(3), 471–486.

Brekke, J. S., Ell, K., & Palinkas, L. A. (2007). Translational science at the National Institute of Mental Health: Can social work take its rightful place? *Research on Social Work Practice, 17*, 123–133.

Brunson, R. K., & Miller, J. (2006). Young Black men and urban policing in the United States. *British Journal of Criminology, 46*(4), 613–640.

Bushway, S. D., & Piehl, A. M. (2001). Judging judicial discretion: Legal factors and racial discrimination in sentencing. *Law and Society Review, 35*(4), 733–764.

Campana, D. (2013, May 13). Kane "second chance" program gets high marks. *Chicago Tribune.* Retrieved from http://www.chicagotribune.com/suburbs/aurora-beacon-news/news/ct-abn-kane-states-st-0506-20150505-story.html

Carson, E. A. (2015). *Prisoners in 2014*. Washington, DC: Bureau of Justice Statistics. Retrieved from https://www.bjs.gov/content/pub/pdf/p14.pdf

Carson, E. A., & Anderson, E. (2016). *Prisoners in 2015*. Washington, DC: Bureau of Justice Statistics. Retrieved from https://www.bjs.gov/content/pub/pdf/p15.pdf

Clear, T. R. (2007). *Imprisoning communities: How mass incarceration makes disadvantaged neighborhoods worse*. New York, NY: Oxford University Press.

Clement, M., Schwarzfeld, M., & Thompson, M. (2011). *The National Summit on Justice Reinvestment and Public Safety: Addressing recidivism, crime, and corrections spending*. New York, NY: The Council of State Governments Justice Center.

Dembo, R., Walters, W., Wareham, J., Burgos, C., Schmeidler, J., Hoge, R., & Underwood, L. (2008). Evaluation of an innovative post-arrest diversion program: 12-month recidivism analysis. *Journal of Offender Rehabilitation, 47*(4), 356–384.

Draine, J., & Muñoz-Laboy, M. (2014). Commentary: Not just variation in estimates: Deinstitutionalization of the justice system. *Psychiatric Services, 65*(7), 873.

Durose, M. R., Cooper, A. D., & Snyder, H. N. (2014). *Recidivism of prisoners released in 30 states in 2005: Patterns from 2005 to 2010*. Washington, DC: Bureau of Justice Statistics. Retrieved from https://www.bjs.gov/content/pub/pdf/rprts05p0510.pdf

Epperson, M. W., & Pettus-Davis, C. (2015a). *Smart decarceration: Guiding concepts for an era of criminal justice transformation* (CSD Working Paper No. 15-53). St. Louis, MO: Center for Social Development, George Warren Brown School of Social Work, Washington University in St. Louis. Retrieved from https://csd.wustl.edu/Publications/Documents/WP15-53.pdf

Epperson, M. W., & Pettus-Davis, C. (2015b, November 24). *Formerly incarcerated individuals are a crucial element in building a decarceration movement*. Retrieved from http://www.safetyandjusticechallenge.org/2015/11/formerly-incarcerated-individuals-are-a-crucial-element-in-building-a-decarceration-movement

Epperson, M. W., Roberts, L. E., Ivanoff, A., Tripodi, S. J., & Gilmer, C. N. (2013). To what extent is criminal justice content specifically addressed in MSW programs? *Journal of Social Work Education, 49*(1), 96–107.

Epperson, M. W., & Pettus-Davis, C. (Eds.) (2017). *Smart Decarceration: Achieving criminal justice transformation in the 21st Century*. NY: Oxford University Press.

Fazel, S., & Danesh, J. (2002). Serious mental disorder in 23,000 prisoners: A systematic review of 62 surveys. *Lancet, 359*(9306), 545–550.

Fraser, M. W. (2004). Intervention research in social work: Recent advances and continuing challenges. *Research on Social Work Practice, 14*, 210–222. doi:10.1177/1049731503262150

George, C., Orwat, J., Stemen, D., Cossyleon, J., Hilvers, J., & Chong, E. (2015, June). *An evaluation of the Cook County State's Attorney's Office deferred prosecution program*. Retrieved from http://www.icjia.state.il.us/assets/pdf/ResearchReports/Cook_County_Deferred_Prosecution_Evaluation_0715.pdf

Gopnik, A. (2012, January 30). The caging of America. *The New Yorker*. Retrieved from http://www.newyorker.com/magazine/2012/01/30/the-caging-of-america

Gottschalk, M. (2009). Money and mass incarceration: The bad, the mad, and penal reform. *Criminology & Public Policy, 8*(1), 97–109.

Gray, K., Staff, T., Gest, T., & News, C. A. (2017). *Friends in court: The growing impact of "participatory defense."* Retrieved from https://thecrimereport.org/2017/03/29/friends-in-court-the-growing-impact-of-participatory-defense

Greenberg, G. A., & Rosenheck, R. A. (2008). Homelessness in the state and federal prison population. *Criminal Behavior and Mental Health, 18*(2), 88–103.

Hagan, J., & Dinovitzer, R. (1999). Collateral consequences of imprisonment for children, communities, and prisoners. *Crime and Justice, 26,* 121–162.

Harlow, C. W. (2003). *Education and correctional populations.* Washington, DC: Bureau of Justice Statistics. Retrieved from https://www.bjs.gov/content/pub/pdf/ecp. pdf

Human Rights Watch. (2013). *World report 2013: United States.* Retrieved from https:// www.hrw.org/world-report/2013/country-chapters/united-states

Jacobson, M. (2005). *Downsizing prisons: How to reduce crime and end mass incarceration.* New York, NY: NYU Press.

Jayadev, R. (2014). *"Participatory defense": Transforming the courts through family and community organizing.* Retrieved from https://acjusticeproject.org/2014/ 10/17/participatory-defense-transforming-the-courts-through-family-and-community-organizing-by-raj-jayadev

Johnson, B. (2003). Racial and ethnic disparities in sentencing departures across modes of conviction. *Criminology, 41*(2), 449–490.

Johnson, C. L., & Cullen, F. T. (2015). Prisoner reentry programs. *Crime and Justice, 44*(1), 517–575.

Kaeble, D., & Bonczar, T. P. (2016). *Probation and parole in the United States, 2015.* Washington, DC: Bureau of Justice Statistics. Retrieved from https://www.bjs. gov/content/pub/pdf/ppus15.pdf

Kaeble, D., & Glaze, L. (2016). *Correctional populations in the United States, 2015.* Washington, DC: Bureau of Justice Statistics. Retrieved from https://www.bjs. gov/content/pub/pdf/cpus15.pdf

Kingsnorth, R. F., MacIntosh, R. C., & Sutherland, S. (2002). Criminal charge or probation violation? Prosecutorial discretion and implications for research in criminal court processing. *Criminology, 40*(3), 553–578.

Kyckelhahn, T. (2012). *State corrections expenditures, FY 1982–2010.* Washington, DC: Bureau of Justice Statistics, Office of Justice Programs, US Department of Justice.

Lipsey, M. W., & Cullen, F. T. (2007). The effectiveness of correctional rehabilitation: A review of systematic reviews. *Annual Review of Law and Social Science, 3,* 297–320.

Lowenkamp, C. T., VanNostrand, M., & Holsinger, A. M. (2013). *The hidden costs of pretrial detention.* Retrieved from http://www.arnoldfoundation.org/wp-content/ uploads/2014/02/LJAF_Report_hidden-costs_FNL.pdf

Mallik-Kane, K., & Visher, C. A. (2008). *Health and prisoner reentry: How physical, mental, and substance abuse conditions shape the process of reintegration.* Washington, DC: Urban Institute. Retrieved from http://www.urban.org/sites/default/files/ publication/31491/411617-Health-and-Prisoner-Reentry.PDF

McLaughlin, M., Pettus-Davis, C., Brown, D., Veeh, C., & Renn, T. (2016). *The economic burden of incarceration in the United States.* St. Louis: Institute for Advancing Justice Research and Innovation. Retrieved from https://advancingjustice. wustl.edu/SiteCollectionDocuments/The%20Economic%20Burden%20of%20 Incarceration%20in%20the%20US.pdf

Minton, T. D., & Zeng, Z. (2015). *Jail inmates at midyear 2014.* Washington, DC: Bureau of Justice Statistics.

Moore, J., Sandys, M., & Jayadev, R. (2015). Make them hear you: Participatory defense and the struggle for criminal justice reform. *Albany Law Review*. Retrieved from https://papers.ssrn.com/sol3/papers.cfm?abstract_id=2594926

National Center on Addiction and Substance Abuse at Columbia University. (2010). *Behind bars II: Substance abuse and America's prison population*. New York, NY: Author.

Nellis, A. (2016). *The color of justice: Racial and ethnic disparity in state prisons*. Retrieved from http://www.sentencingproject.org/publications/color-of-justice-racial-and-ethnic-disparity-in-state-prisons

Obama, B. (2017). The president's role in advancing criminal justice reform. *Harvard Law Review, 130*(3), 811–866.

Petersilia, J., & Cullen, F. T. (2014). Liberal but not stupid: Meeting the promise of downsizing prisons. *Stanford Journal of Criminal Law and Policy, 2*, 1–43. Retrieved from https://law.stanford.edu/publications/liberal-but-not-stupid-meeting-the-promise-of-downsizing-prisons

Pettus, C. A., & Severson, M. (2006). Paving the way for effective reentry practice: The critical role and function of the boundary spanner. *The Prison Journal, 86*, 206–229.

Pettus-Davis, C. (2012). Reverse social work's neglect of justice-involved adults: The intersection and an agenda. *Social Work Research, 36*(1), 3–7.

Pettus-Davis, C. (2014). Social support among releasing men prisoners with lifetime trauma experiences. *International Journal of Law and Psychiatry, 37*(5), 512–523.

Pettus-Davis, C., Epperson, M. W., & Grier, A. (2017). *Guideposts for the era of smart decarceration: Smart decarceration strategies for practitioners, advocates, reformers, and researchers*. St. Louis, MO: Center for Social Development, Washington University in St. Louis. Retrieved from https://csd.wustl.edu/OurWork/SocialJustice/Decarceration/Documents/Guideposts_akg.pdf

Pettus-Davis, C., Epperson, M. W., Taylor, S. & Grier, A. (2017). Guideposts for the smart decarceration era: Recommended strategies from researchers, practitioners, and formerly incarcerated leaders. In M. W. Epperson & C. Pettus-Davis (Eds.), *Smart decarceration: Achieving criminal justice transformation in the 21st century*. New York, NY: Oxford University Press.

Pew Center on the States. (2008). *One in 100: Behind bars in America, 2008*. Washington, DC: Author. Available at http://www.pewtrusts.org/~/media/legacy/uploaded-files/wwwpewtrustsorg/reports/sentencing_and_corrections/onein100pdf.pdf

Pew Research Center. (2013). *King's dream remains an elusive goal; Many Americans see racial disparities*. Washington, DC: Author. Retrieved from http://www.pewsocialtrends.org/2013/08/22/kings-dream-remains-an-elusive-goal-many-americans-see-racial-disparities/4/#incarceration-rate

Pinals, D. A. (2017). Jail diversion, specialty court, and reentry services: Partnerships between behavioral health and justice systems. In R. Rosner & C. L. Scott (Eds.), *Principles and practice of forensic psychiatry* (p. 237). Boca Raton, FL: CRC Press.

Roberts, D. E. (2004). The social and moral costs of mass incarceration in African American communities. *Stanford Law Review, 56*(5), 1271–1305.

Rojek, J., Rosenfeld, R., & Decker, S. (2012). Policing race: The racial stratification of searchers in police traffic stops. *Criminology, 50*(4), 993–1024.

Rosenberg, T. (2017, February 14). Even in Texas, mass imprisonment is going out of style. *The New York Times*. Retrieved from https://www.nytimes.com/2017/02/14/opinion/even-in-texas-mass-imprisonment-is-going-out-of-style.html

Rosenfeld, R., Wallman, J., & Fornango, R. (2005). The contribution of ex-prisoners to crime rates. In J. Travis & C. Visher (Eds.), *Prisoner reentry and crime in America* (pp. 80–104). New York, NY: Cambridge University Press.

Rossman, S. B. (2011). *The multi-site adult drug court evaluation: The drug court experience: Volume 3.* Washington, DC: Urban Institute.

Rubin, R., & Turner, N. (2014, December 25). The steep cost of America's high incarceration rate. *The Wall Street Journal.* Retrieved from https://www.wsj.com/articles/robert-rubin-and-nicholas-turner-the-steep-cost-of-americas-high-incarceration-rate-1419543410

Sampson, R. J., & Loeffler, C. (2010). Punishment's place: The local concentration of mass incarceration. *Daedalus, 139*(3), 20–31.

Sampson, R. J., Morenoff, J. D., & Raudenbush, S. (2005). Social anatomy of racial and ethnic disparities in violence. *American Journal of Public Health, 95*(2), 224–232.

Sarteschi, C. M., Vaughn, M. G., & Kim, K. (2011). Assessing the effectiveness of mental health courts: A quantitative review. *Journal of Criminal Justice, 39*(1), 12–20.

Scheyett, A., Pettus-Davis, C., McCarter, S., & Bringham, R. (2012). Social work and criminal justice. Are we meeting in the field? *Journal of Teaching in Social Work, 32,* 438–450.

Sered, D. (2017). *Accounting for violence: How to increase safety and break our failed reliance on mass incarceration.* New York, NY: Vera Institute of Justice. Retrieved from https://storage.googleapis.com/vera-web-assets/downloads/Publications/accounting-for-violence/legacy_downloads/accounting-for-violence.pdf

Snyder, H. (2012). *Arrests in the United States, 1990 to 2010.* Washington, DC: US Department of Justice, Office of Justice Programs, Bureau of Justice Statistics.

Spelman, W. (2009). Crime, cash, and limited options: Explaining the prison boom. *Criminology & Public Policy, 8*(1), 29–77.

Steadman, H. J., Osher, F. C., Robbins, P. C., Case, B., & Samuels, S. (2009). Prevalence of serious mental illness among jail inmates. *Psychiatric Services, 60*(6), 761–765.

Stevenson, M., & Mayson, S. G. (2017). *Bail reform: New directions for pretrial detention and release.* Retrieved from http://scholarship.law.upenn.edu/faculty_scholarship/1745

Subramanian, R., Delaney, R., Roberts, S., Fishman, N., & McGarry, P. (2015). *Incarceration's front door.* Retrieved from http://www.vera.org/sites/default/files/resources/downloads/incarcerations-front-door-report_02.pdf

Taxman, F. S., Perdoni, M. L., & Harrison, L. D. (2007). Drug treatment services for adult offenders: The state of the state. *Journal of Substance Abuse Treatment, 32*(3), 239–254.

Teplin, L. A., Abram, K. M., & McClelland, G. M. (1996). Prevalence of psychiatric disorders among incarcerated women: I. Pretrial jail detainees. *Archives of General Psychiatry, 53*(6), 505–512.

The Pew Charitable Trusts. (2010). *Collateral costs: Incarceration's effect on economic mobility.* Washington, DC: Author.

Torrey, E. F., Kennard, A. D., Eslinger, D., Lamb, R., & Pavle, J. (2010). *More mentally ill persons are in jails and prisons than hospitals: A survey of the states.* Arlington, VA: Treatment Advocacy Center. Retrieved from http://www.treatmentadvocacycenter.org/storage/documents/final_jails_v_hospitals_study.pdf

Travis, J., & Waul, M. (2003). *Prisoners once removed: The impact of incarceration and reentry on children, families and communities.* Washington, DC: Urban Institute Press.

Overall unemployment has declined during the past 6 years, but this decline has not been equally distributed (Economic Policy Institute, 2015), and there remains marked differences in unemployment by racial and ethnic classification. The 2016 annual average civilian unemployment rate was 4.3% for White adults, 8.4% for Black/African Americans, 5.4% for Hispanic/Latinos, and 3.6% for Asian Americans (US Bureau of Labor Statistics, 2017a/c); in 2013, it was greater than 10% for Native Americans (Austin, 2013). (Not all data sources provide information on all subgroups.) The youth unemployment rate of 15.7% (for 16- to 19-year-olds) is strikingly high: 14.1% of White youth and 10.9% of Asian youth reported being unemployed in 2016, whereas the rate was considerably higher for youth classified as African American/Black (26.7%) (US Bureau of Labor Statistics, 2017b). Unemployment rates also vary with level of education. In March 2017, the rate was 8.6% for individuals older than age 16 years who had completed only 1–3 years of high school. By contrast, the rate for individuals with a bachelor's degree or higher was 2.4% (Federal Reserve Bank of St. Louis, 2017).

Underemployment occurs when skilled workers are employed at low-skilled jobs or when employees who would prefer to work full-time are only able to find part-time employment (Economic Policy Institute, 2015; McKee-Ryan & Harvey, 2011). Although the underemployment rate has also been declining, in January 2017, the Gallup survey found an overall underemployment rate of 14.1% (Statista, 2017). This rate also reflects racial and ethnic inequalities. In January 2017, the underemployment rate for African Americans was twice that for Whites, and the rate for Hispanics was one and a half times higher than that for Whites (Economic Policy Institute, 2017a). Education also affects underemployment rates. In 2017, 19.3% of individuals older than age 16 years who had completed 1–3 years of high school were underemployed compared to 4.9% of individuals with a bachelor's degree or higher (Economic Policy Institute, 2017b).

Working Conditions and Benefits

The work conditions and benefits associated with higher paid jobs protect and stabilize income, whereas the more challenging work conditions and lack of benefits diminish and destabilize the income from jobs held by workers at the lower end of the labor market. As noted previously, wages and hours together determine earnings. If wages are low, employees must work long hours for adequate take-home pay. Higher wages, when coupled with sufficient and stable hours, allow workers to earn sufficient, predictable earnings. Unfortunately, low wages and underemployment (i.e., working too few hours) tend to characterize jobs with limited benefits and precarious work conditions.

Whereas low-wage jobs are typically paid by the hour, higher paying jobs are more often salaried and include other forms of compensation that help support and stabilize workers' financial and personal well-being. Paid sick leave protects earnings when a worker or family member becomes ill or needs to take time off for medical care. Among civilian workers, 41% of workers in the lowest quartile and 87% of workers in the highest quartile have at least some paid sick leave benefits tied to their employment. Similar differences apply with paid vacations, personal leave, and jury duty leave, suggesting that higher status workers have more access to rest, wellness, and even civic participation. These disparities affect workers in later life as well. Less than one-fourth of the lowest paid workers have access to and participate in employer-sponsored retirement plans, whereas 79% of earners in the top quartile take advantage of retirement benefits (US Bureau of Labor Statistics, 2016).

Consequences of Employment Inequality

Employers often try to minimize labor costs by setting schedules with limited advance notice, adjusting workers' hours to meet immediate demand, and maintaining a relatively large pool of part-time hourly employees to fill labor gaps when needed (Lambert, 2008; Lambert et al., 2012). These scheduling practices can translate into unpredictable and variable work schedules over which employees have limited input or control (Henly, Shaefer, & Waxman, 2006; Lambert, 2008). Unpredictable, erratic work schedules are most common among workers paid by the hour, and they disproportionately affect workers of color, workers in low-wage occupations, and low-income parents (Lambert, Fugiel, & Henly, 2014). In addition, nonstandard work hours—work outside of the standard daytime, weekday workweek—have become the norm in today's economy, and disproportionately affects low-income workers (Presser & Cox, 1997). Although some employees prefer these hours, they are more often a requirement of the job (Presser, 2003). Work conditions such as these are negatively associated with employee well-being (e.g., stress, fatigue, and depression) and often interfere with non-work-related responsibilities including child care (Han, 2004; Henly & Lambert, 2014; Henly et al., 2006). Moreover, maternal nonstandard work schedules show negative associations with children's cognitive outcomes (Han, 2005).

Such jobs can destabilize families, often levy high costs for services such as child care, and leave parents torn between their responsibilities to their families and their responsibilities to their employers. Low wages can require parents to work multiple jobs, exacerbating child care difficulties and reducing the time available for parenting (Illinois Action for Children, 2016; Yoshikawa, Weisner, & Lowe, 2006). Low-wage jobs also typically fail to provide paid parental leave, which affects both child development and employee performance (Berger, Hill, & Waldfogel, 2005; Ybarra, 2013).

Although earned income is distinct from the accumulation of assets (wealth), low-wage employment restricts opportunities for investment in a variety of ways. In addition to limiting opportunities for asset accumulation through home ownership, low-wage employment complicates the ability of workers to save for future expenditures such as their children's college and their own retirement. For these workers, low levels of disposable income are often exacerbated by the lack of employer-sponsored retirement plans (Callahan, 2013).

Approximately 15 million children live in families with incomes below the federal poverty threshold (National Center for Children in Poverty, 2015). During the past 30 years, the child poverty rate in the United States has remained 1.7 times higher than the adult rate. On average among OECD member countries, more than 13% of children experience income poverty. In 11 nations, including Germany, Denmark, Sweden, and Finland, less than 10% of children live in poverty. The United States, however, is in a group of five nations in which more than 20% of children experience income poverty (OECD, 2016).

A majority of low-income children in the United States have parents who work, but low wages and unstable employment leave their families struggling to make ends meet. Poverty has a negative impact on children, which can interfere with children's learning and contribute to social, emotional, and behavioral difficulties. A disturbing characteristic of the growth in income inequality is the corresponding inequality in access to high-quality child care, schools, and other enrichment resources it portends (Kalil, 2016). This resource-access gap contributes to a learning and achievement gap between economically better and worse off children that continues into adulthood.

DIMENSIONS OF INEQUALITY IN ASSETS

Wealth is the stock of economic resources in place as opposed to the flow of resources that comes via income to meet immediate needs. It is typically defined as net worth, or the total value of all assets owned by a household minus any debt or liabilities, including cash/monetary equivalents, vehicles, home equity, other property, stocks/bonds/financial securities, and business equity (Nam, Huang, & Sherraden, 2008; Sherraden, 1991). Some definitions refer primarily to liquid assets, sometimes called net financial assets (Shapiro, 2004) or non-home wealth (Wolff, 2014), to only include assets that could be quickly and easily sold in times of need.

Levels of Wealth: Differences Across the Economic Spectrum and by Race and Gender

Between 1983 and 2010, high-wealth families in the top 20% of the wealth distribution experienced an average growth in net worth of nearly 120%. In contrast, families in the middle of the wealth distribution saw an average increase of 13%, whereas families in the bottom 20% of the wealth distribution on average had a net worth of zero, meaning that their average debt was higher than their assets (McKernan, Ratcliffe, Steuerle, & Zhang, 2013). The gap between the wealth of the highest income families and the lowest income families is at its greatest point since these data were first collected in 1983. In 2013, the median wealth of all upper income families was $639,000, whereas that for middle-class families was $96,500, and that for lower income families was $9,300–70 times less than that of upper income families (Fry & Kochhar, 2014).

Racial disparities in wealth are much greater than racial disparities in income and have grown larger since the recession of 2007–2009. In 2012, non-Hispanic Black households and Latino households received a median income 56% and 59%, respectively, of the median income received by non-Hispanic White households (Wolff, 2014). By contrast, in 2007, non-Hispanic Black and Latino households had only 10 and 12 cents, respectively, for every dollar of median wealth held by non-Hispanic White households. After the recession, by 2013, non-Hispanic African American median net worth had fallen to less than 8 cents and Latino median net worth had fallen to 10 cents for every dollar held by non-Hispanic White households. The total median wealth for non-Hispanic White families in 2013 was approximately $141,900, compared to that of Latinos at approximately $13,700 and that of non-Hispanic Blacks at approximately $11,000 (Kochhar & Fry, 2014).

There are also major gender disparities in wealth. In 2013, single women had only 32 cents in median wealth for every dollar of wealth held by single men. Married couples tend to be wealthier, but low-income couples do not reap the same economic benefits from marriage (Chang, 2015).

Financial Accounts: Differences Across the Economic Spectrum and by Race and Ethnicity

Overall, in 2016, 7% of US households were unbanked, meaning that no one in the household had a checking or savings account; 19.9% of US households were underbanked, meaning someone had an insured account, but he or she still used non-bank alternative financial services (AFS); and 68% of US households were fully banked, meaning they had an account and did not use AFS in the past 12 months (Federal Deposit Insurance Corporation [FDIC], 2016).

Households with less than $15,000 in family income were more than three times more likely to be unbanked (25.5%) and were approximately one-third less likely to be fully banked (45.1%). The number of Black and Latino households that were unbanked was more than double (18.2% and 16.2%, respectively), and they were approximately one-third less likely to be fully banked at 45.5% and 48.9%, respectively (FDIC, 2016).

Home Ownership

Home ownership is the largest contributor to net worth for families in the United States, particularly for those of low to moderate income (Wolff, 2014). There are both financial benefits and positive social impacts to home ownership. However, low-wage families face significant obstacles in purchasing and sustaining their homes (Herbert & Belsky, 2008). In addition, both rates of home ownership and returns to ownership vary with race and ethnicity. When the overall housing rate was at its highest in 2004, 76.2% of non-Hispanic White households, 49.1% of non-Hispanic Black households, and 48.9% of Latino households owned their homes (US Census Bureau, 2016). The most recent statistics from 2016 show that homeownership rates have dropped to 72.2% for non-Hispanic White households, 41.7% for non-Hispanic Black households, and 46.3% for Latino households, and the rate is 56.6% for Asian households (US Census Bureau, 2017). Equally important, Blacks and Latinos who did own homes saw less return in wealth from homeownership. For every $1 in wealth that median Black households gained through homeownership, the rate of return for median White households was $1.34. For every $1 in wealth gained by median Latino households through homeownership, median White households received $1.54 (Sullivan, Dietrich, Traub, & Ruetschlin, 2015).

Finding affordable housing is an issue whether one owns or rents. There is currently no housing market in the country where a minimum wage job will pay for a two-bedroom apartment at a fair market rate, defined by the federal government as rental that costs no more than one-third of gross monthly income (National Low Income Housing Coalition [NLIHC], 2016). In some housing markets, such as San Francisco and Washington, DC, rents are too high for even middle-income families (NLIHC, 2016).

Consequences of Wealth Inequality

The United States' extreme wealth inequality has critical consequences. The most immediate consequence is the inability of low-resourced households to meet emergency expenses. There is no official definition of asset poverty, but consistently approximately one-fifth of US households have zero or negative net worth (Wolff, 2014). A more formal asset–poverty measure is insufficient wealth resources to maintain a family at the poverty line for 3 months (Caner & Wolff, 2004; Nam et al., 2008). Based on data from 2011, more than two-thirds of Black and Latino households (67% and 71%, respectively) lack the savings necessary to subsist at the poverty level for 3 months in the event of an unexpected income disruption. In contrast, slightly more than one-third of White households are in a similar financial position (Asante-Mohammed et al., 2016). Thus, if these households face a job loss, medical emergency, or major unexpected expense, they do not have a cushion to cover such emergencies.

In the longer term, wealth inequality means that the majority never experience what Tom Shapiro terms "transformative assets," wealth or inheritance that lifts families beyond where their own achievements would lead (Shapiro, 2004). More than half of US households and two-thirds of Black and Latino households do not have sufficient financial assets to invest in opportunities for mobility, which includes buying a home, starting a business, or paying for their children's education (Shapiro, Oliver, & Meschede, 2009). Black, Latino, and American Indian children are more likely to be born into less advantaged households with modest income and little wealth (Shanks, 2011). Thus, disparities in wealth also have consequences for the next generation. For example, the lack of down payment assistance means that, on average, African Americans take 8 years longer than Whites to build home equity; similarly, the lack of assistance with college costs depresses college graduation rates (Asante-Mohammed et al., 2016).

Wealth inequality leads to an inability for many to achieve a secure retirement. Although Social Security provides a strong safety net for many older Americans, recipients can still live near poverty if it is their only source of income, and many older people have little investment outside of social security. More than 39 million working-age households (45%) do not own any retirement account assets. In addition, households that hold such accounts have significantly higher income and wealth—more than double the income and five times the non-retirement assets—compared to households with no retirement accounts (Rhee & Boivie, 2015). However, even among those that own accounts, the median account value is approximately $50,000—resulting in 80% of working households not having enough saved to replace their annual income for 1 year (Rhee & Boivie, 2015).

Retirement security is lower for households of color. Blacks and Latinos are less likely to have access to employer-sponsored retirement plans and have much lower average retirement savings compared to White households. The average Black and Latino household has $19,049 and $12,329, respectively, in retirement savings, whereas the average White household has $130,472 (Asante-Mohammed et al., 2016). There are a range of approaches that could help reduce such racial inequities among older Americans, from increasing pre-retirement income and assets to making progressive changes in Social Security (Williams Shanks & Leigh, 2015).

SPECIFIC POLICY RESPONSES

A range of policy initiatives alone or in concert can begin to address the entrenched economic inequities that mark the United States. These initiatives aim at both income and assets inequality. To significantly reduce economic inequality, a multipronged approach is necessary, and there are endless opportunities for social workers to contribute to this work.

Policies Addressing Income Inequality

Several policies can be developed and strengthened to address the large and growing inequalities in earned income.

Tax Credits

Social workers can work with agencies and policymakers to extend tax credits and to increase their usefulness to clients. Refundable tax credits serve as the largest mechanism redistributing income to poor and near-poor Americans. Together, the Earned Income Tax Credit (EITC) and Child Tax Credit (CTC) transfer approximately $80 billion per year to low- and moderate-income working families in addition to offsetting income taxes owed (Congressional Budget Office, 2017). Most benefits flow to families with children, although childless workers can claim small EITC benefits. In 2016, more than 27 million individuals received EITC credits. Maximum amounts range from $506 for childless workers to $6,269 for workers with three or more qualifying children; the average amount received was more than $2,455 (Internal Revenue Service [IRS], 2017).

The design and administration of tax credits provide several practical and political advantages. Most notably, the EITC is a highly effective anti-poverty program, in part because it targets its benefits to households just below the poverty line. By one 2012 estimate, it moved 9.4 individuals, including 5 million children, out of poverty (IRS, 2017). Administered by the IRS as part of the annual income tax filing process, the EITC and CTC have high take-up rates and very low operating costs. Unlike other programs for the poor, tax credits do not require annual appropriation, and Congress and the president can only remove them via tax legislation, making them less vulnerable to attack.

These same features create drawbacks as well. The economic benefits that the EITC and the CTC provide to low-income families with children are predicated on employment. Neither program helps the unemployed poor nor those kept out of the labor force by disability or family health or caregiving circumstances. Childless workers do not become eligible for the EITC until age 25 years, and the credit amounts that they receive do not offset payroll taxes so that, after taxes, their net income is often below the poverty line (Marr, Hung, Murray, & Sherman, 2016). Noncustodial parents, including those who actively support their children through caregiving and financial support, receive no benefits beyond the small amounts available to childless workers. Finally, many EITC claimants rely on paid tax preparers to file their returns, meaning some portion of the refund typically benefits financial services.

Universal Child Allowance

A universal child allowance would address some of the remaining weaknesses in family support. Social workers can assess the need for such a program and its likely results. The safety net for families with children has continued to erode as the number of families living in poverty and deep poverty has increased and income in these families has become increasingly volatile (Edin & Shaefer, 2016). Most US safety net programs require employment as a condition of eligibility or are designed to move low-income individuals into employment. Families in which the parents are unemployed or sporadically employed have few options for obtaining assistance (Moffitt, 2015). The Supplemental Nutrition Assistance Program (SNAP) benefits provide food but cannot be used for expenses such as rent and utilities. The Temporary Assistance for Needy Families (TANF) program provides cash assistance, but enrollment has been declining during the past two decades: When TANF was initially enacted, 68 families received assistance for every 100 families in poverty; that number has since fallen to 23 families receiving assistance for every 100 families in poverty (Center on Budget and Poverty Priorities, 2016).

To address these issues, the child tax allowance and the child tax exemption could be replaced with a monthly universal child tax credit. The amount of the credit could vary with the child's age to reflect the higher costs and demonstrated benefits of providing cash support to very young children (Duncan, Magnuson, & Votruba-Drzal, 2014).

This allowance system promises an increased level of basic income support to families in poverty. Furthermore, it is relatively straightforward to administer and to understand, and it provides dependable resources to families who are supporting children. This program could provide family stability for families that currently experience irregular employment, underemployment, as well as unemployment. Regular basic income benefits children's health, school achievement, and overall well-being (Dahl & Lochner, 2012; Marr et al., 2016; Milligan & Stabile, 2011; Strully, Rehkopf, & Xuan, 2010).

Although clearly of significant benefit to families, the costs of a child allowance system are considerable and not entirely offset by the concurrent proposed elimination of tax credits and exemptions (Harris & Shaefer, 2017). These costs, and the politics of introducing a new universal program, may make this a difficult program to implement.

Public Employment Programs

Public employment programs, sometimes referred to as active employment policy, hire people directly on government projects, and the United States has a history of such programs. Public employment has the potential to reduce unemployment, provide income for families, and build experience and skills for future employment in the private sector (Sherraden, 2014). The Works Progress Administration (WPA) and the Civilian Conservation Corps (CCC) are classic examples of public employment from the 1930s Depression era. At any one time, the WPA employed several millions of people, peaking in 1936 at 40% of all those who were unemployed (Levine, 2010, p. 4). Harry Hopkins, a social worker and advisor to President Roosevelt, led the vision and implementation of the WPA to produce public goods and create jobs. Social workers need to understand and explore the benefits of job support and creation.

The CCC was created in 1933 by executive order of President Franklin Roosevelt to undertake conservation work and employ younger workers. The CCC enrolled a total of 3 million young people, mostly men, between 1933 and 1942, in "essential, imperative" conservation work. During a divisive political period, the CCC enjoyed broad bipartisan support, and CCC alumni continued to express positive views of their CCC experience and its impact on their lives many decades later (Sherraden, 1979; Sherraden & Eberly, 1982).

As demonstrated by these Depression-era policies, public employment, with a little imagination, can become much more than "make work" or "jobs of last resort." With daunting environmental and social tasks facing the United States and other countries in the 21st century, public employment can become a vital response to major issues that are not addressed in the private market, including resource conservation, the transition to non-fossil fuel use, work with disadvantaged children, and support for a growing elderly population. Indeed, such essential tasks are better conceived as "jobs of first resort." Compared to the size of the current US labor force, a CCC for the 21st century would create 1 million new jobs, and a new WPA would create 10 million. Such programs are expensive, but they can also support the infrastructure needs of our changing society. As President Roosevelt and Harry Hopkins believed in the 1930s, when the challenge is great, there is no reason to think small.

Employment and Work-Family Policies

To comprehensively address extreme economic inequality and its consequences, policies must also deal with job quality and the numerous aspects of work and family life affecting the quality of life of low-income individuals and families.

Place-Based Wages

During the past 30 years, the US economy has doubled, but a large proportion of these earnings have gone to the top 1% of earners (Reich, 2013). Wages for most earners have been stagnant for the past 30 years, without adjusting for inflation and the rising cost of living in American cities. Care for workers may require a more nuanced approach to wages. The federal minimum wage is set at $7.25 per hour and is not responsive to changes in cost of living or geographic variation. Despite the fact that many states have worked to increase the minimum wage in their respective state, most families find it extremely difficult to make ends meet with a minimum wage job. Social work advocacy at the federal, state, and local levels for higher minimum wages is critical to reversing unequal wage trends. Advocacy for living wage legislation is needed to support individuals living in areas with a high cost of living.

Workplace Benefits

America's 28 million part-time workers earn one-third less per hour compared to their full-time counterparts, and they do not qualify for critical employer-provided benefits (Center for Popular Democracy, Local Progress, & Fair Workweek Initiative, 2016). Many part-time employees are not eligible for benefits such as paid parental leave, short-term disability, and paid sick leave. Moreover, employee earnings are a function of wages and hours; hence, the benefit of wage increases such as those discussed in the previous section can be offset by corresponding reductions in work hours. Thus, policies that encourage employers to hire full-time workers in jobs that provide employer-sponsored benefits are critical.

There are several promising efforts to improve work conditions, benefits, and work hours. For example, in addition to recent local and state minimum and living wage successes, several local governments have passed ordinances that require employers to provide paid sick days and to address erratic and unpredictable scheduling practices. For example, Chicago passed a paid sick day ordinance in 2016, and San Francisco, Seattle, and New York have all enacted legislation designed to reduce schedule unpredictability and increase employees' control over their work hours. At the state level, several states have paid family leave policies or use state disability insurance to address parental leave supports (Ybarra, 2013). The effects of these new initiatives are presently unknown.

Child Care and Early Education Supports

Three-fourths of young children spend time in nonparental child care and early education settings while their parents work (Laughlin, 2013). The landscape of care ranges widely from preschool and center-based programs to home-based arrangements with licensed child care providers and informal caregivers. These care settings provide essential caregiving support to working parents and to parents in higher education and training; they also serve as critical developmental contexts for children—who typically spend more than 30 hours per week in nonparental care (Laughlin, 2013). Thus, the developmental well-being of children and the economic livelihood of families are threatened without access to stable, high-quality, safe, and affordable care (Chaudry, Henly, & Meyers, 2010).

However, despite the almost universal demand for child care and early education services among working families, families face significant barriers finding and maintaining child care that meets their needs in terms of cost, quality, scheduling, and convenience. These caregiving challenges are exacerbated by geographic inequities in child care access and by nonstandard and variable work schedules that do not match the schedules of most formal child care and early education programs (Henly & Lambert, 2005).

The considerable public resources that support the caregiving needs of families are insufficient to meet demand. The federal Child Care Development Block Grant (CCDBG) subsidizes the cost of child care across a range of settings for eligible low-income families with the goal of improving the education, training, and employment outcomes of parents and the developmental well-being of their children in care. However, CCDBG program funding covers only 15% of eligible families (Chien, 2015), and subsidy spells are brief—median spells are 4–8 months across states (Swenson, 2014)—due to a range of factors, including complex program rules; administrative hassles; and instability in families' employment, housing, and other life domains (Ha & Meyer, 2010; Henly, Sandstrom, & Pilarz, 2017; Sandstrom & Chaudry, 2012). The 2014 reauthorization of CCDBG does not address the revenue shortfalls necessary to meet its key objectives for program improvement and increased coverage. Other government programs, such as federal Head Start and state preschool programs (some funded with a combination of federal and state dollars), focus directly on expanding children's early education opportunities, with less attention to the needs of working parents. The return on investment of high-quality preschool and Head Start is clear (Heckman, 2011; Magnuson & Duncan, 2016). However, preschool remains underfunded, program availability and quality vary, many programs do not serve infants and toddlers, and many preschool programs are part-time and provide only daytime weekday care.

Social workers can support state and federal expansion of supports for child care to ensure that they are available for all families, regardless of their ability to pay or their work schedules. Policies should promote access to all types of safe, legal, quality care (care in centers and preschools, licensed family child care, and informal home-based care) to address the diverse caregiving needs and preferences of families. It is critical that policies operate to reduce families' out-of-pocket expenses (e.g., refundable tax credits and child care subsidies) and increase child care supply (e.g., direct investments in early care and education). Families need high-quality and affordable arrangements that are proximate to home and/or work and available during their work, school, and training hours. In addition, explicit attention to the training, technical support, and infrastructure needs of providers, as well as their salary and benefit opportunities, is critical to improving both provider job quality and program quality.

Policies for Lifelong Inclusive Asset Building

There are many possible approaches to help families build wealth. This section discusses several ideas, but it ends with the primary recommendation for a lifelong asset-building policy that is inclusive and progressive (Sherraden, 1991). One possibility is to focus on emergency savings. Offering low- to moderate-income households access to safe accounts and/or financial instruments with incentives for maintaining short-term savings is a promising strategy. Many programs incorporate this concept, especially with refunds received at tax time (Azurdia & Freedman, 2016).

Another approach is to capitalize business start-ups, including microenterprise and other individual entrepreneurship ventures as well as cooperatives and community-initiated ventures. Such investment could spark employment and generate pride in producing quality local products and services. Federal loan programs administered by the Small Business Administration and the Treasury Department's Community Development Financial Institution Fund are limited, and new funding pathways are necessary. In addition, start-ups could require protection from unfair competition by large firms (Cramer, 2014). Cooperatives combine social and economic development and historically have been a source of economic independence in the African American community (Gordon Nembhard, 2014).

Hundreds of billions of dollars in tax benefits each year subsidize retirement, housing, and other financial investments. However, almost 80% of these dollars go to the top quintile of income earners, whereas the bottom 40% of income earners see only approximately 3% of these dollars (CFED, 2014). These funds could be redeployed to ensure everyone has retirement savings and access to affordable housing and secure pathways to homeownership; the tax code would be more equitable, and the country would be in better shape economically.

Finally, we have proposed child development accounts (CDAs) as a national platform for universal and progressive asset building (Huang et al., 2017; Sherraden, 1991). By automatically enrolling all newborns in existing financial platforms and providing additional financial incentives to financially vulnerable groups, everyone has access to asset-building mechanisms and saving. Such investments would reduce wealth inequality by ensuring that no individual begins life without assets. A rigorous experiment on CDAs, across a full state population, with oversamples of subpopulations of color (African Americans, Hispanic Americans, and Native Americans), found that (1) all children can be included and (2) positive impacts are as great or greater for disadvantaged populations; in other words, inclusive CDA policy can benefit everyone (Sherraden et al., 2015).

SOCIAL WORK POLICY, ADVOCACY, AND PRACTICE

In the context of growing extreme inequality, social workers can work with a renewed focus on economic justice. Our future efforts require strong coalitions with like-minded professional allies, the integration of economic inequality issues with social work education, and evaluation of our progress with both process and outcome measurements. For instance, social workers and allies should recognize and work to bring to fruition the possibilities and promise of, as well as increase the value of, refundable tax credits. In practice, social workers should educate families about the EITC and about the costs and benefits of using paid preparers to file (Beverly, 2002). Social workers should advocate expanded access for childless workers and noncustodial parents and either increased benefits or integration with other supports such as a Universal Child Credit. Finally, social workers should advocate for the development of low-cost or nonprofit tax-preparation services and should educate consumers about their advantages.

Social workers can work with unions, employers, and agencies to obtain more humane and regular working conditions, wages, and benefits. They can support programs that provide families with regular schedules and income. They can help develop and support a full range of child care options for low-income working parents.

Social workers can advocate at both the local level and the federal level for emergency savings programs, a more equitable distribution of tax benefits for retirement and housing, and greater economic support for college access initiatives and for child care. Ideally, the passage of a lifelong asset-building policy that is progressive and inclusive could help achieve all these goals.

The extreme and growing income and wealth inequality that exists in the United States is troubling on many levels. When power and economic resources are concentrated in the hands of a few, it threatens our democratic institutions and leads to undue suffering for families and children. Social work research, teaching, and practice working in concert can generate and advocate for practical solutions to reducing these inequalities. It is a grand challenge worthy of our focused effort and engagement. The issues and policy directions described in this chapter align with requirements of the profession's educational credentialing agency, the Council on Social Work Education. For instance, advancing "human rights and social and economic justice" is a core competency, and educational programs training bachelor's- or master's-level social workers should develop this competency. As a Grand Challenge working group, we seek to better understand and support how social work educational programs serve these aims. This work may lead to developing new learning materials or strategies to help student social workers learn practice skills for combatting modern economic inequality.

Widespread economic change requires political, economic, and policy intervention at federal, state, and local levels. Social workers need to be educated to develop metrics for success in this arena and also to assess and evaluate services, programs, and policies. Progress requires the development of measurable goals for reducing extreme economic inequality and also ways of assessing the contributions of a range of efforts to such goals. During the coming years, workgroups within this Grand Challenge will continue to build models of change and develop metrics for evaluating our efforts.

REFERENCES

Asante-Mohammed, D., Collins, C., Hoxie, J., & Nieves, E. (2016). *The ever-growing racial wealth gap*. Washington, DC: Institute for Policy Studies. Retrieved from http://www.ips-dc.org/wp-content/uploads/2016/08/The-Ever-Growing-Gap-CFED_IPS-Final-2.pdf

Austin, A. (2013, December 17). *High unemployment means native Americans are still waiting for an economic recovery*. Washington, DC: Economic Policy Institute. Retrieved from http://www.epi.org/publication/high-unemployment-means-native-americans

Autor, D. (2010). The polarization of job opportunities in the U.S. labor market: Implications for employment and earnings. *Community Investments, 23*(2), 11–41.

Azurdia, G., & Freedman, S. (2016). *Encouraging nonretirement savings at tax time: Final impact findings from the SaveUSA Evaluation.* Retrieved from https://www.mdrc. org/sites/default/files/SaveUSA_FinalReport_ExecSummary.pdf

Berger, L. M., Hill, J., & Waldfogel, J. (2005). Maternity leave, early maternal employment and child health and development in the US. *The Economic Journal, 115*(501), F29–F47.

Beverly, Sondra G. (2002). What Social Workers Need to Know about the Earned Income Tax Credit. *Social Work, 47*(3), 259–266.

Callahan, D. (2013, August 20). Low-wage work and the coming retirement crisis. *Demos Policyshop.* Retrieved from http://www.demos.org/blog/8/20/13/ low-wage-work-and-coming-retirement-crisis

Caner, A., & Wolff, E. N. (2004). Asset poverty in the United States, 1984–99: Evidence from the Panel Study of Income Dynamics. *Review of Income and Wealth, 50*(4), 493–518.

Center for Popular Democracy, Local Progress, & Fair Workweek Initiative. (2016). *Restoring a fair workweek.* Retrieved from https://populardemocracy.org/campaign/restoring-fair-workweek

Center on Budget and Poverty Priorities. (2016). *Chart book: TANF at 20.* Retrieved from https://www.cbpp.org/research/family-income-support/chart-book-tanf-at-20

CFED (2014). *Upside Down: Tax Incentives to Save and Build Wealth.* Washington, DC: CFED.

Chang, M. (2015). *Women and wealth.* Evanston, IL: Asset Funders Network.

Chaudry, A., Henly, J., & Meyers, M. (2010). *Conceptual frameworks for child care decision-making.* Washington, DC: Office of Planning, Research and Evaluation, Administration for Children and Families, US Department of Health and Human Services. Retrieved from https://www.acf.hhs.gov/sites/default/files/opre/conceptual_frameworks.pdf

Chien, N. (2015). *Estimates of child care eligibility and receipt for fiscal year 2012* (ASPE Issue Brief). Washington, DC: Office of the Assistant Secretary for Planning and Evaluation, Office of Human Services Policy, US Department of Health and Human Services. Retrieved from https://aspe.hhs.gov/sites/default/files/pdf/ 153591/ChildEligibility.pdf

Congressional Budget Office. 2017. Spending Projections (supplemental data file). *The Budget and Economic Outlook: 2017 to 2027.* Retrieved from www.cbo.gov/publication/52370

Cramer, R. (2014). Foundations of an Asset-based Social Policy Agenda. In Reid Cramer and Trina R. Williams Shanks (Eds.), *The Assets Perspective: The Rise of Asset Building and its Impact on Social Policy.* Chapter 12, pp. 245-261. New York, NY: Palgrave Macmillan.

Dahl, G. B., & Lochner, L. (2012). The impact of family income on child achievement: Evidence from the Earned Income Tax Credit. *American Economic Review, 102*(5), 1927–1956.

Duncan, G. J., Magnuson, K., & Votruba-Drzal, E. (2014). Boosting family income to promote child development. *Future of Children, 24*(1), 99–120.

Economic Policy Institute. (2015, June 15). *A more comprehensive measure of slack in the labor market.* Retrieved from http://stateofworkingamerica.org/charts/ number-of-underemployed

Economic Policy Institute. (2017a). *State of working America: Underemployment highest for those with least education.* Retrieved from http://www.stateofworkingamerica.org/charts/underemployment-education

Economic Policy Institute. (2017b). *State of working America: All races and ethnicities hurt by recession, racial and ethnic disparities persist.* Retrieved from http://www.stateofworkingamerica.org/charts/underemployment-by-race-and-ethnicity

Edin, K., & Shaefer, H. L. (2016). *$2.00 a day: Living on almost nothing in America.* New York, NY: Houghton Mifflin.

Elsby, M., Hobijn, B., & Şahin, A. (2013, Fall). The decline of the U.S. labor share. *Brookings Papers on Economic Activity,* 1–63. doi:10.1353/eca.2013.0016

Federal Deposit Insurance Corporation. (2016). *2015 FDIC national survey of unbanked and underbanked households.* Washington, DC: Author.

Federal Reserve Bank of St. Louis. (2017). *Unemployment rate by educational attainment and age, monthly, not seasonally adjusted.* Retrieved from https://fred.stlouisfed.org/release/tables?rid=50&eid=48713

Fry, R., & Kochhar, R. (2014). *America's wealth gap between middle-income and upper-income families is widest on record.* Washington, DC: Pew Research Center. Retrieved from http://www.pewresearch.org/fact-tank/2014/12/17/wealth-gap-upper-middle-income

Gordon Nembhard, J. (2014). *Collective Courage: A History of African American Cooperative Economic Thought and Practice.* University Park, PA: Pennsylvania State University Press.

Gould, E. (2016). *Wage inequality continued its 35-year rise in 2015.* Washington, DC: Economic Policy Institute. Retrieved from http://www.epi.org/publication/wage-inequality-continued-its-35-year-rise-in-2015

Grusky, D. B., Mattingly, M. J., & Varner, C. E. (2016). The poverty and inequality report. *Pathways* [Special issue]. Retrieved from http://inequality.stanford.edu/sites/default/files/Pathways-SOTU-2016.pdf

Ha, Y., & Meyer, D. R. (2010). Child care subsidy patterns: Are exits related to economic setbacks or economic successes? *Children and Youth Services Review, 32,* 346–355.

Han, W.-J. (2004). Nonstandard work schedules and child care decisions: Evidence from the NICHD study of early child care. *Early Childhood Research Quarterly, 19,* 231–256.

Han, W.-J. (2005). Maternal nonstandard work schedules and child cognitive outcomes. *Child Development, 76*(1), 137–154.

Harris, D., & Shaefer, H. L. (2017, April 19). Fighting child poverty with a universal child allowance. *The American Prospect.* Retrieved from http://prospect.org/article/fighting-child-poverty-universal-child-allowance

Heckman, J. (2011). The economics of inequality: The value of early childhood education. *American Educator, 35*(1), 31–35.

Henly, J. R., & Lambert, S. J. (2005). Nonstandard work and child-care needs of low-income parents. In S. M. Bianchi, L. M. Casper, & R. Berkowitz King (Eds.), *Work, family, health, and well-being* (pp. 473–492). Mahwah, NJ: Erlbaum.

Henly, J. R., & Lambert, S. J. (2014). Unpredictable work timing in retail jobs: Implications for employee work–life conflict. *Industrial and Labor Relations Review, 67*(3), 986–1016. doi:10.1177/0019793914537458

Henly, J. R., Sandstrom, H., & Pilarz, A. (2017). Child care assistance as work–family support: Meeting the economic and caregiving needs of low-income working families in the US. In M. las Heras, N. Chinchilla, & M. Grau (Eds.), *Work–family balance in light of globalization and technology* (pp. 241–265). Newcastle upon Tyne, UK: Cambridge Scholars Publishing.

Henly, J. R., Shaefer, H. L., & Waxman, R. E. (2006). Nonstandard work schedules: Employer- and employee-driven flexibility in retail jobs. *Social Service Review*, *80*, 609–634.

Herbert, C. E., & Belsky, E. S. (2008). The home ownership experience of low-income and minority households: Review and synthesis. *Cityscape*, *10*(2), 5–61.

Holzer, H. J. (2008). *Living wage laws: How much do (can) they matter*. Washington, DC: Urban Institute. Retrieved from http://www.urban.org/sites/default/files/publication/32126/411783-Living-Wage-Laws.PDF

Holzer, H. J. (2015). *Job market polarization and U.S. worker skills: A tale of two middles*. Washington DC: Brookings. Retrieved from https://www.brookings.edu/research/job-market-polarization-and-u-s-worker-skills-a-tale-of-two-middles

Huang, J., Sherraden, M.S., Clancy, M., Sherraden, M., & Shanks, T. (2017). Start Lifelong Asset Building with Universal and Progressive Child Development Accounts. (Grand Challenges for Social Work Policy Action Statement) Retrieved from American Academy of Social Work & Social Welfare website: http://aas-wsw.org/wp-content/uploads/2017/03/PAS.11.1-v2.pdf.

Illinois Action for Children. (2016, June). *Child care needs of families with nonstandard and unstable schedules* (Policy brief). Retrieved from http://www.actforchildren.org/wp-content/uploads/2016/06/CCAP-Work-Schedules-Policy-Brief-FINAL-6.16.16.pdf

Internal Revenue Service. (2017). *EITC and other refundable credits*. Retrieved from https://www.eitc.irs.gov/EITC-Central/abouteitc

Kalil, A. (2016). *How economic inequality affects children's outcomes*. Washington, DC: Washington Center for Equitable Growth. Retrieved from http://equitablegrowth.org/human-capital/how-economic-inequality-affects-childrens-outcomes

Kalleberg, A. L. (2011). *Good jobs, bad jobs: The rise of polarized and precarious employment systems in the United States, 1970s–2000s* (American Sociological Association Rose Series in Sociology). New York, NY: Russell Sage Foundation.

Karabarbounis, L., & Neiman, B. (2013). *The global decline of the labor share* (NBER Working Paper No. 19136). Retrieved from http:// www.nber.org/papers/w19136

Kochhar, R., & Fry, R. (2014). *Wealth inequality has widened along racial ethnic lines since end of Great Recession*. Washington, DC: Pew Research Center.

Lambert, S. J. (2008). Passing the buck: Labor flexibility practices that transfer risk onto hourly workers. *Human Relations*, *61*(9), 1203–1227.

Lambert, S. J., Fugiel, P. J., & Henly, J. R. (2014, August). *Precarious work schedules among early-career employees in the US: A national snapshot* (EINet (Employment Instability, Family Well-Being, and Social Policy Network Research Brief). Retrieved from https://ssascholars.uchicago.edu/sites/default/files/work-scheduling-study/files/lambert.fugiel.henly_.precarious_work_schedules.august2014_0.pdf

Lambert, S. J., Haley-Lock, A., & Henly, J. R. (2012). Schedule flexibility in hourly jobs: Unanticipated consequences and promising directions. *Community, Work and Family*, *15*(3), 293–315.

Lambert, S. J., & Henly, J. R. (2012). Frontline managers matter: Labour flexibility practices and sustained employment in US retail jobs. In C. Warhurst, F. Carré, P. Findlay, & C. Tilly (Eds.), *Are bad jobs inevitable? Trends, determinants and responses to job quality in the twenty-first century* (pp. 143–159). Basingstoke, UK: Palgrave Macmillan.

Laughlin, L. (2013). *Who's minding the kids? Child care arrangements: Spring, 2011.* Washington, DC: US Census Bureau. Retrieved from https://www.census.gov/prod/2013pubs/p70-135.pdf

Levine, L. (2010). *Job creation programs of the Great Depression: the WPA and CCC.* Retrieved from http://digitalcommons.ilr.cornell.edu/cgi/viewcontent.cgi?article=1713&context=key_workplace

Lui, M., Robles, B., Leondar-Wright, B., Brewer, R., & Adamson, R. (2006). *The color of wealth: The story behind the U.S. racial wealth divide.* New York, NY: The New Press.

Magnuson, K., & Duncan, G. (2016). Can early childhood interventions decrease inequality of economic opportunity? *Russell Sage Foundation Journal of the Social Sciences, 2*(2), 123–141. https://muse.jhu.edu/article/616923/pdf

Marr, C., Hung, C.-C., Murray, C., & Sherman, A. (2016). *Strengthening the EITC for childless workers would reward work and reduce poverty.* Washington, DC: Center on Budget and Policy Priorities. Retrieved from https://www.cbpp.org/research/federal-tax/strengthening-the-eitc-for-childless-workers-would-promote-work-and-reduce

McKee-Ryan, F. M., & Harvey, J. (2011). "I have a job, but . . .": A review of underemployment. *Journal of Management, 37*(4), 962–996.

McKernan, S.-M., Ratcliffe, C., Steuerle, E., & Zhang, S. (2013). *Less than equal: Racial Disparities in wealth accumulation.* Washington, DC: Urban Institute.

Milligan, K., & Stabile, M. (2011). Do child tax benefits affect the well-being of children? Evidence from Canadian child benefit expansions. *American Economic Journal: Economic Policy, 3*(3), 175–205.

Moffitt, R. A. (2015). The deserving poor, the family, and the U.S. welfare system. *Demography, 52,* 729–749.

Nadeau, C. (2015). *New data: Calculating the living wage for US states, counties and metro areas: MIT living wage calculator.* Retrieved from http://livingwage.mit.edu

Nam, Y., Huang, J., & Sherraden, M. (2008). Asset definitions. In S.-M. McKernan & M. Sherraden (Eds.), *Asset building and low-income families* (pp. 1–31). Washington, DC: Urban Institute.

National Center for Children in Poverty. (2015). *Child poverty.* Retrieved from http://www.nccp.org/topics/childpoverty.html

National Conference of State Legislatures. (2017). *State minimum wages: 2017 wages by state.* Retrieved from http://www.ncsl.org/research/labor-and-employment/state-minimum-wage-chart.aspx

National Employment Law Project. (2015, December 21). *14 cities & states approved $15 minimum wage in 2015* [News release]. Retrieved from http://www.nelp.org/content/uploads/PR-Minimum-Wage-Year-End-15.pdf

National Low Income Housing Coalition. (2016). *Out of reach 2016.* Retrieved from http://nlihc.org/oor

Organization for Economic Co-operation and Development. (2014). *OECD employment outlook 2014.* http://www.oecd-ilibrary.org/employment/oecd-employment-outlook-2014/summary/english_45c7c585-en?isSummaryOf=/content/book/empl_outlook-2014-en

Organization for Economic Co-operation and Development. (2016). *Family database.* Retrieved from http://www.oecd.org/els/CO_2_2_Child_Poverty.pdf

Presser, H. B. (2003). *Working in a 24/7 economy: Challenges for American families.* New York, NY: Russell Sage Foundation.

Presser, H. B., & Cox, A. G. (1997, April). The work schedules of low-educated American women and welfare reform. *Monthly Labor Review,* 25–34.

Reich, R. B. (2013). *Income inequality in the United States: Testimony to the United States Congress.* Retrieved from https://www.jec.senate.gov/public/_cache/files/3455c373-7557-4581-8cd8-34b43b759f53/reich-testimony.pdf

Rhee, N., & Boivie, I. (2015). *The continuing retirement savings crisis.* Washington, DC: National Institute on Retirement Security.

Sandstrom, H., & Chaudry, A. (2012). You have to choose your childcare to fit your work: Childcare decision-making among low-income working families. *Journal of Children and Poverty, 18,* 89–119.

Shanks, T. (2011). *Diverging pathways: How wealth shapes opportunity for children.* Oakland, CA: INSIGHT Center for Community Involvement. Retrieved from http://ww1.insightcced.org/uploads/CRWG/DivergingPathways.pdf

Shapiro, T. (2004). *The hidden cost of being African American: How wealth perpetuates inequality.* New York, NY: Oxford University Press.

Shapiro, T., Oliver, M. L., & Meschede, T. (2009). *The asset security and opportunity index.* Waltham, MA: Institute on Assets and Social Policy.

Sherraden, M. (1979). *The civilian conservation corps: Effectiveness of the camps.* PhD dissertation, University of Michigan, Ann Arbor, MI.

Sherraden, M. (1991). *Assets and the poor: A new American welfare policy.* Armonk, NY: Sharpe.

Sherraden, M. (2014). Asset building research and policy: Pathways, progress, and potential of a social innovation. In R. Cramer & T. R. Williams Shanks (Eds.), *The assets perspective: The rise of asset building and its impact on social policy* (pp. 263–284). London, UK: Palgrave Macmillan.

Sherraden, M., Clancy, M., Nam, Y., Huang, J., Kim, Y., Beverly, S. G., . . . Purnell, J. Q. (2015). Testing universal accounts at birth: Early results from the SEED for Oklahoma Kids experiment. *Journal of the Society for Social Work and Research, 6*(4), 541–564. doi:10.1086/684139

Sherraden, M., & Eberly, D. J. (Eds.). (1982). *National service: Social, economic, and military impacts.* New York, NY: Pergamon.

Smeeding, T. M. (2005). Public policy, economic inequality, and poverty: The United States in comparative perspective. *Social Science Quarterly, 86*(1), 955–983.

Statista. (2017). *US underemployment rate from January 2016 to January 2017.* Retrieved from https://www.statista.com/statistics/205240/us-underemployment-rate

Strully, K. W., Rehkopf, D. H., & Xuan, Z. (2010). Effects of prenatal poverty on infant health. *American Sociological Review, 75*(4), 534–562.

Sullivan, M., Dietrich, S., Traub, A., & Ruetschlin, C. (2015). *The racial wealth gap: Why policy matters.* Washington, DC: Demos. Retrieved from http://www.demos.org/publication/racial-wealth-gap-why-policy-matters

Swenson, K. (2014). *Child care subsidy duration and caseload dynamics.* Washington, DC: US Department of Health and Human Services. Retrieved from https://aspe.hhs.gov/report/child-care-subsidy-duration-and-caseload-dynamics-multi-state-examination

The PEW Chairitable Trusts. (2015). *The role of emergency savings in family financial security: What resources do families have for financial emergencies.* Retrieved from http://www.pewtrusts.org/~/media/assets/2015/11/emergencysavingsreport-nov2015.pdf

US Bureau of Labor Statistics. (2016). *Employee benefits survey.* Retrieved from https://www.bls.gov/ncs/ebs/retirement_data.htm

US Bureau of Labor Statistics. (2017a). *Economic news release: Employment statistics of the civilian population by age, race and sex*. Retrieved from https://www.bls.gov/news.release/empsit.t02.htm

US Bureau of Labor Statistics. (2017b). *Household data annual average: Employment status of the civilian noninstitutional population by age, sex and race*. Retrieved from https://www.bls.gov/cps/cpsaat03.pdf

US Bureau of Labor Statistics. (2017c, January 13). Unemployment rate and employment-population ratio vary by race and ethnicity. *The Economics Daily*. Retrieved from https://www.bls.gov/opub/ted/2017/unemployment-rate-and-employment-population-ratio-vary-by-race-and-ethnicity.htm

US Census Bureau. (2016). *Housing vacancies and homeownership (CPS/HVS): Historical Table 16*. Retrieved April 2017 from https://www.census.gov/housing/hvs/data/histtabs.html.

US Census Bureau. (2017, April). *Quarterly residential vacancies and homeownership, fourth quarter 2016*. Retrieved from https://www.census.gov/housing/hvs/files/currenthvspress.pdf

Williams Shanks, T. R., & Leigh, W. A. (2015). Assets and older African Americans. In N. Morrow-Howell & M. S. Sherraden (Eds.), *Financial capability and asset holding in later life: A life course perspective* (pp. 49–68). New York, NY: Oxford University Press.

Wolff, E. N. (2014). *Household wealth trends in the United States, 1962–2013: What happened over the Great Recession?* (NBER Working Paper No. 20733). Retrieved from http://www.nber.org/papers/w20733

Ybarra, M. A. (2013). Implications of paid family leave for welfare participants. *Social Work Research, 37*(4), 375–387.

Yoshikawa, H., Weisner, T. S., & Lowe, E. D. (Eds.). (2006). *Making it work: Low-wage employment, family life, and child development*. New York, NY: Russell Sage Foundation.

investments, retirement savings, college savings, health savings, and medical savings (Levin, Greer, & Rademacher, 2014). Low-income and marginalized populations receive almost none of these benefits. In 2013, only 41% of Black families and 26% of Latino families owned retirement savings accounts—percentages substantively lower than that of White families (61%). Moreover, the mean assets in retirement savings accounts for Whites ($73,000) were approximately 330% greater than those for African Americans and Latinos ($22,000) (Morrissey, 2016).

Recent Developments to Improve FCAB in LMI and Marginalized Populations

To improve financial capability in LMI and marginalized populations, the FCAB framework suggests two strategies: (1) expanding financial inclusion and (2) improving individual financial knowledge and skills. This section summarizes recent developments that apply these strategies in practice.

Expanding Financial Inclusion

Low-income families and marginalized populations face access barriers to financial products and services, such as not having enough money, distrust or dislike of financial institutions, high and unpredictable fees, and privacy concerns (FDIC, 2016a). Some demographic groups, such as immigrants, report language barriers, unreceptive financial institutions, and lack of familiarity with the US financial system (Osili & Paulson, 2005). Expanding financial inclusion includes both removing barriers to banking services, affordable credit, and asset building and expanding access to financial protection and regulation. Doing so requires several approaches. The following approaches can be used separately or in combination:

- Lowering service fees: Banking services that offer low minimum account opening deposits, low monthly maintenance fees, no overdraft or nonsufficient funds fees, and free and linked savings accounts can successfully reach financially vulnerable households (Cities for Financial Empowerment Fund, n.d.; FDIC, 2012).
- Using new financial technology: New financial technology, such as mobile banking, offers ways to reach the unbanked and underbanked with accessible products at low costs (The Pew Charitable Trusts, 2016b).
- Motivating desirable financial behaviors: Small-dollar loans and credit-builder loans that are not based on credit scores but, rather, on borrowers' ability to make installment payments help LMI families overcome credit

constraints. This may motivate desirable financial behavior (National Federation of Community Development Credit and Filene, 2015).

- Facilitating program participation: A number of state-sponsored college savings plans have developed automatic and incentivized savings programs to encourage low-income families to participate in asset accumulation plans for children (Clancy, Sherraden, & Beverly, 2015).
- Integrating financial and social services: The Refund-to-Savings initiative integrates an asset-building opportunity for low-income families in tax services by creating a default allocation of tax refund to savings in free online tax filing services (Grinstein-Weiss et al., 2015).
- Creating new policies and institutions: myRAs were created by the US Department of Treasury in 2015 as a flexible retirement savings program for workers without access to employer-sponsored retirement plans (Commito, 2015). The creation of the CFPB, under the Dodd–Frank Wall Street Reform and Consumer Protection Act of 2010, was a landmark development to eliminate "unfair, deceptive, or abusive acts or practices" in the financial services industry (CFPB, n.d.).

Improving Financial Knowledge and Skills

Financial education has widespread support, even from former Federal Reserve Chairman Ben Bernanke, who in 2006 proclaimed that it "leads to better outcomes for individual consumers and for our economy generally." Since then, federal efforts to improve financial knowledge and skills have intensified. The US Financial Literacy and Education Commission (2011) created a national strategy for financial education to promote financial success, and it developed a national website (http://www.MyMoney.gov) to disseminate financial knowledge and skills. The FDIC's Money Smart program uses a game format to teach key FCAB concepts to individuals at various stages of the life cycle, and it offers specialized curricula for young people and small business owners (FDIC, 2016b).

Several organizations provide financial education resources for social service providers. For example, the CFPB (2015) created a toolkit called Your Money, Your Goals. Other public, private, and nongovernmental providers— such as the Federal Reserve, financial institutions, nonprofit organizations, municipalities, the armed forces, colleges and universities, and employers— also offer financial education in seminars, workshops, online, and in person. Specialized financial education also is available for groups such as college students (National Financial Educators Council, 2013a), immigrants (Lutheran Immigration and Refugee Service, 2012), low-income consumers (Collins, 2010), adults planning retirement (US Department of Veterans Affairs, 2016), prospective homeowners (NeighborWorks America, 2017), and service members and their families (National Financial Educators Council, 2013b).

Although these efforts provide important resources to improve FCAB, many of the existing initiatives do not systematically reach LMI and marginalized families with progressive and universal measures.

RECOMMENDATIONS FOR FINANCIAL CAPABILITY AND ASSET BUILDING FOR ALL

Social work's grand challenge is to build financial capability and assets in ways that include everyone and provide additional supports and resources for marginalized populations. We propose four initiatives that promote financial inclusion and knowledge and skills, especially in marginalized populations. Because both social and economic justice are central tenets of social work, each of these initiatives is also progressive; that is, they aim to reduce inequality and promote upward mobility of people on the bottom rungs of the economic ladder. Some of these recommendations are based on a strong scientific foundation, including large-scale experiments. Others are less well-developed but warrant implementation and evaluation.

Promote Lifelong Asset Building with Universal and Progressive Child Development Accounts

Child Development Accounts (CDAs) are lifelong savings or investment accounts. They encourage asset accumulation for long-term developmental purposes, such as post-secondary education, homeownership, business investment, and retirement. We recommend that every child receive a CDA at birth. Universal and progressive CDAs can achieve the goal of full inclusion, reduce asset inequality early in life, and improve children's early development (Huang, Sherraden, Kim, & Clancy, 2014; Huang, Sherraden, & Purnell, 2014; Kim, Sherraden, Huang, & Clancy, 2015; Nam, Kim, Clancy, Zager, & Sherraden, 2013).

Automatic enrollment, automatic initial deposit, target investment options with growth potential, low administrative costs, and progressive incentives are key features to ensure that CDAs are inclusive, effective, and sustainable (Clancy & Beverly, 2017). They would also be progressive if children from LMI families would receive financial subsidies (Beverly, Clancy, & Sherraden, 2016; M. Sherraden, 1991).

Efforts are underway in some states to provide a CDA for each child (Clancy & Sherraden, 2014). CDAs have received attention in the US Senate (ASPIRE Act, 2010) and the US Congress (USAccounts: Investing in America's Future Act, 2015). The next step is to integrate CDAs into a nationwide policy platform to maximize the policy's effects and efficiency. We recommend creating universal and progressive CDAs that are based on existing nationwide asset-building policy platforms (e.g., 529 college savings plans and the proposed Dependent Care Savings Accounts), that automatically enroll all newborns, and that provide financial incentives to LMI families and marginalized groups (Huang, Sherraden, Clancy, Sherraden, & Shanks, 2017).

Eliminate Asset Limits for Public Assistance Programs

Eliminating asset limits would permit beneficiaries of public assistance to build assets. Means-tested public assistance programs such as the Supplemental Nutrition Assistance Program (SNAP) and Temporary Assistance for Needy Families (TANF) typically place limits on the maximum allowable assets for eligibility. Such asset limits constrain program participants' opportunities to build assets and may result in families spending down their assets to qualify for public assistance programs. There is no evidence of an association between higher asset limits and welfare uptake (Hamilton, Alexander-Eitzman, & Royal, 2015; Rice & Bansak, 2014; The Pew Charitable Trusts, 2016c). Therefore, we recommend eliminating asset limits from all public assistance programs.

Moreover, there are cost savings to eliminating asset limits because workers are not required to investigate the assets of applicants (Corporation for Enterprise Development [CFED], 2011; The Pew Charitable Trusts, 2016c). Relaxed asset limits in SNAP also reduce the likelihood that recipients will cycle on and off the program (Ratcliffe, McKernan, Wheaton, & Kalish, 2016).

Asset limit reforms have been made at the federal, state, and administrative levels. For example, Medicaid asset limits were eliminated by the Patient Protection and Affordable Care Act of 2010. Thirty-four states have eliminated SNAP limits largely via an administrative fix known as categorical eligibility, and 8 states have eliminated the asset test for TANF (Hamilton et al., 2015) through legislative and administrative actions. One state, Louisiana, lifted its TANF asset limit legislatively in 2008 after an administrative study determined that the asset limit was impeding the state's efforts to encourage low-income families' participation in Individual Development Accounts, or matched savings accounts for homeownership, small businesses, and postsecondary education (CFED, 2011). A complete elimination of asset limits from public assistance programs will expand asset-building opportunities for low-income and marginalized families and save public sector funds.

Create FCAB Opportunities in Public Services

We recommend promoting FCAB in marginalized populations through integrating financial opportunities into public services. Increasingly, financial services are being integrated into social, health, mental health, housing, and community development services. For example, at the federal level, Social Security and Supplemental Security Income benefits are delivered electronically through direct deposit (US Social Security Administration, n.d.). Free tax preparation assistance, such as the Internal Revenue Service's Volunteer Income Tax Assistance, is offered by community organizations to encourage LMI families to receive tax benefits and save money (Administration for Children and Families, Office of Community Services, 2015). At the municipal level, the Cities for Financial Empowerment Fund promotes integration of financial counseling into basic city services, such as housing and homeless prevention and workforce development (Cities for Financial Empowerment, n.d.; Mintz, 2014). Youth in employment programs open bank accounts, save, and gain financial knowledge and skills through programs such as MyPath (Loke, Choi, & Libby, 2015), Fun Money (Loke, 2016), and America Saves for Young Workers (America Saves, n.d.).

In addition to integrating FCAB into social policies and programs, we also recommend creating a web-based Financial Capability Gateway (Sherraden et al., 2015). As a public platform, the Gateway would reach everyone as a comprehensive and universal infrastructure for expanded integration of public services and financial services. The Gateway would synthesize all individuals' financial records from their financial service providers in one place, allowing individuals to organize, track, understand, and manage their financial transactions; streamline access to public and financial services through automatic enrollment and other strategies; improve financial knowledge and skills by providing customized, client-oriented financial education; and facilitate the interactive effects of financial education and financial inclusion.

Enhance FCAB Education for Social Work Professionals

Social workers work directly and indirectly with millions of LMI and financially marginalized populations. Future social workers must be equipped with the ability to help clients understand, explore, and access financial services and asset-building opportunities (Loke, Birkenmaier, & Hageman, 2016; Sherraden, Laux, & Kaufman, 2007). They also must be prepared to develop programs and policies that expand financial inclusion, education, and guidance to LMI and marginalized populations. Therefore, we recommend preparing all social workers for FCAB practice through strong curricular offerings in social work education.

Social work education in FCAB has made progress since the 2000s (Birkenmaier, Kennedy, Kunz, Sander, & Horwitz, 2013; Sherraden, Birkenmaier, McClendon, et al., 2017). University-based social work curricula have been developed by the Center for Social Development, the University of Maryland School of Social Work, and a collaboration of social work programs in New York City (Frey, Sherraden, Birkenmaier, & Callahan, 2017; Horwitz & Briar-Lawson, 2017; Sherraden, Birkenmaier, McClendon, et al., 2017). A textbook on FCAB is in press (Sherraden, Birkenmaier, & Collins, 2017), and the Council on Social Work Education, in collaboration with the Center for Social Development, has created the *Economic Well-Being Curricular Guide* and a website that offers teaching resources and guidance for linking social work education competencies and behaviors with FCAB practice.

Educators are expanding FCAB content in social work education by introducing it within existing courses (Doran & Bagdasaryan, in press), as separate courses, and through extracurricular and continuing education (Birkenmaier et al., 2013; Frey, Sherraden, et al., 2017). Teaching resources for faculty include financial educators in university-based services and staff of community-based financial institutions. Field practicums provide valuable learning opportunities for students to apply classroom learning about FCAB with vulnerable clients and communities (Doran & Avery, 2016).

MEASURING AND EVALUATING FCAB PROGRESS IN SCIENTIFIC RESEARCH

Although there is not yet consensus among researchers on metrics, evaluating the progress of the FCAB grand challenge is important. In accordance with the FCAB framework, we propose measuring progress by outputs and outcomes on and impacts of financial inclusion, knowledge, and skills. These three aspects of metrics are defined in Box 12.1.

Although we currently lack consensus on specific FCAB metrics, the authors agree that scientific research must play a central role in measuring progress and advancing FCAB for All. Currently, two critical questions concern what scientific metrics to use and how to evaluate the baseline status of these metrics. To answer these questions, the design and development of FCAB research and measurement should carefully consider three principles (Box 12.2): (1) Engage people served by FCAB efforts in research, (2) frame the context clearly, and (3) implement comprehensive methods to test the research questions.

ORGANIZATION OF THE FCAB GRAND CHALLENGE

To advance the grand challenge of FCAB for All, educators, scholars, and practitioners have organized themselves into four workgroups: research, education, policy, and practice. The members set each group's goals and strategies.

Box 12.1: MEASUREMENT METRICS: OUTPUTS, OUTCOMES, AND IMPACTS

Outputs refer to FCAB activities and services provided by the social work profession and other sectors. They may include, but are not limited to, financial education, financial coaching, financial and credit counseling, credit building, tax preparation, and asset-building programs. Output efforts could be indicated by the number of FCAB programs, the total number of professionals in these programs, the total program expenditures, and the population receiving these services.

Outcomes are improved access to financial products and services and increased financial knowledge and skills at the individual level. Ideally, financial inclusion should include access to basic banking services, asset-building programs, credit, insurance, public assistance programs, financial education, and counseling. One goal of the grand challenge is for all individuals, by 2030, to achieve full access to bank accounts, asset-building accounts, and financial education and to reach a financial literacy rate of 60% in the US adult population.

Impacts are the combined effects of financial inclusion, knowledge, and skills on desirable financial management and well-being. Impact measures could be categorized into main elements of FCAB on income generation, consumption and credit management, insurance and protection, and asset building. For example, the amount of emergency savings or assets accumulated for retirement are two indicators of asset building.

The FCAB Research Workgroup

The research workgroup's goals are to generate scientific FCAB knowledge to support and inspire the agenda of the other three workgroups. The primary research questions include conceptual development and advancement of FCAB as an area of inquiry, including FCAB curricula and education in social work; FCAB in social work practice; and FCAB policies. In addition, the group will focus on developing and evaluating FCAB metrics. It will also identify current and future FCAB scholars and assist them in developing their research agendas.

The FCAB Education Workgroup

The education workgroup's goals are to identify best practices in teaching FCAB content, increase curricular offerings in social work education, and conduct research on educational outcomes. It aims to create and promote

Box 12.2: THREE PRINCIPLES OF FCAB RESEARCH AND MEASUREMENT

Engage people served by FCAB efforts. Racial and social identities matter in the assessment of financial outcomes. Therefore, the grand challenge of FCAB for All must ensure that people served by the efforts—including those with different socioeconomic, racial, and cultural backgrounds—be engaged in the research process. In addition to using a community-based participatory research approach, FCAB research should include input from community members, stakeholders, and marginalized groups.

Frame the context clearly. The context for FCAB research questions and metrics should be clearly framed. Researchers should take care in how questions are asked and the political contexts in which the questions are framed. The framing of questions and measurement should reflect a clear specification of contexts and conditions and not be limited to dichotomized terms (Small & Feldman, 2012).

Implement comprehensive methods to test the research questions. By leveraging a variety of methodological techniques, researchers can evaluate FCAB progress comprehensively and with different points of view. For example, CDA research uses qualitative interviews, administrative data, longitudinal and secondary survey findings, and randomized experiments to understand the various effects and impacts of CDAs on social-emotional and cognitive development, educational expectations and outcomes, and asset accumulation (Beverly, Clancy, & Sherraden, 2016). As another example, the Mapping Financial Opportunity project triangulates data from several sources—geographic information systems data, linked administrative, community, and household data, and original data collection—to examine the relationships between availability of financial services by LMI households and their financial well-being, such as paying bills and saving for emergencies (Friedline & Despard, 2017a, 2017b).

teaching models and best practices that are effective in different degree programs and in different educational contexts. Currently, nearly 20 social work programs either integrate FCAB content into existing courses or offer stand-alone courses. The goal is to reach 50 programs implementing some form of FCAB content in their curriculum by 2022.

The FCAB Policy Workgroup

The policy workgroup's goals include universal access to safe and affordable financial products and progressive lifelong asset accumulation opportunities, as well as expanded FCAB programs in public services. Background papers, policy briefs, policy action statements, and dissemination plans are underway for the policy recommendations discussed previously. The group recognizes the value of partnership and strength in numbers and, when appropriate, seeks to align its policy priorities with the policy agendas of organizations such as the FDIC, CFPB, New America, the Annie E. Casey Foundation, CFED, and the Consumer Federation of America.

The FCAB Practice Workgroup

The practice workgroup's goals are to ensure competent, high-quality, and ethical FCAB practice. It aims to connect FCAB practitioners in social work nationwide to build awareness of the importance of FCAB for All in social work practice. The group is identifying and advancing evidence-based FCAB interventions, such as online tools that provide assistance and encouragement to people with their financial goals. The group is also exploring avenues for collaborating with other disciplines engaged in FCAB practice with vulnerable groups. Finally, the workgroup is examining the potential for an FCAB practice certification.

COLLABORATION AND CROSS-SECTOR INVOLVEMENT FOR FCAB

It is important to note that FCAB is connected with the goals of other social work grand challenges, creating opportunities for collaboration. For example, the Reduce Extreme Economic Inequality grand challenge proposes lifelong asset building as a policy recommendation for narrowing economic inequality. Together, the two grand challenge groups developed a joint policy action statement for universal and progressive CDAs (Huang et al., 2017). Multiple FCAB programs aim to improve financial well-being for children and youth, including CDAs (Beverly et al., 2016), financial education and asset building for youth in the foster care system and those in youth employment programs (Loke et al., 2013; Peters, Sherraden, & Kuchinski, 2016; Shanks & McGee, 2010), and many others. Research (Huang et al., 2014) shows that such programs have impacts on nonfinancial outcomes, such as children's attitudes and behaviors, and can be considered an important prevention strategy for the social work grand challenge Ensure Healthy Development for All Youth. In addition, new financial technology has become a powerful tool to promote FCAB. The creation of a Financial Capability Gateway built on Internet and computer technology is a specific example that intersects with the grand challenge of Harness Technology for Social Good.

To achieve FCAB for All, strategic partnerships with people and organizations across sectors are essential. Through such partnerships, the FCAB group amplifies its impact by drawing on the expertise, skills, and networks of other disciplines and organizations. Potential collaborators include scholars, practitioners, and policy leaders from a number of disciplines (e.g., family and consumer sciences, economics, psychology, business, finance, law, public policy, and education) who work in a variety of contexts (e.g., community, human service, advocacy, business, financial, and government organizations). Efforts to promote FCAB-related policy for vulnerable families bring social workers together with local, state, and federal policy actors, such as public officials, policy experts, lawyers, activists, and others (Weiss-Gal, 2013).

For example, social workers, financial professionals, public officials, and politicians have worked together to advance progressive and universal CDA policies (Beverly et al., 2016). Together, they use the 529 college savings plan infrastructure to create opportunities for financially vulnerable families to build assets for children. Another example is collaboration between human service organizations and financial institutions that offer traditional social services along with financial counseling and coaching, in addition to financial services such as account opening, depositing, withdrawals, and financial education and advice to agency clients (Administration for Children and Families, Office of Community Services, 2015; Mintz, 2014; Roder, 2016).

CONCLUSION

Since its founding as a profession, social work has played an important and unique role in ensuring that everyone has access to societal benefits and an ability to achieve social and economic well-being. As key elements of well-being, financial capability and assets are among social work's grand challenges. Today, social workers are taking the lead in shaping social institutions to promote FCAB for All. This grand challenge provides a rare opportunity to systematically synthesize and institutionalize FCAB as a core social good.

ACKNOWLEDGMENTS

We are grateful for contributions by other network members of the FCAB for All grand challenge, including Clark Peters, Leah Hamilton, Min Zhan, Gabrielle D'Angelo, Bonita Sharma, Jodi Frey, Margaret Clancy, Vernon Loke, Michael Sherraden, Trina Williams, Youngmi Kim, and Mahasweta Banerjee. We thank the Center for Social Development's Gena McClendon for her support of the FCAB grand challenge network, and we thank John Gabbert for his editorial assistance.

REFERENCES

Administration for Children and Families, Office of Community Services. (2015). *Building financial capability: A planning guide for integrated services*. Retrieved from https://www.acf.hhs.gov/ocs/resource/afi-resource-guide-building-financial-capability

America Saves. (n.d.). *America saves for young workers*. Retrieved from https://americasaves.org/organizations/current-initiatives/first-time-workers

American Psychological Association. (2015). *Stress in America: Paying with our health*. Retrieved from https://www.apa.org/news/press/releases/stress/2014/stress-report.pdf

ASPIRE Act of 2010, S. 3577, 111th Cong. (2010). Retrieved from https://www.congress.gov/bill/111thcongress/senate-bill/3577

Banerjee, M., Friedline, T., & Phipps, B. (2017). *My children are actually a barrier: Financial capability of parents of kindergarteners*. Manuscript submitted for publication.

Baradaran, M. (2015). *How the other half banks: Exclusion, exploitation, and the threat to democracy*. Cambridge, MA: Harvard University Press.

Bernanke, B. (2006, May 23). *Financial literacy. Testimony before the Committee on Banking, Housing, and Urban Affairs of the United States Senate*. Retrieved from https://www.federalreserve.gov/newsevents/testimony/Bernanke20060523a.htm

Beverly, S. G., Clancy, M. M., & Sherraden, M. (2016). *Universal accounts at birth: Results from SEED for Oklahoma Kids*. St. Louis, MO: Washington University, Center for Social Development. Retrieved from http://csd.wustl.edu/Publications/Documents/RS16-07.pdf

Birkenmaier, J. M., Kennedy, T., Kunz, J., Sander, R., & Horwitz, S. (2013). The role of social work in financial capability: Shaping curricular approaches. In J. M. Birkenmaier, M. S. Sherraden, & J. Curley (Eds.), *Financial capability and asset development: Research, education, policy, and practice* (pp. 278–301). New York, NY: Oxford University Press.

Birkenmaier, J. M., Sherraden, M. S., & Curley, J. (2013). *Financial capability and asset development: Research, education, policy, and practice*. New York, NY: Oxford University Press.

Brown, A. (2012, October 30). With poverty comes depression, more than other illnesses. *Gallup*. Retrieved from http://www.gallup.com/poll/158417/poverty-comesdepression-illness.aspx?utm_source=alert&utm_medium=email&utm_campaign=syndication&utm_content=morelink&utm_term=All%20Gallup%20Headlines

Cities for Financial Empowerment Fund. (n.d.). *Bank On national account standards (2017–2018)*. Retrieved from http://joinbankon.org/wp-content/uploads/2017/05/Bank-On-National-Account-Standards-2017-2018-final.pdf

Clancy, M. M., & Beverly, S. G. (2017). *Statewide Child Development Account programs: Key design features* (Unpublished manuscript). St. Louis, MO: Washington University, Center for Social Development.

Clancy, M. M., & Sherraden, M. (2014). *Automatic deposits for all at birth: Maine's Harold Alfond College Challenge*. St. Louis, MO: Washington University, Center for Social Development. Retrieved from http://csd.wustl.edu/Publications/Documents/PR14-05.pdf

Clancy, M. M., Sherraden, M., & Beverly, S. G. (2015). *College savings plans: A platform for inclusive and progressive Child Development Accounts* (CSD Policy Brief No.

15-07). St. Louis, MO: Washington University, Center for Social Development. Retrieved from https://csd.wustl.edu/Publications/Documents/PB15-07.pdf

Collins, M. (2010). Effects of mandatory financial education on low-income clients. *Focus, 27*(1), 13–18.

Commito, T. F. (2015). Department of Treasury releases information on and implements myRAs. *Journal of Financial Service Professionals, 69*(4), 11–13.

Consumer Financial Protection Bureau. (2015, April). *Your money, your goals: A financial empowerment toolkit for social services programs.* Retrieved from http://files.consumerfinance.gov/f/201407_cfpb_your-money-your-goals_toolkit_english.pdf

Consumer Finance Protection Bureau. (2016). *Who are the credit invisibles? How to help people with limited credit histories.* Retrieved from http://files.consumerfinance.gov/f/documents/201612_cfpb_credit_invisible_policy_report.pdf

Consumer Finance Protection Bureau. (n.d.). *The Bureau.* Retrieved from https://www.consumerfinance.gov/about-us/the-bureau

Corporation for Enterprise Development. (2011). *Resource guide: Lifting asset limits in public benefit programs.* Retrieved from https://cfed.org/assets/scorecard/2011_2012/rg_AssetLimits.pdf

Cruce, A. (2002). *School-based savings programs, 1930–2002.* St. Louis, MO: Washington University, Center for Social Development. Retrieved from https://csd.wustl.edu/Publications/Documents/wp02-7.pdf

Cynamon, B. Z., & Fazzari, S. M. (2015). Household income, demand, and saving: Deriving macro data with micro data concepts. *Review of Income and Wealth, 63*(1), 53–69.

De Marco, A., De Marco, H., Biggers, A., West, M., Young, J., & Levy, R. (2015). Can people experiencing homelessness acquire financial assets? *Journal of Sociology and Social Welfare, 42*(4), 55–78.

Deaton, A. S. (2011). *The financial crisis and the well-being of Americans.* Cambridge, MA: National Bureau of Economic Research. Retrieved from http://www.nber.org/papers/w17128

Doran, J. K., & Avery, P. (2016, October 14). *Financial empowerment through social work.* Paper presented at the National Association of Social Workers conference, Burbank, CA.

Doran, J. K., & Bagdasaryan, G. (In press). Testing infusion of financial capability and asset building content in social work courses. *Journal of Social Work Education.*

Edin, K. J., & Shaefer, H. L. (2015). *$2.00 a day: Living on almost nothing in America.* New York, NY: Houghton Mifflin.

Federal Deposit Insurance Corporation. (2012). *FDIC Model Safe Accounts Pilot: Final report.* Retrieved from https://www.fdic.gov/consumers/template/SafeAccountsFinalReport.pdf

Federal Deposit Insurance Corporation, (2016a). *2015 FDIC national survey of unbanked and underbanked households.* Retrieved from https://www.fdic.gov/householdsurvey

Federal Deposit Insurance Corporation. (2016b). *Money Smart—A financial education program.* Retrieved from https://www.fdic.gov/consumers/consumer/moneysmart

Financial Industry Regulation Authority Investor Education Foundation. (2016, July). *Financial capability in the United States.* Retrieved from http://www.usfinancial-capability.org/downloads/NFCS_2015_Report_Natl_Findings.pdf

Frey, J. J., Hopkins, K., Osteen, P., Callahan, C., Hageman, S., & Ko, J. (2017). Training social workers and human service professionals to address the complex financial needs of clients. *Journal of Social Work Education*, 53(1), 118–131.

Frey, J. J., Sherraden, M. S., Birkenmaier, J., & Callahan, C. (2017). Financial capability and asset building in social work education. *Journal of Social Work Education*, 53(1), 79–83.

Friedline, T., & Despard, M. (2017a). *How do the features of banks' entry-level checking accounts compare to Bank On national account standards?* Lawrence, KS: University of Kansas, Center on Assets, Education, and Inclusion.

Friedline, T., & Despard, M. (2017b). *Mapping financial opportunity*. Washington, DC: New America. Retrieved from https://www.newamerica.org/in-depth/mapping-financial-opportunity

Grinstein-Weiss, M., Perantie, D. C., Russell, B. D., Comer, K., Taylor, S. H., Luo, L., . . . Ariely, D. (2015). *Refund to Savings 2013: Comprehensive report on a large-scale tax-time saving program*. St. Louis, MO: Center for Social Development, Washington University in St. Louis.

Hamilton, L., Alexander-Eitzman, B., & Royal, W. (2015). Shelter from the storm: TANF, assets and the Great Recession. *SAGE Open*, 5(1), 1–6.

Horwitz, S., & Briar-Lawson, K. (2017). A multi-university economic capability-building collaboration. *Journal of Social Work Education*, 53(1), 149–158.

Huang, J., Sherraden, M., Clancy, M. M., Sherraden, M., & Shanks, T. R. (2017, March). *Start lifelong asset building with universal and progressive Child Development Accounts* (Grand Challenges for Social Work Initiative Policy Action No. 11.1). Cleveland, OH: American Academy of Social Work & Social Welfare.

Huang, J., Sherraden, M., Kim, Y., & Clancy, M. (2014). An experimental test of Child Development Accounts on early social–emotional development. *JAMA Pediatrics*, 168(3), 265–271.

Huang, J., Sherraden, M., & Purnell, J. (2014). Impacts of Child Development Accounts on maternal depression: Evidence from a randomized statewide policy experiment. *Social Science & Medicine*, 112, 30–38.

Hudner, D., & Kurtz, J. (2015). *Do financial services build disaster resilience? Examining the determinants of recovery from Typhoon Yolanda in the Philippines*. Retrieved from https://www.mercycorps.org/sites/default/files/Philippines%20Resilience%20ToC%20Testing%20Report_Final_03.06.15.cm_.pdf

Kahn, J. R., & Pearlin, L. I. (2006). Financial strain over the life course and health among older adults. *Journal of Health and Social Behavior*, 47(1), 17–31.

Killewald, A., Pfeffer, F. T., & Schachner, J. N. (2017). Wealth inequality and accumulation. *Annual Review of Sociology*, 43, 379–404.

Kim, Y., Sherraden, M., Huang, J., & Clancy, M. (2015). Impacts of Child Development Accounts on change in parental educational expectations: Evidence from a statewide social experiment. *Social Service Review*, 89(1), 99–137.

Kochhar, R., & Fry, R. (2014). *Wealth inequality has widened along racial, ethnic lines since end of Great Recession*. Washington, DC: Pew Research Center. Retrieved from http://www.pewresearch.org/fact-tank/2014/12/12/racial-wealth-gaps-great-recession

Lassar, T., Clancy, M., & McClure, S. (2011). *College savings match programs: Design and policy* (CSD Working Paper No. 11-28). St. Louis, MO: Washington University, Center for Social Development. Retrieved from https://csd.wustl.edu/Publications/Documents/RP11-28.pdf

Levin, E., Greer, J., & Rademacher, I. (2014). *From upside down to right-side up: Redeploying $540 billion in federal spending to help all families save, invest, and build wealth.* Washington, DC: CFED.

Loke, V. (2016). *Evaluation of Fun Money, Inc.: Final report.* Spokane, WA: Spokane County United Way.

Loke, V., Birkenmaier, J., & Hageman, S. A. (2016). Financial capability and asset building in the curricula: Student perceptions. *Journal of Social Work Education, 53*(1), 84–98.

Loke, V., Choi, L., & Libby, M. (2015). Increasing youth financial capability: An evaluation of the MyPath Savings Initiative. *Journal of Consumer Affairs, 49*(1), 97–126.

Loke, V., Libby, M., & Choi, L. (2013). *Increasing financial capability among economically vulnerable youth: MY Path.* San Francisco, CA: Federal Reserve Bank of San Francisco, Community Development Investment Center. Retrieved from http:// www.frbsf.org/community-development/publications/working-papers/2013/ march/financial-capability-economically-vulnerable-youth-my-path

Lusardi, A. (2011). *Americans' financial capability.* Cambridge, MA: National Bureau of Economic Research.

Lutheran Immigration and Refugee Service. (2012). *Financial literacy for newcomers: Weaving immigrant needs into financial education.* Retrieved from http://www. higheradvantage.org/wp-content/uploads/2012/05/rw_financial_literacy.pdf

McCallion, P., Ferretti, L. A., & Park, I. (2013). Financial issues and an aging population: Responding to an increased potential for financial abuse and exploitation. In J. Birkenmaier, M. S. Sherraden, & J. Curley (Eds.), *Financial education and capability: Research, education, policy, and practice* (pp. 129–155). New York, NY: Oxford University Press.

Mintz, J. (2014). Local government solutions to household financial instability: The supervitamin effect. *Federal Reserve Bank of San Francisco Community Investment, 26*(6), 16–19, 40–41.

Mishel, L., Gould, E., & Rivens, J. (2015, January 6). *Wage stagnation in nine charts.* Washington, DC: Economic Policy Institute. Retrieved from http://www.epi. org/publication/charting-wage-stagnation

Morris, M., & Goodman, N. (2015, July). *Integrating financial capability and asset building strategies into the Public Workforce Development System.* Washington, DC: National Center on Leadership for the Employment and Economic Advancement of People with Disabilities. Retrieved from http://www.leadcenter.org/system/files/resource/downloadable_version/integrating_fin_cap_asset_dev.pdf

Morrissey, M. (2016). *Retirement inequality chartbook: The state of American retirement— How 401(k)s have failed most American workers.* Washington, DC: Economic Policy Institute. Retrieved from http://www.epi.org/files/2016/state-of-american-retirement-final.pdf

Morrow-Howell, N., & Sherraden, M. S. (2015). *Financial capability and asset holding in later life: A life course perspective.* New York, NY: Oxford University Press.

Nam, Y., Kim, Y., Clancy, M., Zager, R., & Sherraden, M. (2013). Do Child Development Accounts promote account holding, saving, and asset accumulation for children's future? Evidence from a statewide randomized experiment. *Journal of Policy Analysis and Management, 32*(1), 6–33.

National Federation of Community Development Credit Unions and Filene. (2015). *Borrow and Save feasibility study report.* Retrieved from http://www.cdcu.coop/ wp-content/uploads/2016/03/BorrowandSave_FeasibiltyStudy_FINAL.pdf

National Financial Educators Council. (2013a). *College student financial literacy curriculum*. Retrieved from https://www.financialeducatorscouncil.org/college-student-financial-literacy

National Financial Educators Council. (2013b). *The military financial literacy American dream movement campaign*. Retrieved from https://www.financialeducatorscouncil.org/military-financial-literacy

NeighborWorks America. (2017). *National industry standards for homeownership education and counseling.* Retrieved from http://www.neighborworks.org/Training-Services/Resources-for-Counselors-Educators/National-Industry-Standards

Nussbaum, M. C. (2000). *Women and human development: The capabilities approach.* Cambridge, MA: Cambridge University Press.

Osili, U. O., & Paulson, A. (2005). *Individuals and institutions: Evidence from international migrants in the U.S.* Chicago, IL: Federal Reserve Bank of Chicago.

Padua, L. A., & Doran, J. K. (2016). From being unbanked to becoming unbanked or unbankable: Community experts describe financial practices of Latinos in East Los Angeles. *Journal of Community Practice, 24*(4), 428–444.

Peters, C. M., Sherraden, M., & Kuchinski, A. M. (2016). Growing financial assets for foster youths: Expanded child welfare responsibilities, policy conflict, and caseworker role tension. *Social Work, 61*(4), 340–348.

Purnell, J. (2015). Financial health is public health. In Federal Reserve Bank of San Francisco & Corporation for Enterprise Development (Eds.), *What it's worth: Strengthening the financial future of families, communities and the nation* (pp. 163–172). San Francisco, CA: Federal Reserve Bank of San Francisco & Corporation for Enterprise Development.

Ratcliffe, C., McKernan, S.-M., Wheaton, L., & Kalish, E. C. (2016, July 26). *The unintended consequences of SNAP asset limits*. Washington, DC: Urban Institute. Retrieved from http://www.urban.org/research/publication/unintended-consequences-snap-asset-limits

Rice, L., & Bansak, C. (2014). The effect of welfare asset rules on auto ownership, employment, and welfare participation: A longitudinal analysis. *Contemporary Economic Policy, 32*(2), 306–333.

Roder, A. (2016, September). *First steps on the road to financial well-being: Final report from the evaluation of LISC's Financial Opportunity Centers*. New York, NY: Economic Mobility Corporation. Retrieved from http://www.lisc.org/our-resources/resource/liscs-financial-opportunity-centers-surpass-other-programs

Sanders, C. K. (2013). Financial capability among survivors of domestic violence. In J. Birkenmaier, M. S. Sherraden, & J. Curley (Eds.), *Financial capability and asset development: Research, education, policy, and practice* (pp. 85–107). New York, NY: Oxford University Press.

Sen, A. (1985). *Commodities and capabilities*. Oxford, UK: Elsevier.

Sen, A. (1993). Capability and well-being. In M. Nussbaum & A. Sen (Eds.), *The quality of life* (pp. 30–53). New York, NY: Oxford University Press.

Servon, L. J. (2017). *The unbanking of America: How the new middle class survives*. New York, NY: Harcourt Brace.

Shanks, T., & McGee, K. (2010). *Detroit summer youth employment program: Results of employer and youth employee exit surveys*. Ann Arbor, MI: University of Michigan, School of Social Work.

Sherraden, M. (1991). *Assets and the poor: A new American welfare policy*. New York, NY: Sharpe.

Sherraden, M. (2014). Asset building research and policy: Pathways, progress, and potential of a social innovation. In R. Cramer & T. Shanks (Eds.), *The assets perspective: The rise of asset building and its impact of social policy* (pp. 263–284). New York, NY: Palgrave Macmillan.

Sherraden, M. S. (2013). Building blocks of financial capability. In J. Birkenmaier, M. S. Sherraden, & J. Curley (Eds.), *Financial education and capability: Research, education, policy, and practice* (pp. 3–43). New York, NY: Oxford University Press.

Sherraden, M. S., Birkenmaier, J. M., & Collins, J. M. (2017). *Financial capability and asset building in vulnerable households: Theory and practice.* New York, NY: Oxford University Press.

Sherraden, M. S., Birkenmaier, J., McClendon, G. G., & Rochelle, M. (2017). Financial capability and asset building in social work education: Is it "the big piece missing?" *Journal of Social Work Education, 53*(1), 132–148.

Sherraden, M. S., Huang, J., Frey, J. J., Birkenmaier, J., Callahan, C., Clancy, M. M., & Sherraden, M. (2015). *Financial capability and asset building for all* (Grand Challenges for Social Work Initiative Working Paper No. 13). Cleveland, OH: American Academy of Social Work and Social Welfare.

Sherraden, M. S., Laux, S., & Kaufman, C. (2007). Financial education for social workers. *Journal of Community Practice, 15*(3), 9–36.

Shonkoff, J. P., & Garner, A. S. (2012). The lifelong effects of early childhood adversity and toxic stress. *Pediatrics, 129*, e232–e246.

Small, M., & Feldman, J. (2012). Ethnographic evidence, heterogeneity, and neighbourhood effects after Moving to Opportunity. In M. van Ham, D. Manley, N. Bailey, L. Simpson, & D. Maclennan (Eds.), *Neighbourhood effects research: New perspectives* (pp. 55–77). Dordrecht, the Netherlands: Springer.

Specht, H., & Courtney, M. E. (1995). *Unfaithful angels: How social work has abandoned its mission.* New York, NY: Free Press.

Stuart, P. H. (2013). Social workers and financial capability in the profession's first half-century. In J. Birkenmaier, M. S. Sherraden, & J. Curley (Eds.), *Financial education and capability: Research, education, policy, and practice* (pp. 44–62). New York, NY: Oxford University Press.

Stuart, P. H. (2016). Financial capability in early social work practice: Lessons for today. *Social Work, 61*(4), 297–304.

Swanstrom, T., Winter, W., Sherraden, M., & Lake, J. (2013). Civic capacity and school/community partnerships in a fragmented suburban setting: The case of 24:1. *Journal of Urban Affairs, 35*(1), 25–42.

The Pew Charitable Trusts. (2016a). *Payday loan facts and the CFPB's impact.* Retrieved from http://www.pewtrusts.org/~/media/assets/2016/06/payday_loan_facts_and_the_cfpbs_impact.pdf

The Pew Charitable Trusts. (2016b). *Is this the future of banking? Focus group views on mobile payments* [Issue brief]. Retrieved from http://www.pewtrusts.org/~/media/assets/2016/01/cb_futurebankingissuebrief.pdf

The Pew Charitable Trusts. (2016c). *Do limits on family assets affect participation in, costs of TANF?* Retrieved from http://pew.org/29n0ICJ

US Department of Veterans Affairs. (2016). *Retirement and Financial Literacy Education Program.* Retrieved from https://www.va.gov/ohrm/worklifebenefits/rflep.asp

US Financial Literacy and Education Commission. (2011). *Promoting financial success in the United States: National strategy for financial literacy.* Retrieved from https://www.treasury.gov/resource-center/financial-education/Documents/NationalStrategyBook_12310%20(2).pdf

US Social Security Administration. (n.d.). *Social Security direct deposit*. Retrieved from https://www.ssa.gov/deposit/index.htm

USAccounts: Investing in America's Future Act, 2015, 114th Cong. (2015). Retrieved from https://www.congress.gov/bill/114th-congress/house-bill/4045

Venkatesh, S. A. (2006). *Off the books: The underground economy of the urban poor.* Cambridge, MA: Harvard University Press.

Weiss-Gal, I. (2013). Social workers affecting social policy: An international perspective on policy practice. In J. Gal & I. Weiss-Gal (Eds.), *Social workers affecting social policy: An international perspective on policy practice* (pp. 59–78). Chicago, IL: Policy Press.

Grand Challenges
for Social Work
Achieve equal opportunity and justice

CHAPTER 13

Achieve Equal Opportunity and Justice

ROCÍO CALVO, MARTELL TEASLEY, JEREMY GOLDBACH,
RUTH McROY, AND YOLANDA C. PADILLA

The United States is better off today than ever before. However, living conditions have not improved for all Americans—quite the contrary. For example, the unequal distribution of wealth between the *haves* and the *have-nots* has widened substantially in the past three decades (Heathcote, Perri, & Violante, 2010). Families in the top 10% of the income distribution have increased their assets substantially during this period, from 67% to 76% of all wealth in the country. By contrast, the wealth of families in the bottom half of the distribution—50% of all US families—decreased from 3% to 1% during the same period (Congressional Budget Office, 2016). Because of the unequal distribution of wealth, the ideal that America is a land of opportunity, where anyone can pull themselves up by their own bootstraps if only they work hard, is more difficult to achieve today for American children than it was for their parents. Growing up in low-income neighborhoods with low-quality schools, deprived of health care access and economic stability, these children are denied equal access to critical life chances for upper mobility (Heathcote, Perri, & Violante, 2010; Quillian, 2014).

The systematic denial of opportunity and equal access to basic resources, such as quality health care and education, results in a range of unjust outcomes that marginalize entire segments of the population. The lack of opportunity and justice in society stifles individual and family well-being and weakens the social fabric. In many ways, the lack of economic and social opportunity and justice is the foundation of many of the social problems addressed by the other grand challenges, including incarceration, poverty, and even the extent to which communities will be affected by the changing environment. Also, because lack of opportunity and justice results in lack of resources, it indirectly affects healthy youth development, a nurturing family life, a productive and fulfilling life into old age, social engagement, and access to housing. As it is true with all 12 Grand Challenges for Social Work, the challenge to Achieve Equal Opportunity and Justice is intrinsically intertwined with all the others.

Achieving equal opportunity and justice for new generations and, as a result, for all is one of the most complex challenges as well as an exciting opportunity for our society. It is an opportunity that social work—from its interdisciplinary, asset-based, and translational approach from research to practice—is well positioned to lead. The focus of the scholars working on this grand challenge has been twofold. First, it is designed to seek ways to address power dynamics that underlie inequality: policies, institutions, and programs. Second, the work explores the role of social dynamics—focusing on the role of stigma—in creating and maintaining systemic social inequality. We highlight evidence-based social innovations that have demonstrated measurable progress toward closing the opportunity gap and improving economic and educational opportunities for Latinx[1] communities and African American children and youth. For Latinx populations, a promising approach has been health care legislation under the Affordable Care Act. For African American children and youth, a promising approach has been restorative justice programs.

We also bring attention to the role of stigma in creating and maintaining systemic inequality. We discuss how systems produce and maintain disparities through policies, institutions, and programs, and we present successful interventions that have helped to close the *opportunity gap* for populations at risk to remain at the margins of society. As Pinderhughes (2017) suggests, it is important to examine these issues from the perspective of those who are powerful and those with less power:

> Power holders are vulnerable to using bias and stereotyping in their perceptions
> of subordinates when it would facilitate the goals they pursue and not when
> it would interfere with their goal strivings. Power holders in the system ben-
> efit from perceiving and treating subordinates as societal problems, as inferior,
> incompetent and weak. (p. 15)

We must find ways to address these underlying power dynamics in order to meet the challenge of removing stigma, achieving equal opportunity and justice by transforming educational settings for African American children and youth, and improving opportunities for integration among Latinx immigrants.

---

1. The term *Latinx* is used to include the wide variety of gender identities within the Latinx population.

More than 40 million individuals, or 13% of the current US population, were born in a different country. The US-born children of these immigrants, or the second generation, represent another 12% of the population. The largest proportion of these immigrants, greater than 50%, trace their origins to Latin America (Waters & Pineau, 2015).

The United States is on the brink of a demographic transformation. If current trends continue, by 2060, one out of four people in the United States will be of Latinx descent (Stepler & Brown, 2015). The successful integration of these immigrants and their descendants is one of the most underrecognized opportunities for American society (Calvo et al., 2016).

Who Is Considered Latinx in the United States?

This is an interesting question that does not have a unique answer. In 1976, the US Congress passed the only law in the history of the country that mandates the collection and analysis of data for a specific ethnic group: "Americans of Spanish origin or descent." Since then, Hispanics—or Latinos—have been defined as members of an ethnic group that, regardless of race, trace their origins to more than 20 Spanish-speaking nations from Latin America and Spain (Flores-Hughes, 2006).

Although this definition is used by the US Census Bureau to gather information about Latinxs, the identities of millions of individuals that fall into this description are much more complex and fluid than what any definition can muster. Latinx identity comprises countless aspects as diverse as country of origin, language, race, religion, immigrant generation, or immigration status (Passel & Taylor, 2009; Rumbaut, 2011).

Where Do Latinxs Come from, Are They All Immigrants, and When Did They Get Here?

Most Latinxs, 7 out of 10, trace their origins to Mexico. Mexicans constitute not only the largest group of Latinxs but also the largest immigrant group in the United States. Other predominant countries of origin are Puerto Rico, Cuba, El Salvador, the Dominican Republic, and Guatemala (Calvo et al., 2016; López & Patten, 2015).

Since 2000, both a decline in immigration and high birth rates among Latina immigrants have led to a nativity shift in the composition of the Latinx community. Most Latinxs, nearly two-thirds, in the United States are native-born (Krogstad & López, 2014). A significant proportion of these citizens are children growing up in mixed-status families (Stepler & Brown, 2015). A mixed-status family is a family that includes immigrants and citizens. An example of a mixed-status family is one in which the parents are immigrants and the children are US-born citizens (Waters & Pineau, 2015). The number of mixed-status families is growing. More than one-fourth of children in the United States are children of immigrants, and more than 90% of these children are US citizens (Waters & Pineau, 2015).

Although it may seem that Latinx communities are new to the country, it is important to acknowledge that Latinxs have been in the United States for more than four centuries. In fact, Latinxs have been in the country longer than any other group besides Native Americans (Rumbaut, 2006). However, the Immigration and Naturalization Act of 1965, which effectively opened up an unparalleled increase in immigration from Latin America, coupled with the arrival of Latinxs to new destinations within the United States, portrays the Latinx community as a recent emerged group (Rumbaut, 2006; Stepler & Brown, 2015).

What Is Integration, and How Are Latinxs Doing?

Integration is a two-way process by which immigrants and native-born communities become similar to one another (Brown & Bean, 2006). Greater integration implies the same access as that of the native-born American majority to opportunities to advance socioeconomically (Waters & Pineau, 2015). Although the Latinx community in the United States is very diverse in terms of origin, race, education, socioeconomic status, and immigration pathways, significant numbers of Latinx families still face a system that limits opportunities for their integration (Calvo et al., 2016).

Latinx immigrants tend to concentrate in economic sectors characterized by intense physical labor, low compensation, and lack of benefits, which makes them more vulnerable to poverty (Calvo, Jablonska-Bayro, & Waters, 2017). Latinx families are almost three times more likely than are non-Latino Whites to live below the poverty line (Lichter, Sanders, & Johnson, 2015; Macartney, Bishaw, & Fontenot, 2013). The poverty of Latinx families is especially troublesome among mixed-status families, in part because immigrant parents often do not access social programs for which their children are eligible. This contributes to food insecurity, lack of health care, and other unmet needs that have lasting developmental consequences (Suárez-Orozco, Yoshikawa, Teranishi, & Suárez-Orozco, 2011; Yoshikawa, 2011). In addition, despite higher rates of employment, lack of employer health benefits and unaffordability of insurance premiums make Latinx immigrants the most likely group in the country to lack health insurance (Calvo et al., 2017; Kaiser Family Foundation, 2015). Although they tend to have a more favorable mortality rate compared to other groups (Markides & Gerst, 2011), lack of educational and occupational oppor-tunities and inadequate access to health care result in substantially higher rates of chronic conditions such as diabetes (Cowie et al., 2010). These condi-tions intersect on one aspect crucial to the unequal status of the Latinx popula-tion: the lack of access to health care (Calvo et al., 2016, 2017).

Evidence Indicates That Integration Is Possible

The enactment in 2010 of the Patient Protection and Affordable Care Act (ACA) promised to be a defining moment in the integration of Latinx immigrants through equal access to health care. Making health insurance affordable was the cornerstone of the legislation. To achieve this goal, the ACA established health insurance exchange marketplaces in which moderate-income people could purchase their own private insurance. It also expanded Medicaid, a federal–state joint program, to subsidize the coverage of people younger than age 65 years with incomes up to the 138% of the federal poverty level. The eligibility increase was intended to provide poor working-age individuals with low-cost access to health care regardless of income, disability, family status, or other criteria needed to access Medicaid prior to the ACA (Joseph & Marrow, 2017; Rosenbaum, 2011).

The ramifications of health care policy for the full inclusion of the Latinx community and the integration of immigrants were quite significant and provided a natural experiment on the potential of policy reform to advance opportunity. The ACA was passed in order to reduce disparities in health care coverage and utilization. The ACA has had a real measurable impact on Latinxs' coverage and access to health care. For instance, the proportion of uninsured working-age Latinxs decreased from 43% in 2010 to 24% in 2016 (Doty & Collins, 2017).

Although the ACA made great strides toward health equality, it did not ensure universal coverage. The ACA excluded unauthorized immigrants and granted limited coverage to short-term legal permanent residents who had lived in the country for less than 5 years (Joseph, 2016). These limitations put new generations of Latinxs at risk for poor health outcomes. Lack of universal access to health care is a concern. It precludes Latinx communities from accessing preventive health care and heightens their financial stress because people must pay out of pocket for their health care costs (Chavez, 2012; Portes, Fernández-Kelly, & Light, 2012). Providing access to health care *to all* could contribute to the integration of Latinx communities not only by improving their health and sense of belonging (Calvo et al., 2017) but also by preventing the development of complex conditions among one of the largest populations in the country. This, in turn, would increase the efficiency of the US health care system (Tarraf, Vega, & González, 2014).

So far, we have discussed how the systemic lack of health care access results in the exclusion of Latinx communities. Next, we address another systematic inequality that hampers the academic success of African American children and youth.

INCREASING SCHOOL SUCCESS FOR AFRICAN AMERICAN CHILDREN AND YOUTH

Research shows that African American children and youth outpace all racial and ethnic groups attending public schools in school suspension and expulsion rates (Skiba, Shure, Middelberg, & Baker, 2011; Smith & Harper, 2015), reflecting acute racial disproportionality. *Racial disproportionality* refers to the difference between a racial group's representation in a service population and its representation in the general population; it often signals unfairness or nonresponsiveness to the needs of a minority racial group. Although African American children and youth account for 15% of the US public school population, they represent 48% of those suspended from school. However, there is no evidence that they engage in misbehavior at higher rates. Suspensions and expulsions, which are associated with zero tolerance policies, lead to a host of negative academic and social outcomes, increasing the probability of falling behind academically and school failure (Losen, Hodson, Keith, Morrison, & Belway, 2015). Strategies to reduce racial disproportionality in school discipline are critically needed in order to increase school success for African American children and youth.

The urgency of the need to reduce racial disproportionality in public school discipline has gained national attention. In July 2015, the White House Convening to Rethink School Discipline focused on evidenced-based methods in the design of programming to reduce disciplinary disproportionality in schools and to close the school-to-prison pipeline. The conference was part of the US Department of Education's newly developed Rethink Discipline campaign. The campaign's goals include creating "a supportive school climate—and decreasing suspensions and expulsions." The department recognizes that the undertaking will require "close attention to the social, emotional, and behavioral needs of all students." The campaign works from the premise that teachers and students deserve a safe and supportive school environment that is conducive to classroom education. The conference emphasized restorative justice and other evidence-based approaches to reducing disciplinary disproportionality in schools. Each is discussed briefly here.

Restorative justice (sometimes referred to as restorative discipline) is an evidence-based alternative to zero tolerance, which has demonstrated success in strengthening relationships in schools, reducing violence, and decreasing disruptive behaviors. Its primary aim is to address racial and ethnic disproportionality in suspensions and expulsions (Sumner, Silverman, & Frampton, 2010). This model is a system-wide intervention that involves not only schoolchildren and youth but also teachers, principals, counselors, social workers and other school-based professionals, parents, community members, and local organizations in addressing the needs of students and creating a climate to facilitate education and students' emotional development. It is designed to use data to inform practice and the training of essential personnel in techniques that improve school climate, and it involves using student mentoring and community-based interventions. Moreover, this approach can facilitate the amelioration of disciplinary disproportionality and its effects on African American children and youth. This model moves away from zero tolerance and, instead, highlights positive disciplinary approaches, including peer mediation, conflict resolution, affirmation of student dignity and rights, mentoring, and the development of positive behavioral supports and practices. It is based on an ecological perspective that views the child, school, home, and community as parts of a continuum. Its primary aim is to address racial and ethnic disproportionality in suspensions and expulsions (Sumner et al., 2010).

Another evidence-based approach, which has been utilized in more than 7,500 schools nationwide, is the Positive Behavioral Interventions and Supports (PBIS) model. This three-tiered approach involves (1) fostering a universal or school-wide environment of support; (2) individualization of targeted interventions that provide specialized services for identified youth who do not respond to Tier 1; and (3) intensive clinical intervention, including individualized mental health services (Losen, 2011). Positive results have included reductions in school violence, bullying, special education placements, school suspension, and expulsion (Bradshaw, Koth, Thornton, & Leaf, 2009; Horner, Sugai, Todd, & Lewis-Palmer, 2005; Skiba, Eckes, & Brown, 2009; Skiba et al., 2015). Although more research is needed to demonstrate a clear pathway to reducing disciplinary disproportionality for African American school-aged children, PBIS promises to be part of innovative efforts to address cultural bias among teachers, exclusionary discipline, hyperdisciplinary referrals, low expectations for academic achievement, and overreliance on special education placement.

Multidisciplinary service teams that include clinical counselors, clinical social workers, school psychologists, and school nurses, along with teachers, administrators, and other school personnel often part of behavioral health teams, can be instrumental in developing programming aimed at ameliorating disproportionate use of suspension and expulsion (Lardieri, Lasky, & Raney, 2014). Research has shown the effectiveness of behavioral health teams in prevention, successful interventions, and collaborative practice. Coupled with restorative justice practices, this approach can address school challenges faced by African American children and youth. By creating a meaningful, data-driven, and culturally responsive team process for working with students, teachers, and parents, behavioral health teams seek to create contexts in which African American youth can get the help they need without facing unnecessary disciplinary actions or special education labeling (Losen et al., 2015). Other models that broaden collaboration include the Family and School Partnership Program started in 1996, which has delivered advanced consultation and training to more than 800 school-based mental health professionals to assist them in dealing with disciplinary disproportionality in schools. This model offers a 15-credit certificate in advanced school mental health practice for master's-level practitioners.

PATHS (Promoting Alternative Thinking Strategies) is another evidence-based approach designed to reduce disciplinary disproportionality in preschool and elementary schools. Using direct discussion, storytelling, modeling, direct instruction, role play, and video presentations, this program is designed to work with children on socioemotional development, social skills training, self-control, self-awareness, emotional awareness, friendship development, problem-solving, aggression reduction, and role modeling. A classroom behavior management strategy that has been shown to be effective in reducing rates of violence, criminal behavior, and aggression is the Good Behavior Game (Patras et al., 2008).

By using restorative justice and other evidence-based approaches, the social work profession can mount a strong and sizable effort to reduce disciplinary disproportionality for school-aged African American children. Interdisciplinary and collaborative networks with evidenced-based practices tailored to the particular needs of given locations are needed.

Collaborative teamwork is needed to create academic success for children and youth. The time is now to address this major problem faced by our children and youth. It is essential that the social work profession develop a multidisciplinary, sustainable collaborative agenda, drawing on evidence-based innovative strategies, that will strengthen efforts to reduce the disproportionate suspension and expulsion of African American children and youth and ultimately improve their opportunities to achieve their highest potential.

MECHANISMS BEHIND INEQUALITY: WHY ARE WE OKAY WITH THIS?

As described previously, Latinxs and African American children, youth, and families are subjected to an intense lack of opportunity, which research suggests has many negatives for them and for society and very few (if any) positives. Thus, the question remains, Why are we okay with this?

The answer may be found in a better understanding of the role of stigma. Stigma negatively affects members of a wide array of societally marginalized and disenfranchised groups. Link and Phelan (2001) defined stigma as the co-occurrence of interrelated components of labeling, stereotyping, separating, emotional reaction, status loss, and discrimination. Stigmatization is a process that begins with groups being identified and ascribed negative labels or stereotypes (Corrigan, 2004). Society forms negative stereotypes about a particular group based on generalizations, misinformation, attitudes, and beliefs. Stigma results in blame, prejudice, and discrimination against the stigmatized group, which can be manifested through overt or covert words, actions, or policies, whether conscious or unconscious. This social stigmatization can then be internalized by individuals in the stigmatized group, resulting in self-stigma, whereby an internalized societal view of a group norm adversely influences self-perception (Corrigan & Watson, 2002). According to Link and Phelan, stigmatization involves the exercise of power of a dominant group over less powerful groups. Stigma can affect the life opportunities of individuals and groups, including health outcomes, housing opportunities, academic achievement, income, and the likelihood of criminal involvement (Link & Phelan, 2001; Major & O'Brien, 2005).

Stigma produces inequality through broad mechanisms. Link, Phelan, and Hatzenbuehler (2014) identified four: (1) direct person-to-person discrimination, (2) discrimination that operates through the internalization of negative ascriptions among stigmatized individuals (i.e., self-stigma), (3) interactional discrimination involving the perceptions of stigmatized individuals, and (4) structural discrimination. Stigma scholars suggest that the concerns described in previous sections cannot be overcome until we recognize that stigma is a *fundamental cause* of poor outcomes (Hatzenbuehler, Phelan, & Link, 2013; Link & Phelan, 1995; Phelan, Link, & Tehranifar, 2010). That is, poor health conditions will forever persist in some populations despite prevention and treatment efforts because of underlying social and structural conditions that must be addressed first. These fundamental causes, which can be readily found in the previous sections concerning Latinx immigrants and African American children and youth, have four key characteristics: (1) They influence multiple disease outcomes, (2) they affect disease outcomes through multiple risk factors, (3) they involve access to resources that can be used to avoid risk or minimize the consequences of disease once they occur, and (4) the association between the fundamental cause and health is reproduced over time (Phelan et al., 2010). For example, the persistent influence of low socioeconomic status on health has led thought leaders to categorize it as a fundamental cause of health inequality (Phelan et al., 2010). Like those of lower socioeconomic status, individuals who belong to a socially stigmatized group are granted fewer opportunities and thus experience inequality across numerous domains (Sernau, 2014). Thus, the intersection of stigma, identity, and socioeconomics cannot be understated.

How Do We Stigmatize?

Most of us do not consider ourselves as proponents of stigma; generally, all people believe they are "good people" who strive to treat everyone with equity. However, stigma is a peculiar enemy that allows us to both treat others poorly and still be good people. Social stigma involves attribution of negative ascriptions to a person or group based on characteristics that others perceive as undesirable and distinguishing them from society. Link and Phelan (2001) defined stigma as the co-occurrence of interrelated components of labeling, stereotyping, separating, emotional reaction, status loss, and discrimination. In truth, it is this stigmatizing of individuals as "the other" that allows us to treat individuals and groups poorly while maintaining a positive regard of ourselves.

However, stigmatization does not originate with discrimination. Rather, it begins with our ability to partition individuals into those considered deserving of attention and resources and those who are not (i.e., groups being identified and ascribed negative labels or stereotypes; Corrigan, 2004). If one is unsure of who fits within these two groups, one can quickly see that all people are born into a world that has already provided the blueprint. Society, at a collective level, forms negative stereotypes about a particular group based on generalizations, misinformation, attitudes, and beliefs. This stigma results in blame, prejudice, and discrimination against the stigmatized group, which can be manifested through overt or covert words, actions, or policies, whether conscious or unconscious. This social stigmatization can also be internalized by individuals within the stigmatized group, resulting in self-stigma, whereby an internalized societal view of a group norm adversely influences self-perception (Corrigan & Watson, 2002). According to Link and Phelan (2001), stigmatization involves the exercise of power of a dominant group over less powerful groups. Stigma can affect the life opportunities of individuals and groups, including, as previously described, health outcomes, housing opportunities, academic achievement, income, and the likelihood of criminal involvement (Link & Phelan, 2001; Major & O'Brien, 2005).

Can It Be Fixed?

Historical examples suggest that social stigma and inequality can be addressed simultaneously. Women's suffrage, the civil rights movement, voting acts, fair housing acts, the end of "Don't Ask, Don't Tell," and marriage rights for lesbian, gay, bisexual, and transgender (LGBT) individuals are examples of strategies that have pushed forward equality and redistribution of resources to the benefit of marginalized populations. These approaches, which have targeted racism, have also been successful in reducing inequality. For example, the passage of the Civil Rights Act of 1964, which targeted discrimination, led to a significant decrease in Black infant mortality rates (Almond, Chay, & Greenstone, 2006). Likewise, research preceding the repeal of "Don't Ask, Don't Tell" clearly indicated the policy's impact on stigmatization, victimization, depression, anxiety, substance use, and feelings of isolation (Burks, 2011; Estrada, Probst, Brown, & Graso, 2011; Moradi, 2009), and although related stigma is still evident (Mount, Steelman, & Hertlein, 2015), it may be slowly changing for the better (Ramirez et al., 2013).

Scientific evidence foretells significant progress regarding reducing stigma. History shows that many types of stigma—against divorced people, people becoming parents outside of marriage, and people with tattoos—have been markedly reduced (Akerlof, Yellen, & Katz, 1996; Amato, 2010; Emery, 2011; Gerstel, 1987; Jones, 2000; Wegar, 2000). Lessons learned from these changes, social psychological research, and specifically constructed stigma reduction strategies all favor a positive outcome for tackling this challenge. Social movements are one way that the stigmatization process has been reversed in the past. The gay rights movement, for example, has been quite effective at transforming shame and guilt into righteous indignation and pride (Britt & Heise, 2000). Although stigmatization as a social process is unlikely to be fully eradicated, there is strong evidence that many specific forms of stigmatization can be eliminated or significantly reduced.

Regardless of the type of intervention, programs that seek to reduce stigmatization should include a focus on institutions and groups that wield power and influence in society. Examples include schools, hospitals, religions, mental health workers, law enforcement, politicians, government agencies, and employers. These groups control resources, help socialize cultural views toward out-groups, and often maintain and promote the stereotypes that drive the stigmatization process. They are therefore important targets for stigma reduction interventions, particularly those seeking to address structural forms of social stigmatization. Generating change in these areas can be accomplished through information, education, communication, and social marketing campaigns to generate compassion for and reduce blame placed on stigmatized groups (Weiss, Ramakrishna, & Somma, 2006).

A key feature of addressing stigma is that it enables us as a society to resolve the dissonance between our ideals and facts about inequality in our country. Social status and the roles assigned to groups based on certain characteristics (e.g., gender, race, class, and sexual orientation) are integrated into the fabric of inequality. As long as stigma exists and is not systematically addressed as a fundamental cause of inequality in American society, we are susceptible to blaming the victim, thereby obscuring a more effective analysis of the conditions that affect our most vulnerable communities and delaying the resolution of critical issues. With an organized effort to address stigma at multiple levels, however, our society can reverse the adverse effects of oppression through stigmatization and produce greater equity for all.

CONCLUSION

Our challenge is to build a society filled with equal opportunity and justice for all. We know that lack of access to opportunities is not a behavioral issue; thus, changing the behaviors of those affected will not fix the problem. Rather, we need to examine, and change, the systems in which groups are embedded. Specifically, the policy goals for this grand challenge are the universalization of health care access, the elimination of zero tolerance policies in schools, and the identification of key strategic approaches to address structural aspects of stigma that contribute to inequality. Examples include policies that remove barriers to housing and employment among individuals with a history of incarceration, promote a living wage, and reduce gentrification and displacement in poor communities.

To achieve these goals, a timeline based on specific objectives should be advanced by research teams in order to develop local reports on each of the issues presented in this chapter. For instance, the repeal of the ACA may return to states the responsibility to provide health care. Monitoring how this legislative action impacts coverage and access to health care among vulnerable communities across states, cities, and neighborhoods will be of utmost importance. Similarly, documenting regional racial disciplinary disproportionality and exclusionary practices would be the mechanism to document progress toward restoring academic success for African American children and youth. Here, *progress* refers to change over a defined period; *effort* refers to the methods and resources dedicated to a given project. This evidence-based approach will highlight programming successes and continuing challenges. It will make strategic suggestions for eradicating exclusionary policies and practices concerning access to health and education.

Simultaneously, as a profession, we must embrace the challenge of self-reflection. We need a focused agenda to understand the various manifestations of stigma, particularly how they foster inequality and affect health and opportunity, including how social stigma "gets into the body" to produce health inequities and disempowers individuals from engaging in effective problem-solving.

Implications for social work education and practice include understanding how interactions with social work professionals influence access to health care. Similarly, for professionals working in kindergarten through grade 12 school settings, school discipline practices should be tied to performance appraisals for schoolteachers and administrators. This will make individuals within health care and school settings accountable for clients' success navigating the system of care as well as for suspension and expulsion rates. This accountability will require agencies to place a greater focus on client-centered care and will require schoolteachers to place a greater focus on classroom management. Second, clients' termination rates should be linked to agencies' annual performance reviews, and disciplinary practices in schools should be linked to campus report cards.

State reporting of these data by ethnoracial and socioeconomic characteristics of beneficiaries should be mandated. Currently, only school districts are held accountable for school discipline outcomes. This measure would make providers of health care and school administrators more accountable for developing alternatives to health care utilization and to exclusionary school discipline practices. Third, the fees of Medicaid providers should be increased so that they are equivalent to the fees of private practitioners. Fourth, we must identify, implement, and report on specific evidence-based training for health-related professionals, schoolteachers, and administrators working with Latinx and African American communities and also with students who exhibit problem behaviors or who have been diagnosed with disabilities. Fifth, outcome-based research should be conducted on accountability measures and evidence-based practices related to unconscious bias in training of practitioners. Such research has been conducted in other health professions (Haider et al., 2011; Paradies, Truong, & Priest, 2014; van Ryn & Fu, 2003) and can provide a model and approach for similar studies within social work. It is vital to develop and test interventions at individual and community levels to reduce stigma in the general population and internalization of negative ascriptions among stigmatized groups. Ultimately, group resistance training against stigma could be important in reducing or eliminating stigma at the individual level, but strategies for deliberate stigma reduction at a social level are also needed. Finally, "big data" studies can document the burden of stigma (and measure change) as it relates directly to early pathways leading to health problems, and large-scale comparative studies are needed to understand how stigma manifests in the developmental sequence, presaging onset of distinctive health, behavioral, and functional conditions (Weiss et al., 2006).

Our hope is that this chapter serves as a practical resource for educators and students, researchers, policymakers, program administrators, and others to conceptualize and confront the various forms of marginalization faced by many in our society. It will take imaginative social innovations to close the opportunity gap as we pursue the grand social agenda for social work.

ACKNOWLEDGMENTS

Research reported in this chapter was supported by the Spencer Foundation. The content is solely the responsibility of the authors and does not necessarily represents the views of the Foundation.

REFERENCES

Akerlof, G. A., Yellen, J. L., & Katz, M. L. (1996). An analysis of out-of-wedlock childbearing in the United States. *Quarterly Journal of Economics, 111*, 277–317. doi:10.2307/2946680

Almond, D. V., Chay, K. Y., & Greenstone, M. (2006). *Civil rights, the war on poverty, and Black–White convergence in infant mortality in the rural South and Mississippi* (Working Paper No. 07-04). Cambridge, MA: Massachusetts Institute of Technology, Department of Economics.

Amato, P. R. (2010). Research on divorce: Continuing trends and new developments. *Journal of Marriage and Family, 72,* 650–666. doi:10.1111/j.1741-3737.2010.00723.x

Bradshaw, C. P., Koth, C. W., Thornton, L. A., & Leaf, P. J. (2009). Altering school climate through school-wide positive behavioral interventions and supports: Findings from a group-randomized effectiveness trial. *Prevention Science, 10*(2), 100–115. doi:10.1007/s11121-008-0114-9

Britt, L., & Heise, D. (2000). From shame to pride in identity politics. In S. Stryker, T. J. Owens, & R. W. White (Eds.), *Self, identity, and social movements* (pp. 252–268). Minneapolis, MN: University of Minnesota Press.

Brown, S. K., & Bean, F. D. (2006, October 1). Assimilations models, old and new: Explaining a long-term process. *Migration Information Source,* 3–41.

Burks, D. J. (2011). Lesbian, gay, and bisexual victimization in the military: An unintended consequence of "Don't Ask, Don't Tell"? *American Psychologist, 66,* 604–613. doi:10.1037/a0024609

Calvo, R., Jablonska-Bayro, J. M., & Waters, M. C. (2017, June 12). Obamacare in action: How access to the health care system contributes to immigrants' sense of belonging. *Journal of Ethnic and Migration Studies.* https://doi.org/10.1080/1369183X.2017.1323449

Calvo, R., Ortiz, L., Padilla, Y. C., Waters, M. C., Lubben, J., Egmont, W., . . . Villa, P. (2016). *Achieving equal opportunity and justice: The integration of Latina/o immigrants into American society* (Grand Challenges for Social Work Initiative Working Paper No. 20). Baltimore, MD: American Academy of Social Work & Social Welfare.

Chavez, L. R. (2012). Undocumented immigrants and their use of medical services in Orange County, California. *Social Science & Medicine, 74*(6), 887–893.

Congressional Budget Office. (2016). *Trends in family wealth, 1989 to 2013.* Washington, DC: Congress of the United States.

Corrigan, P. (2004). How stigma interferes with mental health care. *American Psychologist, 59,* 614–625. doi:10.1037/0003-066X.59.7.614

Corrigan, P. W., & Watson, A. C. (2002). The paradox of self-stigma and mental illness. *Clinical Psychology: Science and Practice, 9,* 35–53. doi:10.1093/clipsy.9.1.35

Cowie, C. C., Rust, K. F., Byrd,-Holt, D. D., Gregg, E. W., Ford, E. S., Geiss, L. S., . . . Fradkin, J. E. (2010). Prevalence of diabetes and high risk for diabetes using A1C criteria in the U.S. population in 1988–2006. *Diabetes Care, 33*(3), 562–568.

Doty, M. M., & Collins, S. R. (2017, January 19). Millions more Latino adults are insured under the Affordable Care Act. *To the Point.* Retrieved from http://www.commonwealthfund.org/publications/blog/2017/jan/more-latino-adults-insured

Emery, R. E. (2011). *Renegotiating family relationships: Divorce, child custody, and mediation.* New York, NY: Guilford.

Estrada, A. X., Probst, T. M., Brown, J., & Graso, M. (2011). Evaluating the psychometric and measurement characteristics of a measure of sexual orientation harassment. *Military Psychology, 23,* 220–236. doi:10.1080/08995605.2011.559394

Flores-Hughes, G. (2006). The origin of the term "Hispanic." *Harvard Journal of Hispanic Policy, 18,* 81–84.

Gerstel, N. (1987). Divorce and stigma. *Social Problems, 34*, 172–186. doi:10.2307/800714

Haider, A.H., Sexton, J., Sriram, N., Cooper, L.A., Efron, D.T., Swoboda, S . . ..Cornwell, E.E. (2011). Association of unconscious race and social class bias ith vignette-based clinical assessments by medical students. *JAMA, 306*(9), 942-951. doi: 10.1001/jama/2011/1248

Hatzenbuehler, M. L., Phelan, J. C., & Link, B. G. (2013). Stigma as a fundamental cause of population health inequalities. *American Journal of Public Health, 103*, 813–821. doi:10.2105/AJPH.2012.301069

Heathcote, J., Perri, F., & Violante, G. L. (2010). Unequal we stand: An empirical analysis of economic inequality in the United States, 1967–2006. *Review of Economic Dynamics, 13*(1), 15–51.

Horner, R. H., Sugai, G., Todd, A. W., & Lewis-Palmer, T. (2005). Schoolwide positive behavior support. In L. M. Bambara & L. Kern (Eds.), *Individualized supports for students with problem behaviors: Designing positive behavior plans* (pp. 359–390). New York, NY: Guilford.

Jones, C. P. (2000). Stigma and tattoo. In J. Caplan (Ed.), *Written on the body: The tattoo in European and American history* (pp. 1–16). London, UK: Reaktion Books.

Joseph, T. D. (2016). What health care reform means for immigrants: Comparing the Affordable Care Act and the Massachusetts Health Care reforms. *Journal of Health Politics and Law, 41*(1), 101–116.

Joseph, T. D., & Marrow, H. B. (2017). Health care, immigrants and minorities: Lessons from the Affordable Care Act in the United States. *Journal of Ethnic and Migration Studies.* https://doi.org/10.1080/1369183X.2017.1323446

Kaiser Family Foundation. (2015). *Uninsured rates for the nonelderly by race/ethnicity.* Retrieved from http://www.kff.org/uninsured/state-indicator/rate-by-raceethnicity/?currentTimeframe=0&sortModel=%7B%22colId%22:%22Locati on%22,%22sort%22:%22asc%22%7D

Krogstad, J. M., & López, M. H. (2014). *Hispanic nativity shift: U.S. births drive population growth as immigration stalls.* Washington, DC: Pew Research Center.

Lardieri, M. R., Lasky, G. B., & Raney, L. (2014). *Essential elements of effective integrated primary care and behavioral health teams.* Retrieved from https://www.integration.samhsa.gov/workforce/team-members/Essential_Elements_of_an_Integrated_Team.pdf

Lichter, D. T., Sanders, S. R., & Johnson, K. M. (2015). Hispanics at the starting line: Poverty among newborn infants in established gateways and new destinations. *Social Forces, 94*(1), 209–235.

Link, B. G., & Phelan, J. (1995). Social conditions as fundamental causes of disease [Extra issue]. *Journal of Health and Social Behavior, 35*, 80–94. doi:10.2307/2626958

Link, B. G., & Phelan, J. C. (2001). Conceptualizing stigma. *Annual Review of Sociology, 27*, 363–385. doi:10.1146/annurev.soc.27.1.363

Link, B. G., Phelan, J. C., & Hatzenbuehler, M. L. (2014). Stigma and social inequality. In J. D. McLeod, E. Lawler, & M. Schwalbe (Eds.), *Handbook of the social psychology of inequality* (pp. 49–64). Dordrecht, the Netherlands: Springer.

López, G., & Patten, E. (2015). *The impact of slowing immigration: Foreign-born share falls among 14 largest U.S. Hispanic origin groups.* Washington, DC: Pew Research Center. Retrieved from http://www.pewhispanic.org/2015/09/15/the-impact-of-slowing-immigration-foreign-born-share-falls-among-14-largest-us-hispanic-origin-groups

Losen, D. J. (2011). *Good discipline: Legislation for education reform*. Boulder, CO: National Education Policy Center. Retrieved from http://nepc.colorado.edu/files/NEPC-SchoolDiscipline-Losen-2-LB_FINAL.pdf

Losen, D. J., Hodson, C., Keith, M. A., II, Morrison, K., & Belway, S. (2015). *Are we closing the school discipline gap?* Los Angeles, CA: University of California, Los Angeles, Civil Rights Project, Center for Civil Rights Remedies. Retrieved from http://civilrightsproject.ucla.edu/resources /projects/center-for-civil-rights-remedies/school-to-prison-folder/federal-reports/are-we-closing-the -school-discipline-gap

Macartney, S., Bishaw, A., & Fontenot, K. (2013). *Poverty rates for selected detail race and Hispanic groups by state and place: 2007–2011* (American Community Survey Briefs). Washington, DC: US Census Bureau.

Major, B., & O'Brien, L. T. (2005). The social psychology of stigma. *Annual Review of Psychology, 56*, 393–421. doi:10.1146/annurev.psych.56.091103.070137

Markides, K. S., & Gerst, K. (2011). Immigration, aging, and health in the United States. In R. A. Settersen, Jr., & J. L. Angel (Eds.), *Handbook of sociology and aging* (pp. 103–116). New York, NY: Springer.

Moradi, B. (2009). Sexual orientation disclosure, concealment, harassment, and military cohesion: Perceptions of LGBT military veterans. *Military Psychology, 21*, 513–533. doi:10.1080/08995600903206453

Mount, S. D., Steelman, S. M., & Hertlein, K. M. (2015). "I'm not sure I trust the system yet": Lesbian service member experiences with mental health care. *Military Psychology, 27*, 115–127. doi:10.1037/mil0000071

Paradies, Y., Troung, M., & Priest, N. (2014). A systematic review of the extent and measurement of healthcare provider racism. *Journal of General Internal Medicine, 29*(2), 364-387. doi: 10.1007/s11606-013-2583-1

Passel, J. S., & Taylor, P. (2009). *Who's Hispanic?* Washington, DC: Pew Research Center.

Patras, H., Kellam, S. G., Brown, C. H., Muthén, B. O., Ialongo, N. S., & Poduska, J. M. (2008). Developmental epidemiological courses leading to antisocial personality disorder and violent and criminal behavior: Effects by young adulthood of a universal preventive intervention in first- and second-grade classrooms. *Drug and Alcohol Dependence, 95*(Suppl.), S45–S59. doi:10.1016/j.drugalcdep.2007.10.015

Phelan, J. C., Link, B. G., & Tehranifar, P. (2010). Social conditions as fundamental causes of health inequalities: Theory, evidence, and policy implications. *Journal of Health and Social Behavior, 51*, S28–S40. doi:10.1177/0022146510383498

Pinderhughes, E (2017). Conceptualization of how power operates in human functioning. In E. Pinderhughes, V. Jackson, & P. Romney (Eds.), *Understanding power. An imperative for human services* (pp. 1–23). Washington, D.C: NASW Press.

Portes, A., Fernández-Kelly, P., & Light, D. W. (2012). Life on the edge: Immigrants confront the American health care system. *Ethnic and Racial Studies, 35*(1), 3–22.

Quillian, L. (2014). Does segregation create winners and losers? Residential segregation and inequality in educational attainment. *Social Problems, 61*(3), 402–426.

Ramirez, M. H., Rogers, S. J., Johnson, H. L., Banks, J., Seay, W. P., Tinsley, B. L., & Grant A. W. (2013). If we ask, what they might tell: Clinical assessment lessons from LGBT military personnel post-DADT. *Journal of Homosexuality, 60*, 401–418. doi:10.1080/00918369.2013.744931

Rosenbaum, S. (2011). The Patient Protection and Affordable Care Act: Implications for public health policy and practice. *Public Health Reports, 126*(1), 130–135.

Rumbaut, R. (2006). Hispanics and the future of America. In M. Tienda & F. Mitchell (Eds.), *The making of a people* (pp. 16–65). Washington, DC: National Academies Press.

Rumbaut, R. (2011, April 27). Pigments of our imagination: The racialization of the Hispanic–Latino category. *Migration Information Source*. Retrieved from http://www.migrationpolicy.org/article/pigments-our-imagination-racialization-hispanic-latino-category

Sernau, S. (2014). *Social inequality in a global age* (4th ed.). Thousand Oaks, CA: Sage.

Skiba, R. J., Chung, C.-G., Trachok, M., Baker, T., Sheya, A., & Hughes, R. (2015). Where should we intervene? Contributions of behavior, student, and school characteristics to out-of-school suspension. In D. J. Losen (Ed.), *Closing the school discipline gap: Equitable remedies for excessive exclusion* (pp. 132–146). New York, NY: Teachers College Press.

Skiba, R. J., Eckes, S. E., & Brown, K. (2009). African American disproportionality in school discipline: The divide between best evidence and legal remedy. *New York Law School Law Review, 54*(4), 1071–1112.

Skiba, R. J., Shure, L. A., Middelberg, L. V., & Baker, T. L. (2011). Reforming school discipline and reducing disproportionality in suspension and expulsion. In S. R. Jimerson, A. B. Nickerson, M. J. Mayer, & M. J. Furlong (Eds.), *Handbook of school violence and school safety: International research and practice* (2nd ed., pp. 515–528). New York, NY: Routledge.

Smith, E. J., & Harper, S. R. (2015). *Disproportionate impact of K–12 school suspension and expulsion on Black students in southern states*. Philadelphia: University of Pennsylvania, Center for the Study of Race and Equity in Education.

Stepler, R., & Brown, A. (2015). Statistical portrait of Hispanics in the United States, 1980–2013. Washington, DC: Pew Research Center. Retrieved from http://www.pewhispanic.org/2016/04/19/statistical-portrait-of-hispanics-in-the-united-states-key-charts

Suárez-Orozco, C., Yoshikawa, H., Teranishi, R. T., & Suárez-Orozco, M. M. (2011). Growing up in the shadows: The developmental implications of unauthorized status. *Harvard Educational Review, 81*(3), 438–472.

Sumner, M. D., Silverman, C. J., & Frampton, M. L. (2010). *School-based restorative justice as an alternative to zero-tolerance policies: Lessons from west Oakland*. Berkeley, CA: University of California, Berkeley, School of Law, Thelton E. Henderson Center for Social Justice. Retrieved from https://www.law.berkeley.edu/files/thcsj/10-2010_School-based_Restorative_Justice_As_an_Alternative_to_Zero-Tolerance_Policies.pdf

Tarraf, W., Vega, W., & González, H. M. (2014). Emergency department services use and non-immigrant groups in the United States. *Journal of Immigrant and Minority Health, 16*, 596–606.

Van Ryn, M., & Fu, S. S. (2003). Paved with good intentions: Do public health and human service providers contribute to racial/ethnic disparities in health? *American Journal of Public Health, 93*(2), 248–255.

Waters, M. C., & Pineau, M. G. (Eds.). (2015). *The integration of immigrants into American society*. Washington, DC: National Academies Press.

Wegar, K. (2000). Adoption, family ideology, and social stigma: Bias in community attitudes, adoption research, and practice. *Family Relations, 49*, 363–369. doi:10.1111/j.1741-3729.2000.00363.x

Weiss, M. G., Ramakrishna, J., & Somma, D. (2006). Health-related stigma: Rethinking concepts and interventions. *Psychology, Health & Medicine, 11*, 277–287. doi:10.1080/1354850060059505

Yoshikawa, H. (2011). *Immigrants raising citizens: Undocumented parents and their young children*. New York, NY: Russell Sage Foundation.

CHAPTER 14

Conclusion

RICHARD P. BARTH, ROWENA FONG, JAMES E. LUBBEN,
AND SARAH CHRISTA BUTTS

The Grand Challenges for Social Work (GCSW) is an innovation that aims to solve big, compelling problems and make social progress that is powered by science. Inspired by the conviction that social work and its allies can galvanize the helping professions, as well as our colleagues in the arts and sciences, to embark on bold, exciting, and, in some instances, strangely productive pathways, social work and its friends are working within each of the identified 12 Grand Challenges, making progress in identifying measurable outcomes, setting up networks, creating implementation plans, determining metrics to monitor those outcomes, and drafting policy recommendations to profoundly and measurably impact the societal problems being considered (see Appendix 4 for a list of policy recommendations from the 2016 Grand Challenges policy conference). Lessons learned from activities already undertaken will influence the future directions for GCSW and, we assert, the future of the profession and society.

WE ARE NOT ALONE, IN ACADEMIA, IN WANTING TO SOLVE MAJOR SOCIAL PROBLEMS

Each grand challenge is about solving significant social problems faced by people in communities throughout the United States. The complexity of these grand challenge problems calls for innovative and collaborative solutions, many of which are areas of work of great interest to students and faculty across campuses and throughout the nation.

Homelessness is a major and compelling societal problem in many communities. This has long been a focus of federal, state, and especially local government and a few nonprofits. Universities such as the University of Southern California (USC), the University of California at Los Angeles, and the University of Albany have now expressly taken on this problem. They are joined by statisticians, demographers, and engineers in thinking about ways to combat homelessness and achieve other grand challenge goals. We believe that this will offer new, interdisciplinary engagement and innovative solutions that we have not generated in prior decades.

The two Grand Challenge co-leads on End Homelessness have been in the midst of efforts in California and New York. Combined efforts are joining resources at the community, university, and state levels in solving common problems such as homelessness. As Padgett and Henwood discuss in Chapter 7, after making Housing First an international standard, they are helping lead a national movement to apply the historically successful "Housing First" approach (Padgett, Henwood, & Tsemberis, 2016) to new ventures, including work with homeless families involved with child welfare services. We know that economists, attorneys, and statisticians are also working on solutions to homelessness. The University of Maryland's Grand Challenges for Social Work inspired Coalition on Homelessness has representatives from medicine, nursing, pharmacy, and law, along with agency, academic, and field personnel. Although social work is often a leading voice in addressing each of the Grand Challenges, we know that there are many other professionals eager to be actively involved.

BUILDING COALITIONS AND MAXIMIZING WORK EFFORTS

Joining forces by creating coalitions is another way to maximize work efforts, and some of the grand challenges have been joining forces with allies and other disciplines. The co-leads for the Grand Challenge to Eradicate Social Isolation are working with the AARP Foundation who together with the National Academy of Science, Engineering and Medicine are considering a consensus study on social isolation among older adults. The healthy development of children and youth has united social workers, researchers, informaticians, and primary medical care practitioners in examining behavioral health problems in childhood and adolescence. Preventing problems such as anxiety, depression, and alcohol and drug use has been the driving vision of the Grand Challenge to Ensure Healthy Development for All Youth. Prevention has also been a primary aim for the 40-member Coalition for the Promotion of Behavioral Health. Creative ventures as discussed in Chapter 9 on the Grand Challenge to Harness Technology for Social Good also illustrate coalition building. As noted previously, there is a joint venture underway between social work and engineering through the USC Center for Artificial Intelligence in Society, which is a byproduct of the Viterbi School of Engineering and the Suzenne Dworak Peck School of Social Work; the venture fosters the application of technology and artificial intelligence to problems related to HIV and homelessness among youth.

Many examples of building coalitions through strong community involvement and partnerships are emerging. Hazards related to a changing global environment and natural disasters require a societal response, as indicated in Chapter 8. Strengthening community resiliency and having an "urban community adaptation" is another example of starting with the community priorities. The Grand Challenge to Close the Health Gap is using community-based approaches, place-based approaches, and setting-based interventions to solve problems that affect population health, such as alcohol misuse. Joining forces with communities represents a more urgent call for action in solving the major and compelling societal problems mentioned previously.

At least two schools of social work have decided to lift up their own areas of concern and expertise within a grand challenges framework. The University of California at Berkeley School of Social Welfare has had both a domestic and an international focus with its Grand Challenges for Social Work presentations on "The Challenge of an Aging Society," "Poverty and the Empowerment of Women: Lessons from Developing Countries for the US," "Harnessing Technology to Enhance Behavioral Interventions and Improve Service Delivery," "Promoting the Nation's Health and Mental Health," and "Upstream Thinking- Beyond Individual Practice" (for more information, see http://socialwelfareberkeley.edu/berkeley-social-welfare-grand-challenges-social-work). The University of Pennsylvania School of Social Practice and Policy (SP) has developed the SPT Penn Top 10 Social Justice & Policy Issues designed to serve as a bridge between the work at SP2 and practical problem-solving—to meet the challenge of translating lofty concepts into everyday improvements in society. Some of its top 10 topics are interventions for youth, urban food desserts, youth aging out of foster care, and mass incarceration (for the remainder and more about this initiative, see http://www.penntopten.com).

REFRAME AND USE A POSITIVE APPROACH

Negative stereotyping of some populations has prompted innovative and transformative missions for some of the Grand Challenges. This has been the case with the Grand Challenge to Achieve Equal Opportunity and Justice. The working paper "Increasing Success for African American Children and Youth" confronts the frequently negative stereotype of this population and reframes the goal as indicated by its title. This positive approach adapts the restorative justice model used in school systems to support the US Department of Education's "Rethink Discipline" campaign. The Positive Behavioral Intervention and Supports (PBIS) model is an evidence-based, three-tiered approach employing environmental supports, specialized services, and clinical interventions, all of which reinforce the restorative justice model to reduce disciplinary disproportionality in schools. Some of our programs to reduce the preschool-to-prison pipeline, while attentive to the impact of complex trauma, discuss healing circles and healing schools as part of their restorative practice models.

Another population that often meets harsh negative stereotypes is the subject of the Grand Challenge to Promote Smart Decarceration. To change society's view of persons in prisons, stop mass incarceration, and promote smart decarceration have been major challenges, but co-leads of this grand challenge have been very successful in efforts to reframe and promote strategies to build social capital by encouraging social and financial investments in communities most affected by incarceration. Social capital is very much evident in the aging population, and the Grand Challenge of Advance Long and Productive Lives perceives and promotes elders as engaged rather than disengaged.

USING THE STRENGTH OF NETWORKS

GCSW has required and benefitted from an organic organization and implementation. We sometimes say that we are using Mao's Zedong's "let a thousand flowers bloom" approach to organizing the Grand Challenges. Indeed, the 12 Grand Challenges is an organizing framework for research, practice, and policy that is quite decentralized. The Grand Challenges are organized around *networks*, not the more common organizing construct of *centers*. Networks of partnerships have the capacity to obviate the common shortcoming of centers, which is that they generate siloed activities and may stunt innovation that is not generated from the core of a center. Just as social networks allow for anyone to communicate with vast audiences—in the case of "going viral"—the Grand Challenge networks will allow for exponential growth of communications to help innovations arise and go to scale. Although the networks have two or more leaders, they are not intended to be managed; the intent is that they flow to follow the best opportunities for success (see Appendix 5 for a roster of the Grand Challenge network co-leaders).

The potential of these networks is an expansion of leadership and accelerated development of 12 national implementation networks, the onboarding of sister social work organizations, and an ever-growing interest from students and budding awareness from the public. The networks are being led by

38 senior and junior scholars from 21 universities throughout the country. The early accomplishment of network development provides a foundation for progress over the established 10-year timeline.

One type of network is a practice-based research network (PBRN). PBRNs are an innovation arising largely out of the disciplines of medicine and primary care that are being adapted for social work. We anticipate that social work will adapt PBRNs in ways that arise from our current network structure and help us achieve our Grand Challenges. In their most basic form, PBRNs represent networks composed of academic researchers and practitioners, who are committed to ongoing and productive collaboration with the purpose of advancing both a research and a practice agenda. Network organization ranges from informal to formal, with the most sophisticated networks having prescribed components including strong infrastructures and criteria that include mission and statement of purpose, staffing, an organizational structure, and communication processes (Gehlert, Walters, Uehara, & Lawlor, 2015).

The potential of PBRNs to advance solution-focused science in support of Grand Challenges is promising. Strong network collaborations allow interdisciplinary teams to identify research questions that are mutually beneficial; rapidly implement, test, and modify research-informed interventions in community-based settings; establish a common set of data points for collection; support multisite data collection and sharing; and collectively analyze and disseminate results (Kelly et al., 2015). In addition, PBRNs can be expected to reduce the research to practice gap and accelerate.

As network organization is tailored for specific Grand Challenges, we can imagine evolution of powerful research and practice collaborations. One example is the pioneering effort illustrated in the development of the Recovery-Oriented Care Collaborative (ROCC) in Los Angeles designed to improve services for people with serious mental illness; it is led by a team that includes USC professor John Brekke (Kelly et al., 2015). The ROCC PBRN has infrastructure, defined roles, expectations of partners, and shared goals; key replicable components of ROCC's development and activities have been published (Kelly et al., 2015). The establishment of ROCC represents a new frontier that has the potential to be transformative for social work research, practice, and education and also improve outcomes for clients.

A formalized PBRN concept has been suggested to address the Grand Challenge of Close the Health Gap in the Health Equity working paper (Gehlert et al., 2015). Gehlert et al.'s proposed National Health Social Work Practice Based Research Network would represent an opportunity to collect high-quality data on populations of interest, and they state that a key benefit would be to increase research participant sample sizes for subpopulations with which social work is typically concerned. In this example, a national network could yield larger sample data sets, recruit multisite participation, and allow social work researchers to rigorously test interventions on subpopulations

(Gehlert et al., 2015). Thus, GCSW networks and their adaptations of PRBRNs are a promising vehicle to foster transdisciplinary team science, bringing evidenced-based interventions to scale and aiding in the translation of research findings to practice and policy.

Expanded leadership substructure is emerging for the GCSW. In January 2017, the Grand Challenges Executive Committee expanded from being composed of fellows and deans of the American Academy of Social Work and Social Welfare (AASWSW) to include more deeply engaged national social work leaders. Under the leadership of the steering committee—Marilyn Flynn, Michael Sherraden, and Edwina Uehara—the Grand Challenge Executive Committee invited leaders of the National Association of Social Workers, the Council on Social Work Education, the Congressional Research Institute for Social Work and Policy, and the Fund for Social Policy. Bringing the heads of major organizations on board is a step toward institutionalizing grand challenges across the profession and represents an evolution whereby the original founding committee was composed of academics who took on the task of identifying the challenges and the new group needs to implement plans to achieve the goals of the challenges, cultivate partners, communicate, and determine how to measure progress over a decade and beyond. Social work now has an agenda for the 21st century, and the Executive Committee is just one of many forces that will shape how to advance the goals that have been set. The advantage of such a structure is that it builds in social work's major organizations for education (the Council on Social Work Education) and practice (the National Association of Social Workers) and also brings in key policy partners (the Congressional Research Institute for Social Work and Policy and the Fund for Social Policy).

Broad university support is also being cultivated. There are now National Association of Deans and Directors (NADD) and St. Louis Group (SLG) subcommittees on the Grand Challenges, led by identified representatives in those organizations. A mechanism for universities to support the Grand Challenges has also been established. To date, 19 schools of social work have contributed funds as sustaining sponsors, which requires an annual contribution to the AASWSW (see Appendix 6 for a list of GCSW sustaining sponsors).

Regional consortia development is expected to engage universities of all sizes in the effort (Flynn, 2017). In order to fully engage smaller colleges and universities with regional missions, multistate consortia are being formed with a focus on curriculum innovation, campus engagement, and PBRNs. The first consortium was organized in the western United States, with 44 participants representing 23 schools from seven states. The meeting highlighted examples of campus-wide leadership, pedagogical experimentation, student leadership, and successful PBRN development around the Grand Challenges. The meeting offered an opportunity to clarify the purposes of the Grand Challenges and an affirmation of the many ways in which faculty and communities can offer leadership to this initiative. This inaugural meeting was sponsored by the USC, the University of Washington, and Portland State University and held on the campus of Portland State in spring 2017. Subsidies were offered to schools unable to participate without assistance. Since that time, two additional western states have asked to join the consortium, subsequent meetings are being scheduled for fall 2017, and other consortia in the South and Midwest are planned. This volume is the first of a series that will, in time, also help spread the opportunity of the Grand Challenges by including a short book volume for each of the 12 Grand Challenges. Each will, in nontechnical terms, discuss the way that each Grand Challenge is meeting the standard of being important, interdisciplinary, innovative, measurable, and creating a platform for taking society-changing ideas to scale. We also are receiving inquiries from other countries (e.g., Korea and Israel) about assisting them with their own Grand Challenges for Social Work efforts.

The demands of such an initiative are many, and accomplishment is not at all guaranteed. The work cannot be so grand that we fail to do the granular work of planning how we will track progress; developing measurement schemes that are feasible; getting ourselves and our colleagues to forego some of their independence as investigators to share in common practice (and measurement networks); and putting needed resources into the Grand Challenges that we might have otherwise invested in our own schools, departments, agencies, and careers. Focusing our efforts on the 12 Grand Challenges brings the benefit of accelerated progress but may also mean less focus on other areas of advancement. We believe that many other efforts—to advance gender and racial equity, for example—can be paired with work on the Grand Challenges to ensure that progress is fairly distributed.

CONCLUSION

Grand challenges are galvanized in energy and foster sustainable determination when there is a concerted effort to solve societal problems by joining with community-driven initiatives. Positive reframes to the approaches used with stereotyped populations have garnered enthusiasm and innovative thinking. Innovation is very important to engage future social workers and to keep the pipeline of the profession doing significant and transformative work to solve the major and challenging problems facing the clients they choose to impact through cross-disciplinary practice, policy, and research activities.

The Grand Challenges initiative has an infectiously energizing quality that is both inspirational and galvanizing—especially for social work, a "social values"-based profession. However, the Grand Challenges framework is also a mechanism for advocacy beyond values and one that has a scientific basis to support social justice aims. Future steps most likely will involve deeper engagement of practitioners, engagement of scholars in more universities throughout the country, influencing the pipeline and recruitment of new social work students at the elementary and high school levels, better informing the public, more robust communications, and focused efforts to influence public policy and expose barriers to success—especially in those challenges in which political will is required.

REFERENCES

Flynn, M. (2017). The grand challenges concept: Campus strategies for implementation. *Journal of the Society for Social Work and Research, 8*(1), 87–98.

Gehlert, S., Walters, K., Uehara, E., & Lawlor, E. (2015). The case for a national health social work practice-based research network in addressing health equity. *Health & Social Work, 40*(4), 253–255.

Kelly, E. L., Kiger, H., Gaba, R., Pancake, L., Pilon, D., Murch, L., . . . Brekke, J. S. (2015). The Recovery-Oriented Care Collaborative: A practice-based research network to improve care for people with serious mental illnesses. *Psychiatric Services, 66*(11), 1132–1134.

Padgett, D., Henwood, B, & Tsemberis, S. (2016). *Ending homelessness, transforming systems, and changing lives*. New York, NY: Oxford University Press.

APPENDIX 1

Grand Challenge 85 Ideas

Grand Challenges for Social Work ideas were invited and submitted online and in person between October 2013 and May 2015. Ideas were accepted and considered throughout the process of identifying and refining Grand Challenges for Social Work. The following ideas were submitted online and included a description of 500 words or less:

1. Value women in social work.
2. End sexism.
3. Harnessing the digital age: Practice innovation through technology.
4. Human environment and community evolution.
5. Weight management and nutrition.
6. Exploring the archeology of social practice.
7. Workforce development and readiness.
8. Harnessing big data for social policy innovation.
9. Financial empowerment for social workers.
10. Our guiding practice frameworks must be broadened to include genetic variation as a core feature of developmental, social, and environmental assessment.
11. Uplifting a culture of peace from hearth and home to community.
12. Empower and integrate individuals with autism through teaching social skills and healthy living.
13. Addressing urban poverty in informal settlements through the use of passive biotecture and community development.
14. Can we eliminate racist and sexist messages in media to transform our community?
15. Providing employment for developmentally disabled adults and offering them the opportunity to be independent.

16. Transforming our society to dismantle gender oppression and create equality for women and girls.
17. The challenge aims to eliminate the recycling of women in and out of prison.
18. Re-entry is our next civil rights movement.
19. Reduce the high rates of mental illness in our nation's jails and prisons.
20. Redefining the federal roles in social welfare.
21. Close the 30-million word gap.
22. Identify cost-effective evidence-based approaches to address low-income neighborhood factors that contribute to disparities in well-being.
23. Creating a space for unaccompanied youth and young adults without homes.
24. Better quantitative training means better answers for practice and intervention.
25. Increase social work's involvement in the complex issues facing our society.
26. Reduce child neglect in the United States by 50%.
27. Prepare the profession to address structural racism and its impact on our clients and ourselves.
28. Translational research and effective interventions in a multicultural and multilingual world.
29. Social work students need a standardized means to learn practice in the context of a healthy and authentic use of self.
30. Help increase children's chances of upward mobility by improving the quality of parenting.
31. Decarcerate America.
32. Globalize social welfare education.
33. Food security, environmental justice, and protection.
34. Developing a broader range of policies and practices to all, and help the terminally ill die on their terms.
35. Creating healthy roots: Design and implement curriculum for recognizing and removing institutional, racialized policies and practices within social work systems given its negative impact on people of color.
36. Take back urban parks and streets, cut down on crime, through beautification projects by youth.
37. Interrupt the patterns of cumulative disadvantage across the lifespan by promoting equity and choice.
38. How can America provide and pay for long-term services and supports for the elderly and people with disabilities?
39. Reduce the incarceration and re-incarceration of vulnerable populations.
40. Optimizing the productive engagement of older adults.

41. Maximize the choices older adults have for participating in the life of their community.
42. Challenge of an aging society: Creating aging-friendly communities and program models.
43. Create policies and programs that draw on strengths and capacity of older adults to build healthy communities for all ages.
44. Increase access to services and supports necessary to decrease depression among older adults.
45. Develop communities that provide opportunities for positive intergenerational interaction to reduce intergenerational conflict.
46. Increase access to home-based services necessary to reduce institutionalization of older adults and people with disabilities.
47. A grand challenge is to create a transportable coordinated health, mental health, and social service care delivery system.
48. Maximize individual and societal opportunities presented by increased longevity.
49. Integrate health, mental health, and social services for people of all ages.
50. Foster intergenerational communities enabling older people to age in place.
51. Advance open and rational conversations about death and dying.
52. Strengthen social protection to eradicate poverty and social disparities.
53. Reduce social isolation among older populations.
54. Redesign physical structures and social institutions to promote health, well-being, and choice for all ages.
55. Social work needs to identify a framework to define and measure the term "well-being."
56. Promoting behavioral health and preventing negative developmental outcomes from birth through age 24.
57. Reducing the impact of stigma.
58. Use the science of research synthesis to build reliable evidence for practice, programs, and policy.
59. Social work and technology training for social workers by social workers.
60. To reduce the number of children who develop a preventable mental illness.
61. The quest for home.
62. Diagnosis and treatment of children with attachment disorders.
63. Effectively use technology in social work practice.
64. Can social work promote Eco city citizenship?
65. My grand challenge is to eliminate the political gender gap in the United States.
66. Advance equity and choice in aging in all contexts across the life course.
67. Strengthen entitlements and safety net programs across the lifespan.

68. Build truly family-centered care that is pragmatic and aspirational, not charity modeled using technology.
69. Advance conversations about dying across the lifespan.
70. Developing a mobile app for educating mental health professionals about the array of resources available to survivors processing trauma.
71. Responding to the effects of global ecological degradation.
72. Integrating innovative platforms for health care reform into community-based organizations to empower these organizations to create interdisciplinary teams to tackle high rates for chronic and mental illnesses in large urban communities.
73. Affordable housing.
74. Eliminate homework in elementary school, preserving childhood and family life.
75. Empowering women and girls to enable reproductive health and choice for personal, community, and global health.
76. Social emotional skills are extremely important in becoming a successful adult. These skills need to be taught in and out of school with the same importance as education.
77. Reclaiming social work.
78. To place social work on the forefront of the Affordable Care Act by developing patient-centered integrative care.
79. Application of systems thinking in social work research and practice.
80. Corporate personhood.
81. Changing the US child welfare system as we know it.
82. Identifying, documenting, and advocating for the needs of older adults in developing countries.
83. End violence against children.
84. Significantly decrease incidence of low-birth-weight and pre-term babies who are at highest risk for early mortality and morbidity.
85. Create a comprehensive system for early detection and intervention to reduce the odds of early onset psychosis.

CALL FOR PAPERS: ROUND 1 CONCEPT PAPER TOPICS

Concept papers had to meet five established criteria and were 10 pages in length with supporting reference list:

1. Leadership, Literacy, and Translational Expertise in Genomics: A Grand Challenge for Social Work
2. Taking Back Urban Parks and Streets and Cutting Down on Crime Through Beautification Projects by Youth

3. Social Safety and Gun Violence
4. Eradicating Homelessness
5. Reducing Health Inequities: The Most Pressing Social Justice Crisis of Our Time
6. Decarcerate America
7. No Child Hungry
8. Refocusing Social Work Practice & Education on Outcome Values Via Deep Pragmatism
9. Social Work and the Affordable Care Act: Maximizing the Profession's Role in Health Reform
10. Changing the Way Society Views Women as Commodities
11. Social Isolation Presents a Grand Challenge for Social Work
12. Reduce the High Rates of Mental Illness in Our Nation's Jails and Prisons
13. Behavioral Health for All
14. Eliminating the Political Gender Gap
15. Re-entry Is Our Next Civil Rights Movement
16. Prevention of Schizophrenia and Severe Mental Illness
17. Revolutionizing Social Work Education to Prepare for a Super-Diverse Global Society
18. The Global Mental Health Crisis as a Challenge for Social Work
19. Grand Challenges in Global Environmental Change
20. Financial Capability for All
21. Empowering Women Despite Gender Inequality Refashioning Itself in the Modern World
22. Measuring and Framing Well-Being in a Globalized World
23. Responding to the Effects of Global Ecological Degradation
24. Innovations for Inclusion: Reducing Stigma Against Marginalized Groups in Society, Self, and Social Work
25. Media Uprising
26. Interrupting the Patterns of Cumulative Disadvantage Across the Lifespan by Promoting Equity and Choice: The Life Course Impacts of Poverty and Possibilities for Improvement
27. Increasing the Productive Engagement of Older Adults
28. Illegal Immigrants Have a Right to Safety as Much as Any Citizen
29. Safe Children: Ending Severe and Fatal Maltreatment of Children
30. Healthier Births: Reducing Pre-Term Births and Their Hazardous Outcomes
31. Prepare the Profession to Address Structural Racism and Its Impact on Our Clients and Ourselves
32. No Child Unhoused: The Homelessness of Children Is Rare and Brief
33. The Integration of Harm Reduction Practice and Principles into Social Work with Substance-Using Populations: A Grand Challenge for the Profession

34. Decreasing Childhood Poverty Rates in the US by 50% in the Next Decade
35. Full Employment—A Central Challenge for Social Work

CALL FOR PAPERS: ROUND 2 CONCEPT PAPER TOPICS

Round 2 criteria was broadened to capture more macro, policy, and organizational challenges:

1. Reducing and Preventing Negative Consequences Associated with Alcohol Misuse
2. Ending Gender-Based Violence
3. Promoting Equality by Addressing Social Stigma
4. Stepping Up to Harness Big Data for Social Good: A Grand Challenge for Social Work
5. Harnessing the Digital Age: Practice Innovation Through Technology
6. Increasing Success for African American Children and Youth

APPENDIX 2

AASWSW Working Papers

Grand Challenges for Social Work

Individual and family well-being

ENSURE HEALTHY
DEVELOPMENT FOR ALL YOUTH

Unleashing the Power of Prevention

Preventing Schizophrenia and
Severe Mental Illness

CLOSE THE HEALTH GAP

Health Equity: Eradicating
Health Inequalities for
Future Generations

Reducing and Preventing
Alcohol Misuse and Its Consequences:
A Grand Challenge for Social Work

STOP FAMILY VIOLENCE

Ending Gender-Based Violence:
A Grand Challenge for Social Work

Safe Children: Reducing Severe
and Fatal Maltreatment

ADVANCE LONG AND
PRODUCTIVE LIVES

Increasing Productive
Engagement in Later Life

Stronger social fabric

ERADICATE SOCIAL ISOLATION

Social Isolation Presents a
Grand Challenge for Social Work

END HOMELESSNESS

The Grand Challenge of
Ending Homelessness

CREATE SOCIAL RESPONSES TO
A CHANGING ENVIRONMENT

Strengthening the Social Response
to the Human Impacts of
Environmental Change

HARNESS TECHNOLOGY
FOR SOCIAL GOOD

Practice Innovation through
Technology in the Digital Age:
A Grand Challenge for Social Work

Harnessing Big Data for
Social Good: A Grand Challenge
for Social Work

Just society

PROMOTE SMART
DECARCERATION

From Mass Incarceration
to Smart Decarceration

BUILD FINANCIAL
CAPABILITY FOR ALL

Financial Capability and
Asset Building for All

REDUCE EXTREME
ECONOMIC INEQUALITY

Reversing Extreme Inequality

ACHIEVE EQUAL
OPPORTUNITY AND JUSTICE

The Grand Challenge of
Promoting Equality by
Addressing Social Stigma

Achieving Equal Opportunity
and Justice: The Integration of
Latina/o Immigrants into
American Society

Increasing Success for
African American
Children and Youth

Achieving Measurable Progress for Society Through Social Work and Science

Grand Challenges for Social Work
Supporting Working Papers

Individual and family well-being

ENSURE HEALTHY DEVELOPMENT FOR ALL YOUTH

Unleashing the Power of Prevention

Preventing Schizophrenia and Severe Mental Illness

CLOSE THE HEALTH GAP

Health Equity: Eradicating Health Inequalities for Future Generations

Reducing and Preventing Alcohol Misuse and Its Consequences: A Grand Challenge for Social Work

STOP FAMILY VIOLENCE

Ending Gender-Based Violence: A Grand Challenge for Social Work

Safe Children: Reducing Severe and Fatal Maltreatment

ADVANCE LONG AND PRODUCTIVE LIVES

Increasing Productive Engagement in Later Life

Stronger social fabric

ERADICATE SOCIAL ISOLATION

Social Isolation Presents a Grand Challenge for Social Work

END HOMELESSNESS

The Grand Challenge of Ending Homelessness

CREATE SOCIAL RESPONSES TO A CHANGING ENVIRONMENT

Strengthening the Social Response to the Human Impacts of Environmental Change

HARNESS TECHNOLOGY FOR SOCIAL GOOD

Practice Innovation through Technology in the Digital Age: A Grand Challenge for Social Work

Harnessing Big Data for Social Good: A Grand Challenge for Social Work

Just society

PROMOTE SMART DECARCERATION

From Mass Incarceration to Smart Decarceration

BUILD FINANCIAL CAPABILITY FOR ALL

Financial Capability and Asset Building for All

REDUCE EXTREME ECONOMIC INEQUALITY

Reversing Extreme Inequality

ACHIEVE EQUAL OPPORTUNITY AND JUSTICE

The Grand Challenge of Promoting Equality by Addressing Social Stigma

Achieving Equal Opportunity and Justice: The Integration of Latina/o Immigrants into American Society

Increasing Success for African American Children and Youth

Achieving Measurable Progress for Society Through Social Work and Science

APPENDIX 3

The Grand Challenges for Social Work Initiative

The Grand Challenges for Social Work are designed to focus a world of thought and action on the most compelling and critical social issues of our day. Each grand challenge is a broad but discrete concept where social work expertise and leadership can be brought to bear on bold new ideas, scientific exploration and surprising innovations.

We invite you to review the following challenges with the goal of providing greater clarity, utility and meaning to this roadmap for lifting up the lives of individuals, families and communities struggling with the most fundamental requirements for social justice and human existence.

The Grand Challenges for Social Work include the following:

- Ensure healthy development of all youth
- Close the health gap
- Stop family violence
- Eradicate social isolation
- End homelessness
- Promote smart decarceration
- Reduce extreme economic inequality
- Build financial capability for all
- Harness technology for social good
- Create social responses to a changing environment
- Achieve equal opportunity and justice
- Advance long and productive lives

EXECUTIVE COMMITTEE

Co-Chairs

Marilyn L. Flynn
University of Southern California

Michael Sherraden
Washington University in St. Louis

Edwina Uehara
University of Washington

Richard P. Barth
University of Maryland

John S. Brekke
University of Southern California

Darla Spence Coffey
Council on Social Work Education

Rowena Fong
University of Texas at Austin

Sarah Gehlert
University of South Carolina

J. David Hawkins
University of Washington

Charles E. Lewis Jr.
Congressional Research Institute for Social Work & Policy

James E. Lubben
Boston College

Ronald W. Manderscheid
National Association of County Behavioral Health & Developmental Disability Directors

Angelo McClain
National Association of Social Workers

Yolanda C. Padilla
University of Texas at Austin

Gail Steketee (ex officio)
American Academy of Social Work & Social Welfare and *Boston University*

Karina L. Walters
University of Washington

Patricia White
Hunter College

James Herbert Williams
Arizona State University

STAFF

Sarah Christa Butts, Executive Director, Grand Challenges for Social Work initiative
American Academy of Social Work & Social Welfare and *University of Maryland*

Michele Clark, Senior Project Coordinator, Grand Challenges for Social Work initiative
University of Southern California

Lissa Johnson, Director of Policy Initiatives, Grand Challenges for Social Work initiative
Washington University in St. Louis

GRAND CHALLENGES FOR SOCIAL WORK INITIATIVE

APPENDIX 4

 **Grand Challenges**
for Social Work

March 2017

Policy Recommendations to Address the Grand Challenges for Social Work

Ensure Healthy Development for All Youth
- Provide family-focused interventions without cost to patients and families through primary health-care providers in order to prevent behavioral health problems.
- Ensure that 10% of all public funds spent on young people support effective prevention programs.
- Increase local and state capacity to support the high-quality implementation of effective preventive interventions.
- Develop community-level systems to monitor risk, protection, and behavioral-health outcomes.
- Reduce the duration of untreated mental illness in young people.
- Train and enable a workforce for effective prevention practice.

Close the Health Gap
- Focus on settings-based research and interventions to improve the conditions of daily life.
- Advance community empowerment and advocacy for sustainable health solutions and prevention.
- Cultivate health innovation in primary care and community-based centers.
- Promote access to health care and insurance for all.
- Foster development of an interprofessional health workforce.
- Develop a global health policy agenda on reducing alcohol misuse.

Stop Family Violence
- Increase federal funding for prevention and intervention activities, including efforts to reduce the structural inequalities that perpetuate gender-based violence.
- The National Institute of Justice, the National Institutes of Health, and the Administration for Children and Families should increase funding for research on evidence-based interventions that strengthen and enhance safety in families victimized through abuse and violence.
- Encourage and facilitate linkages among birth, child-welfare, criminal-justice, health, and social-service data systems to identify opportunities for preventive services and improvements in the outcomes of older children.

Advance Long and Productive Lives
- Expand paid family and medical leave.
- Create flexible and transitional employment arrangements.
- Expand the Corporation for National and Community Service's support for engaging older adults.

Eradicate Social Isolation
- Increase access to high-quality child care that strengthens social connections.
- Build more age-friendly communities that strengthen social connections.
- Reform solitary confinement.

End Homelessness
- Expand access to housing subsidies, including Housing Choice Vouchers.
- Ensure that evidence-based psychosocial interventions accompany housing assistance for those in need.
- Develop and evaluate housing-led interventions for specific populations.

Create Social Responses to a Changing Environment
- Charge the Federal Emergency Management Agency (FEMA) with guiding and facilitating planned relocations due to environmentally induced displacement in the United States.
- Task FEMA with development of standards for evidence-based practice as well as with determining the locations most at risk for relocation, who might need to move, how soon, and to where.
- Drawing upon recommendations from the US Conference of Mayors Stafford Act Task Force and others, detail a governance structure for planned relocation assistance at the federal level and for coordination with state, tribal, and local entities.

- Create community advisory boards to participate in planning and implementation of relocation.
- Fund research to identify at-risk communities suitable for relocation and to document experiences with planning and implementation.

Harness Technology for Social Good
- Expand Internet connectivity for underserved households.
- Unlock government data to drive solutions to social problems.
- Open the possibility for social work practice across state lines.

Promote Smart Decarceration
- Reverse civic and legal exclusions.
- Use incarceration primarily for incapacitation of the most dangerous.
- Make reduction of disparities a key outcome in decarceration efforts.
- Reallocate resources to community-based supports.

Reduce Extreme Economic Inequality
- Convert the Child Tax Credit into a universal child allowance.
- Strengthen labor standards and reform employment policies.
- Expand active employment creation through public programs and support for business start-up and capitalization.
- Expand the Earned Income Tax Credit.
- Expand child care access to enable stable employment in the context of healthy child development.
- Create new lifelong policies for inclusive and progressive wealth building.

Build Financial Capability for All
- Start lifelong asset building with universal and progressive Child Development Accounts.
- Support a strong Consumer Financial Protection Bureau to help ensure the transparency, safety, fairness, and affordability of financial products and services.
- Create a web-based Financial Capability Gateway to build financial capability for all.
- Prepare social work and human service practitioners to build financial capability and assets for all.

Achieve Equal Opportunity and Justice
- To accelerate Latino immigrant integration, expand coverage under the Patient Protection and Affordable Care Act.
- Enhance, expand, and strengthen federal antidiscrimination laws, including the Voting Rights Act.

- Eliminate zero tolerance policies in schools and promote the use of evidence-informed practices and policies to address racial disciplinary disproportionality.

ABOUT THESE POLICY RECOMMENDATIONS

These policy recommendations emerged from Social Innovation for America's Renewal, a policy conference organized by the Center for Social Development at the George Warren Brown School of Social Work at Washington University in collaboration with the American Academy of Social Work & Social Welfare, which is leading the Grand Challenges for Social Work initiative to champion social progress through a national agenda powered by science.

Grand Challenges Network Co-Leads

ENSURE HEALTHY DEVELOPMENT FOR ALL YOUTH

J. David Hawkins, PhD
Endowed Professor of Prevention
Founding Director, Social
    Development Research Group
University of Washington, School of
    Social Work
jdh@uw.edu

Jeffrey M. Jenson, PhD
Philip D. and Eleanor G. Winn
    Professor for Children and Youth
    at Risk
University of Denver, Graduate
    School of Social Work
jeffrey.jenson@du.edu

CLOSE THE HEALTH GAP

Michael S. Spencer, PhD
Fedele F. Fauri Collegiate Professor
    of Social Work
University of Michigan, School of
    Social Work
spencerm@umich.edu

Karina L. Walters, PhD
William P. and Ruth Gerberding
    Endowed University Professor and
    Associate Dean for Research
University of Washington, School of
    Social Work
kw5@uw.edu

STOP FAMILY VIOLENCE

Richard P. Barth, PhD
Dean and Professor
University of Maryland, School of
    Social Work
rbarth@ssw.umaryland.edu

Patricia Kohl, PhD
Washington University, Brown
    School of Social Work
pkohl@wustl.edu

Shanti J. Kulkarni, PhD
Associate Professor of Social Work
University of North Carolina at
    Charlotte, College of Health &
    Human Services
skulkar4@uncc.edu

Jill T. Messing, PhD
Associate Professor
Arizona State University, School of
Social Work
Jill.Messing@asu.edu

ADVANCE LONG AND PRODUCTIVE LIVES

Ernest Gonzales, PhD
Assistant Professor
Boston University, School of
Social Work
geg@bu.edu

Jacqueline James, PhD
Co-Director of the Boston College
Center on Aging & Work
Research Professor in the Boston
College Lynch School of Education
Boston College, School of
Social Work
jacquelyn.james@bc.edu

Christina Matz-Costa, PhD
Professor
Boston College, School of Social Work
matzch@bc.edu

Nancy Morrow-Howell, PhD
Bettie Bofinger Brown Distinguished
Professor of Social Policy Director
Harvey A. Friedman Center for Aging
Washington University in St. Louis,
Brown School of Social Work
morrow-howell@wustl.edu

Michele Putnam, PhD
Professor and Associate Dean
for Research
Simmons College, School of
Social Work
michelle.putnam@simmons.edu

ERADICATE SOCIAL ISOLATION

Sandra Edmonds Crewe, PhD
Professor and Dean
Howard University, School of
Social Work
secrewe@howard.edu

James E. Lubben, PhD
Louise McMahon Ahearn Chair in
Social Work
Boston College, School of
Social Work
Professor Emeritus
University of California, Los Angeles
lubben@bc.edu & lubben@ucla.edu

Erika L. Sabbath, ScD
Assistant Professor
Boston College, School of
Social Work
erika.sabbath@bc.edu

Elizabeth M. Tracy, PhD
Grace Longwell Coyle Professor of
Social Work
Case Western Reserve University,
Jack, Joseph and Morton Mandel
School of Applied Social Sciences
elizabeth.tracy@case.edu

END HOMELESSNESS

Benjamin F. Henwood, PhD
Assistant Professor
University of Southern California,
Suzanne Dworak-Peck School of
Social Work
bhenwood@usc.edu

Deborah K. Padgett, PhD
Professor, McSilver Faculty Fellow
Silver School of Social Work,
  New York University
Professor of Psychiatry
New York University School of
  Medicine
deborah.padgett@nyu.edu

CREATE SOCIAL RESPONSES TO
A CHANGING ENVIRONMENT

Susan P. Kemp, PhD
Charles O. Cressey Endowed Professor
University of Washington, School of
  Social Work
spk@uw.edu

Lisa Reyes Mason, PhD
Assistant Professor
University of Tennessee, College of
  Social Work
mason@utk.edu

Lawrence A. Palinkas, PhD
Albert G. and Frances Lomas
  Feldman Professor of Social Policy
  and Health
Director, Behavior, Health and
  Society Research Cluster
University of Southern California,
  Suzanne Dworak-Peck School of
  Social Work
palinkas@usc.edu

HARNESS TECHNOLOGY
FOR SOCIAL GOOD

Stephanie Cosner Berzin, PhD
Associate Professor
Assistant Dean, Doctoral Program
Boston College, School of Social
  Work stephanie.berzin@bc.edu

Claudia J. Coulton, PhD
Distinguished University Professor
Lillian F. Harris Professor of Urban
  Social Research
Case Western Reserve University,
  Jack, Joseph and Morton Mandel
  School of Applied Social Sciences
claudia.coulton@case.edu

Rowena Fong, PhD
Ruby Lee Piester Centennial
  Professor in Services to Children
  and Families, University of Texas
  at Austin, School of Social Work
rfong@austin.utexas.edu

Melanie Sage, PhD
Assistant Professor
University of North Dakota, School
  of Social Work
Melanie.sage@UND.edu

Jonathan Singer, PhD
Associate Professor
Loyola University Chicago, School of
  Social Work
jsinger1@luc.edu

PROMOTE SMART
DECARCERATION

Matthew W. Epperson, PhD
Associate Professor
University of Chicago, School of
  Social Service Administration
mepperson@uchicago.edu

Carrie Pettus-Davis, PhD
Assistant Professor
Director, Concordance Institute for
  Advancing Social Justice
Washington University in St. Louis,
  Brown School of Social Work
cpettusdavis@wustl.edu

REDUCE EXTREME ECONOMIC INEQUALITY

Laura Lein, PhD
Katherine Reebel Collegiate
    Professor of Social Work
University of Michigan, School of
    Social Work
Professor of Anthropology
College of Literature, Science, and
    the Arts
leinl@umich.edu

Jennifer Romich, PhD
Associate Professor
University of Washington, School of
    Social Work
romich@uw.edu

Trina Shanks, PhD
Associate Professor
Faculty Associate
Survey Research Center, Institute for
    Social Research
University of Michigan, School of
    Social Work
trwilli@umich.edu

BUILD FINANCIAL CAPABILITY FOR ALL

Julie Birkenmaier, PhD
Professor of Social Work
Saint Louis University, College for
    Public Health & Social Justice
birkenjm@slu.edu

Jin Huang, PhD
Associate Professor of Social Work
Saint Louis University, College for
    Public Health & Social Justice
jhuang5@slu.edu

Margaret S. Sherraden, PhD
Founder's Professor of Social Work
University of Missouri–St. Louis,
    School of Social Work
sherraden@umsl.edu

ACHIEVE EQUAL OPPORTUNITY AND JUSTICE

Rocío Calvo, PhD
Associate Professor
Boston College, School of
    Social Work
Rocio.calvo@bc.edu

Jeremy Goldbach, PhD
Assistant Professor
University of Southern California
Suzanne Dworak-Peck School of
    Social Work
goldbach@usc.edu

Ruth McRoy, PhD
Donahue and DiFelice Endowed
    Professor of Social Work at Boston
    College
Research Professor
Ruby Lee Piester Centennial
    Professor Emerita University
    of Texas at Austin, School of
    Social Work
ruth.mcroy@bc.edu and r.mcroy@
    mail.utexas.edu

APPENDIX 6

Sustaining Sponsors of Grand Challenges for Social Work

Boston College
Boston University
Case Western Reserve University
Colorado State University
Michigan State University
New York University
Ohio State University
Rutgers University
University of Alabama
University of California Berkeley
University at Buffalo
University of California Los Angeles
University of Chicago
University of Connecticut
University of Denver
University of Georgia
University of Houston
University of Maryland
University of Michigan
University of North Carolina
University of Pennsylvania
University of Southern California
University of Tennessee
University of Texas at Austin
University of Washington
Washington University in St. Louis

INDEX

Page references for figures are indicated by *f,* for tables by *t,* and for boxes by *b.*

prevalence, 59
prevention and intervention evidence
    base, 64–66
research strategies, stronger research-
    driven interventions, 71–72
risk factors and contexts, 60–62
social work focus on, 56–58
strategies, promising and emerging,
    67–73 (*see also under* stop
    family violence)
isolation, social, eradicate, 11, 103–116.
    see also social isolation, eradicate

jails. *see* incarceration
James, J. B., 92
Jenson, J. M., 21
Johnson, C., 182
Johnson, M. J., 106
Johnson, R. W., 84
justice
    achieve equal, 12, 248–260 (*see also*
        equal opportunity and justice,
        achieve)
    restorative, 253–254

Kemp, S. P., 26, 141, 142, 143, 144, 146,
    147, 153
Kenney, K., 87
Koop, C. Everett, 103
Korr, W., 14

labor market
    employment and income, 204, 205
    older adults, 86–87
        transitions, 92–93
Latinx, 249n1, 250–253. *see also specific
    topics*
    definition, 250
    integration, 251–253
    origins and immigration, 250–251
    stigmatization, 249, 255–257
Levey, E. J., 63
lifelong inclusive asset building, 218–219
Link, B. G., 256, 257
loans, small-dollar and credit-builder,
    231–232
loneliness, 104. *see also* social isolation,
    eradicate
long and productive lives, advance,
    10–11, 81–97

age distribution and aging
    population, 81–82
innovation, 94–95
next steps, 89–94
    caregiver financial support, 89–90
    discrimination and bias, 93–94
    employer support of older
        workers, 91–92
    federal recognition and
        local support, elderly
        volunteers, 90–91
    physical and social environments,
        for productive engagement, 93
    transition between working,
        volunteering, and
        caregiving, 92–93
problem analysis and improvement
    opportunities, 82–84
productive aging, 82
productive engagement, 82
    outcomes, potential, 84–86, 85b
    realities and innovations, 86–89
    caregiving, 88–89
    volunteering, 87–88
    working, 86–87
social work profession, 95–96
Lubben, J. E., 4, 104, 107, 109, 110, 111
Lubben Social Network Scale, 109

machine learning algorithms, 169
Macy, R. J., 66
maltreatment, child, 56–73. *see also* child
    maltreatment
Mapping Financial Opportunity
    project, 238b
Martin, A. B., 61–62
Mason, Lisa, 153
mass incarceration, 181–187. *see also*
    incarceration, mass
Matz-Costa, C., 82
McClain, A., 14
McGuire, J. F., 87
McKinney–Vento funding, 130,
    132, 134
McPherson, K. E., 103–104
McRoy, R., 14
Medicaid, 252
    asset limits, 234
    on homelessness, 125, 132, 135
    older adults, caregiver support, 90

Printed in the USA/Agawam, MA
July 7, 2021

777518.003